Benjamin Tyson Dske

VIRTUAL LAW

Navigating the Legal
Landscape of Virtual Worlds

Defending Liberty
Pursuing Justice

Cover design by ABA Publishing.

Library of Congress Cataloging-in-Publication Data

Duranske, Benjamin Tyson.
  Virtual law / by Benjamin Tyson Duranske.—1st ed.
    p. cm.
  Includes index.
  ISBN 978-1-60442-009-8
  1. Computer networks—Law and legislation—United States—Cases. 2. Internet—Law and legislation—United States—Cases. I. Title.

  KF390.5.C6D87 2008
  343.7309'944—dc22

                                                                          2008008091

For Sarah

Every place from which justice is pronounced is a veritable *temenos,* a sacred spot cut off and hedged in from the "ordinary" world. The old Flemish and Dutch word for it is *vierschaar,* literally a space divided off by four ropes, or, according to another view, four benches. But whether square or round, it is still a magic circle, a play-ground where the customary differences of rank are temporarily abolished.

—Johan Huizinga
Homo Ludens: A Study of the
Play-Element in Culture, 1938

Contents

Chapter 10
Criminal Law and Virtual Worlds *197*

Chapter 11
Privacy Law and Virtual Worlds *211*

Acknowledgments

I gratefully acknowledge the following individuals, whose previous and ongoing work informs this and all future inquiries into virtual law: Richard Bartle, Bryan Camp, Edward Castronova, Julian Dibbell, Joshua Fairfield, Dan Hunter, Raph Koster, Greg Lastowka, Leandra Lederman, and Tal Zarsky. All were personally generous with their time by telephone, by e-mail, in person, and in-world, and all were instrumental in helping me understand the history of this fascinating area of law.

Thanks also go to Lynn Wolf, who graciously gave permission to reprint portions of an article that her husband (Paul Joseph, 1951–2003) wrote on vigilante justice in early Ultima Online. Also to Bettina Chin, who gave permission to excerpt portions of her student note on defamation in virtual worlds. And to Kate Fitz, who gave permission to reprint the "Galileo Law Directory," her comprehensive compilation of legal resources in Second Life, in its entirety.

I also thank Thayer Preece for her guidance regarding real money trading in World of Warcraft, Steven Teppler for his comments on electronic evidence collection, and Steven Davis for his notes regarding game security. Also, thanks to Cristina Burbach and Sean Kane, my cochairs on the American Bar Association's committee on Virtual Worlds and Multiuser Online Games of the Section of Science & Technology Law, for their support and feedback.

Finally, I wish to thank Stephen Wu, whose early encouragement, enthusiasm for virtual law, and introduction to the ABA's publishing division were instrumental in bringing *Virtual Law* to press.

About the Author

Benjamin Tyson Duranske is a writer and an intellectual property attorney. He edits the website http://virtuallyblind.com, which tracks issues related to virtual law, and co-chairs the Committee on Virtual Worlds and Multiuser Online Games of the American Bar Association's Section of Science & Technology Law.

Introducing Virtual Worlds and Virtual Law

1

What Are Virtual Worlds?

If you ask ten people who participate in virtual worlds to tell you what a virtual world is, you will get ten different answers. The lawyer with an office in a virtual world will tell you virtual worlds are tools that let him stay in touch with high-tech clients. The CEO of a brick-and-mortar company trying to find a foothold in the virtual space will say virtual worlds are the new World Wide Web and will cite Gartner's prediction that eighty percent of all Internet users will have a presence in a virtual world by 2011.[1] A technology writer will tell you that virtual worlds provide a glimpse into the next major computing interface evolution. A college-age game player will tell you that she uses virtual worlds to do "real money" transactions for virtual goods. The marketing director who is running a person-to-person "buzz" campaign for a new movie will talk about virtual worlds' unparalleled potential for personal communication. A digital artist will tell you that virtual worlds are fantastic platforms for distributing his artwork. A musician will tell you about her live concerts on "the grid." A stay-at-home mom who has taught herself to "script" in virtual worlds will explain how she makes thousands of dollars a month in microtransactions selling tiny programs she writes to other users. A virtual land baron will tell you how he supplements his real-world income renting virtual homes and offices. Each description reveals a different experience, and each experience raises serious legal questions in the emerging field of virtual law.

Although these examples illustrate that different users experience different aspects of virtual worlds, closer examination of what they are doing reveals three constants. First, all virtual worlds are computer-based simulated environments, as opposed to just programs. They look like a "place," sometimes a real place, sometimes a fanciful one, but always a visual environment. Second, all are designed to be populated by "avatars"—visual representations of virtual world users. And third, all virtual worlds allow for communication between users, either by text, via the keyboard, or by voice, using a microphone.

From a legal perspective, two additional attributes of most (though not all) virtual worlds are also important: persistence of user-created content, and a "real money" market for in-world items.

■■■■■

What Is a Virtual World?

All are computer-based simulated environments.

All are designed to be populated by "avatars."

All allow for communication between users.

Most offer persistence of user-created content.

Many offer functional economies.

■■■■■

What Hardware Do I Need to Use in a Virtual World?

Computer—Most modern computers can run most virtual worlds and many multiuser games. However, some laptops—particularly business-oriented laptops without dedicated graphics cards—have trouble with the more graphically intense worlds like Second Life, and with more recent games. There.com (a social virtual world with fairly restricted content creation ability) and Ultima Online (a game with many virtual world attributes) will run on nearly every desktop and laptop computer manufactured in the last few years. Not all virtual worlds and games run under the Mac and Linux operating systems, though many do.

Keyboard/Mouse—Most users of both virtual worlds and games prefer a conventional keyboard/mouse combination to any other form of input device.

Microphone—Many virtual worlds offer voice communication. Most users find that a headset or earphones with an attached microphone is the most practical way to use voice features.

Persistence of user-created content is a feature of almost all non-youth-oriented mainstream social virtual worlds. It means that if I create something in the world and then I log out and turn off my computer, the thing I created will stay there so that others can see it and interact with it when I am not online. In other words, what one user does can impact another user's subsequent experiences, even if the first user is no longer logged in to the virtual world. It is tempting to include this as a requirement for "virtual world" status, but doing so eliminates some game-based spaces that raise interesting legal questions. The twenty-four-hour-a-day population of these places via social structures such as "guilds" gives them a comparable sense of permanence, however, which can be said to replace the persistent user-created content that typically exists in social virtual worlds.

"Real money trade" (RMT) of virtual goods for real-life currency is also a feature of many virtual worlds and multiplayer games. Sometimes, as in the popular social virtual world Second Life, an exchange is created by the company that runs the world where the in-world currency ("Linden Dollars" or "Lindens" in the case of Second Life) can be bought and sold. Some games, like Entropia Universe, also feature RMT. Other virtual worlds and games specifically disallow RMT under the Terms of Service that users must agree to when they first sign up or log in. Even where RMT is prohibited by contract, however, thriving black markets exist. One estimate places the worldwide value of RMT at more than US$2 billion per year.[2]

In sum, for the purposes of our exploration of virtual law, virtual worlds are all avatar-based simulations where user alterations of the physical, social, or economic environment of the world are persistent. *Virtual Law* will examine a few games and worlds that do not have persistent content or RMT in relation to specific legal questions, but will focus mainly on virtual worlds and games that meet the preceding definition.

What Do You Call "Virtual Worlds"?

No real consensus yet exists on what these spaces should be called, although "virtual worlds," as the term is used herein, is currently the most common phrase. Some commentators have urged the use of the term "networked virtual environments" rather than "virtual worlds"[3] (which has a certain business and professional appeal), but "virtual worlds" is now used at a rate of 20 to 1 over "networked virtual environments" on the web, and it appears to be the term that will stick.[4] "Virtual reality" is also occasionally used, but that term generally refers to the interface between the user and the environment, and typically involves complex hardware that is not generally available to consumers. Much of the current advances in "virtual reality" equipment are in the fields of commercial-grade flight simulators and military training equipment. In the long run, convergence between "virtual reality" equipment and "virtual worlds" is likely, but at the moment, the terms describe different things. The term "synthetic worlds" is also used by some commentators, and although it may well be more accurate, it also is not used as widely as "virtual worlds."

In any case, the terminology is of more concern to writers than it is to virtual world users, who happily log in to these spaces to run businesses, slay dragons, make conference calls, discover new music, and chat with old friends—all without caring whether they are entering virtual reality, playing a multiplayer online game, using a networked virtual environment, or participating in a virtual world.

What Kinds of Virtual Worlds and Games Exist?

As virtual worlds are still, to a degree, in their infancy, the marketplace is changing rapidly. As this edition of *Virtual Law* goes to press, examples of general interest or social virtual worlds include Second Life, There.com, Active Worlds, and The Sims Online (the last also involves game-play components). Special interest virtual worlds dedicated to a particular experience, typically entertainment, also exist. These include Kaneva (focusing on entertainment generally) and vSide (focusing on music). All these worlds, with the exception of The Sims Online, are essentially "free-form" virtual worlds. That is, there are no goals to achieve, points to accumulate, or levels to unlock. Though there are many game-like features to social virtual worlds, they are not, in a traditional sense, games. In fact, users of social virtual worlds often bristle at game terminology, particularly at being called "players" or having their virtual worlds referred to as "games."

Games should not be excluded from this discussion, however. Many multiplayer online games share key characteristics with virtual worlds, and many of the legal questions that apply to virtual worlds apply equally to multiplayer online games. For the purposes of examining questions related to virtual law, multiplayer games should be considered "virtual worlds" to the extent that they fit the rest of the requirements for these spaces. That is, if they are avatar-based computer-simulated environments that allow for communication between users, they are for our purposes virtual worlds, and they will be governed by the same legal principles that govern virtual worlds. World of Warcraft, Ultima Online, EverQuest II, Entropia Universe, and Eve Online are all multiplayer online games that also qualify as virtual worlds. Moreover, the line between games and virtual worlds is eroding, as products like Sony's Home—a virtual world for Sony's PlayStation 3 game platform—are introduced.[5]

One final category of virtual worlds is worth special mention at the outset: virtual worlds for children. These spaces represent the fastest-growing and largest segment of the virtual world market.[6] One of the most popular, Club Penguin, reported more than 12 million subscribers (exceeding any non-youth-oriented world or game) when it was purchased by Disney in August 2007.[7] Mattel's Barbie Girls registered 3 million subscribers during its first two months of operation.[8] Some of these worlds are designed for children as young as very early elementary school.

There are some key differences between virtual worlds for children and traditional virtual worlds that are meant for adult users. For example, many virtual worlds for children do not allow for the creation or ownership of in-world content, in contrast to most mainstream virtual worlds. Most virtual worlds for children also employ much more active content filtering and removal schemes than do adult-targeted virtual worlds. Most virtual worlds for children also have optional, highly restricted chat controls. Certain legal questions involving virtual worlds for children will be resolved differently as well, because the companies running virtual worlds for children must comply with information collection laws like the 1998 Children's Online Privacy Protection Act, designed to protect children from Internet predators. Questions of liability and criminal law also, of course, differ when children are involved. These differences mean that the questions in virtual law arising from virtual worlds for children will differ somewhat from those that arise in virtual worlds targeted at adults.

Virtual Law will chiefly focus on virtual worlds for adults, largely because most of the legal issues related to virtual worlds come from these less-restricted spaces, but readers should bear in mind that virtual worlds for children exist and are immensely popular and that these spaces also involve some specific legal issues.

■■■■■
What Do I Do with an Avatar?

Interact—Your avatar will interact with everyone else in the virtual world on your behalf. Your avatar's appearance will send a message about yourself to the people you interact with in a virtual world.

Explore—Your avatar is your eyes and ears in the virtual world. You will use your avatar to explore the environment.

Build—You will use your avatar to manipulate the environment. When "you" make something in a virtual world, you will do so via your avatar.

What Is an Avatar and How Do I Get One?

An "avatar" is a visual representation of yourself that you use to interact with other users and with the environment in a virtual world. It is usually a three-dimensional representation and typically (though not always) has a humanoid form with arms, legs, and a head in roughly the right places. The term originally comes from Hindu philosophy, where an "avatar" is the physical manifestation of a higher being in the real world.[9] In the virtual world, the tables are turned: the "higher being" is the user, and the avatar is the user's digital manifestation in the virtual world.

In most social virtual worlds and multiplayer online games, you are presented with a few basic avatar designs when you sign up. You will generally be given a choice of a few fairly generic humanoid avatars, and you may be able to customize your avatar's gender, hairstyle, face and body shape, skin tone, and initial clothing on the virtual world provider's website or in your first few moments in the virtual world during the sign-up process. In multiplayer games (which are often science fiction- or fantasy-based) you will also generally choose a "race" (e.g., elf, human, orc) and a number of traits and skills that control your character's initial abilities and appearance. You may have some options for customizing the look of your character/avatar as well.

Once you have an avatar, what do you do with it? In free-form virtual worlds, you will use your avatar in several ways: to represent yourself to other users, to communicate with other users, to manipulate the environment, and to participate in interactive content. In games, you'll be doing all of that, but you'll also be using your avatar/character to accomplish game tasks.

In both games and free-form virtual worlds, one of your avatar's primary roles will be to represent you to other users. Your avatar will do this whether or not you intend it. Though the unwritten rules of appearance in virtual worlds are vastly different from those in the real world (see Chapter 14: Establishing a Professional Virtual World Presence), you should be aware that everyone who is participating in a virtual world will inevitably judge you by the choices you make regarding the appearance of your avatar, just as people are inevitably judged by the choices they make regarding their real-life appearance. If a user chooses a photorealistic avatar that looks exactly like he does, that sends one message. If the user chooses a relatively nondescript avatar, or chooses not to modify the base avatar significantly, that sends another. Choosing an avatar with exaggerated features or a nonhuman avatar will send a different signal as well.

Hairstyles, the appearance of makeup, and clothing are also typically user-selectable. For better or worse, just as in the real world, presenting yourself as an avatar with a green-tipped blond mullet, theatrical Kabuki makeup, and an orange jumpsuit will say something different to people you interact with than will showing up as an avatar with a pageboy cut, business-appropriate makeup, and a tailored suit. Neither is "better" than the other, and, in some situations, the former will actually appear far less out of place than the latter, but it is important to remember that the choices you make regarding your avatar's appearance will send a message to everyone you interact with; you should make sure it is the message you want to send.

Beyond physical appearance, even the way an avatar moves can send a message. Some virtual worlds let users create custom animations. If a user buys or creates walking animations that make her avatar move like a candidate for office, that sends one message. Selecting animations that make one's avatar move like a baboon, a superhero, or a cowboy sends another.

It is, at bottom, all a matter of personal choice, but you need to be aware that people will undeniably pay attention—either consciously or subconsciously—to every aspect of the appearance of your avatar. Happily, most virtual worlds make changing avatar shapes, dress, skin, hairstyle, and movement animations very simple. The decisions you make initially are generally not permanent, and it is very likely that you will change the appearance of your avatar many times as you learn more about virtual worlds.

You will also interact with other users via your avatar. In virtual worlds, when you type something and hit enter, everyone within a certain distance of your avatar sees the text you typed. You are, essentially, "talking" via your avatar. If you are using a microphone to communicate using voice, the same applies. Users whose avatars are within a certain distance of your avatar will be able to hear you speak, while users beyond that distance will not. As discussed in greater detail later, confidentiality of communication is largely illusory in many virtual worlds.

Manipulation of the environment on your behalf is also the job of your avatar. Your avatar acts as your proxy in a virtual world. So, if you want to build a house, you'll usually start by clicking a button that causes your avatar to appear to make an object in the world. If you want a brick wall, you'll stretch the object to wall size, then paint it with a brick pattern. Want to plant a tree? You'll take one from your avatar's inventory and stick it in the virtual ground. Although you are controlling all of this, of course, on the screen it appears that your avatar is doing the work. And if you need to get a better perspective on your project, you just move your avatar to a better vantage point.

Finally, you participate in the virtual world using your avatar. Exploring means moving your avatar around, either under his own power (by walking, running, or, in some worlds, flying), by "teleporting" (using a common software feature to move instantly from one location to another), or in a virtual vehicle. Once you find something that looks interesting, you interact with it using your avatar. Many social virtual worlds are composed at least partly of user-created content. If you want to try out a user-created roller coaster, you have to sit down in the seat using your avatar. If you are making a presentation to a group, you'll want to have your avatar appear to stand at a podium at the front of the auditorium. If you want to go shopping for some new clothes for your avatar, you'll need to have your avatar visit the virtual mall.

Although you can typically customize your appearance in free-form virtual worlds at will, there is one choice that you make at sign-up that is usually not reversible: your avatar's name. Some virtual worlds allow you greater control over your name than others. For example, There.com currently allows you to choose any name you like as long as it does not violate the site's Terms of Service and has not been taken by another user. On the other hand, Second Life allows you to select anything you like for a first name, but requires you to pick from a set of preapproved last names (making it impossible for most people to use their real name as an avatar's name). Linden Lab has said that it intends to allow Second Life users to select customized names for their avatars for a fee, but as of the publication of *Virtual Law*, no timetable has been set.

Whether you choose to associate your real name with your virtual world identity is up to you. For now, a substantial majority of virtual world avatars are pseudonymous—that is, the avatar is not publicly tied to a real identity. Both social custom and the Terms of Service for most virtual worlds prohibit "outing" an avatar. Many users, however—including the author of *Virtual Law*—do publicly associate their real identities with their virtual world avatars, and as more people arrive who use virtual worlds professionally, more avatars will be associated with real-world identities. Some services, like Second Life, are even introducing identity verification, whereby a third-party service will verify a user's identity and, thus, allow that user to assure other users that her avatar represents a real person with verifiable information on file with the provider. This may be particularly useful for professionals who wish to use virtual worlds for business and academic purposes.

What Should I Expect in a Virtual World?

There is no requirement that virtual worlds look anything like the real world, but most do. Because of this, when you log in to a virtual world for the first time, the experience is closer to visiting a foreign country (albeit one with some very strange customs and technology) than being dropped off on a new planet.

You'll have to adjust to some serious differences—for example, in some virtual worlds your avatar can fly, and, in others, you may find yourself in a conversation with a purple tiger wearing a tuxedo—but generally, once you figure out how the interface works, the world will behave at least roughly as you expect it to. You will generally see a sky above your avatar and ground below. You will generally see a number of other avatars around you, some of whom are just as new as you are. There will typically be buildings (some user-created, some created by the people who run the virtual world), and there will often be signs in the area in which you initially appear explaining what you should do next. Movement within a virtual world typically involves either clicking where you want to go with the mouse or using keys on the keyboard, usually either the arrow keys, the numeric keypad, or the A, S, D, and W keys (these keys form an inverted T where your left hand naturally falls on the keyboard).

Because all virtual worlds are different, it is hard to generalize exactly what you will find, but there's usually some kind of obvious orientation system, and you should try to participate in that if you can find it. You can always just play with the interface yourself as well. Common interface features of virtual worlds include a map that shows you where your avatar is in relation to the rest of the world, an inventory window that shows you a list of the items in your avatar's possession, an appearance window that allows you to modify the physical appearance of your avatar, and an object creation window containing tools that you use to create objects within the virtual world environment.

A few books exist that can give you an introduction to virtual worlds, but the best way to put this area of law in context is to visit a virtual world and get yourself an avatar. In fact, participating in a virtual world is essentially a prerequisite to really understanding much of what this book will discuss. The marketplace is incredibly dynamic, but as this book goes to press, Second Life is the most popular free-form virtual world, and World of Warcraft is the most popular game. Both appear likely to retain those positions for at least the near future. If your interest is primarily in free-form virtual worlds, you can download the Second Life software from http://secondlife.com, register on the website (it is free), choose a name for your avatar, and you will be exploring the environment in a matter of minutes. If you'd like to see what the gaming side of virtual worlds looks like, most (including the popular World of Warcraft) offer a free trial.

Once you arrive with your shiny new avatar, you will find that there are many resources in virtual worlds for new users, though they are not always easy to find. Often more immediately helpful are other users, who are generally happy to lend a hand and answer new users' polite questions.

How Do People Use Virtual Worlds?

People use virtual worlds for many purposes. By far the most popular in-world activity is shopping.[10] Other popular activities include exploring; chatting with friends; listening to music (often accompanied by animated avatar "dancing"); and creating new objects, buildings, and items in the virtual world. All these activities, even shopping, are usually done with other people. It is actually somewhat uncommon to see a lone avatar; most people who enter virtual worlds do so to interact with other users. This makes virtual worlds highly social spaces and well suited for collaborative projects.

Collaboration takes many forms, from art projects to business formation to education. Because so much of virtual world content in many virtual worlds is user-created, and because virtual worlds are still relatively young, there's a lot to do. It sometimes feels a bit like the Wild West likely felt, with people creating everything from scratch-built government and justice systems to railroads to commercial districts to art installations. Most virtual worlds have the ability to create "groups," guilds, or "clubs," so you can easily meet people with similar interests and find ongoing projects that are a good fit for your skills.

How Do Companies Use Virtual Worlds?

There are two kinds of businesses in virtual worlds: small businesses that have grown up organically in these spaces, and bigger companies that are trying to establish their own virtual world presences. Although much will change over the next few years, the markedly different early results experienced by these two groups help illustrate, and are somewhat explained by, their different approaches.

Many in-world small businesses are succeeding by selling user-created content to other users, by renting virtual land to other users, and by selling services in-world.[11] In short, they succeed by providing opportunities for people to spend money doing the things that top the most popular activities list: shopping and socializing. According to Linden Lab's CEO Philip Rosedale, nearly one thousand Second Life users were making more than US$1000 each month in-world as of August 2007.[12] One user, Ailin Graef (better known as Second Life avatar "Anshe Chung"), is famous for having a net worth of more than US$1 million, made entirely from profits earned inside virtual worlds, mainly from real estate and content creation.[13] Alyssa LaRoche, better known as Second Life avatar "Aimee Weber," has written a book on content creation in Second Life under her avatar's name and runs a successful design studio. Weber even registered a trademark on her avatar's distinctive appearance—a green tutu, pigtails, blue butterfly wings, zebra-striped kneesocks, and stompy boots.[14]

On the other hand, some bigger businesses that primarily exist outside virtual worlds have struggled to find success in-world.[15] Many have begun to find niches—for example, Coca-Cola ran a well-received contest encouraging users to create Coca-Cola–branded vending machines,[16] and MTV has partnered with There.com on several significant projects, including Virtual Laguna Beach and Virtual Hills.[17] A few mainstream companies have had unmitigated successes, such as a 2007 promotion for the IMAX version of a Harry

Potter film that personally reached 15,000 members of the marketing company's target demographic in seven days.[18] But overall, companies have struggled to find a way to interact with and take advantage of this new medium. Wagner James Au, a commentator who writes on Second Life, observes that "the top ten corporate sites were attracting about 40,000 weekly visits" during June 2007 and says that "[c]orporate marketing in Second Life fails when it doesn't serve or celebrate the community, or refuses to integrate its greatest virtues."[19] The space is new, and just as companies struggled to use the web in its early days,[20] some are struggling with this new medium. As time goes on, companies will find ways to use virtual worlds for advertising, lead generation, product sales, and market positioning, just as they have learned to use the web.

What Is Virtual Law?

Virtual law is like "Internet law," in that it refers to a wide body of generally preexisting law that is applied somewhat differently in a new context. In fact, much of what we think of as "Internet law" applies to virtual worlds. In sum, virtual law is the statutory and case law that impacts virtual worlds and the application of that law to these spaces. It also refers to the internal governance structures that are beginning to appear in some virtual worlds (such as community "court" systems, mediation programs, and private organizations with contract-based codes of conduct) to the degree that those mimic, draw on, and sometimes interact with "real-world" law. Virtual law includes aspects of civil procedure, constitutional law, contract law, copyright law, criminal law, tort law, patent law, property law, publicity law, securities law, tax law, trade secret law, trademark law, international law, and Internet law. In each area, questions similar to those that arise in relation to real-world activity arise when law is applied to activity that takes place in virtual worlds, though with different, sometimes surprising, implications.

Because virtual worlds are designed to mirror the real world, many of the same problems that require attorneys in the real world arise in virtual worlds as well. Users (via their avatars) form and break contracts, create works of art, invent new technologies, make money, lose money, buy and develop virtual property, create new brands, defraud each other, defame each other, steal from each other, and attack each other. Though many of these acts are clearly covered by existing laws, fundamental differences between virtual worlds and the real world leave the application of these laws to in-world activity fraught with uncertainty. New laws may be written to specifically cover activity that takes place in virtual worlds, but more often, particularly in the short term, existing laws will be interpreted to cover in-world activities. A few cases are already reaching the courts.

One case, which settled shortly before *Virtual Law* went to press, was poised to determine whether Second Life creator Linden Lab's advertisement that users could "own virtual land" really was an offer of ownership of property in a traditional sense, and whether a user's purchase of undervalued land by manipulating web addresses amounted to a crime under California's Penal Code.[21] Another case, a copyright action filed in the Middle District of Florida, recently established content creators' ability to bring suit against a defendant who was identified in the original complaint only by the name of his avatar.[22] Game-based worlds raise different questions. For example, a class action suit was filed in 2007 in the Southern District of Florida on behalf of World of Warcraft players against a company that allegedly sold that game's currency to players for real money, in violation of World of Warcraft's Terms of Service.[23]

As this first edition of *Virtual Law* goes to press, there are many more questions than answers. Will a real-world lawsuit help clarify the status of digital property? Will criminal charges result from in-world activity? Will someone's in-world private legal system become the de facto dispute resolution standard? Will attorneys practicing law in-world get in trouble with real-world ethics bodies? Will someone bring a civil suit for emotional distress inflicted by an avatar? As more people create avatars and begin using virtual worlds, these questions will inevitably arise, and virtual law will just as inevitably become part of the modern legal landscape.

Open Questions on the Future of Virtual Law

1. As virtual worlds become more specialized, what new legal questions will appear?

2. What features are most important to make virtual worlds business and law friendly?

3. Do business-oriented and play-oriented virtual worlds need separate environments?

4. What particular skills do attorneys practicing virtual law need, and how can law schools prepare students for this specialization?

Notes

1. *Gartner Says 80 Percent of Active Internet Users Will Have a "Second Life" in the Virtual World by the End of 2011* (Apr. 24, 2007), *available at* http://www.gartner.com/it/page.jsp?id=503861 (last visited Jan. 4, 2008).

2. Posting of Tuukka Lehtiniemi with contributions from Vili Lehdonvirta, How Big Is the RMT Market Anyway?, http://virtual-economy.org/blog/how_big_is_the_rmt_market_anyw, Mar. 2, 2007, (last visited Jan. 4, 2008).

3. Posting of Christian Renaud, A Warm Welcome, http://blogs.cisco.com/virtualworlds/2007/08/a_warm_welcome.html (Aug. 15, 2007) .

4. A Google search for "Virtual Worlds" yielded 1.7 million hits as of August 2007. "Networked virtual environments" yielded 76,000.

5. Brian Crecente, *Sony Unveils Home*, http://kotaku.com/gaming/gdc07/gdc07-sony-unveils-home-242332.php (Mar. 3, 2007).

6. Matthew Wall, *Virtual Worlds for Kids Take Off* (Aug. 9, 2007), *available at* http://www.guardian.co.uk/technology/2007/aug/09/guardianweekly technologysection.internet.

7. Eric Eldon, *Disney Buys Club Penguin in $700 Million Deal* (Aug. 1, 2007), *available at* http://venturebeat.com/2007/08/01/disney-buys-club-penguin-in-700-million-deal/.

8. Christopher Mims, *Guess Who Just Launched the Fastest-growing Virtual World Ever?* (July 13, 2007), *available at* http://science-community.sciam.com/thread.jspa?threadID=300004405.

9. Avatars of Lord Vishnu, http://www.hindunet.org/avatars/ (last visited Jan. 4, 2008).

10. Linda Zimmer, *Second Life Entertainment Study Released: SL Accounts for More Time Than All Other Forms of Entertainment Combined* (July 16, 2007), http://freshtakes.typepad.com/sl_communicators/2007/07/second-life-ent.html.

11. Kathleen Craig, *Making a Living in Second Life*, WIRED (Feb. 8, 2006), *available at* http://www.wired.com/gaming/virtualworlds/news/2006/02/70153.

12. Jon Fortt, *Linden Lab: Second Life Entrepreneurship Is Booming* (Aug. 1, 2007), *available at* http://bigtech.blogs.fortune.cnn.com/2007/08/01/linden -lab-second-life-entrepreneurship-is-booming/.

13. *Anshe Chung Becomes First Virtual World Millionaire*, Nov. 26, 2006, http://www.anshechung.com/include/press/press_release251106.html.

14. Trademark Application Serial No. 77110299 (filed Feb. 18, 2007), *available at* http://tarr.uspto.gov/servlet/tarr?regser=serial&entry=77110299.

15. Frank Rose, *How Madison Avenue Is Wasting Millions on a Deserted Second Life*, WIRED, July 24, 2007, http://www.wired.com/techbiz/media/ magazine/15-08/ff_sheep?currentPage=all.

16. *See* http://www.virtualthirst.com/ (last visited Jan. 4, 2008).

17. Daniel Terdiman, *MTV Launches "Virtual Hills" Based on There.com Platform* (Jan. 15, 2007), http://news.com.com/8301-10784_3-6150206-7.html.

18. Gail Schiller, *"Phoenix" Soars into Second Life*, HOLLYWOOD REPORTER (Aug. 3, 2007), *available at* http://www.hollywoodreporter.com/hr/content_ display/news/e3i7ba34c61f8b25ae278dc647741c6f273.

19. Posting of Wagner James Au, Unwired (Updated), http://nwn.blogs .com/nwn/2007/07/unwired.html (July 23, 2007).

20. Kent German, *Top 10 Dot-Com Flops*, *available at* http://www.cnet .com/4520-11136_1-6278387-1.html (last visited Jan. 4, 2008).

21. Bragg v. Linden Research Inc., *available at* http://dockets.justia.com/ docket/court-paedce/case_no-2:2006cv04925/case_id-217858/ (last visited Jan. 4, 2008).

22. Eros, LLC v. Doe, *available at* http://dockets.justia.com/docket/ court-flmdce/case_no-8:2007cv01158/case_id-202603/ (last visited Jan. 4, 2008).

23. Hernandez v. Internet Gaming Entertainment, Ltd., *available at* http:// news.justia.com/cases/392882/ (last visited Jan. 4, 2008).

Big Picture Questions in Virtual Law 2

Before delving into narrower questions, it is important to understand a few big picture questions that arise in relation to most areas of virtual law. Big picture questions include whether virtual worlds are just fancy communication tools or something more, how virtual worlds are currently governed, where virtual worlds are located for jurisdictional purposes, and how virtual currency should be viewed.

Augmentationists, Immersionists, and Experimentalists

If you have already downloaded and installed a virtual world client, you have undoubtedly noticed that different people with whom you have interacted view virtual worlds in very different ways. The lens through which each person views virtual worlds has a dramatic impact on how that person views virtual law and on how he or she views the presence of lawyers in virtual worlds. Because virtual world users are frequently passionate about their take on virtual law and in-world governance, it is important to understand a little bit about the various kinds of users you will meet.

One frequently cited classification divides users into "augmentationists" and "immersionists."[1] Robert Bloomfield, a professor of accounting and management at Cornell University who studies economic issues in virtual worlds, argues for a third classification: "experimentalists."[2] This book will adopt these three classifications with twin caveats: (1) most users fall into more than one of these classifications; and (2) the classifications are slowly disappearing, as discussed in greater detail later in this section.

Augmentationists generally view the virtual world chiefly as augmenting their real-life experiences. They might identify one corner of the virtual world as their virtual law office, virtual classroom, or virtual boardroom, but in essence, they view virtual worlds as not much different than e-mail software, a text chat system, or a conference call center. Augmentationists often disclose their real-life identity in their avatar's profile and tend to have no particular loyalty to any specific virtual world. Most attorneys, executives, and other professionals involved in virtual worlds consider themselves chiefly augmentationists. Many augmentationists take pride in having avatars that look rather like themselves. Particularly in relation to free-form and social virtual worlds, I am primarily an augmentationist.

Immersionists, on the other hand, view virtual worlds as alternate realities. They generally keep the virtual world and their virtual identity separate from their real lives. When they log in to virtual worlds, they sometimes adopt different appearances, attitudes, genders, and even species. Nearly everyone who logs in to game worlds is, to some degree, an immersionist. You can't really trick yourself into believing that you're killing an Abyssal Flamebringer Demon with your e-mail client, after all, but it is surprisingly easy to perform the necessary mental gymnastics when you are playing World of Warcraft.

It would be overly simplistic (and insulting) to say that all immersionists are merely playing roles in games, however. Although game players are certainly immersionists (when playing games, I am undeniably an immersionist), some users of free-form social virtual worlds are immersed in different, sometimes serious ways. Many who would chiefly identify themselves as immersionists have relationships, run businesses, and build governments that only exist in virtual worlds.

Many immersionists believe that virtual worlds are at a fundamental level different from the real world and that real-world laws either do not or should not apply. In fact, a surprising number of users believe that they have little or no real-world responsibility for their in-world actions—that if the software code as written by the world-builders allows them to do something, it must be legal.

Virtual world providers have, in some cases, done little to dispel the myth that real-world laws do not apply in their virtual worlds. For example, Linden Lab, the creator of Second Life, only took steps to ban gambling in Second Life in July 2007, four years after the world was launched and after hundreds of residents had spent tens of thousands of hours building functional casinos in-world.[3] This phenomenon—where real-life law is perceived as not applying to virtual spaces—generates a certain amount of conflict between immersionists and anyone who finds it necessary to discuss legal issues related to virtual worlds (e.g., most augmentationists).

Finally, experimentalists, according to Professor Bloomfield (who first used the term in this context) use virtual worlds "as a laboratory in which to conduct controlled experiments."[4] Bloomfield writes:

> By allowing participants to take on natural roles in business settings, virtual worlds can help students understand factory floors and trading floors; supply chains for potato chips and computer chips, marketing strategy, and (my own particular interest) how financial reporting regulations affect capital flows and financial markets. Outcomes in such worlds can also allow researchers to push their own frontiers of knowledge, much as experimental researchers have done, by constructing controlled environments designed to test specific hypotheses, rather than attempting to test hypotheses by looking at data generated for another purpose (and therefore not ideal data for testing the hypothesis in question).[5]

Certain legal questions lend themselves to the experimentalist perspective as well. In particular, legal scholars considering questions of governance and alternative dispute resolution may be able to use virtual worlds as laboratories for experiments that are simply impossible in the real world.

Although classifications of users into neat categories has a certain appeal and, indeed, some use, it is impossible to neatly label everyone who uses a virtual world because most users experience virtual worlds from more than one perspective. For example, one U.K. attorney who is active in Second Life has spent a great deal of time and energy trying to start governmental systems within the virtual world—he also, however, constructs replicas of antique furniture in the virtual world that he sells to other users. Another attorney who regularly attends in-world meetings with the creators of Second Life spent her early days in the virtual world working as a virtual exotic dancer and managing a nightclub. I spend most of my time in virtual worlds attending Second Life Bar Association meet-

■■■■■

Augmentationists, Immersionists, and Experimentalists

Augmentationists view the virtual world as chiefly augmenting their real-life experiences, often disclose their real-life identity in their avatar's profile, and often have no particular loyalty to any specific virtual world. They are often professionals and real-world business owners.

Immersionists view virtual worlds as alternate realities, generally keep the virtual world and their virtual identity separate from their real lives, and sometimes believe that real-world laws either do not or should not apply to virtual spaces. They tend to be gamers, virtual business owners, and people seeking virtual world relationships.

Experimentalists use virtual worlds as laboratories in which to conduct controlled experiments. They are typically educators.

ings, conducting interviews, and giving talks on legal issues, but occasionally I take off my virtual necktie and attend live, in-world concerts.

Indeed, it is impossible to participate in a virtual world as a pure augmentationist because, if nothing else, an augmentationist will find himself wanting to change his avatar's generic appearance shortly after he logs in, and that requires shopping, which means going to a virtual store, browsing around, and buying new clothing. So within moments of arriving in a virtual world, a self-described augmentationist may find himself asking a seven-foot-tall purple tiger wearing a tuxedo for fashion advice, and the augmentationist instantly becomes—at least a little bit—an immersionist. The process is inevitable. As I became more and more immersed in virtual worlds while writing this book, I found my definition of myself as an augmentationist shifting. For example, reporting on a financial fraud in Second Life led to long discussions with dozens of avatars, some of whom had lost thousands of very real dollars. It takes but a few conversations with avatars who lost a real-world mortgage payment's worth of in-world currency to the fraudulent scheme of another user to start viewing virtual worlds from a more immersionist perspective.

This all means that the line between immersionist and augmentationist (and, to a degree, experimentalist) is slowly disappearing. As more and more attorneys, professors, writers, executives, and other professionals get involved in virtual worlds and find themselves interacting with people who use virtual worlds primarily for recreation, that process will only accelerate.

Rights for Players, Users, and Avatars

One fundamental question in virtual law is whether a special set of laws should be created to cover virtual spaces. The question typically comes from academics and game design theorists rather than from practicing attorneys. It is a constant source of tension in the evaluation of any legal question that impacts virtual worlds. The question takes many forms. One noted game designer, Raph Koster, famously discussed the issue of player rights in the context of his hypothetical "Declaration of the Rights of Avatars."[6] The document contains nineteen provisions covering a range of "rights" that Koster felt should guide virtual world creators. They reflect generally accepted principles of due process, free speech, and privacy, and include the following notable provisions:

4. Liberty consists of the freedom to do anything which injures no one else including the weal of the community as a whole and as an entity instantiated on hardware and by software; the exercise of the natural rights of avatars are therefore limited solely by the rights of other avatars sharing the same space and participating in the same community. These limits can only be determined by a clear code of conduct.

5. The code of conduct can only prohibit those actions and utterances that are hurtful to society, inclusive of the harm that may be done to the fabric of the virtual space via hurt done to the hardware, software, or data; and likewise inclusive of the harm that may be done to the individual who maintains said hardware, software, or data, in that harm done to this individual may result in direct harm done to the community.

  . . . .

7. No avatar shall be accused, muzzled, toaded,[7] jailed, banned, or otherwise punished except in the cases and according to the forms prescribed by the code of conduct. Any one soliciting, transmitting, executing, or causing to be executed, any arbitrary order, shall be punished, even if said individual is one who has been granted special powers or privileges within the virtual space. But any avatar summoned or arrested in virtue of the code of conduct shall submit without delay, as resistance constitutes an offense.

  . . . .

11. The free communication of ideas and opinions is one of the most precious of the rights of man. Every avatar may, accordingly, speak, write, chat, post, and print with freedom, but shall be responsible for such abuses

of this freedom as shall be defined by the code of conduct, most particularly the abuse of affecting the performance of the space or the performance of a given avatar's representation of the space.

. . . .

18. Avatars have the right to be secure in their persons, communications, designated private spaces, and effects, against unreasonable snooping, eavesdropping, searching and seizures, no activity pertaining thereto shall be undertaken by administrators save with probable cause supported by affirmation, particularly describing the goal of said investigations.[8]

The full text of Koster's "Declaration of the Rights of Avatars" can be found at Appendix VII.

Although Koster suggests that these guidelines should be followed voluntarily by virtual world and game providers and integrated into the Terms of Service and End User License Agreements that users must agree to in order to access these worlds, others take a more direct approach. Advocates of the more direct approach argue that the law should proactively protect certain rights of virtual world users and game players, via either legislation or interpretation of existing law.

One law professor, Joshua Fairfield, in a paper entitled "Anti-Social Contracts: The Contractual Governance of Online Communities" (currently in draft form), argues that Terms of Service and End User License Agreements are poor vehicles for defining the rights of a community and the obligations of community members to one another.[9] In the abstract to the article, Fairfield writes: "Contracts cannot, by their very nature, provide for every legal need of large and shifting online communities [but] courts can use basic common law principles to provide online communities with the private property, dignitary and personal protections, and freedom of speech that communities need to thrive."[10]

Fairfield's approach would have the courts outline these rights as cases arise challenging game and virtual world companies on the validity of their Terms of Service. Fairfield's approach seems to be, in the short term at least, the most likely outcome. One court has already declared a dispute resolution clause in a virtual world provider's Terms of Service unconscionable.[11] Though the holding itself was relatively fact-specific, the decision highlights the fact that courts are willing to tackle these issues. "This case," the decision begins, "is about virtual property maintained on a virtual world on the Internet."[12]

Another approach comes from Edward Castronova, an expert on the economies of large-scale online games. Castronova has expressed concern that the creation of virtual worlds with augmentationist properties (typically where business is at least as much a focus as play) may make it more difficult for virtual worlds to stand as immersive play spaces. In a *New York Law School Law Review* article, "The Right to Play," Castronova looks to the legislature rather than the courts to establish player and user rights.[13] Castronova argues that virtual worlds, particularly those that exist chiefly for immersive "play," should be governed by specialized rules that prevent real-life law from entering the space and breaking the "magic circle" that "allow[s] these places to render unique and valuable services to their users."[14]

Castronova posits the concept of "interration," which he views as a parallel to "incorporation."[15] Interration describes a proposed legal status that would govern the creation of "closed worlds."[16] These "closed worlds" would be protected from state intervention, and they would, in turn, impose restrictions (such as prohibitions against "real money trade") that would theoretically prevent them from bleeding into real life. Castronova explains that "lack of good faith efforts to maintain the space as a play space could lead to the revocation of the charter."[17]

If there is a theme to this book, it is this: real-world laws apply to virtual worlds to exactly the degree that virtual worlds attempt to offer real-world possibilities. In other words, Castronova and Fairfield are both right. The magic circle must protect spaces that are operated as pure play spaces, but to the degree that providers wish to offer real-life benefits (e.g., the potential to make real money and own virtual property, advanced social and business interaction outside a game context, and pseudo-governmental services), courts can and will apply real-life law to activity that takes place in these spaces.

End User License Agreements and Terms of Service

Until legislation is passed to protect users of virtual worlds, or protection evolves from court cases, users are no more protected from providers—or from each other—than providers say they are. Virtual world providers articulate whatever protections exist in two documents that stand as a form of "law" in virtual worlds— the End User License Agreement (EULA) and Terms of Service (TOS; also sometimes referred to as the Terms of Use or TOU). Virtual world providers require each user to agree to one or both of these documents either when the user initially installs a virtual world client or, in some cases, every time the user accesses the virtual world. Many provisions in these agreements are standard terms that have been found enforceable in other contexts, and most—though not all—existing provisions in these documents seem likely to be deemed enforceable, going forward.

Though generally enforceable, these agreements are subject to a fair amount of scrutiny, and particular clauses are potentially susceptible to the argument that they are unconscionable in context. This is partly because these agreements are contracts of adhesion. A contract of adhesion is a "standardized contract, which, imposed and drafted by the party of superior bargaining strength, relegates to the subscribing party only the opportunity to adhere to the contract or reject it." [18] The lack of negotiation between the parties does not, of course, mean that EULAs and Terms of Service agreements are unenforceable, but it does raise the level of scrutiny that courts will subject them to, and leaves them open to potential unconscionability arguments.

Only one court, the U.S. District Court for the Eastern District of Pennsylvania, has directly addressed any aspect of virtual world EULAs and Terms of Service agreements, and it found the provision it was considering—an arbitration provision—unconscionable. The case, *Marc Bragg v. Linden Research Inc. and Philip Rosedale*, is the first case to test the boundaries of virtual law and will be the subject of several discussions in this book. In the first major decision in the *Bragg* case, the court explained unconscionability as follows:

[U]nconscionability has both procedural and substantive components. The procedural component can be satisfied by showing (1) oppression through the existence of unequal bargaining positions or (2) surprise through hidden terms common in the context of adhesion contracts. The substantive component can be satisfied by showing overly harsh or one-sided results that "shock the conscience." The two elements operate on a sliding scale such that the more significant one is, the less significant the other need be.[19]

The *Bragg* court noted that "Linden presents the TOS on a take-it-or-leave-it basis [where] a potential participant can either click 'assent' to the TOS, and then gain entrance to Second Life's virtual world, or refuse assent and be denied access."[20] The court also found it relevant that "Linden buried the TOS's arbitration provision in a lengthy paragraph under the benign heading 'GENERAL PROVISIONS'" and that there was no reasonable alternative in the marketplace to Second Life, because "Second Life was the first and only virtual world to specifically grant its participants property rights in virtual land."[21] For all these reasons, the court found that the procedural prong of the test for unconscionability had been met.[22]

The court also found that the substantive prong of the unconscionability test was satisfied. In reaching that conclusion, the court largely based its decision on the lack of mutuality in the provision. The court noted that the Second Life Terms of Service "proclaim that 'Linden has the right at any time for any reason or no reason to suspend or terminate your Account, terminate this Agreement, and/or refuse any and all current or future use of the Service without notice or liability to you'" but that end users' only mechanism for dealing with complaints was expensive arbitration.[23] The court held that because "the TOS provide Linden with a variety of one-sided remedies to resolve disputes, while forcing its customers to arbitrate any disputes with Linden" the arbitration provision did not contain even "a modicum of bilaterality."[24] The court also found it significant that Linden Lab could unilaterally modify the provision and that arbitration under the provision (requiring a three-judge panel) would "impose on some consumers costs greater than those a complainant would bear if he or she would file the same complaint in court."[25]

Other courts may treat other provisions in the Terms of Service and End User License Agreements of virtual worlds differently than the *Bragg* court did, but the dicta of the *Bragg* decision are likely encouraging to users, attorneys, and researchers who maintain that virtual worlds are different from other kinds of software. The court, recall, began its decision thus: "This case is about virtual property maintained on a virtual world on the Internet." The first paragraph continues:

> Plaintiff, Marc Bragg, Esq., claims an ownership interest in such virtual property. Bragg contends that Defendants, the operators of the virtual world, unlawfully confiscated his virtual property and denied him access to their virtual world. Ultimately at issue in this case are the novel questions of what rights and obligations grow out of the relationship between the owner and creator of a virtual world and its resident-customers. While the property and the world where it is found are "virtual," the dispute is real.

Although the *Bragg* case settled shortly before this edition of *Virtual Law* went to press, it appears certain that bigger issues of ownership, crime and punishment, and dispute resolution—all long the province of the private "law" set forth in Terms of Service and End User License Agreements—are questions that will eventually end up before judges and juries. It may be in virtual world providers' best interest to recognize this tidal shift in advance, and

■■■■■

Sample Terms of Service and EULAs

Appendix IV: Second Life Terms of Service

Appendix V: World of Warcraft Terms of Use

Appendix VI: Entropia Universe End User License Agreement re-draft their agreements with users to take these concerns into account. To the extent that they do not, courts appear willing to rewrite these contracts, and the *Bragg* arbitration clause decision now provides a framework.

Choice of Forum, Choice of Law, and Arbitration Clauses

"Choice of forum" provisions (dictating, geographically, where a lawsuit or arbitration will occur) and "choice of law" provisions (dictating what state's or country's laws will apply to disputes) are common to all TOS/EULA agreements between virtual world users and providers. Many also include arbitration clauses (dictating when and in what forum arbitration is required or, for some virtual worlds and games, when it is available).

Choice of law provisions typically select the law of the state or country where the virtual world's corporate headquarters are found. For example, There.com, Second Life, and IMVU are all based in California, and all specify that California law controls. Worlds for which the provider's headquarters are in other states (Massachusetts for Active Worlds) and foreign countries (Sweden for Entropia Universe) typically require disputes to be resolved using the rules of their home state or nation. One notable exception is World of Warcraft. World of Warcraft is a property of Blizzard, Inc., which is headquartered in California, but Blizzard is a subsidiary of Vivendi Games, which itself is a subsidiary of Vivendi SA, a French company. World of Warcraft's Terms of Use include a choice of law provision that dictates that Delaware law generally controls disagreements between users and the provider.

Choice of forum provisions are similar, though typically more complex. Some (like Electronic Arts, in a document that covers all Electronic Arts online games) apply different laws depending on the geographic location of the user. Thus, users of The Sims Online (an Electronic Arts game) who access the service from any European Union country must bring disputes against Electronic Arts before a court in England, but disputes between Electronic Arts and users located elsewhere are to be decided in (and, due to the operation of a parallel choice of law provision, under the laws of) the state of California.

Some games and virtual worlds require arbitration; others offer arbitration as an option for certain claims. Arbitration provisions are currently in a state of flux because, as *Virtual Law* goes to press, some virtual world providers are changing their arbitration provisions in apparent response to the *Bragg* decision holding Second Life's arbitration clause unconscionable.

Linden Lab itself changed the Terms of Service for Second Life shortly after the decision. Now, Second Life's TOS agreement includes the following arbitration provision, which governs claims for less than $10,000.

> 7.3 **Optional Arbitration.** For any Claim, excluding Claims for injunctive or other equitable relief, where the total amount of the award sought is less than ten thousand U.S. Dollars ($10,000.00 USD), the party requesting relief may elect to resolve the Claim in a cost-effective manner through binding non-appearance-based arbitration. A party electing arbitration shall initiate it through an established alternative dispute resolution ("ADR") provider mutually agreed upon by the parties. The ADR provider and the parties must comply with the following rules: (a) the arbitration shall be conducted, at the option of the party seeking relief, by telephone, online, or based solely on written submissions; (b) the arbitration shall not involve any personal appearance by the parties or witnesses unless otherwise mutually agreed by the parties; and (c) any judgment on the award rendered by the arbitrator may be entered in any court of competent jurisdiction.

> 7.4 **Improperly Filed Claims.** All Claims you bring against Linden Lab must be resolved in accordance with this Dispute Resolution Section. All Claims filed or brought contrary to this Dispute Resolution Section shall be considered improperly filed. Should you file a Claim contrary to this Dispute Resolution Section, Linden Lab may recover attorneys' fees and costs up to one thousand

U.S. Dollars ($1,000.00 USD), provided that Linden Lab has notified you in writing of the improperly filed Claim, and you have failed to promptly withdraw the Claim.[26]

Second Life's complete Terms of Service can be found at Appendix IV.

This provision provides for voluntary non-appearance-based binding arbitration for claims under US$10,000. Linden Lab subsequently clarified that the arbitration could take place in Second Life itself, giving rise to the likelihood that we will soon see arbitration proceedings with avatar attorneys and arbitrators conducting arbitration hearings entirely within the virtual world.[27]

The following table summarizes the choice of law, choice of forum, and arbitration provisions from the Terms of Service of several virtual worlds and games.

Online World	Choice of Law	Choice of Forum
IMVU	State of California	San Francisco County
Second Life	State of California	San Francisco County for all matters over $10K. Binding non-appearance arbitration (phone, teleconference, avatar) for matters under $10K.
There.com	State of California	Anywhere in California
The Sims Online	England (for EU residents), State of California (for everyone else)	England (for European Union residents), Northern California (for everyone else)
Active Worlds	State of Massachusetts	Arbitration required—either "on-line before the Active Worlds Tribunal" or before a panel of the American Arbitration Association, Boston, Massachusetts.

Online World	Choice of Law	Choice of Forum
Entropia Universe	Sweden	Sweden
World of Warcraft	State of Delaware	Arbitration required except for IP cases, computer crime, and claims for injunctive relief. Arbitration to be initiated in Los Angeles, California (for international players), or at "any . . . location . . . convenient to you" (for U.S. players). All non-arbitration claims are to be filed in Los Angeles, California.

Notably, World of Warcraft and Active Worlds require arbitration, as did Linden Lab regarding disputes with Second Life users before the *Bragg* decision holding the provision unconscionable. There are some differences between Blizzard's and Active Worlds' arbitration provisions and Linden Lab's old arbitration provision, however, which may protect Blizzard and Active Worlds from similar findings. For example, Blizzard specifies arbitration through the American Arbitration Association (AAA), which has provisions for relatively inexpensive consumer arbitration for claims under $75,000.[28] Also, Blizzard allows U.S. users to begin arbitration proceedings "at any reasonable location within the United States convenient for you" (although non-U.S. players must initiate claims "in the County of Los Angeles, State of California, United States of America"). Active Worlds allows for in-world arbitration "before the Active Worlds Tribunal" as an alternative to traveling to Boston, which could make the process less expensive for users with complaints (though notably, the composition of the "Active Worlds Tribunal" is not discussed, and no further information is provided by Active Worlds). The lower cost of these options does mitigate at least one of the factors that led the *Bragg* court to find the clause unconscionable, though neither providers' provision addresses the court's other two chief concerns—lack of mutuality in possible remedies, and the provider's right to unilaterally change the terms of the provision at a later date.[29]

There are other interesting caveats in Blizzard's arbitration provision for World of Warcraft (the most complex provision set forth by any of the virtual world and game providers surveyed). Blizzard requires that both parties "first attempt to negotiate any Dispute (except those Disputes expressly provided below) informally for at least thirty (30) days before initiating any arbitration or court proceeding." This negotiation must be instigated by letter. Notably, the disputes that are exempted from this provision (which are also exempted from the general arbitration provision in Blizzard's agreement) include most of the disputes Blizzard would want to bring against users. These include claims "to enforce or protect, or concerning the validity of, any of your or Blizzard's intellectual property rights," disputes "related to, or arising from, allegations of theft, piracy, invasion of privacy or unauthorized use," and claims for injunctive relief. Because these claims are exempted from the Informal Negotiations and Binding Arbitration provisions, Blizzard preserves its option to bring these claims against a user directly by filing the claim in a court of law.

These clauses are worth keeping in mind as you consider the narrower questions in virtual law, as they dictate where and how lawsuits against virtual world providers can be filed. They are also worth paying close attention to over the next few years, as they may change significantly in response to the *Bragg* decision that forced Linden Lab to modify its arbitration clause.[30]

Virtual Currency

Virtual worlds and games typically have some form of currency. In Warcraft, "gold" is used to buy higher-powered weapons and raw materials. In Second Life, "Linden Dollars," or Lindens," are used to buy literally everything from land to apartments to personal services to a new look for your avatar to "stock" in virtual companies. In There.com, "Therebucks" are used for avatar clothing, recreational equipment (like dune buggies), and other accessories.

The intersection of "real money" and virtual worlds (often referred to as "real money trading" or simply "RMT") is a source of much controversy, particularly in the context of games. RMT in games takes many forms. One of the most common involves buying in-world currency with real currency. After the user completes the purchase (typically by paying for the "gold" or other virtual currency with a credit card via a website), the seller contacts the user in-world and delivers the purchased currency to the user's character. Another common RMT transaction involves goods and equipment such as particularly powerful weapons or rare in-world possessions that are difficult or time-consuming to secure through game play. Finally, people buy and sell entire accounts (by way of disclosure, I was first exposed to RMT in the classic online game Ultima Online, when I decided I didn't need the distraction during my first year of law school and sold my Ultima Online account to another user for approximately $400). RMT, particularly the sale of in-world currency and the sale of high-powered accounts, has turned into a big business. Julian Dibble, author of two popular books and numerous articles on virtual worlds, estimated that in 2007 approximately $1.8 billion changed hands for virtual goods, and "gold farming" companies in China alone employed over 100,000 people.[31]

Richard A. Bartle, a noted game writer and researcher, and creator of what was arguably the first virtual world, "MUD," has taken a strong stand against RMT.[32] Bartle's argument is that virtual worlds, and particularly goal-based games, are fundamentally different from the real world and must remain so in order to preserve that which makes them good.

Bartle refers to what happens to games and virtual worlds that allow or turn a blind eye to RMT as "commodification." Notably, he does not take the position that the practice should be illegal, or even prevented by all providers, but he does believe that game and virtual world publishers ought to be able to prevent commodification and that one avenue for doing so is a strongly worded—and rigidly enforced—EULA.

Bartle focuses his criticism particularly on the "hero's journey" that exists in one form or another in virtually all games and, to a degree, in free-form virtual worlds as well. In essentially all games, your character starts relatively weak, unequipped, and without significant knowledge of his or her environment. With perseverance, your character grows in strength and power until he or she is able to take on the strongest enemies the world has to offer (or, in the case of free-form virtual worlds, masters the intricacies of whatever vocation or avocation the user chooses to have his or her avatar follow). Bartle says, with good reason, that that heroic story trajectory is undermined, destroyed even, when users can simply purchase, with real money, the attributes, equipment, and knowledge that otherwise is only available to higher-level players who have spent dozens (and in some cases hundreds, or even thousands) of hours walking the virtual heroic path. Bartle explains his argument against RMT in the context of a board game:

> Suppose you were one of three people playing the game Clue, and that you were close to winning. The person playing Mrs. White suddenly leans over to the person playing Colonel Mustard and says, "I'll give you $20 if you show me your cards." Colonel Mustard obliges, Mrs. White pays up, and promptly announces that Reverend Green did it in the ballroom with the candlestick.
>
> Understandably, few players would be pleased if this happened to them. Although there are no written rules in Clue about bribery, there are, nevertheless, unwritten rules that say this kind of activity stops a game from being a game. You would probably think twice about playing with Colonel Mustard again, and three times about playing with Mrs. White.[33]

Many game designers agree with Bartle, and, as a result, most (though not all) games explicitly bar RMT. The provisions in various providers' End User License Agreements and Terms of Service barring RMT differ in form, but World of Warcraft's RMT clause provides a robust example:

8. **Ownership/Selling of the Account or Virtual Items.**
    Blizzard does not recognize the transfer of Accounts. You may not purchase, sell, gift or trade any Account, or offer to purchase, sell, gift or trade any Account, and any such attempt shall be null and void. Blizzard owns, has licensed, or otherwise has rights to all of the content that appears in the Program. You agree that you have no right or title in or to any such content, including the virtual goods or currency appearing or originating in the Game, or any other attributes associated with the Account or stored on the Service. Blizzard does not rec-

ognize any virtual property transfers executed outside of the Game or the purported sale, gift or trade in the "real world" of anything related to the Game. Accordingly, you may not sell items for "real" money or otherwise exchange items for value outside of the Game.[34]

World of Warcraft's complete Terms of Use Agreement (as of publication) is reprinted at Appendix V.

Players risk banishment from games and virtual worlds that require agreement with provisions like this when they engage in RMT, but many players simply accept that risk. It can be a very expensive risk. One player bought a World of Warcraft account that included a high-level character and two very rare weapons for almost US$10,000; the account was banned five days later.[35] Blizzard even took the extraordinary step of filing a federal lawsuit against one firm that buys and sells gold, "Peons4Hire."[36] The case settled, resulting in a permanent injunction that essentially shuts down Peons4Hire's parent company's entire World of Warcraft operation—essentially a complete victory for Blizzard.

In spite of game and virtual world providers' best attempts to curtail the practice, many forums exist for black-market RMT sales, and if history is any indication, always will. Until early 2007, eBay allowed auctions for virtual currency, goods, and accounts from all worlds and games, even those where RMT was expressly prohibited by the EULA or TOS. Although these auctions have now been banned at eBay (presumably due to pressure from providers like Blizzard), other sites still allow these auctions, and sellers advertise their gold, power-leveling services, and rare items heavily on the web, via e-mail spam, and through instant messages within the virtual worlds and games themselves.

Not all virtual worlds and games, however, take this approach. Several embrace RMT and refer to their environments as possessing a "Real Cash Economy" (RCE). Some of the games and virtual worlds that embrace RCE and RMT have found success, although depending on the business model, they may be of dubious legality in the United States.

One successful RCE can be found in Entropia Universe. The software that lets a player access the game world is free to download, and the game is nominally free to play. You can log in, wander around,

■■■■■

Different Approaches to RMT/RCE

Second Life—Users can buy and sell Lindens to and from other users on the official Linden Dollar Exchange (LindeX). Linden Lab manipulates the economy to maintain a theoretically stable exchange rate.

There.com—Therebucks can be purchased directly from the provider, from other members, or from third-party online "banks" that usually offer competitive exchange rates. Members can also sell their Therebucks to banks in exchange for real-world currency, usually USD.

IMVU—"Credits" can be purchased from IMVU directly or from third-party resellers; third-party resellers also buy IMVU credits or facilitate sales to other users for a fee.

World of Warcraft—Users are not allowed to buy or sell gold or items for real money.

Kwari—Users must buy ammunition from the provider for real money to play in a match. A separate cash pool is divided among the winners of each match.

Entropia Universe—Players can play for free, but most players find it necessary to buy equipment from the provider. Equipment deteriorates with use and requires "repair" via payment to the provider.

and, indeed, eke out a meager living by—this sort of thing cannot be made up—collecting the sweat of various animals found in the world and picking up "dung" to sell as fertilizer. However, more appealing (and more lucrative) virtual vocations, such as hunting and mining, require the purchase of equipment, which costs real money. Many players report that it is nearly impossible to make significant progress in the game without making at least an initial cash investment in order to buy certain critical in-world items from MindArk, the company that runs Entropia Universe. MindArk explains that its "income base is the fees that the users pay for acquisition, repair and renewal of the different assets and objects that the user chooses to use In-World."[37]

Entropia Universe's in-world currency ("PEDs") is convertible to real currency at a fixed exchange rate of $1 for 10 PEDs. Withdrawing PEDs as dollars to your real-world bank account also involves a fee of 1.5% (minimum $10).[38] A lot of money is at stake in Entropia Universe. A virtual spaceport within the game sold for 1m PEDs (US$100,000).[39]

Although games like Entropia Universe do involve increases in "abilities" over time, they also rely largely on luck. The two most common professions in Entropia ("hunting" and "mining") give players typically low-value but occasionally very high-value rewards and bear a striking resemblance to slot-machine gambling with tokens. In both cases, the player risks something of value ("ammunition" or "mining probes" bought with real cash in Entropia Universe, and a handful of dollar tokens in a slot machine) for a random reward that has immediate cash-out value.

Attempting to avoid legal pitfalls associated with anti-gambling laws, one game (in beta testing at press time) called Kwari promises a purely skill-based contest between players. From Kwari's description: "Every time you hit another player in Kwari you make money. Every time you are hit by another player it costs you. Every shot counts. How much is down to the stake level you play in."[40] In other words, Kwari aims to fall into the same legal classification as sites that host for-fee chess tournaments. Instead of taking a percentage of each pot, Kwari's business model is to act as players' "virtual arms dealer," selling them ammunition at a preset rate, but otherwise only managing the transfer of funds in each match from the losing participants to the winning participants. Though state law differs on the legality of such enterprises, games like Kwari are at least arguably legal in most U.S. states.

Notably, even worlds and games that embrace RMT and RCE attempt to limit their exposure to liability for investments in their currencies in their Terms of Service and End User License Agreements. Linden Lab, for example, maintains a website where Second Life users can sell Lindens to other users for real money,[41] keeps a running total of the amount of in-world spending over the previous twenty-four hours in U.S. dollars on the front page of the Second

Life website,[42] and advertises that you can "[m]ake real money in a virtual world . . . that's right, *real money*" (emphasis in original).[43] Linden Lab also banned gambling in 2007, stating that "Linden Lab and Second Life Residents must comply with state and federal laws applicable to regulated online gambling." However, in spite of a fair bit of evidence that Linden Lab treats Lindens as a valuable currency and Second Life as a Real Cash Economy, the Second Life Terms of Service state:

> 1.4 Second Life "currency" is a limited license right available for purchase or free distribution at Linden Lab's discretion, and is not redeemable for monetary value from Linden Lab.
>
> You acknowledge that the Service presently includes a component of in-world fictional currency ("Currency" or "Linden Dollars" or "L$"), which constitutes a limited license right to use a feature of our product when, as, and if allowed by Linden Lab. Linden Lab may charge fees for the right to use Linden Dollars, or may distribute Linden Dollars without charge, in its sole discretion. Regardless of terminology used, Linden Dollars represent a limited license right governed solely under the terms of this Agreement, and are not redeemable for any sum of money or monetary value from Linden Lab at any time. You agree that Linden Lab has the absolute right to manage, regulate, control, modify and/or eliminate such Currency as it sees fit in its sole discretion, in any general or specific case, and that Linden Lab will have no liability to you based on its exercise of such right.

In spite of this provision, if the question arises in litigation or criminal prosecution in the future (as seems likely), a reasonable argument can be made that Lindens are, functionally, a currency that has real value. The fact that Linden Lab runs and profits from the LindeX (the currency exchange), the widespread advertising referring to the opportunity to make "real money," previous comments in the press by Linden executives that encourage the idea that Lindens are currency, and the visible ease with which one can convert real money to Lindens and back—all are evidence that Lindens have value.

These different approaches to virtual currency—from RCEs like Entropia Universe to fictional currencies like Second Life's Linden to World of Warcraft's outright prohibition against RMT—are worth keeping in mind as we explore a number of areas of virtual law, particularly in regard to criminal law and property law.

Open Questions on the Big Picture of Virtual Law

1. Will laws be written specifically directed at virtual worlds and multiuser games, or will existing laws be interpreted to cover these spaces?

2. Will disputes between residents of virtual worlds give rise to more real-world legal actions, or will in-world mechanisms be developed to address these issues?

3. Should virtual worlds be protected from the intrusion of real-world laws?

4. Are Real Money Trading and a Real Cash Economy compatible with "play" in virtual worlds?

5. What new legislation might help encourage development of virtual worlds as places for expression, creation, and experimentation?

Notes

1. Henrik Bennetsen, *Augmentation vs. Immersion* (August 8, 2006), http://slcreativity.org/wiki/index.php?title=Augmentation_vs_Immersion.

2. Robert J. Bloomfield, *Studying Real-World Business in Virtual Worlds* (May 31, 2007), http://terranova.blogs.com/terra_nova/2007/05/studying_realwo.html.

3. Posting of Robin Linden to Second Life blog, *Wagering in Second Life: New Policy,* http://blog.secondlife.com/2007/07/25/wagering-in-second-life-new -policy/ (July 25, 2007, 16:05 PST).

4. Robert Bloomfield, *Metanomics 101 Suggested Reading* (Sept. 11, 2007), http://metanomics.metaversed.com/11-sep-2007/metanomics-101-suggested -reading.

5. Robert J. Bloomfield, *Worlds for Study: Invitation—Virtual Worlds for Studying Real-World Business (and Law, and Politics, and Sociology, and. . .)* (May 25, 2007), http://ssrn.com/abstract=988984.

6. Raph Koster, *Declaring the Rights of Players* (Aug. 27, 2000), http://www.raphkoster.com/gaming/playerrights.shtml.

7. "Toading" refers, literally, to a game or virtual world administrator's turning a user into a toad, although it has become shorthand for removing a user and all history of his or her existence from a virtual world or game.

8. Koster, *supra* note 6.

9. Joshua Fairfield, "Anti-Social Contracts: The Contractual Governance of Online Communities," Washington & Lee Legal Studies Paper No. 2007-20 (July 2007), http://ssrn.com/abstract=1002997.

10. *Id.*

11. Eric Krangel, a/k/a Eric Reuters, *Judge Rules Against "One-Sided" TOS in Bragg Lawsuit,* May 31, 2007, http://secondlife.reuters.com/stories/2007/05/31/judge-rules-against-one-sided-tos-in-bragg-lawsuit/.

12. Memorandum, Bragg v. Linden Research, Inc., (No. CIV.A.06-4925, May 30, 2007), http://casedocs.justia.com/pennsylvania/paedce/2:2006cv04925/217858/51/0.pdf; *see also infra* Appendix IX.

13. Edward Castronova, *The Right to Play,* 49 N.Y.L. Sch. L. Rev., 185–210 (2004), http://ssrn.com/abstract=733486.

14. *Id.* at 185.

15. *Id.* at 204.

16. *Id.* at 201.

17. *Id.* at 204.

18. Comb v. PayPal, Inc., 218 F. Supp. 2d 1165, 1172 (N.D. Cal. 2002).

19. Memorandum and Order Denying Motion to Dismiss, Bragg v. Linden Lab (No. CIV.A.06-4925, May 30, 2007), http://www.paed.uscourts.gov/documents/opinions/07D0658P.pdf; *see also infra* Appendix IX.

20. *Id.* (internal citations omitted).

21. *Id.* at 29 (internal citations omitted).

22. *Id.* at 31 (internal citations omitted).

23. *Id.* at 34 (internal citations omitted).

24. *Id.* at 32 (internal citations omitted).

25. *Id.* at 36–37 (internal citations omitted).

26. Second Life Terms of Service, http://secondlife.com/corporate/tos .php (last visited Jan. 5, 2008); *see also infra* Appendix IV.

27. Eric Krangel, a/k/a Eric Reuters, *UPDATE—Linden Raises Possibility of Virtual Arbitrations in New ToS* (Sept. 17, 2007), http://secondlife.reuters .com/stories/2007/09/18/linden-revamps-arbitration-in-new-terms-of-service/.

28. "If the consumer's claim or counterclaim does not exceed $10,000, then the consumer is responsible for one-half the arbitrator's fees up to a maximum of $125. . . . If the consumer's claim or counterclaim is greater than $10,000, but does not exceed $75,000, then the consumer is responsible for

one-half the arbitrator's fees up to a maximum of $375." American Arbitration Association Consumer Arbitration Costs, http://www.adr.org/sp.asp?id=22039 (July 1, 2003).

29. Memorandum and Order Denying Motion to Dismiss, *Bragg supra* note 19 at 28; *see also infra* Appendix IX.

30. *See Bragg, supra* note 29, at 32 (internal citations omitted).

31. Julian Dibbell, *The Life of the Chinese Gold Farmer,* N.Y. TIMES, June 17, 2007, (Magazine), *available at* http://www.nytimes.com/2007/06/17/magazine/17lootfarmers-t.html.

32. Richard A. Bartle, *Virtual Worldliness: What the Imaginary Asks of the Real,* 49 N.Y.L. SCH. L. REV. 19 (2005).

33. *Id.*

34. World of Warcraft, Terms of Use Agreement (January 11, 2007), http://www.worldofwarcraft.com/legal/termsofuse.html; *see also infra* Appendix V.

35. Cristina Jimenez, *The High Cost of Playing Warcraft,* BBC NEWS (Sept. 24, 2007), *available at* http://news.bbc.co.uk/1/hi/technology/7007026.stm.

36. Posting of Eyonix, *Gold Spam: Our Continued Efforts,* http://forums.worldofwarcraft.com/thread.html?topicId=106771592 (May 26, 2007) .

37. About Project Entropia, http://www.mindark.com/about_PE_e.html (last visited Jan. 5, 2008).

38. Entropia Universe—Bank Withdrawal, http://www.entropiauniverse.com/en/rich/5675.html (last visited Jan. 5, 2008).

39. US FILM-MAKER PAYS US $100,000 FOR VIRTUAL REAL ESTATE IN THE LARGEST VIRTUAL PURCHASE EVER (Oct. 26, 2005), http://www.mindark.se/docs/pr/October-26-2005.pdf.

40. What Is Kwari?, http://www.kwari.com/what_is (last visited Jan. 5, 2008).

41. Linden Dollar Exchange, http://secondlife.com/currency/ (last visited Jan. 5, 2008, login required).

42. Second Life: U.S. $ Spent Last 24h, http://secondlife.com (last visited Jan. 5, 2008).

43. Second Life: The Marketplace, http://secondlife.com/whatis/marketplace.php (last visited Jan. 5, 2008).

Evidence and Virtual Worlds **3**

Whether for civil lawsuits, criminal defenses or prosecutions, or corporate due diligence on a virtual world company, attorneys and other professionals looking at virtual spaces need to understand the differences between evidence collection in the real world and in virtual worlds. Conversation records, financial histories, and other documentary evidence raise different questions when they come from interaction that takes place in virtual worlds.

Virtual World and Game Hosts as Data Providers

It is important to realize that virtual world providers are, in a sense, simply data hosts. Their primary job is to maintain the virtual world.

Just as a web page host must make periodic backups of critical data on behalf of its customers, virtual world providers make periodic backups of the virtual world itself in order to be able to restore it in the event of data loss. Making sure that end user data are not lost is arguably one of the most important functions of a virtual world provider.

Data can be lost for many reasons. Simple human programming error could easily cause the deletion of data. Environmental catastrophe (e.g., fire or flood) could destroy the hosting facility and, with it, the virtual world. Malicious computer attacks—either external to the virtual world or from within—could wipe out some or all of the virtual world environment or end user data. Because preserving user data is so important and the likelihood of periodic loss nearly certain, all virtual world providers perform regular backups.

Regular backups are typically conducted at the time of day that has the least number of average logins to the virtual world. They are invariably stored off-site, frequently in the form of multiple copies at multiple locations. And, most importantly from the standpoint of evidence preservation, they are typically stored on a rotation and sometimes stored indefinitely.

For example, if a complete backup of the virtual world environment is taken every night, those backups will all be stored for a certain period, such as one week. But each week, one of these backups is preserved for a longer period. In our example, let's say it is

■■■■■

Possible Evidence Sources in Virtual Worlds

Public Chat Logs

Instant Message Chat Logs

Still Screenshots

In-world Video

Webcam Captures

Transaction Logs

Object Histories

Friend Lists

Audio Recordings

Authenticated Documents

Friday's backup. So each week, the backups that were made on Saturday through Thursday are overwritten, but each Friday backup is saved longer, often a month, sometimes a year, sometimes even indefinitely. Then, each month, one of the Friday backups, let's say the last one, is saved longer, perhaps a year, perhaps indefinitely. Some providers will wipe out old backups after a certain period, but information technology directors are notoriously careful about preservation of historical backup data, and a virtual world provider could well store a few extremely old "versions" of the world, complete with user content, indefinitely.

For security and business reasons, information about virtual world providers' schedules for retention of backups is typically not published, although it can and should be a topic for early discovery in litigation involving a virtual world provider.

Chat and User Activity Logs

Beyond simple whole-world backups, and perhaps more interesting from the standpoint of evidence collection, is the incredible volume of information that individual users save about their own virtual world activities and about the activities of others. Chat logs, transaction logs, friend lists, screenshots, object histories, and more all provide levels of evidence that simply do not exist in the real world.

First, consider simple typed chat and associated records. Although voice is rapidly becoming a part of virtual worlds, most users still conduct the majority of their communication using the keyboard. The process is fairly simple: a user types a few words on his or her screen and then hits the "Enter" key. At that point, the words appear either in a personal message window visible only to the intended recipient, or, in the case of public chat, in the windows of everyone within a predefined area of the virtual world surrounding the user. This area might be confined by the boundaries of a building or a property line, or it might be an arbitrary geographic boundary set by the parameters of the virtual world software itself. The text is typically captured by the virtual world host and preserved on the host's storage devices for a period of time.

The level of detail that virtual world providers keep and can access well after an incident is surprising. For example, in the *Bragg* case (which progressed through most of discovery before settling), Linden Lab produced logs from conversations from Second Life that were more than two years old, and cited excerpts from these logs in briefing to the court. It is quite possible (even likely) that Bragg's chat and financial record logs were specially stored outside the whole-world backup rotation and standard document retention policy because Bragg quickly filed a lawsuit after he was banned from the virtual world, but it is notable that other users' chat and financial history logs were also referenced in Linden Lab's briefing. This indicates either that these logs had also been specially stored or that Linden Lab was able to find these logs in its backup rotation two years after the conversations and events that generated them occurred. Although in the *Bragg* case it seems likely that the logs were specifically preserved with an eye on the prospect of litigation, it is not inconceivable that a virtual world provider could store, indefinitely, a record of every word that was typed and every financial transaction that took place within a virtual world. Text files require a static and relatively trivial amount of storage space, and digital storage becomes less and less expensive each year.

Beyond the data stored by the virtual world provider itself, however, the client software (software that is installed on an end user's computer that allows him or her to access the virtual world) also typically offers a number of options for data preservation, some of which are turned on by default when the software is installed. Different virtual world clients offer different options, but at minimum, most offer at least the ability to preserve a perfect record of all text-based chat. This chat also often includes information indicating object usage and creation, because the chat window is typically used to present additional information to a user.

Here is an example of the sort of log (typically referred to as a "chat log") that is automatically stored to the hard drive of a user of Second Life if that option is enabled. I am "Benjamin Avatar" in this example.[1]

[2007/10/08 9:39] *Connected*
[2007/10/08 9:39] *Bill Green is online.*

[2007/10/08 9:39] *Sarah Johnson is online.*

[2007/10/08 9:40] *Sally Smith has given you an object, 'T-Shirt'*

[2007/10/08 9:40] *Private message from Sally Smith: "Here's a sample t-shirt for your group. Can you give me L$300 for it? I can give you a discount on more."*

[2007/10/08 9:39] **John Wu:** So, is this the Second Life Bar Association?

[2007/10/08 9:40] **Benjamin Avatar:** Yes. Feel free to look around.

[2007/10/08 9:40] *Private message to Sally Smith: "Sally, thanks for the shirt. It looks great. Here's L$300 for it. How much can you discount if I get 100?"*

[2007/10/08 9:40] *Sally Smith is not online. Message will be delivered later.*

[2007/10/08 9:40] *You paid Sally Smith L$300.*

[2007/10/08 9:40] **John Wu:** Nice. New offices, right?

[2007/10/08 9:40] *Carl Brown is online.*

[2007/10/08 9:40] **Benjamin Avatar:** Yes. Someone donated the space for us.

[2007/10/08 9:40] *Flight-Helper 3.0a whispers: Flight-Helper activated . . .*

[2007/10/08 9:41] *Teleport-Memory 2.0b: Auto-saving 'Mal-felonius' location . . .*

[2007/10/08 9:41] **John Wu:** That's great. How do I join?

[2007/10/08 9:41] *Carl Brown is off-line.*

[2007/10/08 9:42] **Mary Chavez:** John, search "Group" for it. It's easy!

[2007/10/08 9:42] **John Wu:** Thanks Mary! :)

[2007/10/08 9:43] **Benjamin Avatar:** Yes, thanks, Mary. Nice to meet you John. Hope to see you both at the next meeting.

Breaking this log down, you will see that there is a lot more information here than initially meets the eye.

First, there is a minute-by-minute time and date stamp for every entry. This option is not preset in all virtual world clients, but it is in many, and users tend to demand it. I suspect that it will be optional in most virtual world clients in the future.[2]

Second, there is a wealth of information about who I know, along with a record of their conversations, even though they themselves may have this option disabled. For example, when I log on, the software tells me that avatars "Bill Green" and "Sarah Johnson" are already online. It later tells me that avatar "Carl Brown" logged on at 9:40 and logged off one minute later at 9:41. The software does this because Bill, Sarah, and Carl are listed as my "friends" in a feature that allows us to track each other's online status. It is not uncommon for a user to have hundreds of "friends" and, thus, for hundreds of users to have log files reflecting the exact time the user logs in and logs out. It is not inconceivable that a user could create an avatar and become "friends" with another user for the sole purpose of tracking every second of that user's online status by simply remaining logged in at all times.

Next, the italicized text provides a great deal of information regarding objects that I am using. You can tell from this log that I am using tools with the names Flight-Helper 3.0a and Teleport-Memory 2.0b—these are tools that, respectively, let my avatar fly faster and higher than the virtual world software allows on its own, and record my location when I visit a new place. At 9:41, the object Teleport-Memory 2.0b recorded that I was at the 'Malfelonius' location in Second Life (where the Second Life Bar Association is headquartered). If I were to have interacted with these tools, say, by requesting a list of locations I had previously visited from the Teleport-Memory tool or by programming the Flight-Helper tool to let me fly at a different rate of speed, that would appear in this log as well.

In addition, transactions are reflected in this log, even if they occur off-line. For example, when I logged on, I was immediately given a T-shirt with a logo for the Second Life Bar Association on it created by an avatar named "Sally Smith." Sally had made the shirt at my request between the last time I logged in and this time, and had given it to me while I was off-line. She also asked me to pay her L$300 ("L$" is shorthand for the currency used in Second Life) for the shirt, and offered me a discount on a larger order. Both the transaction in which she gave me the shirt and the text she sent me appeared when I first logged in. I then gave Sally L$300, as she requested, and asked her how much of a discount she'd give me for a larger order. Because Sally was off-line, the information was

■ ■ ■ ■ ■

What You Can Learn from a Chat Log

When the user logged on.

Who the user spoke to.

Who spoke to the user.

Where the user went.

What the user bought.

What the user sold.

What tools the user accessed.

When the user's friends logged on.

When the user's friends logged off.

stored for her for later. The text between me and Sally, the transfer of the shirt, and the transfer of the funds were all logged.

Finally, of course, there is a complete record of my chat history for the four minutes from 9:39 to 9:43 a.m. on October 8, 2007, establishing that I was talking to two users about the Second Life Bar Association, and encouraging them to attend a meeting to take place later in the month.

Some users choose to disable all of these options, of course, but many do not for a variety of reasons. Some professionals use the feature to keep meeting transcripts and records. Many social users enjoy reading their old chat histories. And in many cases— probably the majority—users are simply not aware that they are keeping these records. Even when a user has disabled all logging in his or her virtual world client, there is no way to guarantee that the user's conversational partners (and in the case of public chat, that includes every person within "hearing" range) have also disabled the option. Particularly in the case of public chat or meetings with several participants, it is nearly certain that someone has intentionally or inadvertently compiled a log that details who was at the meeting and records every word "spoken" there.

Other Sources of Evidence in Virtual Worlds

Other sources of evidence can be found within virtual worlds. Many users keep screenshots of their virtual world experiences, a large number of which end up on the Internet. More and more users are also taking video footage of their virtual world experiences and storing it either within their account, on their personal hard drive space, or, sometimes, on the Internet for public consumption. Currently over 300,000 images from Second Life alone are split between two popular photo-sharing sites, with, presumably, tens of millions more residing on users' hard drives.[3] Most virtual worlds provide a "snapshot" option and a "movie" option that allow users to take pictures inside the virtual world and store them indefinitely; exporting them to non-virtual world–based storage is relatively simple as well. Even when screen capture and movie functions are not provided, users can (and do) take screenshots and even video captures using third-party software.

Objects in virtual worlds (e.g., clothing, cars, etc.) contain a great deal of data about their creator and owners. Typically, an object retains its creation date, the name of its creator, and, in some cases, even the names of previous owners, sale prices, and dates of transfer.

Although voice logging has not yet reached virtual worlds in a significant way, users regularly record voice presentations in order to make them available to off-line users later. As voice chat becomes more integrated and common, the likelihood that users will store audio files of their virtual world interactions will only increase.

The Reliability of Evidence Collected in a Virtual World

The admissibility and apparent reliability of evidence collected from virtual worlds raise potential issues. Evidence from virtual worlds is not, of course, any more or less reliable than any other form of electronic evidence, but at least until use of virtual worlds becomes more widespread, there could well be a prejudice against it from judges and juries. Even now, close to a decade since e-mail became essentially a business necessity, some judges still subject it to a higher level of scrutiny than physical letters.[4]

In the long term, nothing about virtual world logs, images, movies, and other files should cause attorneys or courts to subject them to any greater or lesser scrutiny than any other digital media. In fact, it seems likely that virtual world–based evidence will gain traction and acceptance faster than e-mail and web-based evidence both because these earlier electronic tools paved the way and because virtual worlds are themselves easily identifiable with real-world analogs. A written contract in-world could be (and sometimes is) visually handed from one user to another, very much like a paper-based written contract would be in the real world. The user may even store a copy of that contract in a three-dimensional file cabinet in her "office." Similarly, log files look remarkably like deposition transcripts, and video and audio files are documentary evidence that the court is already familiar with. Finally, the ability to match multiple independent chat logs may actually make them less subject to challenge than other forms of evidence. These facts should make evidence collected in virtual worlds less problematic for nontechnical judges and jurors than early e-mail, web pages, and Internet transactions, although attorneys introducing this evidence should make sure that the fact finder can view it in context.

In the one case in which chat log evidence has been before a judge (the *Bragg* case in Pennsylvania), neither party objected to the introduction of the logs or raised authenticity concerns, and there was no indication that the court viewed this evidence with any particular suspicion.

A complete survey of the various hurdles to admission of electronic evidence is beyond the scope of this book, but anyone hoping to rely on such evidence should be prepared, at minimum, to address it with the same level of care—and expect it to be subject to at least the same level of scrutiny—as e-mail or web printouts currently are. Establishing authenticity via deposition, declaration, requests for admission, independent corroboration through the logs of other users and the provider, expert testimony, and metadata (e.g., embedded file creation and modification dates, etc.) may help avoid attacks on the evidence. Submission of this authenticating evidence along with the evidence derived from virtual world logs, images, and audio and video files may avoid the evidence being discounted or ignored at summary judgment, or excluded from trial.

When both parties in a dispute about a transaction or an event involving a virtual world are fairly savvy regarding the nature of evidence collected in virtual worlds (which will often, if not typically, be the case), they may want to consider avoiding some of these issues via stipulation. Depending on the dispute, evidence that comes from a virtual world can often be independently corroborated with data held by the opposite party. This is particularly true of disputes between users and a virtual world provider. In these cases, the parties may want to consider stipulating to the authenticity of some evidence—particularly chat logs—to the extent that there is a match between the two parties' records. This will eliminate areas of unnecessary conflict and allow the fact finder to focus on the genuine issues of dispute between the parties.

Future Authentication of Documents in a Virtual World

One might reasonably wonder why, with the creation tools available to users of virtual worlds, there is no widespread system for authenticating documents. Although several groups have attempted to create notarization schemes in virtual worlds (with varying degrees of success), none has yet garnered sufficiently widespread acceptance that we can expect, as a matter of course, to find documents or other evidence that has been authenticated using one of these services.

That may change, however. As professionals begin using virtual worlds in greater numbers, one can expect these services to gain in popularity. The most promising service at this time is Nota Bene, a Second Life business that advertises digital "signature" authentication. According to its materials, "Nota Bene is a fully automated, easy to use, self-service notary. Built on strong, public cryptographic technology, notarizations are secure, verifiable and tamperproof."[5] The process is remarkably simple. First, users create a document (e.g., a written contract for design work, a chat log that they wish to agree is authentic, an agreement that resulted from a mediation, etc.). They then take this document to what looks like a large ATM at a designated location in the virtual world.[6] When both (or all) avatars who wish to sign the document are present at that location, the document is fed into the ATM. At that point, each user clicks the ATM and is given an identical copy of the document that he or she is contemplating signing. The users read it, click the ATM again to sign the document, and, when all signers have done this, indicate that they are finished. The ATM then gives them each a digital "receipt" that includes each "signature," the text of the agreement, and an authentication key. Nota Bene offers an automated process that verifies the contents using the key, but as the encryption scheme is public, verification can also be done by a user (or an expert) outside the virtual world without any intervention by Nota Bene. This is an important feature because Nota Bene could cease operations without impacting users' ability to authenticate documents processed through the system.

Whether by traditional means of authentication or via creative, in-world solutions like Nota Bene, professionals focusing on virtual worlds should expect a higher level of documentation than in non-virtual world environments. Documentation of virtual world activities—both intentionally and unintentionally created—will feature prominently in deals involving virtual world companies and providers and in disputes arising out of virtual world conduct.

Open Questions on Evidence Collection in Virtual Worlds

1. Should virtual world and game providers store data indefinitely?

2. How should attorneys explain virtual worlds to a judge or jury in order to put evidence collected there in context?

3. What new technologies could be introduced to help authenticate evidence collected in-world?

Notes

1. These are not real names, and this is not a real conversation.

2. Posting of Duckless Vandyke, Logging Chat to Disk Does Not Include Timestamps (Second Life Bug Report/Feature Request), http://jira.secondlife.com/browse/VWR-383 (April 5, 2007).

3. As of January 5, 2008, SLUniverse.com's Snapzilla had 231,019 Second Life screenshots and pictures, and the photo-sharing site Flickr had 105,994.

4. Patrick J. Hatfield, Jon A. Neiditz & Jay G. Safer, From E-Discovery to E-Admissibility? *Lorraine v. Markel* and What May Follow (2007), http://www.lordbissell.com/newsstand/1178.

5. Nota Bene FAQ, http://slurl.com/secondlife/Obscure/31/181/145/ (last visited Jan. 5, 2008); Zarf Vantongerloo, The Notary and Infrastructures for Agreement and Trust, http://nyls.blogs.com/demoisland/2006/01/the_notary_and_.html (Jan. 9, 2006).

6. The appearance of things in a virtual world is, of course, completely arbitrary. This script could be running in an object that looks like a desk, a book, or even a humanoid form, but Nota Bene has chosen to make its authentication machine look like an ATM.

Governance of Virtual Worlds

The question of governance of virtual worlds is surprisingly controversial. Unlike other controversial questions in virtual law, however, there is not much debate among academics or attorneys—most agree that until and unless virtual world–specific legislation is passed, real-world laws apply to real-world activity that takes place in virtual worlds and game spaces. In essence, the law doesn't care that users are selling goods as pixilated purple tiger avatars; if the users are making real money, a sale is a sale, and activity that surrounds it will be regulated. Similarly, the law is already well equipped to draw a distinction between consensual "play" activity (such as "assault" or "theft" in a game where the activity is part of the game) and real activity that could give rise to real-world liability.

Essentially, absent special legislation regarding virtual worlds and games, it is reasonable to assume that the law will simply treat business as business and play as play. Whatever business that takes place inside virtual worlds will be governed as if it is happening via the web or a mail-order catalog, and whatever game-type play that takes place inside them will be treated as if it is happening in a fenced-off paint-ball park or a boxing ring. Governance of virtual worlds seems, to most attorneys, to be a fairly simple question. Either new laws will be written, or old ones will be applied, as necessary. Indeed, much of virtual law is simply a description of the projection of existing real-world law to virtual spaces, and the rest is a discussion of the potential for new laws to be written to address deficiencies. The assumption that this is not only reasonable but essentially a given is largely uncontroversial among attorneys, legal scholars, and people who use virtual worlds to make their living.

It is not at all uncontroversial among some users and designers, however, and this creates many of the controversial issues regarding governance of virtual worlds. Many users and designers take the view that with few exceptions, real-world laws should not be applied to any activity that takes place in virtual spaces. In addition to the questions raised by this school of thought, an entirely separate set of governance issues arises within virtual worlds themselves, as users attempt to create private governments and legal structures to govern each other.

The relationship among the three levels of virtual world governance (real-world law's governance of virtual worlds generally, providers' governance of the users of their individual virtual worlds, and users' governance of other users) also creates many controversies. It is not an accident that this chapter appears early in *Virtual Law*. Questions raised here, and the proposed "magic circle test" for when and where law should be applied to virtual spaces, will come up repeatedly in subsequent chapters.

Johan Huizinga's "Magic Circle"

We begin exploring these questions by focusing on the "magic circle." This term refers to a concept first articulated by Johan Huizinga in his 1938 work, *Homo Ludens* (*Man the Player*). The magic circle is essentially a dividing line between play spaces and reality. From a legal perspective, it gives us a potential bright-line division between that which should be regulated and governed, and that which should not. According to Huizinga, play is "an activity connected with no material interest and no profit can be gained by it [and that] proceeds within its own proper boundaries of time and space."[1] We will return to this definition at the conclusion of this chapter.

The Intellectual Argument Against Real-World Governance

The intellectual argument against real-world governance of virtual worlds and games is, at its core, that these spaces with few exceptions should, by default, be protected as play spaces. For an attorney, speculating whether there is real, legally actionable "theft" involved when one character steals a powerful "Katana of Vanquishing" sword from another character in Ultima Online seems perfectly reasonable, particularly when that Katana can be sold on an auction site for $50. To many players and designers, however, it is no more reasonable to ask whether a "theft" occurred than to speculate whether a "murder" occurred if the victim character tracks down the "thief" who "stole" the Katana and spectacularly "kills" him with a giant ball of blue fire.

This is an entirely valid argument, and it directly supports the idea that some—maybe even most—games and social virtual worlds should qualify for "magic circle" protection. It is a position held by a number of highly regarded game designers, virtual world users, and legal writers, including, to a certain degree, myself. Although there are areas where the law *can*, *should*, and, like it or not, *will* be applied, there are many areas where it *cannot*, *should not*, and ultimately *will not*. Indeed, by defining exactly what makes a protected play space, we also must necessarily define what is *not* a protected play space. This creates places where real-life law should regulate and places where it should not. Along with exploring various governance options, finding a workable approach to this division is the goal of this chapter.

The Emotional Argument Against Real-World Governance

Some arguments have little to do with protecting play spaces or finding a line between play and reality, even if that is the superficial explanation offered. Rather, they are emotional arguments. These arguments must be addressed, because they have a certain appeal, and because they are repeated with sufficient regularity in the mainstream press that they will inevitably be lodged in the minds of many fact finders, both judges and jurors, who are evaluating legal claims.

"It's just a game" is the usual explanation for deception, gloating, and other generally antisocial aspects of game play, and, really, it is not a bad explanation. As any schadenfreude-filled eight-year-old who has just revealed a "Draw 4" card in Uno can tell you, deception, gloating, and antisocial behavior can be a lot of fun in games, so long as nobody is really getting hurt.

Games are, by their very definition, not real, so they can give players the chance to act in ways that are unacceptable in the real world. It is wrong to sabotage a coworker's presentation, but you can play a "back ten spaces" card in a game and feel great about it. It is wrong to lie, but no one would accuse a poker player holding four spades and a heart of doing anything unethical by grinning like she drew a flush. Making and breaking alliances is such an integral part of the television reality-game show *Survivor* that it has spawned a number of websites devoted to analysis of players' strategy and skill at deception. Modern multiplayer role-playing games, particularly those which encourage unsavory character classes (e.g., "rouge," "thief," "spy," and "assassin") even build sneaky, underhanded play right in to the game's motif and mechanisms.

Even in social virtual worlds with no goal-based gaming components, some users have an instinct, frequently encouraged by the virtual world provider, that they are participating in an entirely new kind of world, maybe a better one where things will be different, maybe even one where real-life dos not apply. Because there is an element of escapism and unreality to virtual world participation, it is an easy mistake to make. After all, if the law of gravity doesn't apply, why should the law of fraud?

Enhancing that mistaken impression is the fact that for the first several years of 3-D virtual worlds' existence, prosecutors and civil litigators, particularly in the United States, were simply not paying attention to these spaces. There wasn't enough money involved and the user base was so small that they were just not on the radar screen of most of the legal community. In the early days, 3-D virtual worlds were used by a minuscule number of people. For example, the number of registered Second Life accounts grew one hundred times larger in twenty-two months, between December 2005 and October 2007 (from $100,000^2$ to $10,000,000^3$). Concurrent logins, a better measurement of actual use, increased twenty-fivefold over this period as well, from under $2,000^4$ to over $50,000.^5$ Even multi-user games (which had a larger early user base and experienced earlier success) raised few legal questions because they were, in fact, games, and did not focus on communication and sales like social virtual worlds.

There are two groups of people who argue most strenuously against outside governance of virtual worlds: griefers (who participate in virtual worlds and games for the sole purpose of causing mayhem and disrupting other users' experiences) and militant early adopters (some of whom passionately believe that their favorite world should remain suspended, as if in amber, in the state it was before it became popular).

Griefers and militant early adopters make odd bedfellows, because early adopters have a particular loathing for griefers (borne of years of baiting, battles, complaints to providers, banning, forum posts, and harassment), but both tend to take the same position on the intrusion of real-world institutions, albeit for completely different reasons. In both cases, the users' arguments are not based on any rational understanding of law or game design theory, but are largely the product of an emotional attachment to a romanticized notion of all virtual worlds as potential utopias, free of the meddlesome interference of business and government.

Griefers' motivations are clear—the intrusion of real-world law means that they could be taken to court, in some cases even jailed, for some of the more shockingly antisocial and cruel things that they do.

■■■■■

"Griefing" in Virtual Worlds

- In December 2006, griefers digitally modified a real-life picture of Ailin Graef (better known as virtual property baroness "Anshe Chung") so that she appeared to be cradling a giant penis in her arms. Then, when she was participating in an interview with CNET in Second Life, they bombarded her avatar with thousands of copies of the picture, as well as thousands of flying animated penises created using the Second Life scripting software. They posted a video of the attack on YouTube.*

- In August 2007, griefers crashed seventeen sims on the Second Life grid in a pattern that formed a giant red swastika on the overhead map.**

- In November 2007, griefers used scripted "weapons" that produced a visual depiction of smoke and fire to attack a replica of the World Trade Center in Second Life.***

*Daniel Terdiman, *The Legal Rights to Your "Second Life" Avatar,* Jan. 5, 2007, http://www.news.com/2100-1047-6147700.html.

**Urizenus Sklar, *17 Sims Crashed in Swastika Pattern. Rosedale Sim Among Them,* SECOND LIFE HERALD, Aug. 12, 2007, http://www.secondlifeherald.com/slh/2007/08/17-sims-crashed.html.

***Amanda Wellington, *Weekend Attacks on World Trade Center Replica,* SECOND LIFE HERALD, Nov. 13, 2007, http://foo.secondlifeherald.com/slh/2007/11/weekend-attacks.html.

As discussed in greater detail in Chapter 9, "Tort Law and Virtual Worlds," a reasonable case can be made that some of these attacks, particularly those that target individuals, may give rise to real-world damages claims as "intentional infliction of emotional distress." Similarly, though the First Amendment widely protects generally offensive speech in the United States, many countries, most notably Germany and France, have strict codes prohibiting inciting hatred against ethnic groups. To the extent that the griefers argue that virtual worlds are "just games" and that they are just playing them differently than others, a test that evaluates an act for "magic circle" protection should measure the reasonableness of that stance on a case-by-case basis.

Somewhat oddly, militant early adopters (the other camp of users who argue, from an emotional perspective, that virtual worlds should be generally free of the application of real-world law) include a number of people who are regularly targeted by griefers. Their argument is somewhat more appealing, if rather less rational, as many early adopters stand to gain the most by restrictions on aggressively antisocial (and markedly antibusiness) behavior in virtual spaces.

At bottom, the early adopters just want things to be like they were at the beginning. Having had the privilege of being involved in several games and virtual worlds in early beta testing, and having been involved in many more shortly after launch, I can attest to the nostalgic appeal of the argument. There is something inherently great about being among the first to visit a new space, particularly if it becomes popular. There are few, if any, places left to be the first to visit in the real world, but virtual worlds provide endless opportunity for exploration. Users who get involved in new virtual worlds in the early stages naturally view the resulting world as "theirs" in a sense, and anyone who visits later is a mere tourist by comparison. Watching the world change is hard, and no matter how much these changes might ultimately benefit the early adopters (many of whom own significant virtual property and are both financially and emotionally invested in seeing the world continue successfully indefinitely), they often fiercely resist any change.

Changes in Second Life in 2007, particularly related to user creates content, were, though predictable given the increase in the platform's visibility, seemingly shocking to users who had been involved in the world from the early days. For example, for almost four years of Second Life's existence, any user who bought a spot of virtual land was allowed to run a completely unregulated casino on it, with digital slot machines and craps tables, poker rooms, cocktail waitresses (clothed or unclothed), and bright neon signs. Users played the casino games in Linden Dollars, of course, but there was a ready market, maintained by Second Life's provider, to convert real dollars to Linden Dollars and vice versa. Running a casino often immensely profitable, and casinos proliferated widely. There is no real question that the casinos were illegal,[6] but there were widespread protests that lasted for weeks when Linden Lab finally banned them, after (although Linden Lab claimed not connected to) a report from Reuters that FBI agents had visited several Second Life casinos.[7] A number of upset users claimed that they were under the impression that because casinos had been tolerated for so long, they had to have been legal.

Who Really Governs Virtual Worlds and Games?

The first level of governance is that of the provider over the users. Both game-based and social virtual worlds rely heavily on the policies of the virtual world provider as a sort of informal code of laws. Every provider tells users what they can and cannot do in the virtual world. Some rules are designed to comply with real-world laws (e.g., Linden Lab's decision to ban gambling in Second Life in 2007), some are designed to preserve a play space as free of real-world pressures (e.g., most game companies' prohibition against sales of in-world gold and items for real money), and some are merely designed to make the world a more aesthetically pleasing place (e.g., World of Warcraft's prohibition against names "comprised of [a] partial or complete sentence [such as] 'Inyourface,' [and] 'Welovebeef'"[8]).

In games, the rules of the game themselves can be considered a form of law and, in fact, often include notions of retribution, punishment, and self-defense from criminal law principles long recognized by real-life judicial systems. In the early days of Ultima Online, for example, an ingenious reputation system kept track of a user's transgressions (such as murders), and the penalty for repeatedly killing other players in unprovoked attacks was to become freely attackable oneself. Paul Joseph, one of the first legal scholars to examine questions of virtual law, wrote extensively of this system in a prescient 1998 article:

It was always anticipated that player-controlled characters could come into conflict and even kill each other. It should be noted that the "death" of a character is not final. A "dead" character can be "resurrected" by magic, although the process can result in the loss of some acquired skills which the player may have spent many hours developing. In addition, while the character is "dead," its possessions are at the mercy of anyone who might be tempted to loot the "body." Similarly, it is possible to steal possessions from a character. The loss may represent many hours of game play and cause a player considerable inconvenience.

The game was set up with the assumption that some players would tend to steal and kill and others would resist them. In a sense, issues of justice, morality, and law were built into the structure of the game. One of the fascinating aspects of the game, however, is that, even in its first months of operation, it has developed in ways unanticipated by the game designers.

As originally planned, towns were zones of safety where no crimes could be committed, but the areas outside of towns, the "wilderness," was unregulated. The mechanism of law and order in towns was simple and brutal. Computer-controlled "guards" instantly appear and kill any character who attacks another in town, who steals in town, etc.

Almost immediately, however, an unanticipated problem developed. New players, who started out with 100 gold pieces and a few saleable possessions, were preyed upon by experienced players as soon as the "newbies" left the town. Because it appeared to some players that killing these new players was easier than obtaining wealth by more legitimate means, the level of such activity was much greater than had been anticipated. Players flooded the game staff with complaints, suggestions, and demands for reform. That reform is still in the process of being hammered out, but it has already brought about a number of changes designed to discourage indiscriminate player-killing while not ruling it out altogether.

Under the new rules, many possessions disappear from new player-controlled characters when they are "killed," thus making crimes against them less lucrative. In addition, steps were taken to make it harder to identify new players as new. Thus, the so called "player-killer" can never know for sure whether he or she is attacking a vulnerable opponent. Persistent player-killing of "good" characters can result in the offender being identified as such an evil character that he or she will be killed on sight by the computer-controlled guards merely for entering a town. Essentially, this is a system of "outlawry" in which the condemned are forced to live outside the normal channels of society and commerce available to everybody else. A system of bounties will give players additional incentives to "kill" those who make a habit of indiscriminate "killing."

The "player-killers" have not taken this lying down. Some have established player-controlled fortresses from which they venture out to kill and to steal. Others have found ways to trick "good" players into becoming the aggressors in situations where the guards will kill them, thus doing the player-killer's work.

The most interesting recent development has been the bare beginning of a "good" player vigilante movement. Some players have styled themselves guardians who routinely patrol areas and kill player-killers when they are found. Other ad-hoc groups of players have confronted particularly egregious player-killers. Such players have been told that their actions are unacceptable and must cease. One notorious player-killer was given an ultimatum to change or be hunted down.[9]

The concept of in-world "rules" operating as law is not limited to game-based virtual worlds. Providers of social virtual worlds also get significant pressure from the users to "legislate" against acts that run counter to the community's interest. There.com, for example, has hired a number of employees whose job it is to monitor all uploads of "textures" (which users add to pre-built items and then sell to other users) and police accusations of in-world "texture theft."[10] Because real money is at stake in these actions, users could, theoretically, file a lawsuit rather than bring a copyright claim to There.com's management, but the reality is that most claims would not be financially viable given the relatively low value of the virtual goods in question. So There.com offers its own protection scheme, which, interestingly, includes both penalties for theft (ranging from education to fines to termination of the infringer's There.com account) and a mechanism to discourage false reports of theft (after three false reports, the user's reports will no longer be investigated). According to the policy,

> [w]hen we are notified of a texture theft situation, our Approvers will conduct a thorough investigation. If it is determined the complaint is valid, the following actions will be taken:
>
> **1st Offense:** The product will be retired (with no refund of submission fees) and the offending Developer will be educated and suspended from the Developer Program for a period of at least ten (10) days.
>
> **2nd Offense:** The product will be retired (with no refund of submission fees) and the offending Developer will be suspended from the Developer Program for a period of at least sixty (60) days. The Developer will then be required to pay a reinstatement fee of up to T$100,000 [about US$50] if he or she wishes to reenter the Developer Program.
>
> **3rd Offense:** The product will be retired (with no refund of submission fees) and we will take swift remedial action, up to and including the offending Developer's permanent suspension from There.
>
> If we receive more than two (2) unfounded complaints from a Developer, we reserve the right to no longer investigate claims on behalf of that Developer.[11]

Because of the expense associated with pursuing claims through lawsuits and the relatively low value of most claims arising from microtransactions between users of virtual worlds, the only method of enforcement practically available to a user who perceives a wrong having been done is usually via the "laws" created by the provider. Some of those laws involve the code of the virtual world or game (e.g., one literally cannot "trespass" on the land of another in most virtual worlds, because software restrictions prevent users from going where they are not allowed), and others involve human intervention and enforcement mechanisms (e.g., filing an "abuse report" about certain inappropriate activities in Second Life results in an investigation, and, if the user is found guilty, sanctions ranging from a warning to account suspension are imposed). Because lawsuits are impractical for many users, they are forced to rely on these mechanisms. User complaints about lackadaisical enforcement of rules and widespread allegations of favoritism have plagued nearly every virtual world provider.

Between the expense of lawsuits and the difficulty of getting virtual world providers to enforce their own rules, users have frequently found ways to take matters into their own hands. As previously noted, in the early days of Ultima Online, particularly when it was easy to identify new users, "newbie farming" was a popular pastime. As new users flocked to the game, players who had been around a few weeks longer (and who were, thus, quite a bit more powerful) would camp outside of the "town" borders, where they would not be attacked by nonplayer character guards. They would wait there, systematically kill every new player who dared to leave "town," and take their meager possessions. Although death wasn't permanent, if a character was "killed," the attacker (and anyone on the scene willing to risk a similar fate) got to loot everything the victim was carrying—money, equipment, weapons, and even clothing. New players started with a relatively small amount of gold and a few possessions, but for the effort involved, they were much easier to kill than monsters that carried similar loot. Dying would bankrupt new players, so it was common to see groups of new players begging for food and money near major centers of commerce. The response, which preceded any action by the provider, was the formation of groups of vigilante players who styled themselves guardians of the weak and protected new users, completely voluntarily. Many of these groups went on to found whole cities of like-minded role-players, some of which still exist ten years later.

Technology has come a long way since the early days of Ultima Online, and with the advent of user-programmable objects in worlds like Second Life, users have unprecedented control over the environment. One result is that users are experimenting with their own in-world governments and consumer protection schemes. Because no provider currently backs any of the unofficial governmental experiments, users must come up with their own enforcement mechanisms using the tools at hand. In Second Life, which has by far the most advanced user-governments, the enforcement mechanism of choice is shunning.

So far, shunning is the only punishment any in-world government has been able to codify, because any other sanction short of real-world legal action (from in-world fines to account termination) requires the participation of the virtual world provider. That said, shunning, even in its limited form, can have real impact in a virtual world, particularly a social virtual world where social standing is paramount. One Second Life project, calling itself the "Metaverse Republic," is attempting to create what amounts to a global shunning system based on a fully functioning judiciary. Essentially, landowners who wish to participate in the system will place an object on their land that will prevent access by anyone whose name appears on a list of banned avatars. The list consists of those who have been "convicted" in formal judicial proceedings. The system envisions appeals, a code of civil procedure, advocates, and most of the rest of the trappings of a Western common law system. The project is partly managed by an avatar named "Ashcroft Burnham," who was behind the attempt to create a functional judiciary at a more narrowly focused governmental simulation in late 2006. Other groups have also tried to create gridwide justice systems, with little success.

There are, however, several limited-area governments set up in Second Life. Most are themed around on a certain architectural or cultural style, and most operate both as microgovernment centers and as land rental businesses. The most comprehensive microgovernment system can be found at the Confederation of Democratic Simulators (CDS), which advertises itself as "a virtual, self-governed community of several simulators (sims) in the synthetic world of

Second Life, under the jurisdiction of a common government."[12] To become a citizen of the CDS, one simply rents land there. All citizens are encouraged to participate in governance issues by joining (or starting) a faction. By renting land in the CDS, the citizen agrees to live under the guidelines of the government. The CDS has a constitution and a code of laws. As mentioned earlier, an attempt was made to form a functioning judiciary in late 2006, but it did not succeed.[13] Each "sim" has a relatively strict set of land covenants and is meticulously planned for visual appeal. This is designed both to increase the aesthetic enjoyment of the resident-citizens and to attract and keep shoppers who visit the sims' bustling business districts. The primary benefit of the covenants is that the CDS sims suffer none of the visual blight that plagues much of Second Life. One of the CDS sims is themed in a classic Roman style, and another is medieval Bavarian. A third, in the Alpine Rural Antique style, is planned.

Besides the CDS, which has the most developed government, there are other "microgovernment" projects, most of which are styled as benevolent dictatorships (and a few of which are decidedly malevolent). One of the former, "The Independent State of Caledon," is visually based loosely on Victorian England. It contains over 1.5 million square meters of "virtual property," which, in an undeveloped state, is currently worth approximately $40,000 and costs its owner approximately $4500 per month in maintenance fees (presumably these fees are more than offset by the rental fees). Its owner (as avatar "Desmond Shang") reports that although banishment is an option, he has not had to ban a single user in one and one-half years of operation.[14]

Another Second Life microgovernment, slated to open in 2008, is the "Al-Andalus Caliphate," a private government sim based on what its creator says are "authentic Islamic principles." Al-Andalus plans to eventually incorporate a functioning judiciary, based on Islamic law. According to its inaugural announcement and a subsequent interview with its founder, the Al-Andalus Caliphate Project "reconstructs 13th Century Moor Alhambra and builds around this virtual space a community of individuals willing to explore the modalities of interaction between different languages, nationalities, religions and cultures within a political and juridical space shaped by authentic Islamic principles," specifically, "leading edge research of how authentic Islamic legal principles can be applied in a 21st century context, and be compatible with universal ideals of dignity, equality, democracy, participation and human rights."[15] Other projects—including Extropia, a microgovernment focused on creativity and art, with a "tomorrowland" feel—are slated to open in 2008 as well.

The prospect of microgovernment holds a great deal of promise and is one of the most compelling forms of experimentation that can take place in virtual worlds, but it is limited by the geographic location of the servers. As discussed earlier, declaring one's "state" independent accomplishes little when there are at least two forms of government (the provider's "law," and the actual laws of the city, state, and country where the servers are located) controlling the virtual land. The greatest legal flexibility will be found in interconnected simulators that are, in fact, geographically dispersed. When parts of "the grid" are hosted in different countries, then the local government of the host country will control what can and cannot be made available on that part of the grid, much as control of the web is localized while access is, largely, global.

At the edges of this debate are those who argue that virtual spaces, particularly free-form virtual worlds, do, in fact, constitute brand new, previously undiscovered "lands," where the law of the country hosting the servers does not apply—something along the lines of discovering an uninhabited, previously unmapped island. Although two respected commentators, David G. Post and David R. Johnson, raised this argument as early as 1996 in relation to "cyberspace" as a possible "territory" outside traditional notions of geographic boundaries and renewed that argument in relation to virtual worlds in 2006,[16] the view has not gained a great deal of traction outside academia.

How Questions of Governance Will Reach the Courts

Although fascinating (and likely), a future of dispersed grids and microgovernmental experiments is still speculative. The governance question most likely to end up before a court in the immediate future is much simpler: When should real-life laws be applied to virtual worlds?

It is tempting to duck this question and suggest that the issue be handled on a case-by-case basis. After all, a claim of defamation between users differs significantly from a tax claim by the government against a gold farmer, and neither has much in common with a criminal prosecution for running an illegal stock exchange. The question of when the "magic circle" protecting play spaces should be respected, and when it should not, could first arise in any of these hypothetical cases or any of a dozen others. However, it seems clear that there is a tipping point at which a virtual world or game moves from "play" to "real," and as courts begin the process of defining that point, they will need a framework.

Although the facts could vary, from a practical perspective, the question of the application of the "magic circle rule" is likely to reach the courts in a fairly narrow and predictable form. A defendant—either criminal or civil—will plead that there is nothing of value at stake in the case against him or her because the world where the alleged events took place is "just a game," and the small print in the Terms of Service says that the currency, goods, and property involved are worth nothing more than pink $5 Monopoly bills, silver top hats, and red plastic hotels.

The question will likely first reach a decision point in the context of a motion for summary judgment, which means that both parties will have had the opportunity to conduct significant discovery. A party opposing such a motion would be well served to provide evidence that the virtual world or game provider did not treat the currency as valueless and, in fact, encouraged users to treat it as "real money." Language in the virtual world or game's advertising may suggest as much. Evidence that users did so may be helpful as well.

The fact that this keystone question of when and where virtual worlds and games should have magic circle protection will likely first arise in the context of a motion for summary judgment is notable for another reason: the question is, at its core, a question of fact, not of law. That means that in many cases, the fact finder—the jury, or judge, at trial—should determine whether a game or virtual world is sufficiently "real" to take it outside the protection of play spaces that the magic circle affords. Although in some cases the question will be able to be settled at summary judgment (taking all evidence in a light most favorable to the non-movant), in many cases that will not be possible. The reasons for this will become clear when we examine a possible formal test later in this chapter.

Counsel may be tempted to avoid or gloss over this fundamental question in briefing. This is a particular danger for attorneys who come to a lawsuit already familiar with these spaces. It seems intuitive to people who use these spaces regularly that because real money is changing hands, real agreements are being reached, and real people are living significant portions of their lives in virtual worlds, real-life law will apply there too. This is not remotely obvious to the vast majority of potential jurors, judges, and others who are not already familiar with these spaces.

This bears repeating. Most people do not think, intuitively, that real-life law should apply to something that looks like a game. Articulate, smart, technologically savvy friends of mine, who have heard me rejoice at every science-fiction-turns-real story I encounter, still marvel at the idea that there are lawsuits based on these spaces, often asking, incredulously, "Wait, didn't that happen in a *game*?" If technologically oriented people are skeptical, it should not be surprising that fact finders with less knowledge of high-tech developments are likely to be outright hostile to the idea.

Practitioners contemplating filing a suit involving any aspect of these spaces should read the three complaints (two regarding intellectual property infringement claims, and one regarding real money trading in violation of a Terms of Service agreement in Appendices VIII, X, and XI) for examples of different approaches to adding context for the fact finder. The key is to not lose track of the fact that the judge and jury who will hear the case are likely not already familiar with these spaces.

Although one expects that reaction to diminish as social virtual worlds become more popular, it will never disappear entirely, nor, probably, should it. The instinct that play spaces are "just games" and need to be protected is a good instinct. The questions are: What spaces? and When? There are very good reasons to encourage courts to use a formal test to determine when magic circle protection exists. At the moment, due in no small part to game and virtual world providers' attempts to address the question using click-through contracts (see Chapter 6, Contract Law and Virtual Worlds), the status of virtual property and virtual currency is unclear in the United States. The first cases that test this ground would do well to provide a clear framework for those that follow.

The "Magic Circle Test" and Governance

In the end, the question of governance must to come back to the magic circle. Spaces that wish to avoid the intrusion of real-world governance must, generally, be allowed to do so by taking steps to prevent their play spaces from being used for real-world purposes. On the other hand, virtual worlds and games that do not choose to avail themselves of the protection of the magic circle (by, for instance, encouraging a real cash economy) should, of course, be subject to real-world regulation. Users and designers can take steps to minimize the intrusion, but it is as absurd to think that real-world laws don't apply in a virtual world (where money changes hands, contracts are made, users run full-scale businesses, and many avatars are functionally business identities) as it is to think that real-life laws do not apply at a private costume ball simply because the partygoers are wearing masks.

It is notable that some commentators, including Joshua Fairfield (with whom I agree on a great many points), find the concept of the magic circle lacking.[17] As such, the test proposed here may ultimately be unnecessary, as Fairfield argues. Even if it is not strictly necessary to create a formal test (because the principles already exist), it may still prove useful to describe the framework and to name it. It is useful to do this because attorneys arguing before judges and juries (who will, in some cases, instinctively feel that questions arising from virtual worlds can all be dismissed with "it's just a game") must be prepared to handle this objection head-on. A formal test that addresses the concern will make it that much easier for courts to determine when the magic circle does not provide protection and, in so doing, will also make clear when it does. That can only benefit virtual worlds in the long run.

■■■■■
The Magic Circle Test

An activity that occurs in a virtual world is subject to real-world law if the user undertaking the activity reasonably understood, or should have reasonably understood, at the time of acting, that the act would have real-world implications.

Although I do not intend to offer a complete framework, believing that to be the province of judges and juries who will, as cases with different facts arise, determine how best to apply the test, a baseline test is necessary. The "magic circle test" proposed here is this: *An activity that occurs in a virtual world is subject to real-world law if the user undertaking the activity reasonably understood, or should have reasonably understood, at the time of acting, that the act would have real-world implications.*

Several items are important to note here. First, the test is not whether the user thought that the law would apply, but whether the user reasonably expected or should have reasonably expected the act to have real-world implications. In other words, it is not an inquiry into the user's understanding of the test, but into the user's understanding of the nature of the action. In short, did the user *reasonably* believe that it was really "just a game"?

Second, a reasonable expectation can arise from many sources, but the standards of the virtual community and the provider's rules governing that community are valuable starting points. This is particularly true to the extent that the rules, and the community's general understanding of those rules, could create broad expectations of consent to certain otherwise prohibited activities. This, functionally, provides an exception for most users of game-based worlds, where it is understood, for example, that "theft" using in-game mechanics is consented to by all involved.

Third, this test can be applied just as easily to virtual world providers as it can to virtual world users. When a virtual world provider declares that a virtual world is a play space and takes steps to maintain the space's magic circle protection (by, for example, preventing the virtual property, currency, and possessions of users from being converted to real assets, and by promptly removing users who treat the play space as a source of income), then the law must respect the fact that the provider does not intend its actions to have real-world implications. When the provider devalues gold or items in order to enhance game play, bans accounts and reclaims fictitious assets for any reason—or no reason at all—and claims ownership of any and all intellectual property created with the provider's tools, the law will generally leave it alone, because it is, after all, really *"just a game."*

Users can still be held responsible for their actions (e.g., by allowing tax claims against those who do treat the play space like a source of income, or allowing tort suits against those who use it to defame other users) on an individual basis, in spite of the worlds' and providers' general standing as protected. It must be emphasized that the test targets the activity in question in proceedings before the court, not the nature of the space itself. This means that a provider can retain its general protection of the space even while a few users abandon the protection for their own real-world-impacting activities. In sum, the presence of a few gold farmers doesn't destroy the protection of the magic circle for everyone else. Similarly, this approach preserves the ability for a world to be largely protected by the magic circle (say, a generally social space with lots of games) but have aspects that are not protected as part of the "play" (e.g., the real-life purchase of a limited license to certain copyrighted music to listen to while playing).

Finally, this test puts the Terms of Service for various game worlds in the proper place, as an important, though not determinative, factor in determining the nature of the activity in question. The Terms of Service can, and should, be considered a factor in determining whether a user reasonably expected that her actions would have no real-world implications, but they should not be allowed to override objective indicia of intent that would otherwise cause courts to treat the action as outside the magic circle and thus subject to real-world law. In other words, a user who steals a half-million U.S. dollars' worth of Linden Dollars from other Second Life users via a complicated fraud, and cashes them out as real currency, should not then be able to point to a small-print provision in the Terms of Service that says Linden Dollars merely represent "limited license rights" with no real-world value, in support of a claim that his actions were protected by the magic circle as play when it is clear that at the time of acting he had no such reasonable expectation.

There are undoubtedly ways to express all of this without reference to the magic circle (you can get there, in most cases, just using the concept of consent, as Fairfield rightly observes),[18] and there may even be sound strategic reasons for doing exactly that in some cases. But this idea—that play spaces need to be treated as play spaces—is not just an academic one, and it is likely to be in the back of the mind of any fact finder looking at any lawsuit regarding these spaces in the foreseeable future. Attorneys working in this space should consider confronting the issue directly, as doing so may help clarify what can otherwise seem a sticky issue in cases involving virtual worlds and games.

Open Questions on Governance in Virtual Worlds

1. How can private microgovernment systems in virtual worlds enforce their decisions without the participation of the provider?

2. What are the limitations of the proposed magic circle test? (*"An activity that occurs in a virtual world is subject to real-world law if the user undertaking the activity reasonably understood, or should have reasonably understood, at the time of acting, that the act would have real-world implications."*)

3. Is it important to protect play spaces as play spaces, free of governmental and legal interference?

Notes

1. Johan Huizinga, Homo Ludens (1938), p. 13.

2. *Wooot! 100K Dormant Alts,* Second Life Herald, Dec. 22, 2005, http://www.secondlifeherald.com/slh/2005/12/wooot_100k_dorm.html.

3. Posting of Markus to Otherland Group, 10 Million Residents Registered for Second Life Now http://otherland.blogs.com/group/2007/10/10 -million-resi.html (Oct. 13, 2007).

4. *Wooot!, supra* note 2.

5. Posting of Tateru Nino to Second Life Insider, Second Life Concurrency Passes 50K, http://www.secondlifeinsider.com/2007/09/03/second-life-concurrency-passes-50k/ (Sept. 3, 2007, 21:00).

6. ANITA RAMASASTRY, COULD SECOND LIFE BE IN SERIOUS TROUBLE? THE RISK OF REAL-LIFE LEGAL CONSEQUENCES FOR HOSTING VIRTUAL GAMBLING (2007), http://writ.lp.findlaw.com/ramasastry/20070411.html; *see also* posting by Christine Hurt to Conglomerate, From Virtual Tax to Virtual Gambling, http://www.theconglomerate.org/2007/04/from_virtual_ta.html (April 9, 2007).

7. Eric Krangel, a/k/a Adam Reuters, *FBI Probes Second Life Gambling,* April 3, 2007, http://secondlife.reuters.com/stories/2007/04/03/fbi-probes-second-life-gambling/.

8. "Account Cancelled" posting to http://forums.worldofwarcraft.com/thread.html?topicId=3547731855&sid=1&pageNo=1 (Dec. 24, 2007, 21:48).

9. Paul Joseph, *Ultima Online: Justice in a Virtual World,* PICTURING JUSTICE, Jan. 1998, http://www.usfca.edu/pj/articles/Ultima.htm.

10. There Texture Protection, http://developer.prod.there.com/developer/developer_help_textheft.html (last visited Jan. 5, 2008).

11. *Id.*

12. The Confederation of Democratic Simulators, http://slcds.info/2006/12/16/the-confederation-of-democratic-simulators/ (last visited Jan. 5, 2008).

13. I purchased land in Colonia Nova, a CDS sim, and applied to be a judge as part of this process. The judiciary was never formed, however, chiefly due to what appeared to me to be significant personality conflicts between those who supported it and those who opposed it.

14. Dreamingen Writer, *Interview with Desmond Shang,* SEVENTH SUN, Nov. 2007, http://www.theseventhsun.com/0907_caledon.htm.

15. Posting of Benjamin Duranske to Virtually Blind, Al-Andalus Caliphate Government Sim Opens in Second Life; Judiciary to Be Based on Islamic Law, http://virtuallyblind.com/2007/09/13/al-andalus-caliphate-opens/ (Sept. 13, 2007).

16. David R. Johnson & David G. Post, "Law and Borders—The Rise of Law in Cyberspace," 48 STAN. L. REV. 1367 (1996), http://www.cli.org/X0025_LBFIN.html; http://firstmonday.org/Issues/issue11_2/post/.

17. Joshua Fairfield, *The Magic Circle,* prepared remarks for Itechlaw Conference, Chicago, 2007, http://www.law.indiana.edu/webinit/papers/fairfield_the_magic_circle_weiss.pdf.

18. *Id.* at 3.

Property Law and Virtual Worlds 5

No area of virtual law is more controversial than the application of property law to virtual worlds. This is true because property law analysis is a necessary precursor to many other questions in virtual law. A user cannot be guilty of the crime of theft unless the victim had a right to the property in question in the first place, a resident cannot be held liable for land fraud against a fellow resident if title to the "land" is never rightly held, and there's very little point to enforcing contracts created in a virtual world if the subject matter of the contract can't be owned to begin with.

The question of ownership impacts the relationship between users and virtual world and game providers as well. All virtual world and game providers' Terms of Service and End User License Agreements clearly reserve all rights to in-world non-intellectual property to the providers. A few social virtual worlds do allow users to retain some intellectual property rights, but those attempt to make the distinction between intellectual property and "virtual property" clear.

As controversial as the questions are, most of the questions surrounding virtual property are, at this point, relatively academic. They generally involve calls for the law to rapidly evolve to acknowledge a new form of "virtual property" that falls somewhere between traditional intellectual property and traditional tangible property. These arguments are important, but they are not overwhelmingly likely to win over a judge in a motion for summary judgment absent more practical arguments upon which the court can more easily ground its decision.

At its most basic, the theoretical argument in favor of the acknowledgment of this new class of property—"virtual property"—is that virtual goods do not fit the profile of tangible or intellectual property, but they need recognition anyway. Virtual goods do not fit the profile of tangible property because they exist only on the screen and, even then, only when called forth by software commands. Similarly, virtual goods don't fit the profile of intellectual property because many contain minimal or no user creativ-

■■■■■

The Basic Argument for Recognizing Virtual Property: Virtual goods have clear value to consumers and match society's usual definitions of "property" in most other respects, so they need some form of property law protection.*

The Basic Argument Against Recognizing Virtual Property: Virtual worlds and game spaces serve their primary purpose as experimental, social, and play spaces better if they are not "commodified" (that is, turned into centers of commerce against the desires of the developers).**

*Greg Lastowka & Dan Hunter, *The Laws of the Virtual Worlds*, 92 CAL. L. REV. 1, 49 (Jan. 2004), *draft available at* http://ssrn.com/abstract=402860.
**RICHARD BARTLE, THE PITFALLS OF VIRTUAL PROPERTY (April 2004), *available at* http://www.themis-group.com/uploads/Pitfalls%20of%20Virtual%20 Property.pdf.

ity (rather, they are closer to purchased consumer goods). But because virtual goods have clear value to consumers and match society's usual definitions of "property" in most other respects, they need some form of property law protection.[1]

On the other hand, the argument against the widespread recognition of "virtual property" (also at its most basic) is that virtual worlds and games serve their primary purposes as experimental, social, and play spaces better if they are not "commodified" (that is, turned into centers of commerce against the desires of the developers).[2]

This chapter will argue that the law needs to acknowledge and provide protection for virtual property, but that it must do so in a way that preserves virtual worlds and games as play spaces, at least to the extent that the developers desire their worlds to remain pure play spaces. On one hand, many game and virtual world providers seek to avoid real-life implications in their social and play spaces. Where providers take reasonable steps to draw a line between the real and the virtual, the world or game should be protected by the "magic circle" that protects other play spaces (from theme parks to family Monopoly games) from taking on inadvertent real-world implications. On the other hand, it is both inevitable and desirable that some game and virtual world designers will seek to include real money trade (RMT) and offer a real cash economy (RCE) in their platforms. Users of these platforms need the protection of virtual property law.

Need does not equal action, however, and attorneys must realize that however desirable the recognition of "virtual property" may be, the law is likely to move slowly in accepting this new class of property. Although the concept of virtual property is intriguing, and several well-argued papers exist on the topic (some of which will be referenced later in this chapter), there is no reason to expect that legal recognition of an entirely new class of property will take place any time soon. Remember, intellectual property protection has been around in one form or another since at least 1474 and is still subject to widespread skepticism.[3] Nonetheless, the debate over virtual property takes center stage in most disputes involving virtual worlds, and it is reasonable to expect to see judicial rulings that begin to address it in the near future.

In this chapter we will examine the history of virtual property and the various arguments for and against considering virtual property as a new class of property. We will then examine the status quo and consider arguments that could be raised under *existing* law which—while perhaps less intellectually appealing—probably have a greater likelihood of success before a judge or jury.

A Short History of Virtual Property

A debate exists over the nature of virtual property because, whether it is desirable or not, sales of virtual property are making a lot of people a lot of money. This is a relatively new phenomenon. Until the late 1990s, providers of both game-based and social virtual worlds (to the extent that these spaces existed) operated under the assumption that everything on their servers was theirs to do with as they pleased. Users also understood this to be true. No one thought that objects in early text-based multi-user dungeons (MUDs) might one day be fought over in court. Not only did the virtual worlds' and games' Terms of Service (where they existed) make this clear, but there was never really any question about it. Most MUDs were reset regularly, with all objects redistributed to their original locations. If a user typed a command on Tuesday that caused her character to "pick up" and then "wear" a purple hat, she might log in on Wednesday and find that the hat had been returned to general circulation or that another user's text-based representative was now "wearing" it. To the extent that users had access to a semipermanent personal inventory of items (which was true in at least one very early 2-D avatar-based social virtual world called "The Palace," which is still in operation), the virtual items could only be used to decorate the world's otherwise generic avatars, and no practical mechanism for user-to-user sales existed.

In the late 1990s, twin forces changed this status quo. First, the idea of permanent character-possession of objects gained prominence, originally in games and later in social virtual worlds. Second, a market developed for the goods.

This came about because the Internet, for the first time, allowed an infinitely broad base of otherwise disconnected players to access a shared, stored set of game resources with relative ease. Ultima

Online (UO), released in 1997 (and still in operation), is largely credited with popularizing the game-based virtual world genre, although there were other, earlier attempts.

Ultima Online, like virtually all games, involves a heroic journey. In linear, single-player games, that heroic journey takes a character from a relatively powerless starting point to a relatively powerful end point, where he or she defeats the most difficult obstacle in the game, and the game ends. Because Ultima Online was at least partly a social world, however (and because the business model depends on the indefinite retention of customers), there was no designed "end" or "winning" to the game. Instead, users largely measured their standing in the game by comparing their success to the success of other users. Typical areas for comparison included (1) the player's ability to perform combat moves in the game, (2) the player's knowledge of the game world, (3) the player's characters' social standing in various formal and ad hoc role-playing groups, (4) the statistical abilities ("level") of the player's characters, and, perhaps most of all, (5) the value of the player's characters' land and possessions.

This last, the value of players' land and possessions, is where Ultima Online, particularly in its early years, really broke new ground. The game mechanic was ingeniously simple and stands as the model for most virtual world games that have followed. It started with a very large world—large enough that you'd likely not visit every area in a year of regular play. The world was rich with natural resources. These resources included, among other things, animals that could be killed or tamed, fish that could be caught, veins of rare metals in the mountains that could be mined, and trees that could be chopped.[4] Procuring the resources demanded certain skills. For example, a skilled fisherman (in other words, a character who had spent a significant amount of time fishing) had a higher chance of catching fish and a lower chance of catching boots. A skilled miner could mine more efficiently.

Some of the resources that could be gathered were valuable in and of themselves, but, typically, turning the resources into something usable (e.g., turning iron ore into a suit of iron armor, or turning an animal pelt into a pair of leather boots) required use of still different skills. This feature encouraged players to cooperate and created a thriving in-world economy. Currency (gold) could be earned in the game for various actions or given by one player to another in exchange for goods, further enhancing the economy and encouraging easy trades.

The result of all this was that certain products became very rare (and thus very valuable) based on the frequency with which the necessary resources appeared within the world, the level of skill required to extract these resources, and the level of skill required to manipulate the resources. For example, producing a high-quality set of rare blue "valorite" armor required (1) locating a sufficient quantity of valorite ore (requiring knowledge of the game world), (2) mining the ore (which requires a high "mining" skill"), and (3) fabricating the pieces (which requires a high blacksmithing skill). Sometimes, this was all done by one player, but more often, this single suit of armor would be the result of collaborative efforts of several characters. This made a full suit of valorite armor an expensive purchase and made ownership of such a set a mark of success, or at least wealth. (Somewhat oddly, because powder-blue armor wasn't terribly popular from an aesthetic perspective, these extremely valuable sets tended to end up decorating people's virtual homes and castles.)

On top of the inherent creation of relatively rare products by the game mechanic, the company that managed Ultima Online routinely created extremely rare items and introduced them into the world, occasionally as holiday gifts. Some other items were created due to flaws in the game's mechanics that were subsequently fixed. Some items, particularly those which were introduced intentionally, had significant play-enhancing value (e.g., item bless deeds, which allowed a user to "bless" a weapon and, thus, never lose it when the user's character died), but others were valuable only because of their rarity (e.g., a pair of dark green sandals that I once owned for my Ultima Online character that were made during a brief time when dark green leather could be created because of a programming error). These rare items often decorated the homes of the richest players in the game—homes that themselves stood as demonstrations of the players' wealth and success within the world. It is not an exaggeration to say that even now the vast majority of players in Ultima Online spend most of their time trying to accumulate wealth in order to impress their neighbors.

So where is the heroic journey here? When a new player logs in to the world for the first time, he or she is relatively powerless, poorly equipped, nearly broke, and alone. Slowly, over many hours, days, weeks, and months of play, the user is able to accumulate vast wealth, purchase a home, perhaps find some rare treasures, master various crafts, start a shop, own pets, join guilds, and make friends. Though there is no endgame, there is a definite heroic journey that takes every player from penniless unknown weakling to well-equipped, highly skilled, socially known veteran. And the primary evidence that a player has progressed on the heroic journey in Ultima Online (and in every other online game with no endpoint which has followed) is the accumulation of assets and increases in the character's statistical skills that accompany asset accumulation via the game-play mechanics.

Marking success with wealth, of course, led almost immediately to the creation of a secondary market for in-world Ultima Online assets that existed entirely outside Ultima Online. I was first exposed to this market in 1999, when I began playing Ultima Online. At the time, that market largely existed on eBay, although it has since been moved to other services (eBay banned auctions of intangible property in contravention of game companies' agreements with their customers in early 2007). Discovering this market was an eye-opening experience. People were routinely (at the rate of many dozens of auctions per hour) buying and selling advanced Ultima Online accounts for hundreds of dollars. Item and gold auctions were even more common, with gold available in nearly any quantity at any hour of the day. Auctions for key resources were never more than minutes from closing. One user, a real-world acquaintance of mine, purchased a "tower" in Ultima Online (the second-largest building available in the world) in 1999 for slightly over US$1000.

The market has exploded since 1999, with estimates of sales of virtual goods, in-world currency and gold, and user accounts in game worlds (the last are not, strictly speaking, virtual property themselves, though they are essentially "packages" of virtual property) now reaching as high as US $1.8 billion per year.[5] The phenomenon is not limited to games, of course. Sales of virtual goods within social worlds like Second Life alone routinely exceed US$1.3 million per day and show no signs of slowing.

This robust economy in virtual possessions that don't fit in any traditional property category largely explains why there is now a question over the nature of virtual property. A number of scholars have made real progress defining the category, and while it is not likely that the category will be wholly recognized as a new branch of property law in the immediate future, the question of the definition of virtual property is already arising in the context of legal disputes and will certainly continue to do so. That question is the focus of the remainder of this chapter.

What Is Virtual Property?

"Virtual property" (to the extent that some are beginning to argue for the acceptance of the term) simply refers to in-world objects that can be possessed by one user to the exclusion of others. In games, these can be resources, valuable weaponry, or gold. In social virtual worlds, they can be nearly anything, from "hoverboards" in There.com to clothing for avatars in IMVU to animated stripper poles for entrepreneurial adult entertainers in Second Life.

Joshua Fairfield, in his seminal paper *Virtual Property*, defines virtual property as encompassing three legally relevant qualities: interconnectivity, persistence, and rivalrousness.[6] These concepts are reflected in the rather less precise, if perhaps somewhat more accessible, definition that I offered above.

The first two elements—interconnectivity and persistence— are straightforward and are really part of the generally accepted definition of virtual worlds themselves. The "persistence" of goods simply refers to the fact that they remain available to a user from one session to another, so that after logging off, he can access them again when he logs back on. Similarly, the "interconnectedness" of goods merely refers to their presence in the virtual world. If the existence of a good is apparent to or impacts more than one user (in any sense at all), the good is "interconnected." This is true of essentially everything except interface features in most virtual worlds and games. Finally, "rivalrousness" simply refers to exclusivity of use. If you and your guildmates in World of Warcraft kill a Barnabus and it drops a Conjurer's Vest, only one of you can walk away with the vest. The Conjurer's Vest is, thus, a "rivalrous" good.

For the remainder of this chapter, we will use this simplified version of Fairfield's definition: "virtual property" refers to in-world objects that can be possessed by one user to the exclusion of others. We will find (perhaps somewhat counterintuitively) that virtual land must be dealt with separately. The first portion of this chapter deals only with virtual objects.

The Red Herring of "Value"

The concept of "virtual property" is intuitively attractive not just to academics but to anyone who has ever purchased or sold a virtual item for real money. We have an instinct that because the item has obvious value, it must be an item that can be owned. The reality, however, is that the ability to sell something to someone else for money, while intuitively implying "ownership," doesn't establish anything at all from a legal perspective. There are other, better arguments that we will consider later, but this one frequently arises because of its intuitive appeal, and it is important to understand its limits.

Consider this: you have the ability (providing you can find a sufficiently stupid buyer) to "sell" someone the Statue of Liberty. You could tell someone he can have complete and total ownership of it, from the copper crown to the base, if he gives you $100. And after his "purchase," he may, if he is sufficiently stupid, even go on believing that he owns it for the rest of his days. So what? Finding a willing buyer for something does not prove that the seller originally "owned" it. Along the same lines, it matters not at all if the seller herself was also exceedingly stupid and really thought that she owned the statue in the first place, or even that she sold it in good faith. The combined mistakes of two people who misunderstand both the seller's original ownership and the buyer's purchase of an item do not create legal meaning in an otherwise invalid transaction. Perceived value simply cannot be the foundation of an argument for the existence of virtual property.

The reality is that at the moment, every virtual world and game—even those, like Second Life, that preserve users' ownership of some *intellectual* property—expressly reserve any ownership rights in the virtual items that are periodically created in the virtual world or game. This is true whether the objects appear because the game software creates them as a result of user interactions with it, or, in social free-form worlds, when they appear as a result of users' creative efforts. The providers use relatively unambiguous clauses in their Terms of Service and End User License Agreements to declare this.

For example, consider World of Warcraft's Terms of Service, which fairly unambiguously state:

> **8. Ownership/Selling of the Account or Virtual Items.**
> . . . .
> Blizzard owns, has licensed, or otherwise has rights to all of the content that appears in the Program. You agree that you have no right or title in or to any such content, including the virtual goods or currency appearing or originating in the Game, or any other attributes associated with the Account or stored on the Service. Blizzard does not recognize any virtual property transfers executed outside of the Game or the purported sale, gift or trade in the "real world" of anything related to the Game. Accordingly, you may not sell items for "real" money or otherwise exchange items for value outside of the Game.[7]

Even Second Life, which is widely praised (and justifiably so) for being the first platform to formally recognize users' intellectual property (IP) rights, makes the fact that users do not retain any property rights in the objects on Second Life servers at least as clear as Blizzard does:

> **3.3 Linden Lab retains ownership of the account and related data, regardless of intellectual property rights**

you may have in content you create or otherwise own.
You agree that even though you may retain certain copyright or other intellectual property rights with respect to
Content you create while using the Service, you do not
own the account you use to access the Service, nor do
you own any data Linden Lab stores on Linden Lab servers (including without limitation any data representing or
embodying any or all of your Content). Your intellectual
property rights do not confer any rights of access to the
Service or any rights to data stored by or on behalf of Linden Lab.[8]

One can argue that provisions like these should be found unconscionable; this is particularly true for virtual worlds and games
where the large print says nearly the opposite of the small print.
That is an issue of contract law, however, and it will be considered
in the next chapter. From a *property law* perspective, there is no
good reason to believe that these provisions will not generally be
found to be enforceable (or meaningless, which will turn out to be
equally effective at preventing recourse). The law does not move
quickly to develop new rights, particularly in the time-tested field
of property law, and these provisions do not obviously violate any
existing property right.

Yet most people share the instinct that the billions of dollars
of perceived value here should be recognized. Many users instinctively feel that a virtual object that can only be owned by one person, and has a sale price that can readily be expressed in dollars
and cents, really *is* worth something, particularly when the company that runs the virtual world where it is found says so in its
advertising materials. In the absence of far-off specific protection
for virtual property, the best way to defeat these provisions will not
be by encouraging a court to break new legal ground or by arguing
directly that this perception of value should equate to a new property right, but by giving a judge or jury the opportunity to apply
existing law to these provisions in a way that comports with most
people's instinct. Practical arguments for that position will be considered later in this chapter and in the following chapter on contract law.

The Argument Against Recognizing Virtual Property

Richard Bartle, who is credited with creation of the very first computer-based virtual world (MUD, in 1978), is concerned about virtual property.[9] The fact that Bartle is concerned ought to be enough to give even the most gung-ho virtual property advocate pause. Bartle has watched this entire march toward virtual property from the beginning, and his concerns are valid. They are not, however, entirely incompatible with a recognition of virtual property.

Bartle uses the term "commodification" to refer to "the transformation of previously non-commercial relationships into commercial ones." His central thesis is that markers for achievement in games (at least outside casinos) are generally not subject to market forces. This has allowed game designers a great deal of freedom to experiment with various economic principles that might otherwise be considered horrible abuses of power. When there's no expectation of *real* value, an otherwise horrible abuse of power can simply be seen as a design decision. Bartle feels, and not without cause, that this makes games better.

Bartle outlines several problems with virtual property in a 2004 paper entitled *The Pitfalls of Virtual Property*, which he has graciously granted permission to excerpt here. These are legitimate problems that should not be simply brushed aside, particularly in relation to game-based worlds, where the economy should, in theory, be subservient to the fun of play.

> If you accept (or if the law accepts) virtual property as a concept, you as a developer, become a custodian rather than an owner—you have responsibilities. Of these, the one that seems to attract the most attention from pro-commodification players is an obligation to ensure that virtual property retains its value. . . . This puts severe—perhaps impossible—constraints on [designers]. For example, suppose that as a player you were to buy the Sword of Truth, the most deadly weapon in some particular virtual world. You might expect to pay a premium for it. However, if the very next day the virtual world were to be flooded

(through design, patch or bug) with ten thousand Swords of Greater Truth, your investment would be wiped out. It doesn't have to be a sword, it could be an axe; it doesn't have to be better, it could be the same. Whatever, PayPal isn't going to refund your $5,000.[10]

Anyone who has played a multiplayer online game knows that Bartle is absolutely right that this process (whereby players lose perceived value through design decisions) actually happens. Players even have a term for it: "nerfing" (as in, "The designers nerfed my axe-fighter; now axes only do half as much damage!" or "The designers nerfed chair-building; now you need ten pieces of lumber instead of six!").[11]

Nerfing inevitably happens for a variety of reasons, some intentional and some unintentional. Typically, designers nerf a class of character or weapon type because it becomes apparent through game play that the character class or weapon is too powerful. It is also extremely difficult to predict the long-term consequences of early design decisions because users come up with all sorts of ways to imbalance the world to their benefit; these actions sometimes require responses that reduce perceived value. For example, in the very early days of Ultima Online, the world was structured such that a player who wished to develop a craft-based skill needed to make an extraordinary number of low-value items in order to progress to higher levels. For example, a tailor had to make a huge number of virtual hats—we're talking about thousands and thousands of hats—in order to master the craft. Hats could be disposed of in only two ways—by selling them to other players or by selling them to non-player characters (NPCs). But because Ultima Online's designers wanted something approaching a real economy, the NPCs were programmed to only buy hats if there were users who were, in turn, buying hats from the NPCs. Because there were many times more hats in Ultima Online's "Britannia" than heads to put them on, no one was buying. This resulted in huge piles of hats (and other low-value items) littering the Ultima Online landscape until, ultimately, the designers changed the rules so that NPCs would buy hats from players regardless of demand. This, in turn, caused massive inflation that continues today. For example, one could buy 50,000 UO Gold in an eBay purchase in 2000 for approximately $24.00. Currently, $24.00 buys approximately *ten million* UO Gold. In other words, UO Gold bought in the year 2000 is worth 1/200 as much now, representing a loss that could be attributed to game design changes.

Bartle argues that this sort of situation should not result in a lawsuit against the designers, and, as noted, this argument has a great deal of merit. Keep it in mind as you read the rest of this chapter. In my opinion, Bartle is right, and noncommodified worlds should be preserved as noncommodified worlds—but they are not the only option. More on that after we consider the argument in favor of recognizing virtual property.

The Argument for Recognizing Virtual Property

Although virtual property is not likely to be recognized soon as a new class of property, several very good arguments have been developed as to why it *should* be. These arguments inform the practical arguments against enforcement of certain provisions in providers' Terms of Service, which will be discussed later in this chapter and in the chapter on contracts, and, for that reason, it is important to understand their genesis.

The basic framework for the arguments in favor of the recognition of virtual property was developed by Greg Lastowka and Dan Hunter in a 2004 article, "The Laws of Virtual Worlds."[12] Lastowka and Hunter examined both normative (how things ought to be) and descriptive (how things are) theories of property law and found that under both, "virtual property"—that is, the virtual swords, dresses, and gold pieces that accumulate in the inventories of users of game-based and social virtual worlds—should be understood, in law, to be no less "property" than real swords, dresses, and gold pieces.

It is beyond the scope of this chapter to break down Lastowka and Hunter's excellent analysis item by item, but their conclusions are illustrative. Readers interested in the details behind the conclusions are encouraged to consult the original text. Regarding descriptive theories (in essence, looking at what "virtual property" really is), Lastowka and Hunter found that virtual property matches all the earmarks we use to define property generally. It can be so easily bought and sold.[13] It is no less "real" than a digital book or downloadable computer program, which are also, at their core, merely ones and zeros.[14] It is no less "real" than the formula for Coca-Cola, which is recognized as a trade secret and protected as intellectual property.[15] Yes, the objects are impermanent in a sense, but Lastowka and Hunter observe that many forms of property, from leaseholds to mineral rights, are also fleeting.[16] Permanence is hardly a requirement for property to be property anyway—a chicken lives and has value but a short while, yet one can clearly own chickens.

In sum, Lastowka and Hunter conclude, "the objections to virtual property on the basis that it is intangible or impermanent are descriptively implausible. Our property system cheerfully accommodates these characteristics, in one form or another, in various types of property interests. There appears to be no plausible descriptive objection to granting property interests in virtual assets."[17]

Lastowka and Hunter also looked at the three leading normative theories of property—"the utilitarian theory of Bentham and his economist-acolytes, the labor-desert theory of Locke, and the personality theories that stem from Hegel."[18] They concluded,

> The three main normative theories of property, then, all provide strong normative grounds for recognizing that property rights should inhere in virtual assets, whether chattels, realty, or avatars. Depending on the theory one adopts, the limitations on rights in virtual property may be uncertain. Nonetheless, our conclusion is that there seems to be no reason under traditional theories of property to exclude virtual properties from legal protection. Further, based on the earlier discussion, we can conclude that there is no descriptive disconnection between our real-world property system and virtual assets. From both descriptive and normative positions, owners of virtual assets do, or should, possess property rights.[19]

One of the clearest theoretical arguments for the recognition of virtual property as a new category of property comes from Joshua

Fairfield, who provided the framework for the definition of "virtual property," noted earlier.[20] Fairfield argues that the United States is falling behind other nations in protection of virtual property because, by not protecting virtual property, the law has allowed the attorneys who draft EULAs and Terms of Service for virtual world and game providers to dictate the terms of this debate. That is, the law has effectively abandoned its duties to those who look to it for protection and instead left the foxes in charge of the virtual property henhouse. Fairfield argues:

> In general, we continue to govern virtual property through the law of intellectual property. Even where there has been some recognition that virtual property is somehow "different," no clear articulation of that difference has been offered. As a result, holders of intellectual property rights have been systematically eliminating emerging virtual property rights by the use of contracts called End User License Agreements ("EULAs"). Despite (or perhaps because of) these contracts, no distinct protection for property rights in virtual property has appeared in the United States, even though millions of people and billions of dollars are involved in gray-market transactions in such property. In comparison, China, Taiwan, and Korea have already made significant steps toward protecting ownership interests in virtual property, hoping to attract the burgeoning industry of virtual worlds.[21]

Fairfield posits that the ability to assert true ownership rights over any good that can be possessed by one person to the exclusion of others is fundamental to efficient markets and, thus, to the ongoing growth of the space.[22] He also points out that recognition of virtual property is not without precedent—both e-mail addresses and URLs are, essentially, virtual property that the law has already moved to protect.[23]

Fairfield also argues that a long-standing equilibrium has developed between contract law and property law. In essence, property law provides for a set of limits on what contract law allows parties to bargain away. For example, property law prohibits "unreasonable restraints on alienation" in the context of the purchase of real property (e.g., a provision in a contract that says a homeowner cannot sell the property secured by virtue of the contract is invalid). Intellectual property law also serves as a limit on contract. For example, a person who is not the actual inventor of a patented process or apparatus cannot be listed as the "inventor" on its patent due to the operation of patent law (although the inventor can, of course, contract away her right to the invention). Similarly, community property laws in many states limit a couple's ability to agree to a division of property by prenuptial and postnuptial agreement.[24] Closer to the subject at hand, the law of unconscionability holds that contract provisions that are manifestly unfair for, among other reasons, a gross disparity between the value of the items exchanged, will not be enforced. This, too, can be seen as an extension of property law—when one contracts away something of great value *that one owns* for a mere pittance, that factor weighs against enforcement of the contract provision that created the imbalance.

These are all situations where society has made the decision that it is in its best interest to limit the generally unfettered right to contract on the grounds that it is trumped, or at least matched, by an equally important property right.

Fairfield argues that this equilibrium is necessary for both fair markets and sound contract law. In the absence of recognized property rights that govern virtual property, Fairfield posits, contracts will attempt to limit these rights, perhaps unfairly.

> The law of property and the law of contract typically balance each other. The law of contract permits parties to realize the value of idiosyncratic preferences through trade. The law of property traditionally limits the burdens that parties may place on the productive use or marketability of high-value resources by means of contract. For example, unreasonable contractual restraints on alienation are eliminated by the law of property. But currently in the context of the internet, we have imported the common law of contract wholesale, without the counterbalance of property law. As a result, emergent useful property forms are being eliminated by contract.[25]

One might expect that the net result of this (or at least a result that would bolster Fairfield's claim) would be that game companies would, at this moment, be rubbing their hands with glee and slyly entering the market for the goods that are created by their software and then abandoned by players who leave the game. In fact, and rather ironically, the provider is perhaps the only entity for whom the goods have as great a value when they are destroyed as when they are available in the world. If "virtual property" is recognized, each virtual sword could be seen as a tiny debt owed by the game company to its players. Recognition of virtual property would force game and virtual world providers that do not choose to take advantage of the protection of the magic circle to treat assets in-world as any other assets. In other words, producing a "magic sword" via programming in a game world would be essentially the same as producing a play sword from plastic. Absent enforceable agreements to the contrary, storing it for users in between play sessions would involve some risk and liability, as could making changes to the game world that "nerf" the sword and make it less valuable.

Reconciling the Arguments—How Virtual Property Will Come into Being

Fairfield's theory, while representing an obvious change in the way we would view some current games and virtual worlds, makes a great deal of sense. We know that property law, as it stands, does not recognize the $1.8 billion industry, but as the industry grows, pressure for change will inevitably increase as well. Clarification is appealing not only to scholars but to attorneys, executives, and game designers working in this space as well, who would all very much like to see some general understanding emerge regarding the status of virtual property. Many, myself included, believe this is inevitable and think that Fairfield's definition will prevail.

However—and this is a very big however—the existence of virtual property as described in Fairfield's definition will only be widely accepted by the game design community, and thus implemented in the rules, Terms of Service, and End User License Agreements of virtual worlds and games, *if it is offered in conjunction with something like Raph Koster's theory of interration.* Any effort to legislate the existence of virtual property will—and should—be met by fierce resistance from the game design and user communities on the grounds that such an effort would undermine play spaces as play spaces *unless* the measure is accompanied by a mechanism that allows games and virtual worlds that wish to remain play spaces, clear of the obligations that the notion of virtual property creates, to do so. People should be able to play games, trade goods, and interact socially without real money entering into the transactions uninvited. *Forced* commodification would ruin much of what is good about play spaces.

The solution, as noted, will come from something like Raph Koster's "interration." Interration, recall, is essentially the idea that game and social virtual world providers ought to be able to avail themselves of formal legal protections that arise from the "magic circle" through a process that parallels that of incorporation. That is, if a game company or virtual world provider wishes to create a pure play space, largely, if not entirely, exempt from real-world laws, it ought to be able to do so by following a set of carefully construed rules. Chief among those rules must be a prohibition against treating the game world's currency, property, and items as "virtual property."

It is a reasonable assumption that if one of these theories is adopted as law, the other will be as well. That is, if a new class of property known as "virtual property" is acknowledged and protected from outright grabs via contract law, along with that will come some mechanism whereby game and virtual world providers can create environments that exist without being concerned with the real-world value of every digital sword, hat, and paperclip that is represented in the world.

If that assumption holds—that Fairfield's hypothesis will only be adopted in conjunction with something along the lines of Koster's theory of interration—a company that does choose to avail itself of interration will be free of the restrictions of "virtual property" law and, thus, can manipulate its economy at will, delete items and accounts on a whim, introduce new features that grossly devalue current property, and, generally, treat the world as a true game or environment for social experimentation without fear of lawsuits.

■■■■■
Why Black Market RMT Exists

Scarcity of Rewards—The mechanics of most games make certain high-value rewards very scarce so that there is more incentive to accomplish harder tasks. Some players do not want to "work" for these prizes, but still want the prizes.

Scarcity of Resources—In some games, resources that are necessary to progress are hard to find. Some players prefer to purchase them, paying someone else to do the hunting.

Speculation/Arbitrage Opportunities—Some players speculate in price increases in the secondary market or buy accounts of people who quit the game and then sell the component parts at a profit.

Appearance of Success—Some players want to appear to be better at the game than they are, so they are willing to pay to play advanced accounts.

Early-Stage Boredom—Some games are fun at higher levels, but getting to the higher levels is boring. Some players would rather pay someone else to do the "grunt work" necessary to move up a level. This goes along with . . .

Money vs. Time—Some players, particularly adult players with full-time jobs, find it close to impossible to play online games (which are often scaled for people with hundreds of free hours every year) to earn high-level characters and rewards, and prefer to buy them.

Everybody Else Is Doing It—RMT encourages more RMT. When paying for an advanced account becomes the norm, then players who do not buy an account will not feel they are getting the full game experience.

We can assume that many, if not most, game companies will take this route, preserving via "interration" (or a process like it) what they are finding they have a very difficult time preserving through

■■■■■

Why Black Market RMT Is Bad for Games

Discourages Poorer Players—If cash buys advanced accounts and weapons, then the game quickly becomes a playground for only the richest real-life players.

Undermines the Heroic Journey—Games provide a place for players to experience struggles and success. Buying a pass to the front of the line deprives players of that experience.

Discourages Long-Term Play—Players who can buy advanced accounts will not spend the time (and money) game designers hope they will in the game world generating those results.

contract. Many players will presumably seek out these worlds and games, because they can be relatively confident that their individual heroic journey (in games) or socioeconomic experiments and interaction (in social virtual worlds) will not be overwhelmingly compromised by the presence of a market for the goods and abilities that they are struggling to accumulate (in games) or by the restrictions of real-life law (in social virtual worlds). There will, of course, be no possibility of making real money in these spaces, but just as the vast majority of people choose not to play Monopoly for real money, presumably a large percentage of the players of online games and participants in social virtual worlds will choose to participate for fun. Their fun will be enhanced by the security of a level playing field and the absence of restrictive legal oversight.

On the other hand, a company that chooses to act as a full participant in the notion of virtual property will gain the not insignificant benefits of a new set of potential revenue streams, a more "real" economy with higher stakes for players, and the opportunity to serve a presumably older, more professional, more profitable user base. A company that chooses this path will, however, have to deal with certain ramifications of that decision which, in the absence of such a rule, companies that are flirting with the notion of virtual property have thus far been able to sweep under the rug with broadly phrased contract provisions.

What Will Happen When Virtual Property Comes into Being?

The full impact of this shift (a joint implementation of Fairfield's and Koster's hypotheses) is beyond the scope of this book and, in fact, somewhat unpredictable. A few results, however, *are* predictable and are worth keeping in mind from the perspective of both academic inquiry and practical implementation.

The impact will be markedly different for game providers than it is for providers of social virtual worlds. Taking game providers first, let's consider a hypothetical user named "Wendy," who plays World of Warcraft, a game that has taken every possible step to avail itself of magic circle protection. When Wendy slays a creature (commonly referred to as a "mob," from the programming term "mobile object")[26] and claims an item (let's say, a particularly powerful sword) and some gold "drops" as a reward, then Wendy's character will take the sword and the gold from the mob's fallen corpse and add them to her inventory. At that point, they are hers.

Because they are rivalrous goods, she has exclusive ownership—no other player can possess that particular sword or those particular gold pieces unless she gives them to another player, at which point she will no longer possess them. Because the sword and the gold are "interconnected," other players can see that she has them and will have their game play impacted by Wendy's possession of them. And because the sword and the gold are persistent, they will remain in Wendy's inventory while she is not using the world (in some worlds, like Ultima Online, Wendy could even put the sword and pile of gold on display in her home when she was not using them, and other players could visit the home and see the sword and gold even though Wendy was not logged in at the time). But they are not "virtual property" because World of Warcraft has made it explicitly clear throughout its presentation of the world, its agreements with its users, and its enforcement of its policies that World of Warcraft is not a real cash economy and that it treats the goods as merely part of its "game set," having no outside value at all.

Viewing the virtual objects in a game as part of the "set" makes a great deal of sense. Nearly all games' objects and currency become extant in the world only because the game provider has written software that creates them and distributes them to players as rewards for accomplishing tasks. Even when a user "creates" an object, it is really a programmatic event dictated by the provider, similar to following the plans to assemble a bookshelf using predrilled wood and nuts and bolts provided by a furniture store. No genuine "creation" occurs that is not entirely anticipatable by the game provider based on resources and programming. There are several reasons for this restriction, including aesthetics (if users could create objects without restriction, it would be impossible to preserve the look and feel of a game world), game play (a sword fighting game would quickly lose its appeal if some characters had laser pistols), and liability (unfettered object creation raises both intellectual property and obscenity concerns). The bottom line is that game-based virtual worlds are, generally, restrictive regarding their content. Along with this, the transfer of items and wealth is tightly regulated because these functions (for example, buying and selling items in-world) are usually part of game play.

Interration (whether via a formal process like that described by Koster, or via an informal, consistent application of policy and presentation that avoids giving users the false expectation that the world has a real cash economy) will protect games like World of Warcraft from being treated as having "virtual property" when they do not. The opposite must also be true: a game or virtual world provider that does *not* choose to interrate, and thus implicitly (or explicitly) acknowledges the value of the virtual property that will be created in the game or world, would no longer be allowed to declare objects and currency created in-world completely valueless (as most games do now via a few lines in the game's End User License Agreement or Terms of Service).

Providers that do not interrate, and thus acknowledge the existence of virtual property, would be forced to choose between two options. The provider could either (1) grant ownership of virtual property created in the world to the world's or game's users, who would take possession and ownership of these assets upon receipt in-world, with all that implies, or (2) essentially "lease" the objects to users as part of the provider's agreement with users of the virtual world or game—that is, retain ownership. Either of these options could be accomplished via a game's Terms of Service. And either approach arguably provides far greater clarity, enforceability, and validity than some virtual worlds' current Terms of Service and advertising which try, on the one hand, to deny the existence of virtual property and, on the other, to preserve ownership of it to the game company.

The first option (whereby a provider grants ownership) allows the game provider to have the game software create objects and distribute them to users without concern over the creation of corporate assets (although this does raise concerns regarding whether the game company is essentially running an illegal gambling operation).

The second option—leasing the assets to users as part of their monthly subscription fee—may be more appealing to game designers. After all, it allows the company to retain all that glorious, newly created virtual property. And in a sense, that is what most providers attempt to do now, although because they do not acknowledge the existence of virtual property in the first place, they are reduced to using poorly suited contract provisions that simply declare players in possession of nothing. One significant upside to acknowledging virtual property is that game companies could dispense with this problematic, and potentially invalid, language and replace it with tested provisions that grant the right to use the property to the users so long as they continue paying monthly fees. The downside, of course, is that these created items then become assets, and, at the end of the day, a company will have to account for them. If a provider failed to set up appropriate contractual precautions and shut down the servers while "owing" users their virtual property, everyone who had an account would presumably be able to get in line with the electric company and the provider's real-world landlords to try to collect on the debt of virtual swords and spell-casting reagents, at pennies on the virtual dollar. In addition, the company could be exposed to liability for decisions it makes that devalue some assets at the expense of others, particularly if the net result is an increase in the company's bottom line. None of these are insurmountable legal hurdles, but they are new issues that companies would have to carefully consider in creating their EULAs and Terms of Service agreements.

For social virtual world providers, the challenges regarding currency and objects are rather different. Game providers generally create and control all the content in the game, but many social virtual world providers rely on their users to create the majority of the in-world content.[27] As a result, they will face different challenges if and when they begin to acknowledge virtual property.

In a sense, their decision is simpler than the game companies' decision. If virtual property is acknowledged, social virtual world providers that create little or none of the in-world content (like Second Life's Linden Lab) could be seen to have never owned any of the items in the world in the first place. The users who created or purchased the items own them. Providers could simply acknowledge the existence of virtual property and accept the relatively small additional liability that action creates. Any competent provider is maintaining multiple off-site backups anyway, so the only real risks are going bankrupt without providing a method whereby users can back their objects up and take them elsewhere, and not being able to throw users off the system without giving them the ability to either take their objects with them or sell them in-world. Bankruptcy, of course, is a risk that consumers run when entrusting any data, money, or possessions to any company—from personal photographs stored on photo-sharing websites to deposits at a brick-and-mortar bank to a pair of gym shoes left in a locker. All other risks can reasonably be handled with insurance, contract provisions, and reliable backup and portability schemes. A provider could even promise in its agreements with customers to make its software available as open-source in the event that the company ceases to operate the world, so that people could still access their virtual property. In the end, from a legal perspective, virtual world providers who are not, themselves, populating users' inventories with objects put themselves in a position where the only major new obligation they take on by acknowledging the existence of virtual property consists of not throwing users out of the world without allowing them the opportunity to either take or sell their possessions. That obligation does not seem a wholly unreasonable one for a virtual world provider to take on.

Ownership of Currency

Regarding currency, the problems are also not as complex as current TOS and EULA provisions make them out to be. The simplest way for a social virtual world provider to handle currency under a virtual property regime is to allow transactions between users (either for a fee or not) but otherwise to simply not enter the currency market as a participant. Transactions can take place in real-world dollars and cents, or the company can do conversions to an in-world currency at a set, nonfluctuating rate. The former is simpler and makes it clear that the economy is what it really is—a true "real cash economy." The latter has advantages, however, including the potential for the illusion of greater user-wealth via a themed or "fun" currency (e.g., users may be happier having one thousand in-world "coins" instead of one U.S. dollar), and it offers the significant benefit of allowing transactions at a fraction of a penny. The company would, of course, need to maintain a U.S. dollar reserve to back an in-world currency (if it chooses to issue one, rather than simply facilitating U.S. dollar transactions), but if it is only issuing currency in exchange for dollars in the first place, it obviously can.

Ownership of Virtual Land

This leaves virtual land—essentially the server-based depiction of the piece of real estate upon which users can build objects for others to see, purchase, and interact with. "Virtual land" can exist in either game-based or social virtual worlds. Although World of Warcraft currently does not offer users the ability to "own" parts of the game world, many games, dating back all the way to Ultima Online, do, and there is a near-constant call in the World of Warcraft forums for the creation of private and guild "virtual land."[28] The feature is a staple of social virtual worlds, where customization of a space, whether for entertaining, sales, or simply accommodating individual user taste, is a significant part of the offered experience.

It is important to differentiate virtual land from virtual objects (what we have been referring to as virtual property here) because virtual land, unlike relatively portable virtual objects, is inherently tied to significant hardware resources that are typically owned by the hosting company. It, by definition, isn't portable, as it is part of the virtual world itself. It "resides" on servers owned by the virtual world provider. Whereas virtual objects that are not currently in use or apparent in the world could (technical and security limitations aside) just as easily reside as ones and zeros on users' own hard drives in users' home computers, a parcel of virtual land requires constant server attention. In fact, the use of a parcel of virtual land is really just shorthand for the use of a certain percentage of one of the virtual world provider's many servers' computing resources. By "building" on the land, a user consumes hard-drive space and memory to make his creations constantly available for any user who visits the area. When others "arrive" at the parcel, the server causes the things that are built there to display on the monitor of the person who is "visiting" the land with her avatar. The owner of the land consumes bandwidth as well for every bit of data that is sent over the Internet to the computer of the user who is visiting.

There are different approaches to the problem of "land ownership," all of which are valid and would likely be legally enforceable standing alone, but none of which mixes well. In one approach, a virtual world provider could offer true ownership of all the resources. That is, it could sell hardware, or shares in hardware, to users and essentially act as a specialized collocation ("colo") center, providing constant and reliable power, appropriate environmental cooling systems, security, and automated backup rotation. The provider would charge a monthly fee for the services and might well also offer hardware installation and maintenance, but customers would own the hardware that runs there and could decide what level of server speed and reliability they needed to use for their portion of the virtual world based on their individual purposes. In another approach, the virtual world provider could retain ownership of all the servers and rent the virtual land to users for a monthly fee. In yet another model, the virtual world provider could run a core group of servers where it could retain all land ownership and control content, but license the software that runs the virtual world to third parties to install on their own servers, which would be seamlessly connected to the provider's network, allowing users to easily move between the privately owned areas and the areas owned by the virtual world provider.

Practical Arguments Regarding Virtual Property

Although the preceding arguments are better suited to congressional hearings or to the boardroom of a virtual world start-up company than to a brief in support of a motion for summary judgment or a closing argument to a jury, they make a great deal of sense and have a lot of intuitive appeal. The problem for practicing attorneys who wish to bring a claim on these grounds, of course, is that there currently is no law of virtual property that attorneys can point to in order to justify a finding that, for example, a game company should not be allowed to arbitrarily delete a user's account without at least providing a mechanism for extraction of value. One suit (*Marc Bragg v. Linden Lab*) was filed on exactly these grounds, and although it settled before a decision could be made, it raised questions that forced this issue to the forefront of the legal battle over virtual property.

This issue will come up in lawsuits in several ways. The most direct is in the context of a suit against a provider when a user is banned from the virtual world or game. This allegation was at the heart of the *Bragg* case, discussed in greater detail later in this section. Another way that the issue could arise is in the context of a criminal investigation into fraudulent activity in a virtual world. As discussed in Chapter 10, "Criminal Law and Virtual Worlds," a real cash economy combined with a user base that is primed to believe that traditional economic laws might not apply in virtual worlds provides a fertile field for unscrupulous users. Along the same lines, several civil suits have been filed (and many more threatened) based on alleged trademark misappropriation and copyright infringement. To the extent that the government or plaintiff in these cases must prove that the fraud or infringement was beneficial to the defendant, it must establish that the "currency" in the virtual world where the act took place has value. Defendants quickly turn to the Terms of Service in protesting their innocence, usually by pointing to the provision regarding currency and saying, "See, it's just a game."[29]

This problem is not going to go away unless one of two things happens. Either (1) providers will change their Terms of Service to recognize the value of the objects and currency in their worlds and, with that, the obligations that they may be taking on by encouraging real-world value to accumulate in users' accounts, or (2) a case will hold that provisions depriving users of the contents of their account—their "virtual property"—are (or are not) valid contractual provisions. From a practical perspective, anyone contemplating a suit against a provider should be paying close attention not just to the formal Terms of Service and End User License Agreement but also to the public statements of the company's representatives, the advertising materials for the game or world, and the historical implementation of policy. These factors, of course, not only have a real impact on user expectation but also resonate with judges and juries.

At this point, analysis must again diverge between virtual worlds (and a few games) that actively promote a real cash economy, and those that do not. It seems unlikely that a plaintiff who has been banned from World of Warcraft for violations of the Terms of Service would prevail in a claim against the provider (Blizzard Entertainment) on a theory of virtual property. Blizzard takes significant steps to prevent users from engaging in real money trading and has made clear that it has no tolerance for the practice.

In a sense, Blizzard is trying to informally "interrate." By taking significant steps to prevent users from engaging in real money trading (including the rather extraordinary step of suing gold farming companies), by not offering any of the trappings of a real cash economy such as a currency exchange or the ability to buy or sell items to and from Blizzard, and by completely avoiding any language in advertising materials that implies that any of the virtual items in World of Warcraft have real value, Blizzard has drawn a clear magic circle around its game world. That magic circle would be difficult to break with a lawsuit in the event that a player was banned from the world, no matter what the reason for the banning. That is appropriate—the law should not force game and virtual world providers to manage a real economy in their games if they don't want it as a feature, any more than it should force people who wish to play a family game of Monopoly to risk real money. The fact that some users will inevitably find a way to buy and sell items in games is not a persuasive argument for forcing game companies to accept liability for the black market trades, particularly when they have made the clear decision to try to keep the game world inside the protection of the magic circle.

On the other end of the spectrum, consider the game Entropia Universe, which embraces a real cash economy and appears to make most of its money by selling equipment to players, then charging real money to "repair" that equipment as it "degrades" over time (Entropia Universe does not have a subscription fee). Entropia Universe makes it completely clear that users are spending real money with every action they take and that the rewards are worth real money. Indeed, that feature appears to be the major selling point for the game. From the main page of Entropia's website:

> The Entropia Universe is more than a game. The Entropia Universe is for real. Real people, real activities and a Real Cash Economy in a massive online universe.
>
> Join people from around the globe who use the Entropia Universe currency, the PED, to develop their characters everyday on the untamed planet of Calypso. The unique and secure Real Cash Economy allows you to transfer your accumulated PED back into real world funds.[30]

The site is even more explicit on a subsequent page.

> The Real Cash Economy (RCE) in the Entropia Universe means that the virtual items inside the universe have a real value.
>
> In order to develop your character in the Entropia Universe it is necessary to invest in your character. You may wish to purchase tools, weapons, real estate or a range of other items. These items cost PED (the Entropia Universe currency).
>
> Real world currencies may be transferred into your secure Entropia Universe account where they are then exchanged into PED. The PED currency is directly connected to the real world economy through a fixed exchange rate with the US dollar, where 10 PED = 1US$. So if you deposit

10 US dollars, you will have 100 PED availabel [sic] to use In-World. For a full list of deposit options, please read the Deposit section.

Participants often accumulate PED through the sale of manufactured items and by offering services to others and may at any time withdraw their accumulated PED back into real world currencies according to the exchange rate mentioned above. Read the Withdrawals section of this website for more information.

The Real Cash Economy is a unique and pioneering feature of the Entropia Universe.[31]

Aside from the obvious jurisdictional concerns (MindArk, the company that runs Entropia Universe, is based in Sweden), a lawsuit against Entropia Universe for unfairly depriving a user of his virtual property would seem intuitively more legitimate than one against Blizzard on behalf of a World of Warcraft player on the same grounds. In game design terms, MindArk has chosen not to avail itself of the protections of the magic circle. In legal terms, MindArk has chosen to enjoy the benefits of selling goods to users for money and, thus, has to be accountable for that decision. Somewhat curiously, the Terms of Service for Entropia Universe are far less explicit about the value of PEDs, but the advertising materials are more than sufficient to justify a claim, and, notably, the Terms of Service do not counter the advertising materials.

This brings us to the virtual world of Second Life, which occupies a potentially uncomfortable middle ground that seems to create significant potential for litigation. Second Life is by far the most popular and well-known non-game virtual world. No one outside Linden Lab really knows the history of the development of the economy of Second Life, but either through design or inattention, Linden Lab has ended up in the unenviable position of essentially running what for all intents and purposes appears to be a real cash economy while denying that it is doing so via restrictive provisions in the Terms of Service that define land, currency, and objects as part of a "product"[32] and, thus, entirely the property of Linden Lab.

Consider the Second Life website, which advertises:

- "Make real money in a virtual world. That's right, **real money**."[33]
- "There are as many opportunities for innovation and profit in Second Life as in the Real World. Open a nightclub, sell jewelry, become a land speculator; the choice is yours to make. Thousands of residents are making part or all of their real life income from their Second Life Businesses."[34]
- "Millions of Linden Dollars change hands every month for the goods and services Residents create and provide. This unit-of-trade may then be bought and sold on LindeX (Second Life's official Linden Dollar exchange), or other unaffiliated third party sites for real currency."[35]
- "Second Life has a fully-integrated economy architected to reward risk, innovation, and craftsmanship."[36]
- "Residents create their own virtual goods and services. Because residents retain the IP rights of their creations, they are able to sell them at various in-world venues."[37]
- "Businesses succeed by the ingenuity, artistic ability, entrepreneurial acumen, and good reputation of their owners."[38]
- "Second Life's real estate market provides opportunities for Residents to establish their own communities and business locations."[39]

Now consider, by way of contrast, the Second Life Terms of Service, which state:

> **1.4 Second Life "currency" is a limited license right available for purchase or free distribution at Linden Lab's discretion, and is not redeemable for monetary value from Linden Lab.** You acknowledge that the Service presently includes a component of in-world fictional currency ("Currency" or "Linden Dollars" or "L$"), which constitutes a limited license right to use a feature of our product when, as, and if allowed by Linden Lab. Linden Lab may charge fees for the right to use Linden Dollars, or may distribute Linden Dollars without charge, in its sole discretion. Regardless of terminology used, Linden Dollars represent a

limited license right governed solely under the terms of this Agreement, and are not redeemable for any sum of money or monetary value from Linden Lab at any time. You agree that Linden Lab has the absolute right to manage, regulate, control, modify and/or eliminate such Currency as it sees fit in its sole discretion, in any general or specific case, and that Linden Lab will have no liability to you based on its exercise of such right.[40]

. . . .

5.3 All data on Linden Lab's servers are subject to deletion, alteration or transfer. When using the Service, you may accumulate Content, Currency, objects, items, scripts, equipment, or other value or status indicators that reside as data on Linden Lab's servers.

THESE DATA, AND ANY OTHER DATA, ACCOUNT HISTORY AND ACCOUNT NAMES RESIDING ON LINDEN LAB'S SERVERS, MAY BE DELETED, ALTERED, MOVED OR TRANSFERRED AT ANY TIME FOR ANY REASON IN LINDEN LAB'S SOLE DISCRETION.

YOU ACKNOWLEDGE THAT, NOTWITHSTANDING ANY COPYRIGHT OR OTHER RIGHTS YOU MAY HAVE WITH RESPECT TO ITEMS YOU CREATE USING THE SERVICE, AND NOTWITHSTANDING ANY VALUE ATTRIBUTED TO SUCH CONTENT OR OTHER DATA BY YOU OR ANY THIRD PARTY, LINDEN LAB DOES NOT PROVIDE OR GUARANTEE, AND EXPRESSLY DISCLAIMS (SUBJECT TO ANY UNDERLYING INTELLECTUAL PROPERTY RIGHTS IN THE CONTENT), ANY VALUE, CASH OR OTHERWISE, ATTRIBUTED TO ANY DATA RESIDING ON LINDEN LAB'S SERVERS.

YOU UNDERSTAND AND AGREE THAT LINDEN LAB HAS THE RIGHT, BUT NOT THE OBLIGATION, TO REMOVE ANY CONTENT (INCLUDING YOUR CONTENT) IN WHOLE OR IN PART AT ANY TIME FOR ANY REASON OR NO REASON, WITH OR WITHOUT NOTICE AND WITH NO LIABILITY OF ANY KIND.[41]

Either of these positions, standing alone, is fine. A virtual world can certainly have a thriving real cash economy where it can factually advertise that you can "make real money." On the other hand, a provider could certainly choose to bypass the traditional subscription model and sell "game dollars" without encouraging a market in them or telling users that they were "real" in any sense. That is a reasonable position, and there is no reason that a world or game provider could not take this position—but it must do so entirely. A provider that fails to carefully and consistently articulate that the currency is *not* real and that the virtual property and virtual land do *not* belong to the users—in its advertising material, its Terms of Service, and its implementation of its policies—is running a very real risk of lawsuits.

The most predictable suit (which Second Life's Linden Lab already faced), is a claim that a user was unfairly deprived of real assets when his account was suspended or canceled. I interviewed the attorney who represented Marc Bragg, the plaintiff in that case. Part of that interview is reproduced here. The full text of the interview is available at my website, http://virtuallyblind.com.[42]

Q. Beyond Marc Bragg's individual issues, do you view this case as saying something important about virtual law?
A. Yes. There are a lot of different things that this case will address. The biggest one is the intersection between ownership of and access to virtual items. These are different things, and the question is how the Court will reconcile these.

Also, we want to determine what law will be applied. I've urged a similar law to that of "landlocked property." Basically, if I sell a property that is entirely surrounded by someone else's property, an easement by necessity is going to be created so that the buyer can access the land. Same thing here, if someone sells virtual land or items, that should result in a user or consumer having the right to access things that they bought.

Another line of thought is that buying virtual land or items is like buying a membership in a club. Sure, someone could terminate that membership, but if they do, there's a California law that says the member should be entitled to due process in advance of being terminated from the club. Any contract provision that states otherwise is invalid.

What's happening now is that Linden is contesting the idea that they sold land, even though they told everyone that they were selling it before.

So the first issue is ownership, the second is access, and the third is if access is cut off, what is the recourse for the consumer?

There are other potential suits where these issues could arise as well. It is conceivable that users could file individual or class action lawsuits on the grounds that a provider encouraged fraudulent and illegal activity under the guise of "economic experimentation," or on the grounds that the provider implemented policy in a way that deprived users of some of the value of their possessions or property (e.g., failing to enforce rules that are designed to prevent devaluation of virtual property via "griefing"). The potential for liability simply cannot be overemphasized—a company that tries to have it both ways, by emphasizing the real cash economy of the world while attempting to retain the ability to arbitrarily terminate accounts and deny the value of goods, land, and currency in its Terms of Service, will inevitably be subject to legal claims from users who feel they were misled.

In terms of game design and virtual world philosophy, this means that the magic circle is a take it or leave it proposition. A circle is an apt description. A circle must be continuous; once it is broken, it is no longer a circle. If a company wishes to profit by selling currency and land, and outright encourages users to make their real-life living in the virtual space, it cannot reasonably protest that the fine print says it is "only a game" when faced with users who expect to extract that stored value or expect policies that genuinely protect the assets they have purchased.

Although it settled before judgment on the merits, the case of *Bragg v. Linden Lab* indicates the perils virtual world providers face when confronted with challenges to their Terms of Service that purport to limit the companies' liability for virtual property, when the company has made public statements and presented advertising that appears to endorse the concept of real-world ownership of virtual goods and land. The *Bragg* case will be examined in greater detail in the following chapter on contract law. From a property perspective, however, it should serve as a shot over the bow for providers contemplating the balance between the benefits and liability associated with acknowledging and encouraging the idea of ownership of virtual property in their virtual worlds and games.

Closing Thoughts Regarding Virtual Property

It is notoriously difficult to predict adoption of entirely new legal regimes, but it seems clear that the current situation—where virtual property is recognized by the black market, denied by providers, and limited only by somewhat suspect contract provisions in potentially unenforceable click-through agreements—is simply not tenable in the long term. Virtual property will gain early traction by voluntary adoption, not by fiat. That is, legislation and decisions by courts are, in the short term at least, rather less likely than voluntary action and market demand to force companies to accept the growing reality of virtual property ownership. Companies have already begun this process to a degree, and as more companies enter the space, and greater legal scrutiny is focused on these companies' EULAs and Terms of Service agreements, there will be ever-increasing pressure on virtual world and game providers to either start drawing their own magic circles and "interrating" informally (as Blizzard has done, by aggressively banning those that use its service for profit), or else embrace virtual property and, thus, abandon contract provisions saying that they can ban users and confiscate property and currency without cause.

Open Questions on Virtual Property

1. Do the potential business benefits to a virtual world provider that acknowledges virtual property and runs a true real cash economy outweigh the potential legal liabilities?

2. How can game companies discourage RMT through game mechanics?

3. Besides the proposed "interration" option for game companies that wish to avail themselves of magic circle protection, what current legal structures could a company use to create its own magic circle?

4. Why do some virtual world companies resist implementing true real cash economies?

5. If virtual world providers who wish to run real economies are ultimately unable to declare virtual property nonexistent in their Terms of Service and EULAs, how should they begin to address it?

Notes

1. Greg Lastowka & Dan Hunter, *The Laws of the Virtual Worlds,* 92 Cal. L. Rev. 1, 49 (Jan. 2004), *available at* http://ssrn.com/abstract=402860.

2. Richard Bartle, The Pitfalls of Virtual Property (2004), http://www .themis-group.com/uploads/Pitfalls%20of%20Virtual%20Property.pdf.

3. Ladas & Parry, LLP, *A Brief History of the Patent Law of the United States, available at* http://www.ladas.com/Patents/USPatentHistory.html (last visited Jan. 6, 2008).

4. Zachary B. Simpson, *The In-game Economics of Ultima Online* (April 7, 1999), http://www.mine-control.com/zack/uoecon/uoecon.html.

5. Julian Dibbell, *The Life of the Chinese Gold Farmer,* N.Y. Times, June 17, 2007 (Magazine), *available at* http://www.nytimes.com/2007/06/17/magazine/ 17lootfarmers-t.html.

6. Joshua Fairfield, *Virtual Property,* 85 B.U. L. Rev. 1047, 1050 (Oct. 2005), *available at* http://ssrn.com/abstract=807966.

7. World of Warcraft, Terms of Use Agreement (Jan. 11, 2007), http:// www.worldofwarcraft.com/legal/termsofuse.html; *see also infra* Appendix V.

8. Second Life, Terms of Service, http://secondlife.com/corporate/tos .php (last visited Jan. 5, 2008); *see also infra* Appendix IV.

9. Bartle, *supra* note 2.

10. *Id.*

11. Forum Poll: What EverQuest Nerf Do You Dislike the Most?, http:// eq.stratics.com/content/community/pollarchive.php (last visited Jan. 6, 2008).

12. Lastowka & Hunter, *supra* note 1.

13. *Id.* at 37.

14. *Id.* at 39.

15. *Id.*

16. *Id.* at 41.

17. *Id.* at 56.

18. *Id.* at 49.

19. *Id.*

20. Fairfield, *supra* note 6.

21. *Id.* (citations omitted).

22. *Id.*

23. *Id.* at 1056.

24. Ronald B. Standler, Prenuptial and Postnuptial Contract Law in the USA (Apr. 24, 2004), http://www.rbs2.com/dcontract.pdf.

25. Fairfield, *supra* note 6, at 1051 (citation omitted).

26. Richard A. Bartle, Designing Virtual Worlds 102 (2004).

27. Posting of Mitch Wagner to InformationWeek blog, Building in Second Life, with Links to Web Info, http://www.informationweek.com/blog/main/archives/2007/04/building_in_sec.html (Apr. 24, 2007, 19:30).

28. Posting of Banjo, Add Guild Halls to the Game, http://forums.worldofwarcraft.com/thread.html?topicId=75493078&sid=1 (Feb. 13, 2007, 04:49:11 AM UTC).

29. Kathianne Boniello, *Unreality Byte$,* N.Y. Post (Oct. 28, 2007), *available at* http://www.nypost.com/seven/10282007/news/regionalnews/unreality_byte.htm.

30. Entropia Universe, http://www.entropiauniverse.com/index.var (last visited Jan. 6, 2008).

31. Entropia Universe, Features, http://www.entropiauniverse.com/en/rich/5357.html (last visited Jan. 6, 2008).

32. Caleb Booker, *It's Not an Economy, It's a Product* (Nov. 7, 2007), http://metaversed.com/06-nov-2007/metanomics-reloaded-gene-yoon-aka-ginsu-linden.

33. Second Life, The Marketplace, http://secondlife.com/whatis/marketplace.php (last visited Jan. 5, 2008).

34. Second Life, Business Opportunities, http://secondlife.com/whatis/businesses.php (last visited Jan. 6, 2008).

35. Second Life, Economy, http://secondlife.com/whatis/economy.php (last visited Jan. 5, 2008).

36. Second Life, The Marketplace, *supra* note 33.

37. *Id.*

38. *Id.*

39. *Id.*

40. Second Life, Terms of Service, *supra* note 8.

41. *Id.*

42. Benjamin Duranske, *Interview with Marc Bragg's Lawyer, Jason Archinaco* (Aug. 28, 2007), http://virtuallyblind.com/2007/08/28/jason-archinaco.

Contract Law and Virtual Worlds   6

Contracts, in their most basic form, are simply legally binding agreements between parties governing their relationship. Virtual worlds and multiuser games give rise to a number of interesting contract questions because contracts govern several different relationships that arise in these spaces.

In every game and virtual world, formal clickthrough agreements govern the relationship of users to the provider of the game or virtual world. In most cases, these agreements attempt to govern the relationship between users as well. And increasingly, contracts are being formed within virtual worlds between users. The different types of agreement raise different issues, some legal, some technical. This chapter will consider these issues from both perspectives.

Contracts Between Users and Virtual World Providers

If you have used an online game or a virtual world, you have undoubtedly entered into a contract with the provider of that game or world. Every virtual world and multiuser online game requires that participants agree to various provisions in a formal agreement in order to play the game or visit the world.

Typically, these contracts are presented to users in the form of "click to agree" dialogue boxes when the user installs the software. They are usually entitled Terms of Use or Terms of Service and, in most cases, either incorporate or require additional assent to an End User License Agreement (as is the case with most software users install on their computers).

Some virtual worlds and games require that users agree to the Terms of Service each time the software is launched. Others require assent each time the software is updated. Some only require assent when the Terms of Service are changed. A few require agreement only once, when the software is first installed, and direct users to a website for updates.

These agreements vary significantly in terms of their content, but all include variations on certain basic provisions. Typically, the agreements discuss intellectual property (IP) rights, virtual property rights (or lack thereof), behavioral guidelines, privacy, account

■■■■■
Typical TOS and EULA Provisions

Dispute Resolution Provisions

Choice of Law Provisions

Choice of Forum Provisions

Liability Limitations

Warranty Information

Intellectual Property Limitations

Virtual Property Limitations

Transfer of Account Provisions

Account Closure Provisions

Privacy Policy Provisions

Behavioral Guidelines

transfer, account termination, and, where relevant, the purchase and cashing-out of in-world currency.

Three typical click-through agreements (for Second Life, World of Warcraft, and Entropia Universe) are reproduced in Appendices IV, V, and VI. A few selected provisions are included in this chapter to illuminate the discussion.

Second Life's Terms of Service agreement (considered the standard-bearer for preserving users' IP rights), provides an example of an intellectual property ownership provision. The relevant section begins as follows:

> 3.2 You retain copyright and other intellectual property rights with respect to Content you create in Second Life, to the extent that you have such rights under applicable law. However, you must make certain representations and warranties, and provide certain license rights, forbearances and indemnification, to Linden Lab and to other users of Second Life.[1]

Subsequent paragraphs restrict these rights, but generally, the provision does allow users to retain copyright and trademark rights in content created using the Second Life interface.

An example of a provision concerning virtual property rights (or the lack thereof) comes from MindArk's End User License Agreement (EULA) for Entropia Universe:

> Virtual items will often have names similar or identical to corresponding physical categories such as "people," "real estate," "possessions," and the names of specific items in those categories such as "house," "rifle," "tools," "armor," etc. Despite the similar names, all virtual items are part of the System and MindArk retains all rights, title, and interest in all parts including, but not limited to Avatars and Virtual Items; these retained rights include, without limitation, patent, copyright, trademark, trade secret and other proprietary rights throughout the world.
>
> As part of your interactions with the System, you may acquire, create, design, or modify Virtual Items, but you agree that you will not gain any ownership interest whatsoever in any Virtual Item, and you hereby assign to

MindArk all of your rights, title and interest in any such Virtual Item.[2]

MindArk thus attempts to prohibit "ownership" of virtual items and, at the same time, secure for itself any rights that users might otherwise have in their in-world creations.

An example of a provision regarding behavioral guidelines comes from Second Life's "Community Standards" (incorporated into the click-through agreement by reference):

All Second Life Community Standards apply to all areas of Second Life, the Second Life Forums, and the Second Life Website.

1. **Intolerance**—Combating intolerance is a cornerstone of Second Life's Community Standards. Actions that marginalize, belittle, or defame individuals or groups inhibit the satisfying exchange of ideas and diminish the Second Life community as [a] whole. The use of derogatory or demeaning language or images in reference to another Resident's race, ethnicity, gender, religion, or sexual orientation is never allowed in Second Life.

2. **Harassment**—Given the myriad capabilities of Second Life, harassment can take many forms. Communicating or behaving in a manner which is offensively coarse, intimidating or threatening, constitutes unwelcome sexual advances or requests for sexual favors, or is otherwise likely to cause annoyance or alarm is Harassment.

3. **Assault**—Most areas in Second Life are identified as Safe. Assault in Second Life means: shooting, pushing, or shoving another Resident in a Safe Area (see Global Standards below); creating or using scripted objects which singularly or persistently target another Resident in a manner which prevents their enjoyment of Second Life.

4. **Disclosure**—Residents are entitled to a reasonable level of privacy with regard to their Second Lives. Sharing personal information about a fellow Resident—including gender, religion, age, marital status, race, sexual preference, and real-world location beyond what is provided by the Resident in the First Life page of their Resident

profile is a violation of that Resident's privacy. Remotely monitoring conversations, posting conversation logs, or sharing conversation logs without consent are all prohibited in Second Life and on the Second Life Forums.

5. **Indecency**—Second Life is an adult community, but Mature material is not necessarily appropriate in all areas (see Global Standards below). Content, communication, or behavior which involves intense language or expletives, nudity or sexual content, the depiction of sex or violence, or anything else broadly offensive must be contained within private land in areas rated Mature (M). Names of Residents, objects, places and groups are broadly viewable in Second Life directories and on the Second Life website, and must adhere to PG guidelines.

6. **Disturbing the Peace**—Every Resident has a right to live their Second Life. Disrupting scheduled events, repeated transmission of undesired advertising content, the use of repetitive sounds, following or self-spawning items, or other objects that intentionally slow server performance or inhibit another Resident's ability to enjoy Second Life are examples of Disturbing the Peace.[3]

Most virtual worlds prohibit similar behavior, with greater or lesser restriction depending on the target audience of the world.

An example privacy provision comes from There.com's substantial Privacy Policy, which is incorporated by reference into There.com's Terms of Service. After explaining how private data are used internally, There.com states:

> We may release your personally identifiable information about you and/or your account (a) to a successor entity upon a merger, consolidation or other corporate reorganization in which we participate or to a purchaser of all or substantially all of our assets to which this Site relates. Such successor entity will be bound by the terms and conditions of this Privacy Policy, (b) to comply with valid legal process such as a search warrant, subpoena or court order, or (c) in special cases such as a physical threat to you or others.

Other virtual worlds and games have similar provisions.

Whether and in what circumstances a virtual world or game provider allows for account transfer varies widely by provider. Some offer the service for a fee, others prohibit account transfer, and a few allow it only in special circumstances, such as upon the death of the account holder. Blizzard's World of Warcraft Terms of Use are clear on this point: "Blizzard does not recognize the transfer of Accounts." Other providers, such as Ultima Online's Electronic Arts, offer formal account transfer procedures.[4]

All providers' Terms of Service discuss what happens when accounts are terminated. Most simply inform players that terminated accounts cannot necessarily be reactivated, but those services that do not include a monthly fee (like MindArk's Entropia Universe) have more complex provisions for "expiring" old accounts. Entropia Universe's relatively complex provisions regarding account termination follow:

> MindArk may terminate this Agreement upon notice to the Participant. Such termination may be made without reason, and may be for one or more Participants.
>
> MindArk reserves the right, pursuant to the conditions set forth in Section 17, to terminate your Account and this Agreement without notice, at MindArk's sole discretion, if you fail to comply with the terms of this Agreement.
>
> In the event that your Account is locked or terminated, no refund will be granted. Any delinquent or unresolved issues relating to former participation must be resolved before MindArk will permit you to have a new Account.
>
> You acknowledge and agree that your Entropia Universe Account will be deemed inactive if it is not used for a period of three hundred and thirty (330) consecutive days.
>
> You further acknowledge and agree that your Entropia Universe Account will be purged if [it] is not used for a period of five hundred and ten (510) consecutive days. Upon purging your Account, . . . all your item(s) will be sold for their Trade Terminal (TT) value and the funds will be transferred to the PED balance of your Account.
>
> . . . .
>
> In addition, your virtual real estate will be reclaimed by MindArk and your Avatar skills will be erased. Upon veri-

fication of your identity, MindArk may, at MindArk's sole discretion, reactivate your Account, but you will never be able to retrieve the items, estate deeds or skills that were purged due to Account inactivity.[5]

Although they differ by provider, most virtual worlds and games include some provision such as the one just quoted that allows providers to remove accounts and user data after the passage of a certain period.

Virtual world and game click-through agreements also include other standard contract terms, such as dispute resolution provisions (including alternative dispute resolution requirements, and choice of law and venue clauses), statements limiting the liability of the provider, and warranty information.

Disputes Regarding Contracts Between Users and Virtual World Providers

Disputes between users and providers of virtual worlds will inevitably arise. Currently, the likelihood of user-provider disputes is dramatically increased by the tension noted in Chapter 5 between the formal Terms of Service of many virtual worlds and games (which, generally, preserve the rights of the provider at the expense of the user and minimize the obligations of the provider to the user) and the relatively aggressive advertising that heavily promotes many of these spaces as possessing completely new forms of ownership, governance, and business.

One such case—*Bragg v. Linden Lab*—has already had an impact on contracts between virtual world providers and users, triggering a change in Linden Lab's arbitration provision in the Second Life Terms of Service after the previous version was declared unconscionable by a federal judge in the Eastern District of Pennsylvania. The *Bragg* case was closely watched by attorneys who practice in this emerging field because it was hoped that the case would clarify the status of virtual property. Although the case did not progress to trial, this early decision indicated that the court was not likely to enforce the click-through Terms of Service without subjecting them to significant scrutiny.

Marc Bragg, the plaintiff (and later, counter-defendant), is an attorney. He brought suit against Linden Lab for suspending his account (as Second Life avatar "Marc Woebegone") and failing to compensate him for, or allow him to access, approximately $8,000 worth of virtual land that was in Bragg's account at the time that the account was suspended. His theory was that even if Linden Lab had the right to eject him from the virtual world, it did not have the right to reclaim the virtual property associated with his account because he had been told in advertising materials and in presentations by Linden Lab executives that he "owned" this land.

Bragg's complaint states: "The utopia of Second Life and the promise by Defendants to potential participants that they will retain all rights, title and interest in the virtual land, property and goods was a lie. Apparently, Defendants never intended to perform according to their promises and representations."[6] In addition to Linden Lab, Bragg named Linden Lab's CEO, Philip Rosedale, as a defendant in the suit, on the grounds that Rosedale personally had made statements to induce users to purchase land in Second Life and represented that users would own this land.

For its part, Linden Lab brought counterclaims based on the activity that allegedly led to Bragg's account being banned in the first place. Linden Lab claimed that Bragg had unfairly purchased some of the land in his account at far less than its true value by directly typing in secret web addresses which he had surmised would lead to hidden auction pages for land that was not otherwise available based on the format of the other, live auctions, instead of by clicking on links on the Second Life website. The web pages Bragg allegedly accessed were available using a standard web browser if one knew (or could deduce) what address to type, but they were not linked anywhere on the main land auction page. This practice, which Bragg referred to in later filings as "backward browsing," allegedly allowed Bragg (and others) to access land auctions that were not yet listed on the Second Life website and, consequently, were not being bid on by members of the general public. Linden Lab said that it considered Bragg's actions an "exploit" that violated the Terms of Service. The court, in a subsequent Order, explained what happened next: "[Linden Lab] froze Bragg's account, effectively confiscating all of the virtual property and currency that he maintained on his account with Second Life."[7]

Linden Lab and Rosedale moved to dismiss Bragg's case for various reasons, chiefly that an arbitration clause in the Terms of Service that Bragg had agreed to in order to access Second Life required arbitration "in San Francisco, California under the Rules of Arbitration of the International Chamber of Commerce by three arbitrators appointed in accordance with said rules."[8] Bragg opposed the motion on the grounds that the arbitration clause was unconscionable. To the surprise of many commentators who had expected that the high bar for unconscionability (overly harsh or one-sided results that "shock the conscience"[9]) would prove insurmountable, the court declined to enforce the arbitration provision. Relevant passages of the order follow, and the order, which is likely to become the cornerstone for a number of briefs targeting virtual world and game providers' EULAs and Terms of Service agreements, is reprinted in its entirety in Appendix IX. The *Bragg* court wrote:

> [U]nconscionability has both procedural and substantive components. *Davis v. O'Melveny & Myers,* 2007 WL 1394530, at *4 (9th Cir. May 14, 2007); *Comb v. Paypal, Inc.,* 218 F. Supp. 2d 1165, 1172 (N.D. Cal. 2002). The procedural component can be satisfied by showing (1) oppression through the existence of unequal bargaining positions or (2) surprise through hidden terms common in the context of adhesion contracts. *Comb,* 218 F. Supp. 2d at 1172. The substantive component can be satisfied by showing overly harsh or one-sided results that "shock the conscience." Id. The two elements operate on a sliding scale such that the more significant one is, the less significant the other need be. Id. at 743; *see Armendariz v. Foundation Health Psychcare Servs., Inc.,* 6 P.3d 669, 690 (Cal. 2000) ("[T]he more substantively oppressive the contract term, the less evidence of procedural unconscionability is required to come to the conclusion that the term is unenforceable, and vice versa."). However, a claim of unconscionability cannot be

> determined merely by examining the face of the contract; there must be an inquiry into the circumstances under which the contract was executed, and the contract's purpose, and effect. *Comb*, 218 F. Supp. 2d at 1172.[10]

The court first turned to the "procedural" element, which would be satisfied "by showing oppression through the existence of unequal bargaining positions or surprise through hidden terms common in the context of adhesion contracts."[11] The court found that the procedural unconscionability element was fulfilled because the contract was a contract of adhesion.[12]

> A contract or clause is procedurally unconscionable if it is a contract of adhesion. *Comb,* 218 F. Supp. 2d at 1172; *Flores v. Transamerica HomeFirst, Inc.,* 113 Cal. Rptr. 2d 376, 381-82 (Ct. App. 2001). A contract of adhesion, in turn, is a "standardized contract, which, imposed and drafted by the party of superior bargaining strength, relegates to the subscribing party only the opportunity to adhere to the contract or reject it." *Comb,* 218 F. Supp. 2d at 1172; *Armendariz,* 6 P.3d at 690. Under California law, "the critical factor in procedural unconscionability analysis is the manner in which the contract or the disputed clause was presented and negotiated." *Nagrampa v. MailCoups, Inc.,* 469 F.3d 1257, 1282 (9th Cir. 2006). "When the weaker party is presented the clause and told to 'take it or leave it' without the opportunity for meaningful negotiation, oppression, and therefore procedural unconscionability, are present."[13]

The court also observed that the lack of reasonable market alternatives to Second Life impacted its analysis.[14] At least at the time of the decision, no other virtual world allowed its users to retain any significant intellectual property rights. While that particular point of differentiation is unlikely to remain true for long, it may be a good argument to raise if challenging any successful virtual worlds' Terms of Service in the foreseeable future anyway. Virtual worlds and games all make significant efforts to differentiate themselves from one another, a situation which all but guarantees that the argument that a particular virtual world has a unique feature set will be available in relation to nearly any successful virtual world. The court also noted that the fact that the arbitration provision was (at the time) "buried . . . in a lengthy paragraph under the benign heading 'GENERAL PROVISIONS'" supported the conclusion that this prong was met.[15]

Concerning the court's analysis and virtual world click-through agreements in general, it is worth observing that under California law (which governs many user-provider agreements), *every single agreement* between a virtual world provider and the virtual world's users is subject to attack on the ground that it meets the test for procedural unconscionability. There are reasonable counterarguments in many cases, but because these agreements are always offered on a take-it-or-leave-it basis—a significant factor in favor of a finding of procedural unconscionability in this case—attorneys representing clients with complaints against virtual world providers can be expected to attack nearly any apparently unbalanced provision in the contract on these grounds.

The *Bragg* court notes, however, that meeting the procedural prong does not necessarily compel the result that the contract provision is considered unconscionable. "Even if an agreement is procedurally unconscionable, it may nonetheless be enforceable if the substantive terms are reasonable. . . . Substantive unconscionability focuses on the one-sidedness of the contract terms."[16] Here, the court found that "a number of the TOS's elements lead the court to conclude that Bragg has demonstrated that the TOS are substantively unconscionable."[17]

Chief among the "one-sided" contract terms that the court cited was the arbitration provision itself, which, the court noted, allowed "the stronger party [Linden Lab] a range of remedies before arbitrating a dispute, such as self-help, while relegating to the weaker party [Bragg] the sole remedy of arbitration."[18] Here, the court found that the Terms of Service allow Linden Lab to remove at will users who it believes have violated the agreement (as is the case for all virtual worlds and games) while requiring that an aggrieved user go through a fairly complex arbitration procedure to bring a claim.[19] The court observed:

> The TOS proclaim that "Linden has the right at any time for any reason or no reason to suspend or terminate your Account, terminate this Agreement, and/or refuse any and

all current or future use of the Service without notice or liability to you." TOS ¶ 7.1. Whether or not a customer has breached the Agreement is "determined in Linden's sole discretion." Id. Linden also reserves the right to return no money at all based on mere "suspicions of fraud" or other violations of law. Id. Finally, the TOS state that "Linden may amend this Agreement . . . at any time in its sole discretion by posting the amended Agreement [on its website]."[20]

The court concluded that "[i]n effect, the TOS provide Linden with a variety of one-sided remedies to resolve disputes, while forcing its customers to arbitrate any disputes with Linden."[21]

Finally, the court examined the arbitration provision itself and found that it also supported a finding of unconscionability because it created significantly greater expense for a user who wished to bring a claim than the same claim would cost that user to file in court. The court wrote:

> The court's own estimates place the amount that Bragg would likely have to advance at $8,625, but they could reach as high as $13,687.50. Any of these figures are significantly greater than the costs that Bragg bears by filing his action in a state or federal court. Accordingly, the arbitration costs and fee-splitting scheme together also support a finding of unconscionability.[22]

The court also considered the choice of venue in Linden Lab's home state of California, the confidentiality required by the arbitration scheme, and the lack of "legitimate business realities" supporting the clause in concluding that it was unconscionable.[23] The court concluded:

> Taken together, the lack of mutuality, the costs of arbitration, the forum selection clause, and the confidentiality provision that Linden unilaterally imposes through the TOS demonstrate that the arbitration clause is not designed to provide Second Life participants an effective means of resolving disputes with Linden. Rather, it is a one-sided means which tilts unfairly, in almost all situations, in Linden's favor. . . . [T]hrough the use of an arbitration clause, Linden "appears

to be attempting to insulate itself contractually from any meaningful challenge to its alleged practices."[24]

The *Bragg* suit was settled under undisclosed terms, but we do know that the terms which *were* publicized allowed Bragg to reenter Second Life in good standing and reclaim assets from his previously banned account. It is not unreasonable to assume that there were other provisions in the settlement agreement benefiting Bragg as well.

It is important to bear in mind that this is a single order in a single case, and that the argument may not do as well in other circumstances with other providers. Linden Lab itself changed its arbitration provision after the *Bragg* order was issued and now offers, but does not require, binding arbitration for matters under $10,000. On the other hand, Bragg was hardly a sympathetic plaintiff, having been originally suspended for activity that many users instinctively feel was underhanded, even if they also feel that Linden Lab may have overstepped by confiscating the rest of Bragg's virtual property. One can certainly imagine a plaintiff with a more sympathetic story pushing the issue of the validity of these contracts even farther than Bragg did. In any case, it is very likely that the precise arguments Bragg raised will arise again, because virtual world and game providers show no sign of backing off their use of contracts of adhesion in their interactions with users, and the amount of money users have invested in their accounts is only increasing with time.

Using Contracts to Govern the Relationship Between Users in Virtual Worlds

As noted, the Terms of Service and End User License Agreements just discussed are not used only to govern the relationship between users and providers. There are sections, typically very lengthy sections, that prohibit certain types of behavior directed at other users as well. Among other things, these provisions typically prohibit players from making derogatory racial and sexual comments, abusing loopholes in the game or virtual world programming for personal gain, and impersonating an administrator. Some, as noted in the preceding chapter on virtual property, also prohibit or otherwise govern the circumstances of players' transfer of virtual property to each other. This seems an appealing use of the Terms of Service; a company must protect its users from each other for business reasons, even if not for legal reasons. That said, there is an excellent argument that contracts are not well suited to this task.

The argument comes from Joshua Fairfield, whose academic work in the field of virtual property is discussed at length in Chapter 5. In a paper (currently in draft form) entitled *Anti-Social Contracts*,[25] Fairfield highlights a significant problem with using EULAs and Terms of Service agreements to govern the relationship between users.

Fairfield's argument is, in essence, that EULAs and Terms of Service documents are poorly suited to govern the relationship between users. They are poorly suited to this task because the rights they purport to protect—chiefly property rights and the right to be free of particularly odious abuse—are traditionally rights that bind whole groups of citizens based on common understanding and the universal application of certain laws, not rights that bind individuals based on contract.

That is, contracts, generally, do not bind anyone but the parties involved. This means that absent fairly specific circumstances (see the following section, "Third-Party Beneficiary Enforcement"), whether a user's complaint about another user's potential violation of the Terms of Service or EULA will be handled efficiently, quickly, and fairly by the provider is, at its core, a business decision, not a legal one. A virtual world provider's Terms of Service and EULAs prohibiting sexual and racial harassment aren't couched as an obligation on the part of the *provider* to maintain a world free of sexual and racial harassment—the provider is merely giving itself the *option* of getting rid of people who violate those provisions.

Imagine a situation where a social virtual world provider's biggest land customer is an unmitigated bigot who periodically runs around screaming racial epithets. If that person accounts for, say, five percent of the company's profits, and the users who are complaining about him collectively account for a fraction of a percent, it would be a terrible business decision to get rid of the troublemaker. Some games charge a flat rate to all customers, which would likely lead to somewhat more even enforcement of these provisions, but even in those games and worlds, one can easily envision a situation where the provider simply decides that it is not cost effective to enforce the provisions. After all, it just comes down to economics. Employee time, bad publicity, and possible lawsuits are real costs that will factor into the decision. If a sufficient number of users are willing to keep playing the game or visiting the virtual world in spite of those who violate community standards, some providers will simply decide not to enforce certain provisions of the EULA or Terms of Service agreement.

The virtual world provider has a single overriding obligation, which is to maximize its profitability. Regardless of what it says in the Terms of Service, if it is in the providers' best interests to fail to religiously enforce certain contract provisions—due to the cost of employing sufficient administrators, publicity issues with widespread banning, or simply because the game is designed to cater to players who like to harass others—then it is reasonable to expect that provider to do exactly that.

In addition, "efficient breach" of contracts is both acceptable and contemplated by the law (even if it is not warmly received). From a user perspective, particularly that of those users who are arguably most damaging to the social fabric of an online community, there is good reason to breach the agreement. A gold farmer who is making $100 for every $10 account that gets banned simply does not care if the penalties named in the contract (typically, banishment of a single identity) are enforced against her. And users who are simply there to harass have even less to lose—either they will employ technical workarounds to avoid bans if they are determined to stay in the world, or they will move on to a different environment.

Fairfield's argument has practical application and fits in nicely with one central theme of *Virtual Law*, namely, that courts are soon going to be dealing with issues between users. Consider the point made earlier in this chapter: many modern EULAs and Terms of Service are subject to reasonable attack on the grounds that they are manifestly unfair contracts of adhesion to begin with. Message boards and Internet forums are choked with empty threats of class action lawsuits against providers for failing to enforce their EULAs and Terms of Service, but these threats make little sense legally. Instead, users should consider targeting their lawsuits against the people who are, in fact, causing whatever damage is alleged.

Third-Party Beneficiary Enforcement

Although limited in application to fairly narrow factual circumstances, and cost-prohibitive in many of those, third-party beneficiary contract actions are a potential method of asking courts to assist in enforcing Terms of Service and EULAs to a greater degree than the providers are willing or, in some cases, able to. These actions will appeal to plaintiff attorneys, for they can often be styled as class actions and will frequently target defendants for activities that are facially either widely perceived as reprehensible or fairly obviously against the rules of the virtual world where they took place.

In its most basic form, a third-party beneficiary contract action is based on a contract that directly benefits a third party. The premise is that the third party has a right to sue one of the contracting parties for breaching the agreement, to the extent that the third party is deprived of the intended benefits of the contract. Most providers' contracts do not disclaim third-party beneficiaries, and, in fact, it is not unreasonable to expect that many providers would support a third-party beneficiary contract action on the grounds that it moves the enforcement mechanism from their hands (where it is a constant source of user complaint) to the courts, where their role will be fairly limited. To the extent that providers did intend the user body at large to be third-party beneficiaries of the contract, the providers may even be willing to say so in a declaration in support of a motion (or opposition to a motion) on the matter.

Because the EULAs and Terms of Service universally avoid language that requires the providers to enforce their agreements, the targets of the actions would inevitably be other users. To the extent that users are taking action that is personally profitable (for example, large-scale gold farming operations, schemes to defraud users of their virtual property, and gross devaluation of virtual land through technically sophisticated placement of undesired advertisements), affected users may be able to recover significant class-based damages.

In general, a plaintiff or plaintiff class asserting third-party beneficiary status would have to argue that it is the intended beneficiary of an agreement between the provider and the defendant-user. The argument would be that the provider owes all users who have paid the monthly fee an experience that comports with the advertising for the game or world in exchange for their monthly fee. Plaintiff-users would argue that as part of providing that experience—in fulfillment of its obligation to plaintiff-users—the provider contracted with the defendant-users, requiring that the defendant-users give up certain otherwise available activities to help guarantee that the world or game would comport with the promises made contemporaneously to the plaintiff-users.

One such suit has already been file—a class action lawsuit in the Southern District of Florida on behalf of nearly every World of Warcraft player, naming one of the largest virtual property companies, Internet Gaming Entertainment (IGE), as defendant. World of Warcraft player Antonio Hernandez is named plaintiff.

The plaintiffs' core claims read as if they come straight out of Richard Bartle's *Pitfalls of Virtual Property*. The plaintiffs allege that IGE, by running a gold farming operation, camping spawns (harvesting an unfair percentage of a scarce resource), devaluing gold, spamming chat, and generally making game play less satisfying, has intentionally breached the World of Warcraft Terms of Use and End User License Agreement. IGE's employees must, of course, agree to the Terms of Use and EULA in order to use the World of Warcraft software to accumulate and transfer gold and other virtual property and to increase the abilities of characters in World of Warcraft accounts that they wish to list for sale. The complaint alleges that the plaintiffs were intended "third-party beneficiaries" of the Terms of Use agreement and EULA between IGE's employees and Blizzard, and that the plaintiffs suffered harm as a result of IGE's breach of these agreements. According to the amended complaint,

> While not necessarily the case in all virtual worlds, in order to ensure the integrity of *World of Warcraft's*® virtual world, Blizzard Entertainment's EULA and ToU expressly prohibit

the sale of virtual assets for real money. This prohibition protects the integrity of *World of Warcraft®,* ensures that the competitive playing field within *World of Warcraft®* is level, and makes certain that the time, energy and effort expanded by Subscribers is not negatively impacted by others who use real money to purchase scarce and limited virtual resources.

. . . .

Defendants engage in the fradulent scheme and conspiracy to generate, market, distribute and sell *World of Warcraft®* gold through the efforts of hundreds of employees, agents and affiliates who work at the direction and control of, and/ or for the benefit of, IGE. These employees, agents and affiliates are commonly referred to as gold farmers ("IGE gold farmers"). IGE gold farmers are often citizens of developing third world countries who spend up to 14 hours per day, or more, logged into *World of Warcrqft®* collecting resources and *World of Warcraft®* gold. IGE gold farmers log into *World of Warcraft®* through accounts paid for, and/or controlled, in whole or in part, directly or indirectly, by Defendants. At the direction of Defendants, through channels of distribution designed, established, maintained and/or controlled by Defendants, IGE gold farmers then deliver gold through the *World of Warcraft®* mail system to Subscribers who have paid real money as described above. IGE gold farmers are co-conspirators with Defendants in this fraudulent marketing and sales scheme.[26]

The amended complaint appears as Appendix X. Updates to this case, and all pending cases discussed herein, will continue on my website, http://virtuallyblind.com, after the publication of this edition of *Virtual Law.*

As Fairfield observes, third-party beneficiary actions are fairly limited in their application, and, moreover, "there will always be people who do affect the community from the outside, but who have simply not signed any contract whatsoever."[27] For that reason, among others, third-party beneficiary actions should not be seen as a panacea to the problems created by EULAs and Terms of Service agreements, but attorneys may wish to explore this option if confronted with a situation where some users are diminishing the virtual world experience for others through activity that violates the virtual world or game's behavioral standards.

Contracts Between Users in Virtual Worlds

One theme of this book is that virtual worlds are, above all, communication tools. This function—which is so integrated in virtual worlds as to be essentially invisible—is what gives rise to most disputes in and about social virtual worlds and, to a degree, games. In no area of law is that more apparent than in contract law. As these spaces become more technologically advanced and move from point-of-sale transactions to more robust economies with longer-term agreements between users, the potential for disputes will only increase.

In a sense, virtual worlds are better suited to the resolution of contract disputes than is the real world for at least two reasons. First, record keeping in virtual worlds is generally automated and accurate. Second, in many worlds, the code itself handles transactions in a way that everyone assents to before making a transaction.

On the other hand, in terms of users' ability to create long-term contracts, virtual worlds and games are currently limited for several reasons, most notably, the current expectation of pseudonymity in most virtual worlds. Consider, for example, a user of a social virtual world who wants to build an office complex. This activity will involve using the virtual world's building tools to make walls, ceilings, windows, furniture, and more. It will also involve programming light sources, elevators, and other interactive objects. The user doesn't want to spend the time necessary to learn how to use the complicated building and scripting tools; besides, there are thousands of experts in these tools who use the virtual world every day. The obvious solution is to hire someone to help, but in most social virtual worlds, there is no way to form an enforceable contract for work for hire.

The problem isn't a legal problem. There is no reason that the employer and the contractor can't form a binding contract using a virtual world's communication tools (either text or voice) to negotiate the terms. After all, legally enforceable contracts can be negotiated using telephones, e-mail, and faxes. If the parties do desire a final written document memorializing the terms they've agreed to, there is no reason that cannot be accomplished entirely within a virtual world as well.

The primary problem with contracting in a virtual world is the pseudonymity that virtual worlds provide. It is not legally necessary to know the real name of the party you are contracting with (for example, if someone forms a contract using a pseudonym, the contract is still legally enforceable), but it is, practically, necessary to know who you contracted with in order to enforce the contract. This would not be true in a social virtual world or game where an enforcement mechanism or justice system designed to resolve user disputes was built in to the world or at least supported by the provider, but no current world has such a mechanism. As such, in the event that a contract between pseudonymous avatars is breached, users must resort to lawsuits and subpoenas to determine the name and geographic location of the breaching party in order to enforce the agreement. The associated expense is, in many cases, prohibitive.

Parties do contract in virtual worlds with some regularity, particularly for rental of property, and often at their own peril. In Second Life, for example, a high percentage of the "land" that is available is via a secondary rental market. Linden Lab "sells" the land to users who then divide it into smaller parcels and rent it out on a monthly basis to other users. Linden Lab has traditionally declined to interfere in disputes between residents, leading to relatively widespread abuse of tenants by unscrupulous landowners who operate with some degree of impunity. Typical reports of such abuse involve very simple facts: the parties agreed to a rental period, the tenant paid, and then, prior to the end of the rental period, the landowner used administrative tools available to landowners to remove the tenant from the land and prohibit reentry. Obviously, these cases are well suited to claims based on the rental contract, but the low value of most of the claims renders them poorly suited to full-blown lawsuits. Typically, when a user has made the mistake of trusting an unscrupulous landlord in virtual worlds where the provider has taken a hands-off approach, nothing can practically be done even though the claim may be entirely legitimate. There are virtual better business bureaus and websites that track the bad acts of some virtual world participants, and users who have been victimized may wish to seek those resources.

One possible solution that can bridge the gap is a liquidated-damages contract with the amount in question held by a neutral, reputable third party until both parties have agreed that the contract terms have been fulfilled, or an arbitration proceeding has decided any issues related to breach. This presupposes finding a neutral, trustworthy third party—likely one who has a real-life name and reputation tied to his or her avatar—and a reputable arbitration system, but the prospect is much cheaper than litigation and would give the parties a degree of comfort that blind trust in pseudonymous avatars simply does not.

In some cases, where, for example, both parties have associated real identities with their avatars, the problem is minimized. But, currently, most transactions between virtual world users involve one or more anonymous parties, and, as a result, most transactions are point-of-sale transactions, with payment and purchase changing hands at essentially the same time. Until providers begin taking more proactive enforcement steps on breach of contract claims or users find a way to impose in-world justice or reputation-based systems with real teeth (both of which can be expected at some point in the future, at least in some worlds), contracts will remain difficult to enforce, limiting the growth potential of virtual worlds as platforms for business.

Open Questions on Contracts in Virtual Worlds

1. What solutions (created by providers and users) could help users form long-term agreements without exchanging personal information?

2. What obligations should a provider offering users the chance to "own" aspects of a virtual world be subject to in the event that the provider decides to ban a user from the world?

3. How would a jury have decided *Bragg v. Linden Lab*?

4. Should providers identify the broader user base as the "intended beneficiary" of Terms of Service agreements, and assist users in raising third-party beneficiary claims against those who break the agreements?

Notes

1. Second Life, Terms of Service, http://secondlife.com/corporate/tos .php (last visited Jan. 5, 2008); *see also infra* Appendix IV.

2. Entropia Universe, End User License Agreement, http://www.entropia universe.com/pe/en/rich/107004.html (last visited Jan. 6, 2008); *see also infra* Appendix VI.

3. Second Life Community Standards, *available at* http://secondlife.com/ corporate/cs.html (last visited Feb. 23, 2008).

4. Origin Account Access Transfer: Frequently Asked Questions, http:// www.uo.com/acct_xfer.html (last visited Jan. 6, 2008).

5. *See supra* note 2.

6. Complaint at 23, Bragg v. Linden Lab, *available at* http://lawyers .com/BraggvLinden_Complaint.pdf (last visited Jan. 6, 2008).

7. Memorandum and Order Denying Motion to Dismiss at 6, Bragg v. Linden Lab (May 30, 2007), *available at* http://www.paed.uscourts.gov/ documents/opinions/07D0658P.pdf (last visited Jan. 6, 2008); *see also infra* Appendix IX.

8. *Id.* at 22.

9. *Id.* at 26.

10. *Id.*

11. *Id.*

12. *Id.* at 28.

13. *Id.*

14. *Id.* at 29.

15. *Id.*

16. *Id.* at 31.

17. *Id.* at 31–32.

18. *Id.* at 32.

19. *Id.* at 33.

20. *Id.*

21. *Id.*

22. *Id.* at 37.

23. *Id.* at 37–41.

24. *Id.* at 41–42 (citation omitted).

25. Joshua Fairfield, *Anti-Social Contracts: The Contractual Governance of Online Communities* (July 2007), Washington & Lee Legal Studies Paper No. 2007-20, http://ssrn.com/abstract=1002997. Note that Professor Fairfield graciously permitted excerpts from the current draft of the paper, but readers should know that it is still being revised, and the text may change slightly before publication.

26. Complaint at 23 and 28, Hernandez v. IGE, *see* Appendix X.

27. Fairfield, *supra* note 25.

Intellectual Property Law and Virtual Worlds 7

More mainstream articles have been written about intellectual property (IP) law in virtual worlds than about any other topic in virtual law. Indeed, mainstream articles about virtual worlds invariably note the extent to which these spaces (particularly the virtual world Second Life) offer the ability for users to retain intellectual property rights to their creations. As a result, the existence of intellectual property rights in virtual worlds is both widely acknowledged and poorly understood. Many people conflate virtual property rights (a somewhat speculative concept, as discussed in Chapter 5, "Property Law and Virtual Worlds") with intellectual property rights in virtual creations. Although intellectual property rights in virtual creations are somewhat controversial, they are, at least, grounded in established law.

Five key areas in intellectual property law will be considered in this chapter. Four are traditionally viewed in the realm of intellectual property—copyright, trademark, patent, and trade secret law. The fifth, the right of publicity, is occasionally grouped with intellectual property topics and occasionally with privacy issues. Because the right of publicity law has some potential for crossover with copyright law in relation to virtual worlds, it will be considered here.

History of Intellectual Property and Virtual Worlds

Linden Lab's November 14, 2003, announcement that users would retain certain intellectual property rights to creations in Second Life surprised many industry watchers. Readers who have a background in gaming will understand the surprise. Until this announcement, it had been standard operating procedure for games, even games that had many characteristics of virtual worlds such as significant social interaction and object creation abilities, to insert clauses into their license agreements expressly retaining any intellectual property rights for IP created using the software. In particular, the license agreements generally claimed everything that the user might otherwise assert a claim over, such as screenshots, characters, videos of game play, and even the very text typed to other users while playing the game.

On the other hand, readers with a background in art may not understand the surprise; the news may have seemed completely natural. In fact, creators who have worked in more traditional mediums may be surprised that it was considered news at all. After all, it would seem wholly absurd for Crayola to claim ownership of all drawings done with its crayons, or Microsoft to claim ownership of all novels written using Microsoft Word.

It is relatively uncontroversial that the game or virtual world provider should and does retain all intellectual property rights to the content the *provider* adds to the process (just as Crayola owns the logos on the crayon box, and Microsoft owns the software code for Word). That will, in a lot of games and virtual worlds, amount to most the content. But there is a fair argument that intellectual property rights in the characters users create, homes they build, and "stories" they tell through their interactions with other users should be theirs, just as the drawings users make with crayons and the stories users craft with word processing software should be owned by their creators, not the toolmakers. To head this argument off at the pass, game and virtual world companies, until very recently, universally claimed these rights in the Terms of Service and End User License Agreements to which users were forced to assent in order to use the game or virtual world. Second Life broke that tradition.

Terms of Service and End User License Agreements

Until Linden Lab broke the tradition with Second Life, game and virtual world providers had generally taken steps to secure ownership of all intellectual property rights to users' creations in virtual worlds and games. They did this by inserting provisions in their Terms of Service and End User License Agreements, to which users were required to assent in order to play the game or participate in the virtual world. These provisions expressly claimed ownership of all content created using the game or virtual world engine. Here are three examples of these clauses.

> **Entropia Universe—Ownership:** The System, including, but not limited to, computer code, text, graphics, audio files, logos, button icons, images, characters, items, concepts, data compilation and software, is the property of MindArk and protected by Swedish and international copyright laws.
>
> . . . .
>
> MindArk retains all rights, title, and interest in all . . . Avatars and Virtual Items; these retained rights include, without limitation, patent, copyright, trademark, trade secret and other proprietary rights throughout the world.
>
> . . . .
>
> You hereby grant MindArk the worldwide, perpetual, irrevocable, royalty-free, right to exercise all intellectual property rights for any content you may upload to the Entropia universe, including, but not limited to, user-to-user communications.[1]

World of Warcraft—Ownership: All rights and title in and to the Program and the Service (including without limitation any user accounts, titles, computer code, themes, objects, characters, character names, stories, dialogue, catch phrases, locations, concepts, artwork, animations, sounds, musical compositions, audio-visual effects, methods of operation, moral rights, any related documentation, "applets" incorporated into the Program, transcripts of the chat rooms, character profile information, recordings of games played on the Program, and the Program client and server software) are owned by Blizzard or its licensors.[2]

City of Heroes—(c) Member Content. Members can upload to and create content on our servers in various forms, such as in selections you make and characters and items you create for the Game(s), and in bulletin boards and similar user-to-user areas ("Member Content"). By submitting Member Content to or creating Member Content on any area of the Service, you acknowledge and agree that such Member Content is the sole property of NC Interactive. To the extent that NC Interactive cannot claim exclusive rights in Member Content by operation of law, you hereby grant (or you warrant that the owner of such Member Content has expressly granted) to NC Interactive and its related Game Content Providers a non-exclusive, universal, perpetual, irrevocable, royalty-free, sublicenseable right to exercise all rights of any kind or nature associated with such Member Content, and all ancillary and subsidiary rights thereto, in any languages and media now known or not currently known. You shall indemnify and hold NC Interactive and its affiliates harmless from and against any claims by third parties that your Member Content infringes upon, violates or misappropriates any of their intellectual property or proprietary rights.[3]

Most current virtual worlds and games include language like this in their click-through agreements.

There is a subtle difference between these three provisions that is worth noting. Entropia's provider, like most game providers, requires that users grant it a license to all user-created intellectual property generated in Entropia Universe, but it does not outright declare ownership of it. World of Warcraft, like many others, does not address user-created content at all, presumably because there is no apparent way to "create" anything in these worlds (although there is a fair question as to whether a copyright in obvious user-created content, such as dialogue, is really something that a provider can claim ownership of in a click-through agreement). The last example, City of Heroes (a superhero-themed, game-based virtual world) covers both positions, taking sole ownership of any uploaded content to the extent allowed by law and requiring users to grant an irrevocable, sublicenseable right to exercise any and all intellectual property rights associated with the content. To the extent that these provisions are ultimately found valid (they have not been tested), City of Heroes has given itself the strongest position of the three. Its position is strongest because it claims as much ownership as possible, but also includes a fallback position where it claims a paid-up license, thereby providing additional protection against potential liability if the outright declaration of ownership is found unenforceable.

There.com, a social virtual world, offers somewhat greater intellectual property ownership provisions than do the game-based worlds just referenced. There.com does not explicitly state that developers retain intellectual property rights in their creations, but by not claiming assignment or ownership, it functionally preserves those rights to the user. There.com's intellectual property provision only requires licensing the content to There.com's provider and, even then, only "for any purpose necessary or relating to the Services."[4]

Even farther along the spectrum of allowing users to retain their intellectual property rights, as previously mentioned, is Second Life. Although the creator community rightfully applauds Second Life for taking the remarkable step of formally recognizing users' IP rights, it is important to carefully examine the lengthy terms to which users must agree in order to use the service. The intellectual property rights clause begins with this statement:

3.2 You retain copyright and other intellectual property rights with respect to Content you create in Second Life,

**to the extent that you have such rights under applicable
law. However, you must make certain representations and
warranties, and provide certain license rights, forbearances and indemnification, to Linden Lab and to other
users of Second Life.**[5]

Trademark and copyright ownership are straightforward and
are not seriously undermined by the rest of the terms of the provision. Users only grant Linden Lab the right to delete the content
and use the content in testing, maintenance, and advertising. Linden Lab even provides a mechanism for requesting that material
not be used in advertising, though it limits its obligation to cease
distribution of user material to that which is "commercially reasonable" and appropriately noticed.[6]

The patent clause in Second Life's Terms of Service is worth
focusing on, however, as it may cause serious concern to users who
wish to patent inventions that they implement in Second Life and to
companies with preexisting patents contemplating using the Second Life platform for business. The clause reads:

You also understand and agree that by submitting your Content to any area of the Service, you automatically grant (or
you warrant that the owner of such Content has expressly
granted) to Linden Lab and to all other users of the Service
a non-exclusive, worldwide, fully paid-up, transferable, irrevocable, royalty-free and perpetual License, under any and
all patent rights you may have or obtain with respect to
your Content, to use your Content for all purposes within
the Service. You further agree that you will not make any
claims against Linden Lab or against other users of the Service based on any allegations that any activities by either
of the foregoing within the Service infringe your (or anyone
else's) patent rights.[7]

The first provision says that you agree that Linden Lab, as well
as every user of Second Life, gets an automatic license to any patent you are granted on anything you invent in the virtual world. If
this is enforced, then there is no reason to seek a patent on any
invention that is in Second Life. Millions of people and businesses,
including Linden Lab, would have free licenses.

The second provision says that by signing on to Second Life, you agree not to sue any other user, or Linden Lab, for infringing *any* of your patent rights for activity that takes place in Second Life. That is a significant waiver. If a company sees Second Life as a space it wants to move in to—perhaps to sell virtual versions of products with patented features—it cannot. By simply agreeing to this provision (which users must do in order to log in to Second Life), users agree not to sue anyone, including Linden Lab, who sells infringing products in Second Life. In fact, just by logging in to investigate possible infringement, users would theoretically give up their right to bring a claim for any infringement they find.

Enforcement of Intellectual Property Rights in a Virtual World

Most virtual world providers offer a mechanism for reporting copyright and trademark infringement. Typically, the mechanism for reporting copyright infringement is more robust, as it follows the structure for takedown notification set up by the Digital Millennium Copyright Act (DMCA). By complying with Section 512 of the DMCA, online service providers are protected against claims of copyright infringement made against them that result from the conduct of their users. This "safe harbor" provision is designed to shelter service providers from the infringing activities of their customers. For example, Linden Lab provides a detailed procedure for reporting copyright claims, including seven steps for filing a notification and six separate steps for filing a counter-notification.[8] Only written notifications are accepted.[9] Reports vary regarding the effectiveness of sending such notices to providers.[10]

There is no equivalent law regarding trademark infringement claims, so no provider offers as robust a mechanism for trademark enforcement. Instead, most providers invite users to submit notifications via online or off-line means. Even if no formal procedure is provided, most providers at least refer to steps for preventing trademark infringement on their websites (though it is not always clear how one is supposed to report infringement). Here is the language Linden Lab uses regarding trademark claims:

> Linden staff generally removes content that uses trademarks without apparent authorization, with or without giving notice to the object owner. This generally includes all [Real Life] corporate logos and brand names.
>
> It is often difficult to tell what may or may not be trademarked. However, use of designer logos and brand names without permission, such as Gucci, Nike, Louis Vuiton [sic] etc., are usually not acceptable.[11]

Although it is not entirely clear based on Linden Lab's statement how one is supposed to submit a claim for trademark infringement to Linden Lab, there are reports that Linden Lab has taken action when contacted by attorneys for trademark holders about potential in-world infringement of marks.[12]

One in-world company is attempting to address these concerns. The Second Life Patent and Trademark Office offers Second Life users a suite of intellectual property protection tools, including individual item registration, automated DMCA notices and copyright applications, limited edition numbering, and private, time-stamped storage of evidence of creation.[13] Some of these tools may prove useful if litigation is necessary.

Litigation may well be the only answer in some cases. To the extent that both the alleged infringer and the provider are unwilling to take the material down, users with trademark and copyright concerns may need to turn to the courts. Some lawsuits involving allegations of in-world copyright and trademark infringement have already been filed. We will examine those as we take a closer look at each of the major areas of potential intellectual property infringement in virtual worlds in the sections that follow.

Copyright Law and Virtual Worlds

In very general terms, copyright law protects the expression of an idea, such as books, movies, choreographic works, musical compositions, audio recordings, paintings, drawings, sculptures, photographs, software, and radio and television broadcasts. Copyright is automatic—absent some agreement to the contrary, a creator automatically owns what she creates. Once an idea has been secured in a fixed medium (e.g., by applying fingers to keyboard or brush to canvas), the copyright holder is immediately entitled to enforce her exclusive rights. However, a copyright holder can (and should) register that copyright with the U.S. Copyright Office. The cost of registration is minimal—$45 currently.[14] The process is straightforward, and many individuals choose to register their copyrights themselves, without involving attorneys. The primary reason to register is that registration allows the copyright holder to file a copyright infringement lawsuit. Additionally, if registration is done within three months after publication of the work or before an infringement of the work, statutory damages based on a "per work" calculation and attorney's fees are available as remedies. In the case of infringement for microtransactions in a virtual world (where actual damages may be minimal), the availability of statutory damages is particularly important.

There is widespread potential for copyright infringement in virtual worlds, and, indeed, there is widespread infringement of copyrights. The issue comes up in several different contexts. In one context, residents create objects, buildings, avatar shapes and skins, clothing, sounds, and more using copyrighted material that they do not own. For example, there are entire areas in Second Life that are built to represent the worlds of *Star Wars*, *Star Trek*, and Harry Potter. Users of these areas can don avatar shapes that turn them into perfect replicas of characters from the original material, visit locations that were originally depicted in the copyrighted movie or book, and purchase accessories used by their favorite characters. These builds are, in a sense, similar to "fan fiction" websites, where users write short stories that involve characters from popular books, movies, and television shows.

As with most areas of intellectual property law, there is some resistance to enforcement of copyrights against people who appear to be simply fans expressing admiration of their favorite fantasy world. In regard to web-based infringement, some creators say they don't mind fan sites generally but express concern about fan fiction that takes their characters in entirely unanticipated (often sexual) directions. That possibility is particularly problematic in virtual worlds that allow unfettered scripting and building. While Second Life's "Harry Potter" build itself may simply be a charming and respectful homage by a loving fan, other users can (and, in fact, do) use the available avatar shapes, buildings, and items to create sexual imagery involving the characters from the books and films.[15]

Other potential instances of copyright infringement of major mainstream works include radio stations in virtual worlds that broadcast music, often without a license,[16] in-world distribution of books as text documents,[17] and in-world distribution of full-length copies of movies to watch in one's virtual home.[18]

The potential for direct copying of products within virtual worlds, coupled with the fact that real money is changing hands, creates the possibility of actionable infringement between users. Claims of alleged in-world copying (typically via bugs in the virtual world software) abound. Two of these claims have given rise to lawsuits between users. The complaints for those lawsuits are reprinted as Appendices VIII and XI.

In the first, Eros, LLC, which sells software that allows Second Life users to cause their avatars to appear to engage in sexual intercourse, alleged that a user known at filing only by his avatar's name violated Eros's copyright and trademark on its popular "SexGen" products. In the second lawsuit, six plaintiffs (including, again, Eros) brought a suit against a New York man named Thomas

---

■■■■■
Virtual World Copyright Trends

- Massive unlicensed use of copyrighted works in virtual worlds.
- Significant unlicensed use of in-world content creators' copyrighted works by other virtual world users.
- Large numbers of copyrights registered on virtual world creations.

Simon claiming copyright and trademark infringement. Simon allegedly exploited a flaw in the Second Life software to duplicate thousands of copies of the creators' products and allegedly sold copies of those products to other Second Life users as Second Life avatar "Rase Kenzo." The allegedly infringing items represented nearly every type of product for sale in Second Life, including avatar clothing, skins and shapes, scripted objects, furniture, and more. Both of these suits ended in victories of sorts for the plaintiffs. The first, against the "John Doe" defendant, ended in default, and the second, which involved multiple parties, ended in a consent judgment.

Trademark Law and Virtual Worlds

Trademark law is designed to avoid consumer confusion about the origin of goods. A trademark is a distinctive mark that identifies the source of a product or service. A trademark is typically a name, word, phrase, logo, symbol, design, image, or a combination of these elements (such as "Coca-Cola" or the Nike "Swoosh" emblem). A trademark does not have to be registered with the United States Patent and Trademark Office, but trademark claims based on unregistered marks can only be brought in state courts. In addition, registration creates "a legal presumption of ownership nationwide, and the exclusive right to use the mark on or in connection with the goods or services set forth in the registration."[19] Trademark registration fees start at $325, and additional fees may apply depending on the path the application takes through the approval process. Although it is possible to secure a trademark without legal counsel, the process is somewhat complex, and many applicants find it valuable to have an attorney involved.

In virtual worlds that allow unfettered scripting and building, particularly when a major brand has not chosen to enter the space, unauthorized use of real-world trademarks has proven too tempting for many designers to resist. Some worlds, such as There.com, have teams of employees that monitor all design uploads, partly to prevent real-world trademark and copyright infringement.[20] Others, such as Second Life, take a relatively hands-off approach,

■■■■■
The Value of Linden Dollars in Second Life

Linden Dollars can be sold for U.S. dollars on an official exchange. Linden Lab attempts to maintain a stable rate of exchange. The current exchange rate is roughly 265 Linden Dollars for US$1.

removing content which is alleged to violate trademarks only when it is brought to their attention.[21]

Particularly in worlds that take a relatively hands-off approach, trademark infringement is widespread. Here are a handful of numbers gathered recently in Second Life that begin to illuminate the scope of the problem:

- Sixteen shops in Second Life advertised "Ferrari" cars. One model sold for L$1995 (approximately US$7.75). None was sold by the holder of the Ferrari trademark.

- A "limited-edition" virtual Cartier "Himalia" necklace for avatars was offered for sale for L$10,000 (nearly US$40). It was not being sold by Cartier.

- At least forty stores in Second Life advertised virtual "Rolex" and "Chanel" watches, averaging around L$350 (US$1.61). Neither Rolex nor Chanel ran any of these stores.

- More than fifty stores in Second Life sold virtual sunglasses branded "Gucci," "Prada," "Ray-Ban," and "Oakley." Each pair was priced around L$125 (US$0.75). None of these stores appeared to be owned, sponsored, endorsed, or licensed by any of these companies.

- The term "Gucci" alone generated 106 hits in Second Life classifieds, referring shoppers to stores selling virtual versions of nearly every hot product the company made, including shoes, handbags, and clothing. "Vuitton" generated thirty-nine hits. "Abercrombie" got thirty. "Timberland" got twenty-six. None of these stores appeared to be affiliated with the company behind the name.

- "Nike" held the record, generating 186 hits, many of which linked to stores where shoppers could find avatar shoes bearing the company's distinctive swoosh. Nike itself did not sell any of these shoes.

- Even geek-darling Apple isn't immune. A half-dozen stores in Second Life sold virtual "iPods" for avatars. Some added copyright infringement, preloading the unlicensed "iPods" with songs from artists ranging from Michael Jackson to Gwen Stefani. Apple did not appear to be behind these stores.

- Of ten randomly selected "shopping malls" found in Second Life's classifieds, seven had stores selling goods that exhibited obvious trademark infringement. Several stores appeared to sell nothing but unlicensed brand-name goods.

Currently, over 20 million unique transactions take place in Second Life each month. This number has more than doubled in the last year. There is no way to know exactly how many of these transactions involve knockoff goods, but a quick overview of in-world shopping areas reveals that well over one percent (probably closer to three to five percent) of the goods for sale in-world carry unlicensed trademarks. Assuming that even one percent of the transactions in-world involve unlicensed trademarks, there are well over 200,000 instances of profitable trademark infringement resulting in a sale in Second Life every month—over 2.4 million transactions a year. If the average infringing transaction is just $1.50 (much less than the price of a market-saturated knockoff Rolex), and the other assumptions are accurate, over $3.5 million changes hands in transactions involving counterfeit goods in Second Life every year.

Although $3.5 million is quite a bit of money, the more immediate concern for real-world companies whose products are being knocked off in Second Life has to be the legal requirement to actively enforce their trademarks. Failure to actively enforce a trademark can result in loss of registration for the mark. Moreover, the more dilution of distinctive, famous trademarks is tolerated by a company, the harder it is to later argue that any particular infringer should be enjoined.

There is one particularly interesting issue that courts could be asked to resolve regarding trademarks in virtual worlds, and it involves the nature of the virtual goods themselves. The question is this: If a user who is not affiliated with Nike makes a pair of "Nike" shoes in Second Life and sells them, is he selling shoes, is he selling a picture of shoes, or is he selling something altogether new— virtual shoes? The question is important because lesser-known trademark holders' ability to enforce their marks diminishes with a disconnect between the real product that carries the mark and an alleged infringing product. Although the question doesn't mean much for Nike (the Nike mark is sufficiently famous that Nike can prevent people from entering even unrelated fields with products branded with the swoosh), it is critical for smaller manufacturers, such as in-world companies which create their own in-world brands, that have no such protection.

Some companies have taken creative approaches to the problem. Herman Miller, which makes the high-quality real-life "Aeron" chairs, among other products, established a presence in Second Life in the fall of 2007.[22] Of course, as with most major brands, Second Life users were already building and selling knockoff virtual "Herman Miller" chairs.[23] The real Herman Miller hired a development company (Rivers Run Red) that produced licensed, extraordinarily attractive, virtual versions of its products, which Herman Miller then offered for sale in Second Life. Herman Miller also, however, offered anyone who had previously purchased a knockoff vir-

■■■■■
Virtual World Trademark Trends

- Massive unlicensed sales of mainstream brands' products in virtual worlds with few content controls.
- Unlicensed sales of in-world content creators' brands by other virtual world users.
- Increase in registered trademarks sought for virtual world avatars and company logos.

tual "Herman Miller" a free copy of a licensed Herman Miller virtual chair in exchange for a promise to destroy the knockoff. Herman Miller widely publicized the offer using a "Get Real!" advertising campaign, and the number of infringing chairs for sale in the virtual world plummeted.[24]

Some in-world brands are developing significant reputations in their own right, and a few are starting to register their trademarks. In late 2007, Alyssa LaRoche became the first person to secure a trademark on an avatar. Her avatar, known as "Aimee Weber," is a well-respected Second Life designer. "Aimee Weber" is also part of the name of LaRoche's design studio. The trademark application includes this description of the mark:

> **Description of Mark:** The color blue appears in the wings and the hair accessories. The color green appears in the shirt and skirt. The color black appears in the hair, eyes, eyebrows, lips, glasses, necklace, bra, waistband, in the striped pattern on the arms and stockings, as well as the toe and calf areas of the boots. All the elements of the drawing are also outlined in black. The color white appears in the eyes, the striped pattern on the arms and legs, as highlights on the black toes of the boots, on the front of the boots, and in the laces. The color peach appears in the skin.[25]

One interesting note: the "Aimee Weber" avatar, once trademarked, is basically locked into a persistent image. It is hoped LaRoche is happy with "Weber's" pigtails, butterfly wings, green tutu, zebra leggings, and stompy boots, because that's what she's stuck with as long as she wants to keep the mark.

Patent Law and Virtual Worlds

Patent rights are exclusive rights to an invention granted by the government for a fixed period in exchange for a public disclosure of the invention. They represent a deal between society and the inventor: in exchange for telling everyone precisely how an invention is accomplished, society grants the inventor the exclusive rights to the invention for a specified period—currently twenty years from filing

■ ■ ■ ■ ■

Virtual World Patent Trends

- Terms of Service for Second Life claim license to all inventions users create in the virtual world and waive suit against in-world infringers.
- Large number of patent applications filed on virtual world–related inventions.

or seventeen years from issuance.[26] In very general terms, patents can only be issued on inventions that are new, useful, and nonobvious. It is important to note that patents are issued on inventions, not on products—most patents cover a wide range of products. For instance, an *invention* of a method to instantly change the color of a room's walls using a newly discovered chemical combination in paint could, if the patent application was drafted correctly, cover *products* that accomplish the change with the click of a remote control, the flip of a light switch, or the touch of a hand on the walls themselves.

Patents are inevitable in any new technological space. Some reflect true innovation, and others do not. This space is no different. Here are excerpts from five applications that are currently pending, covering everything from group-to-group entertainment in virtual worlds to advice-tracking in virtual worlds. No patents specific to this space have issued yet, but dozens, if not hundreds, likely will issue during the lifespan of this edition of *Virtual Law*.

- ### Application No. 20070156883: System and Method for Group to Group Entertainment

   Abstract: A hardware and software platform for collaboratively reviewing prior group to group interactions while planning, producing and archiving new group to group interactions. The platform may be used to collaboratively create group to group interactions. The system may be used to link two or more stadia, movie theatres or homes so as to provide interaction between the groups at each location simultaneously as a game or other event takes place.

Claim 1: A method for group to group interaction comprising: planning the group to group interaction involving at least two groups; producing the group to group interaction including said at least two groups; and enabling the group to group interaction between said at least two groups.

- **Application No. 20070087820: Financial Institutions and Instruments in a Virtual Environment**

Abstract: A system and method to allow players of a video game to perform financial transactions in a virtual environment. According to some embodiments, real world financial instruments such as a credit card or other financial instrument may guarantee some or all of the virtual financial operations.

Claim 1: A method comprising: providing a virtual environment including a virtual financial intermediary; providing a means for a player to open an account at a virtual financial intermediary; providing a means for a player to perform transactions at a virtual financial intermediary; and securing said transactions by means of a real world financial security.

- **Application No. 20070087797: Video Game Environment that Tracks Help and Advice Provided to Other Player Characters**

Abstract: A virtual game environment in which characters are allowed to give help to one another and in which the game tracks the amount of helpfulness of each character is provided. Characters may be rewarded or paid for giving help to each other. In some embodiments, help may be given in the form of advice.

Claim 1: A method comprising: providing a virtual video game environment wherein a plurality of characters interact with one another; determining the helpfulness of at least one of the characters.

- **Application No. 20070117615: Securing Contracts in a Virtual World**

Abstract: The disclosure provides novel video game methods and systems for enforcing contracts within video game environments. Methods and systems of the invention include virtual and real world penalties and remedies for entities that breach contracts or other obligations undertaken in the virtual world.

Claim 1: A method comprising: providing a virtual environment in which virtual entities are able to interact with each other; receiving a request from a first entity to enter into a virtual contract with a second entity; determining a contract value for the contract; determining if the first entity is eligible to enter into the virtual contract; determining if the first entity is required to secure the virtual contract; receiving a financial security from the first entity if the first entity is required to secure the virtual contract; forming the virtual contract; and storing terms associated with the virtual contract.

- **Application No. 20070166690: Virtual Counseling Practice**

Abstract: A virtual counseling practice. The practice enables a counselor trained to provide counseling to a patient to hold counseling sessions within a virtual reality world. A counseling server, a counseling application, and a counseling database, supplement the patient and counselor session in the virtual world. The counseling application provides communication tools. The communication tools supplement the counseling section [sic] through heightening of feelings, emotions, and other patient information during the session.

Claim 1: A virtual counseling practice comprising: a. a counselor trained to provide counseling to a patient, a counseling support service comprising a counseling server, a counseling application, and a counseling database; b. said counseling application configured to provide virtual reality communication tools for operation within a virtual reality world, said virtual reality communication tools configured to provide communication between said counselor and said patient; c. said virtual reality communication tools comprising a first group of strong intensity feeling objects, a first group of moderate intensity feeling objects, a first group of mild intensity feeling objects.[27]

To the extent that users are concerned about patent rights in virtual worlds, they also need to pay close attention to the Terms of Service or risk protracted and expensive legal battles. As noted earlier in this chapter, Second Life's patent clause in particular is remarkably broad and largely makes patents on inventions created in Second Life pointless. It can even be interpreted to cause companies who visit Second Life to relinquish their right to sue other companies and individuals for patent infringement that takes place in the virtual world, something that a company concerned about its intellectual property rights must consider carefully before venturing into that particular virtual space.

Trade Secret Law and Virtual Worlds

Very generally, a trade secret can be any formula, pattern, physical device, idea, process, or compilation of information that both (1) provides a competitive advantage in the marketplace, and (2) is treated in a way that can reasonably be expected to prevent its disclosure.[28] Trade secret law effectively allows a perpetual monopoly in secret information. The protection does not expire, as it would if patent protection was sought. On the other hand, there is no formal protection scheme, so once the information is no longer secret, a third party is not prevented from independently using the previously secret information.

The most important aspect of trade secret law from the standpoint of virtual worlds is the requirement that the information be treated in a way that can reasonably be expected to prevent its disclosure. Courts will consider a number of factors, including (1) the extent to which the information is known outside the business, (2) the extent to which the information is known by employees and others involved in the business, (3) the extent of the measures undertaken by an employer to protect the secrecy of the information, (4) the value of the information to the employer, (5) the

■■■■■
Virtual World Trade Secret Trends
- Companies avoid using unsecured features in virtual worlds to communicate sensitive information.
- Third-party encryption in development for communication of sensitive information in virtual worlds.

amount of effort or money expended by the employer in developing the information, and (6) the ease or difficulty with which the information could be properly acquired or duplicated by others.[29]

The current nature of virtual worlds renders them poor forums for maintaining secrecy. Although information could theoretically be communicated through a virtual world using third-party encryption software with a reasonable assurance that it would only be available to the sender and recipient, it rarely is. Nearly all communication in current virtual worlds is vulnerable to eavesdropping from other users and is stored on the servers of the provider for an indefinite period (theoretically available to any employee of the provider with sufficient security rights and interest). Moreover, it is protected only by a generic privacy policy, not a specific nondisclosure agreement. Using current virtual world clients for the communication or storage of unencrypted trade secrets is not recommended.

Right of Publicity and Virtual Worlds

The right of publicity, sometimes considered part of privacy law rather than intellectual property law, very generally is the exclusive right to charge for (or prevent) the commercial exploitation of one's name, likeness, or voice.[30] The extent to which the right of publicity is protected varies greatly by state. California, which is also home to many virtual world providers, has a well-developed body of right of publicity case law backed by a statutory scheme—the "Celebrities Rights Act."[31] The Act not only gives living celebrities the exclusive right to control how their image is used commercially, it extends that protection seventy years past the celebrity's death.[32]

The right to publicity can arise in two ways in virtual worlds. The first is the in-world use of real-world celebrities' images for product endorsements or, somewhat disturbingly, directly *as products*. And the second, which has yet to arise but is on the horizon, is the potential for users to assert the right to publicity based on the fame of their avatars.

Regarding the use of real-world celebrities' images in virtual worlds, the most common is not as decorations on T-shirts, or as photographs or posters to decorate virtual homes (though both exist); rather, it is the painstaking detailed duplication of the face, body, walk, and, sometimes, voice of the celebrity for use as avatar animations, "skins," "shapes," and gestures (with associated sounds). There is a thriving market in these "celebrity skins," with one shop selling dozens of skins of celebrities, both living and dead. The available "skins" include Cameron Diaz, Johnny Depp, Britney Spears, Scarlett Johansson, Brad Pitt, and Elvis Presley, among others.[33] It is notable that the advertising for many of the celebrity skins at this shop depicts the skins applied to naked avatars with exposed genitalia. The images of these naked avatars wearing the "skin" of the celebrity are generally juxtaposed with photographs of the real-life celebrities (the photographs, not surprisingly, are generally taken from websites without attribution or apparent permission). It is also notable that there is really no limit in Second Life to the activities that an avatar can be animated to appear to participate in, aside from the imaginations of the users, and the graphics capabilities of virtual worlds are only improving. Although celebrity avatars are definitely recognizable as counterparts to their real-life inspirations, they are, for now at least, clearly computer simulations. It is certain that the not-far-off future will bring truly photorealistic avatars, compounding the obvious potential problems.

Because these stores are selling "images" of celebrities in-world in three-dimensional, creepily "wearable" form and, further, using the celebrities' real-life pictures in their advertising, they very likely are treading on celebrities' right of publicity. However, there is at least a potential defense. A store accused of infringing a celebrity's right of publicity could claim that the images are sufficiently artistic and interpretative to give them First Amendment protection as artistic works. Though the First Amendment does provide some protection, "commercial speech" gets less protection than other kinds of speech. This is an unsettled field of law, but a recent case helped clarify the interplay between First Amendment protection and the right of publicity. In that case, an Ohio district court held that a painting of Tiger Woods was protected by the First Amendment as an artistic work. On appeal, the Sixth Circuit affirmed the court's holding.[34]

The other potential application of the right of publicity is on behalf of famous avatars. Consider "Aimee Weber," the avatar whose real-life counterpart is the proud owner of the virtual worlds' first registered trademark on an avatar, as discussed earlier. Alyssa LaRoche is not, at the moment, terribly likely to have her own image used as an endorsement. But "Aimee Weber" is one of the best-known avatars in the virtual world, appearing not only as the representative of "Aimee Weber" studios in Second Life but also on the cover of a book on content creation, for which the author is given as "Aimee Weber" (rather than LaRoche's real name). Similarly, though few have heard of Ailin Graef, her avatar, "Anshe Chung," has appeared on the cover of *Business Week* and is widely known as the first "virtual millionaire," based, largely, on her land holdings in Second Life.

■■■■■
Virtual World Right of Publicity Trends

- Celebrities who enter virtual worlds will find their presence already established by users selling "celebrity skins."
- Virtual celebrities known mainly as avatars will be able to assert the right to publicity over their digital "image."

Certainly using a pseudonymous pen name does not disqualify one from protection. For example, "Bob Dylan" is much more likely to be used in an infringing endorsement than "Robert Zimmerman," and there is no real question that a lawsuit could follow. So Alyssa LaRoche could clearly bring a claim based on the use of the *name* "Aimee Weber." Similarly, now that voice is gaining wider acceptance in virtual worlds and musicians are discovering these virtual spaces, it is not at all inconceivable that a pop star will develop who is known only by her avatar, her voice, and her pseudonymous name. The singer would have a claim based on unauthorized use of her voice, just as Bette Midler and Tom Waits prevailed in voice-based claims for radio advertising mimicking their distinctive voices, against, respectively, Ford and Frito-Lay.[35]

The issue is whether the use of the avatar's *image* (which, at least in LaRoche's case, is clearly not an attempt to copy the appearance of the real LaRoche, if, for no other reason, because the avatar sports blue butterfly wings) could give rise to a claim under the right of publicity as well. It probably can. The case that is most applicable here is *Motschenbacher v. R.J. Reynolds Tobacco Co.*[36] The case is notable because it did not involve the name, image, or voice of the actual person who brought suit. Instead, R.J. Reynolds had used a race car that looked remarkably similar (though not identical) to Lothar Motschenbacher's race car to advertise Winston cigarettes. Motschenbacher brought suit, and the court held that the company was infringing Motschenbacher's right of publicity because of the clear association between the car and the driver. The parallel is clear. Put aside the fact that most avatars have humanoid forms; that fact is irrelevant. There is no reason that avatars could not be sufficiently associated with a real person such that that person can claim infringement, just as Motschenbacher prevailed in his suit against R.J. Reynolds based on the appearance of his car.

Content creation is a fundamental part of virtual worlds, and, as a result, intellectual property questions abound. Even seemingly unrelated issues in virtual law typically involve some virtual property issues. It is worth keeping these issues in mind when evaluating any legal situation arising from a virtual world.

Open Questions on Intellectual Property Law and Virtual Worlds

1. Should some virtual worlds permit even greater intellectual property ownership—perhaps simply reserving all intellectual property rights to works created in the virtual world to the creators—in order to encourage business?

2. What legal challenges are likely to arise in relation to Second Life's patent policy?

3. Should virtual worlds be more proactive in removing infringing content, or rely on user-to-user lawsuits to curtail copyright and trademark infringement?

4. What steps short of a lawsuit should companies that find their brand infringed in virtual worlds consider taking?

Notes

1. Entropia Universe, End User License Agreement, http://www.entropia universe.com/pe/en/rich/107004.html (last visited Jan. 6, 2008); *see also infra* Appendix VI.

2. World of Warcraft, Terms of Use Agreement (Jan. 7, 2007), http://www.worldofwarcraft.com/legal/termsofuse.html; *see also infra* Appendix V.

3. City of Heroes User Agreement (Nov. 2007), http://www.plaync.com/help/eula_coh.html.

4. There.com, Privacy and Security: Developer Agreement, http://webapps.prod.there.com/help/201.xml.

5. Second Life, Terms of Service, http://secondlife.com/corporate/tos .php (last visited Jan. 5, 2008); *see also infra* Appendix IV.

6. Second Life, Terms of Service (emphasis in original), *id.*; *see also infra* Appendix IV.

7. Second Life, Terms of Service, *id.; see also infra* Appendix IV.

8. Second Life, DMCA: Digital Millennium Copyright Act, http://secondlife.com/corporate/dmca.php (last visited Jan. 5, 2008).

9. *Id.*

10. Tenshi Vielle, *Our Heroes Are Dead,* SECOND LIFE HERALD, Aug. 27, 2008, http://www.secondlifeherald.com/slh/2007/08/our-heros-are-d.html.

11. Trademarks and Copyrights in Second Life, http://support.secondlife .com/ics/support/KBAnswer.asp?questionID=3966 (login required; last visited Jan. 7, 2008).

12. Posting of Aldon Hynes, A Cease and Desist Letter About Trademarks in Second Life, http://www.orient-lodge.com/node/2575 (Oct. 30, 2007, 14:32).

13. Welcome to the Second Life Patent and Trademark Office, http://www.slpto.com/ (last visited Jan. 7, 2008).

14. Copyright, Current Fees, http://www.copyright.gov/docs/fees.html (last visited Jan. 7, 2008).

15. Posting of Chris "Petey" Peterson, Second Life Sucks, http://www .somethingawful.com/d/second-life-safari/second-life-sucks.php (last visited Jan. 7, 2008).

16. Posting of Eliot Van Buskirk to WIRED Listening Post blog, Does Music on Second Life Infringe Copyright?, http://blog.wired.com/music/2006/11/does_music_on_s.html (Nov. 17, 2006, 15:39:46).

17. Curious Rousselot, *Gorean Copyright Fight,* SECOND LIFE HERALD, Feb. 11, 2007, http://www.secondlifeherald.com/slh/2007/02/gorean_copyright.html.

18. Benjamin Duranske, *Three Things: Hot Issues in Virtual Law* (May 5, 2007), http://virtuallyblind.com/2007/05/05/hot-virtual-law-issues/.

19. Trademark FAQ, http://www.uspto.gov/web/offices/tac/tmfaq.htm (last visited Jan. 7, 2008).

20. There.com, Submission Guidelines, http://developer.prod.there.com/ developer/developer_help_sg.html (last visited Jan. 7, 2008).

21. Trademarks and Copyrights in Second Life, http://support.secondlife .com/ics/support/KBAnswer.asp?questionID=3966 (login required; last visited Jan. 7, 2008).

22. Benjamin Duranske, *Herman Miller Fights Trademark Infringment* [sic] *in Second Life with "Get Real" Campaign* (Oct. 8, 2007), http://virtuallyblind .com/2007/10/08/herman-miller-second-life/.

23. *Id.*

24. *Id.*

25. Trademark Application Serial No. 77110299 (filed Feb. 18, 2007), http://tarr.uspto.gov/servlet/tarr?regser=serial&entry=77110299.

26. 35 U.S.C. § 154(a)–(c)

27. Search for patent applications by number at http://uspto.gov.

28. Trade Secret Basics FAQ, http://www.nolo.com/article.cfm/objectId/ 90781CA8-0ECE-4E38-BF9E29F7A6DA5830/310/119/FAQ/ (last visited Jan. 7, 2008).

29. RESTATEMENT OF TORTS § 757.

30. Comedy III Productions Inc. v. Gary Saderup, Inc., 25 Cal. 4th 387 (Cal. 2001).

31. CAL. CIV. CODE § 3344.1.

32. *Id.*

33. Posting of UrizenusSklar to SECOND LIFE HERALD blog, Body Doubles: Another IP Puzzle for SL, http://www.secondlifeherald.com/slh/2007/03/ body_doubles_an.html (Mar. 2, 2007, 19:35).

34. ETW Corp. v. Jireh Publishing, Inc., 99 F. Supp. 2d 829 (N.D. Ohio, 2000).

35. Midler v. Ford Motor Co., 849 F.2d 460 (9th Cir. 1988); Waits v. Frito-Lay, Inc., 978 F.2d 1093 (9th Cir. 1992).

36. Motschenbacher v. R.J. Reynolds Tobacco Co., 498 F.2d 821 (9th Cir. 1974).

Civil Procedure and Virtual Worlds

For the most part, rules of civil procedure apply to disputes involving virtual worlds transparently and without significant mental gymnastics, though there are a few exceptions. The exceptions typically result from the fact that most virtual world users are pseudonymous. Once the pseudonymity provided by an avatar is stripped away, the civil procedure implications are no different than in any other case. A transaction between avatars is, in fact, just a transaction between two human beings who happen to have the ability to partially obscure their identities. Once the identities are established, rules of civil procedure governing the underlying dispute are no different than if the identities of the participants had been known originally.

However, virtual worlds do provide at least an initial illusion of anonymity, and if a dispute arises that cannot be dealt with amicably between pseudonymous users without revelation of identities, then it becomes important to be able to discover the identity of the person who controls the avatar.

A case (*Eros, LLC v. John Doe*) against a virtual world user who was, at the time of filing, known only by the name of his avatar in the virtual world of Second Life ("Volkov Catteneo") resulted in a default judgment in Florida's Middle District Court. This chapter will focus on the initial steps taken in that case and, thus, will chiefly emphasize the Federal Rules of Civil Procedure, although general principles discussed herein will apply to most state court proceedings as well.[1]

Suing Fictitious Defendants Generally

Anonymous "John Doe" lawsuits, also known as "fictitious defendant" lawsuits, have gained popularity (and notoriety) over the first half of the first decade of this millennium due to their widespread deployment by the Recording Industry Association of America (RIAA) against users of file-sharing services.[2] Fictitious defendants are placeholders—typically named as "John Doe" or, in the case of an unknown number of defendants, "John Doe #1-10" (or 20, 100, etc.). They have been used in a variety of situations, many of which have nothing do with the Internet. For example, medical malpractice cases frequently name John Doe defendants because the plaintiff does not know the names of every doctor who participated in his or her case at the time of filing. Similarly, product defect cases often use fictitious defendants to identify an unknown manufacturer of a part.[3] In fictitious defendant suits, the plaintiff generally amends the complaint to add the real name of the defendant once it is learned during the discovery process. Although these suits have a long history, they have become much more common in the last few years due to their deployment as tools to pierce the pseudonymity provided by most Internet providers. They have become so common that larger Internet service providers have entire teams of attorneys simply to respond to these requests.[4]

Fictitious defendant lawsuits are not without controversy, partly because of the widespread negative publicity generated by the RIAA's aggressive enforcement and somewhat imprecise methods of identification. The RIAA has brought tens of thousands of lawsuits, at least one against a defendant who turned out to be deceased,[5] and one against a family that did not own a computer or have Internet access.[6] Negative publicity associated with John

Doe lawsuits is not limited to the file-sharing lawsuits filed by the RIAA, however. Privacy advocates argue that anonymous speech is an important right protected by the First Amendment of the U.S. Constitution, and that John Doe lawsuits—which reveal identifying information about a user who sought privacy—create a chilling effect on otherwise-protected anonymous criticism of government and corporate bodies and of public figures.[7]

Virtual worlds, by their nature as pseudonymous meeting places, attract a high percentage of users who feel strongly about the protection of this level of pseudonymous privacy, so it is worth bearing in mind that a lawsuit that seeks to dislodge the identity of a user may generate some negative publicity. However, the *Eros* lawsuit mentioned earlier, which asserts a copyright claim on behalf of a virtual world content creator, has been widely heralded as a positive move for virtual worlds.[8]

Kevin Alderman, the owner of Eros, LLC, is a popular and well-known figure in Second Life (as avatar "Stroker Serpentine"), and the suit was generally perceived as a groundbreaking step that has helped everyone who creates content in virtual worlds protect that content. But even that suit attracted some criticism, with one commentator suggesting that rules of procedure should be changed to require plaintiffs to plead specific information sufficient to survive a motion to dismiss before being able to subpoena providers for information.[9] Others disagree and observe that the more difficult it is to find this information using subpoenas and the courts, the more likely it is that aggrieved parties will seek the information by conducting independent investigations, potentially revealing more damaging information than would have been provided in response to a subpoena.[10]

Suing Pseudonymous Internet Users

This text uses the term "pseudonymous" because there is, practically, no real anonymity on the Internet (there are solutions that make it much harder to determine who is behind a keyboard, such as proxy servers and exclusive use of public terminals, but they are well beyond the average user's comfort zone and require rigorously disciplined use to be effective). Because most Internet users generally will never really be anonymous, most virtual world users will not be anonymous. Virtual worlds are, after all, essentially just a new way of communicating. They send and receive data using the same Internet service provider that is used to check e-mail and visit websites, so the same civil procedure steps that are used to track down a pseudonymous Internet user generally will work to track down a virtual world user.

Before considering virtual worlds, which add a few wrinkles to this procedure, consider a simple web-based service with which you may already be familiar, such as Yahoo! or Google. These services offer pseudonymity to their users. For example, if a user wants to set up a pseudonymous online identity, he can simply create a new e-mail address at Yahoo! or Google. He is not even required to fill in a name (real or otherwise) when he does this—he can simply leave all identifying data blank or provide false information. Assume that he then does something using that e-mail address that potentially subjects him to civil or criminal liability—distributes copyrighted material, for example. He may think that he is anonymous and that there are no data associated with that name that can be traced to him because he provided no information to Yahoo! when he signed up for the e-mail address. In fact, he has already identified himself sufficiently that two simple subpoenas will, in most cases, reveal his identity.

Each computer accessing the Internet has a unique number called an "IP address" ("IP" stands for "Internet Protocol"). The IP address is assigned by the Internet service provider—for most home users, their telephone company or cable television provider. This address may change occasionally, but at any given time, it is only assigned to a single account (sometimes more than one computer in a home will share the same external IP address, which raises issues we will discuss later in this chapter, but the IP address will only be associated with a single account).

This IP address, which is, typically, assigned to one computer or at least one household, is available to websites that users browse. In fact, the address must be available to these websites, otherwise the sites would not be able to direct data to the right computer (there are anonymous "proxy" hosts that strip out these data, but they slow browsing significantly, and most users do not use them).

So when our example user logs in to a website, that website is generally sent the IP address.

Websites typically keep logs of the IP addresses that took certain actions. For example, Yahoo! stores—for at least some period—the IP address of the computer that was used to set up the "anonymous" e-mail account discussed earlier.[11] If that account is used to commit a crime or—as relevant here—if appropriate legal process is employed to request the information, Yahoo! will provide that IP address to the authorities in a criminal matter or to attorneys who are prosecuting civil suits.

Yahoo! explains this to users in its Terms of Service:

> You acknowledge, consent and agree that Yahoo! may access, preserve and disclose your account information and Content if required to do so by law or in a good faith belief that such access preservation or disclosure is reasonably necessary to: (a) comply with legal process; (b) enforce the TOS; (c) respond to claims that any Content violates the rights of third parties; (d) respond to your requests for customer service; or (e) protect the rights, property or personal safety of Yahoo!, its users and the public.[12]

So an attorney seeking the identity of our example Yahoo! user who used his pseudonymous e-mail address to distribute copyrighted material only needs to provide Yahoo! a well-formed subpoena. Yahoo! (or any other provider) will respond by producing records that reveal the IP address associated with the e-mail address that is associated with the actions that gave rise to the lawsuit.

Once that IP address is known, it is easy to determine which Internet service provider (telephone company, cable provider, etc.) assigned the address to an individual user because Internet service providers own large, publicly available ranges from which they assign individual addresses to their users. The attorney seeking the identity of the user then simply subpoenas the provider. Providers generally keep records of which user was assigned which IP address at any given time, so with a time and date and an IP address, the provider can generally determine which user was accessing the network using that IP address at that time. The provider will then produce documents that establish which user was using the IP address at the relevant time and will also produce documents sufficient to identify the user. Because the Internet service provider is typically also the user's telephone or cable provider, information available generally includes the user's real name and address.

Occasionally, though not commonly, an IP address is "static" and permanently assigned to one user rather than reassigned on a regular basis to different users. In those cases, the process is even easier, because identifying the person who was using the address does not depend on the extent to which the Internet service provider keeps long- term records. Record retention is rarely a problem when subpoenaing providers, however, as most providers preserve IP address assignment information for a remarkably long time, if not indefinitely. To the extent that they do not do so already, U.S. legislation requiring providers to store these data indefinitely has been proposed,[13] and such legislation has already passed in the European Union.[14]

Finally, it is worth noting that in addition to IP address information, the content provider who gave our example user the e-mail account that was used to distribute copyrighted material (Yahoo! in our example) likely has a wealth of other information on the user that should be sought in a subpoena. It is possible, of course, that the user registered with his real name or geographic location or somehow otherwise associated identifying information with the account. If so, then it may not even be necessary to subpoena the Internet service provider, though the information could still be sought in case the provider has additional details or simply to provide confirmation.

Suing Pseudonymous Avatars

Shifting this discussion to virtual worlds changes a few key issues, most of which make the process somewhat easier. Because virtual worlds are, for many users, chiefly social places, a great deal of information about individual users exists within user profiles, friend networks, group memberships, and other publicly available data sources. Also, many virtual world users write about their experiences in virtual worlds in personal blogs and leave comments on other users' blogs. Many also have social networking presences for their avatars and regularly update both real-world and virtual world details on these spaces. In sum, virtual worlds, by their very nature, encourage users to share a great deal of personal information. A good investigator will be able to find a lot of information on many virtual world users from publicly available sources and, when successful, save months of discovery and significant legal fees that would otherwise be expended securing the identity of a fictitious defendant.

Where investigation is unsuccessful, however, filing a "John Doe" lawsuit may be the most expeditious way to dislodge the identity of a user who is believed to have committed an act that gives rise to civil liability. The *Eros, LLC v. John Doe* complaint, filed in the Middle District of Florida, provides an excellent example of the type of pleading that will be employed in cases like this. According to the complaint,

24. Defendant maintains one or more accounts within Second Life, and is known as Volkov Catteneo within Second Life. On information and belief, based on information obtained through Eros's investigation of Defendant's activities, defendant is an adult male who has in connection with his other on-line activities listed his name as "Aaron Long." Eros does not know whether Aaron Long is a pseudonym.

25. Despite reasonable efforts, Eros does not presently know Defendant's true identity or address but intends to obtain this information by way of subpoenas directed to one or more Internet service providers that are likely to have obtained said information from Defendant.[15]

The complete text of the *Eros, LLC v. John Doe* complaint can be found at Appendix VIII.

On the same day that the complaint was filed, Eros also requested leave to serve subpoenas in advance of the time allowed under Federal Rules of Civil Procedure 26(d) and 26(f), which require that the parties confer before discovery commences. Interestingly, Eros addressed the privacy arguments set forth earlier in this chapter, a seemingly wise move that serves at least three purposes: (1) to dismiss the argument itself, (2) to establish a reputation with the court for candor, and (3) to blunt potential negative publicity from the privacy advocates in the virtual community. Eros argued:

> While Courts have recognized that the First Amendment protects the right to speak anonymously, on the internet and elsewhere, this protection is not absolute. *Sony Music Entertainment Inc. v. Does 1-40,* 326 F.Supp. 2d 556, 562-63 (S.D. N.Y. 2004). In particular, the First Amendment does not protect copyright infringement or other violations of others' intellectual property rights. *Harper & Row Publishers, Inc. v. Nation Enters.,* 471 U.S. 539, 555-56, 569 105 S.Ct. 2218 (1985); *In Re Capital Cities/ABC, Inc.,* 918 F.2d 140, 143 (11th Cir. 1990). For the reasons that follow, even assuming *arguendo* that Defendant's illegal copying and sale of Eros's products qualifies as "speech", the First Amendment does not protect the information Eros seeks to obtain from discovery.
>
> While Eros has not uncovered any controlling 11th Circuit precedent on this precise issue, Eros submits that the *Sony Music* case, *supra,* and the cases cited therein, provide useful guidance here. In *Sony Music,* the court noted that in cases involving subpoenas seeking information from internet service providers and other entities regarding otherwise anonymous subscribers or other persons who are parties to litigation, courts have considered the following factors to weigh the need for disclosure against First Amendment interests: (1) a concrete showing of a prima facie claim of actionable harm; (2) specificity of the discovery request; (3) the absence of alternative means to obtain the subpoenaed information; (4) a central need for the subpoenaed information to advance the claim; and (5) the party's expectation of privacy. *Id.* at 564-65 (citations omitted). All of these factors favor grant of Eros's motion here.[16]

The *ex parte* motion for leave was granted the day after it was filed, and subpoenas issued to Linden Lab (the company that operates Second Life) and payment processing company PayPal, with whom the defendant was believed to maintain an account. Both Linden Lab and PayPal complied with the subpoenas.[17] Presumably, Linden Lab and PayPal provided what identifying information they had in their possession, as well as relevant IP addresses, as discussed earlier.

After Linden Lab and PayPal complied with the subpoenas, Eros returned to the court and sought leave to serve subpoenas on AT&T and Charter Communications, which, according to the motion, provided Internet service to the IP addresses provided by Linden Lab and PayPal. Both complied with the subpoenas, and, based on the information provided, the plaintiffs amended their complaint to add a named defendant.

Serving Documents on Avatars

At least with respect to federal cases, attorneys practicing in virtual worlds may reach agreements between and among themselves to allow for the service of documents via the interface provided by the virtual world, just as they may choose to stipulate to service by e-mail attachment or facsimile. Federal Rule of Civil Procedure 5(b)(1), "Service under Rule 5(a)" (governing services of motions and other documents subsequent to service of the complaint), specifies, in part, that service can be accomplished by delivering a copy to opposing counsel by any means, "including electronic means, consented to in writing by the person served."[18] Of course, corporate attorneys are free to exchange most documents using any mutually agreeable technology as well.

Attorneys contemplating this method should bear in mind that ethical concerns regarding data privacy and practical concerns regarding frequent failures of virtual world software must trump the potential convenience of exchanging documents with opposing counsel—at least for now. Virtual worlds focused on professionals with more robust privacy guards and communication tools are not far off, however, and mutually agreeable service between attorneys' avatars is certainly not out of the question.

Note, however, there are no such provisions in the Federal Rules of Civil Procedure for service of an *initial* summons and complaint by electronic means, and a request for waiver of service must be "dispatched through first-class mail or other reliable means."[19]

Open Questions on Civil Procedure and Virtual Worlds

1. What issues are raised by the use of John Doe lawsuits to learn the identity of users of virtual worlds?

2. Should providers comply with subpoenas for user information?

3. Should providers be required to retain indentifying data regarding users?

Notes

1. All references in this chapter are to the 2006 Federal Rules of Civil Procedure (incorporating the revisions that took effect Dec. 1, 2006).

2. Posting of Grant Robertson to Digital World blog, The RIAA vs. John Doe, a Layperson's Guide to Filesharing Lawsuits, http://digitalmusic .weblogsinc.com/2006/08/07/the-riaa-vs-john-doe-a-laypersons-guide-to -filesharing-lawsui/ (Aug. 7, 2006, 12:30 AM).

3. MICHAEL S. VOGEL, UNMASKING "JOHN DOE" DEFENDANTS: THE CASE FOR CAUTION IN CREATING NEW LEGAL STANDARDS (under revision), http://www.cfp2002.org/ proceedings/proceedings/vogel.pdf (last visited Jan. 7, 2008).

4. Saul Hansell, *Increasingly, Internet's Data Trail Leads to Court,* N.Y. TIMES Feb. 4, 2006, *available at* http://www.nytimes.com/2006/02/04/technology/ 04privacy.html.

5. Andrew Orlowski, *RIAA Sues the Dead,* THE REGISTER, Feb. 5, 2005, *available at* http://www.theregister.co.uk/2005/02/05/riaa_sues_the_dead/.

6. Anders Bylund, *RIAA Sues Computer-less Family, 234 Others, for File Sharing* (Apr. 24, 2006), http://arstechnica.com/news.ars/post/20060424-6662 .html.

7. Frequently Asked Questions (and Answers) About John Doe Anonymity, http://www.chillingeffects.org/johndoe/faq.cgi (last visited Jan. 7, 2008).

8. Posting of Eloise Pasteur to Second Life Insider, Linden Lab Coughs Up Stroker Case Name, Maybe the Law Will Change?, http://www

.secondlifeinsider.com/2007/08/06/liden-lab-coughs-up-stroker-case-name -maybe-the-law-will-chang/ (Aug. 6, 2007, 18:01).

9. Pejman Yousefzadeh, *Virtual Reality "Avatars" Are Now Real Enough to Be Sued,* THE AMERICAN, July 10, 2007, *available at* http://www.american.com/ archive/2007/july-0707/virtual-reality-2018avatars2019-are-now-real-enough-to -be-sued.

10. VOGEL, *supra* note 3.

11. Yahoo! India Privacy, IP Addresses, http://info.yahoo.com/privacy/in/ yahoo/ip/ (last visited Jan. 7, 2008).

12. Yahoo! Terms of Service, http://info.yahoo.com/legal/us/yahoo/utos/ (last visited Jan. 7, 2008).

13. William Baker, *Will Congress Regulate Social Networking Sites?,* PRIVACY IN FOCUS (Wiley Rein & Fielding, LLP), Aug. 2006, *available at* http://wileyrein .com/docs/newsletter_issues/444.pdf.

14. Jo Best, *Europe Passes Tough New Data Retention Laws,* CNET, Dec. 14, 2005, http://www.news.com/Europe-passes-tough-new-data-retention-laws/2100 -7350_3-5995089.html.

15. Eros, LLC v. Doe, http://dockets.justia.com/docket/court-flmdce/case _no-8:2007cv01158/case_id-202603/ (last visited Jan. 4, 2008); Complaint *infra* at Appendix VIII.

16. Eros v. Doe, http://docs.justia.com/cases/federal/district-courts/florida/ flmdce/8:2007cv01158/202603/2/ (last visited Feb. 23, 2008), *Motion for Leave to File Subpoenas.*

17. Eric Krangel, a/k/a Eric Reuters, *Linden Hands Over "John Doe" Information* (Aug. 6, 2007), http://secondlife.reuters.com/stories/2007/08/06/ linden-hands-over-john-doe-information/.

18. FED. R. CIV. P. 5(b)(1).

19. FED. R. CIV. P. 4(d)(2)(B).

Tort Law and Virtual Worlds

Torts are civil wrongs that the law recognizes as grounds for a lawsuit. They include a wide range of actions, from assault to slander to interference with contract. At first glance, virtual worlds and games appear well suited to straightforward application of tort law, given that they are on one hand, approximations of reality, and on the other, born of contractual relationships. Depictions of player-to-player assault are the very point of many game-based virtual worlds, and free-form virtual worlds seem to act as petri dishes for (at least informal) claims of defamation. In reality, however, the underlying technological limitations of most virtual worlds and games and the existence of the "magic circle" render many tort claims problematic. There are, however, a few notable exceptions, and some tort claims could even find new application in virtual worlds. This chapter will first consider limitations on the application of tort law in virtual worlds and multiplayer games, and then examine those torts that do appear to have application in these spaces.

The Magic Circle and the Limits of Tort Law in Virtual Spaces

Before we delve into individual tort claims, consider again Johan Huizinga's discussion of the magic circle, in conjunction with Edward Castronova's current theory of "interration." The theory behind both is that play should be protected from the reach of the real world, and, to a degree, the real world should likewise be protected from activities that are defined as play.

The magic circle, of course, has been drawn around many play events, not just computer-based games. For example, a football game involves a great deal of assault (the threat of violence caused by an immediate show of force). In fact, threatening violence by an immediate show of force essentially defines the job of the defensive linemen, whose task it is to pressure the quarterback and prevent him from successfully completing a pass. When they succeed, the quarterback ends up on his back in the grass. No tort is committed when they succeed, however, because everyone on the field, including the quarterback, has consented to the activity. In formal sporting events, that consent is formalized with a contract, although it can be done just as easily by the informal consent of all participants (e.g., a backyard football game). The key is that the consent only goes as far as the rules of the game permit. It could be said that the magic circle protects this play space from the intrusions of the law.

To the extent that a virtual world is being used as a play space (and not, instead, a new communications tool for a business, for example), the magic circle should protect that space as well. Consider Ultima Online. One character class is "Thief," and players can join the "Thieves Guild." To join the Thieves Guild, you must increase a skill called "Stealing." Once your character has sufficient skill at stealing, he or she can take virtual objects from other players without their consent.[1] To do this, your character literally walks up behind another player's character, rifles through his backpack, and steals something that looks valuable. If your character gets caught with her hand in her target's backpack, the victim can, without penalty, attack and kill the thief, and take all her possessions. Neither act—the thievery nor the vigilante killing—is permissible in real life, of course, and both acts would result in civil liability and criminal charges.

In all modern social virtual worlds, and in some games, stealing virtual property (by compromising a password, for example) is prohibited and can result in a user being suspended, or even reported to the authorities. But in Ultima Online, it is built into the game mechanic, and it is all good, clean fun. The difference is the magic circle. Expressed in legal terms, everyone who plays Ultima Online consents to the potential for thievery, and everyone who plays a thief consents to the possibility of vigilante justice.

Two potential issues arise from this analysis that are worth bearing in mind when we begin exploring individual tort claims later in this chapter. First, what liability should exist in a *social* virtual world, where the protection of the magic circle via shared consent is less clear? For example, in a free-form social world that some people use as a giant role-playing game, and others use to raise money for real business ventures and nonprofit organizations, should magic circle protection apply? Second, is there a point where the law should reject the protection of the magic circle entirely?

Limitations on Touch-Based Torts Arising from Virtual Worlds

Beyond the fact that the magic circle and the doctrine of consent eliminate the possibility of many types of tort actions in virtual worlds and games, current technology also operates as a limit on what sorts of torts can reasonably arise in virtual spaces. If *Virtual Law* makes it to a fifth or sixth edition, you may, by then, be entering a virtual world by stepping into a "holodeck" in your garage or slipping on headgear and a contact suit, and it is certainly conceivable that someone could actually cause a "touch" across vast distances by triggering a response in the gear you are wearing that impacts your physical body. When you consider a recently released vest that lets users "get pounded with body slams, crushed with G-forces, and blasted with bullet fire," science fiction questions of real-life battery arising from virtual world interactions move a bit closer to reality.[2] The adult industry is also working to create products that bridge the gap between reality and fantasy by allowing "touch" via Internet-based communication; early versions of some are already in the marketplace.[3] These, too, could potentially provide grounds for a claim that an offensive "touch" had occurred over a great distance.

Until these products achieve more widespread acceptance, however, we can dispense with the torts of assault and battery. No matter how dangerous a sword-swinging Level 70 Night Elf appears in World of Warcraft, he can't *really* hurt the physical player behind the keyboard, and everyone knows that. The same is true regarding periodic claims of "virtual rape." No matter how offensive, objectionable, and wrong it may be for someone to cause an unwanted sexual animation or text involving a user's avatar to appear on that user's computer screen, it simply does not meet any state's legal definition of "rape," all of which require some form of actual contact. That is not to say that depictions of nonconsensual assault and rape that occur with fairly grim regularity in virtual worlds can't give rise to another tort (for example, intentional infliction of emotional distress, discussed in greater detail later in this chapter), but actual, actionable assault and battery that require physical contact are simply not possible in virtual worlds and games. At least not yet.

Limitations on Property-Based Torts Arising from Virtual Worlds

The nature of virtual property is likely to be a significant focus of virtual law over the next decade. Although it will obviously impact property-based torts (e.g., trespass to property, trespass to chattel, conversion) in virtual worlds, a few notes can be made at this point, even in the absence of judicial decisions that will ultimately help clarify these questions.

Torts related to "real property" (e.g., land) like "trespass to land" are not likely to apply to virtual property. However the questions regarding the nature of "virtual land" and "virtual property" are settled, it is highly unlikely that they will be settled with a holding finding virtual land exactly the same as real land. That is true for a number of reasons, chief among them that (1) rules for real property are based, in large part, on the absolute limit on the resource, (2) the rules for real property are among the oldest in law and have a long history of case law, much of which would prove difficult to adapt to virtual property, and (3) "real property" rules are narrowly tailored to apply to property that is limited by real, physical boundaries.

One may well be able to draw parallels from real property law to virtual property, but direct application is problematic. You hardly require an "easement by necessity" to access your virtual property if you can instantly teleport into it, noise pollution doesn't really matter if a parcel owner can simply turn exterior sounds off on her land, and trespass isn't even possible if the right technical solutions are in place. In short, virtual property, by definition, simply isn't "real property," and torts that arise from ownership of real property are not likely to apply to activity that takes place entirely within a virtual world and that impacts "virtual land."

On the other hand, the outcome of the debate over the nature of virtual property does inform the question of whether torts related to personal property or "chattels" (e.g., conversion and trespass to chattel) apply to virtual property. In fact, these torts would likely apply to "virtual land" in a virtual world more than real property laws would, as "land" in a virtual world is closer in nature to any other virtual possession (e.g., a sword, handbag, or house) than it is actual "land." If courts find that virtual property does amount to something beyond its intellectual property components—that is, if a court finds that it is indeed possible to own a virtual sword or handbag—there is no reason that tort protection of this property should not also spring up. So to the extent that the possessor of an item of virtual property is permanently deprived of his possession of that property due to the unjustified willful interference of another (e.g., through deletion, by a virtual world provider), a suit based on the tort of conversion is not prima facie unreasonable. Similarly, a suit based on trespass to chattel would not be unreasonable in a situation where a user was temporarily deprived of possession of an item of virtual property (at least where the user could show actual damages).

Business Torts Arising from Virtual Worlds

Torts that are based on interference with contract, conspiracy, unfair trade practices, and fraud should apply to activity that takes place in virtual worlds with little, if any, additional analysis. There is nothing about communication in a virtual world that renders that communication any less actionable than if it had occurred in a web-based forum, by e-mail, by postal mail, or over a telephone. Thus, virtual world-based claims of intentional interference with contracts, fraud, restraint of trade, and conspiracy raise no special concerns aside from those concerns of evidence and proof outlined in other chapters. It is notable, however, that contracts in virtual worlds are only just at the cusp of becoming practical. As discussed in Chapter 6, "Contract Law and Virtual Worlds," in greater detail, the current pseudonymity offered by most virtual worlds has discouraged widespread use of contracts, with most users choosing to engage only in point of sale and similar transactions where performance is either guaranteed by code or otherwise expected with a certain degree of immediacy.

Defamation in Virtual Worlds

Generally, a defamatory statement is a negligently or maliciously published false, unprivileged, statement of fact that is harmful to someone's reputation. Various state statutes define defamation differently, but in general, a plaintiff seeking restitution for defamation must prove (1) a publication to one other than the person defamed of (2) a false statement of fact (3) that is understood as (a) being of and concerning the plaintiff and (b) tending to harm the reputation of the plaintiff. In addition (4) if the plaintiff is a public figure, he or she must also prove actual malice.[4]

The "publication" can be either spoken (leading to a claim for slander) or written (leading to a claim for libel). The statement must be a "statement of fact" (something demonstrably provable as either true or untrue). So a statement like "Jim committed malpractice" is an actionable statement of fact, while the statement "Jim is a jerk" is not.

In addition, nearly all states recognize "defamation *per se*" for false statements which are "injurious to another in their trade, business, or profession," statements which falsely claim the subject has a "loathsome disease" (historically leprosy and sexually transmitted disease, now also including mental illness), statements which involve false allegations of "unchastity" (typically in unmarried people, and, in some states, only unmarried women), and false claims of criminal activity (in some states, this only applies to crimes involving dishonesty).[5] When a statement falls into one of these categories, a plaintiff need not prove that the statement was defamatory—it is assumed. As a result, a plaintiff does not need to prove monetary damages to establish liability.

There are, generally, two ways that defamation claims can arise from interaction in a virtual world or game. The first, and simplest, is when a well-known link exists between an avatar and a real-life person, to the extent that talking about one is the same as talking about the other. This is true more often for professionals (typically augmentationists) and educators (often experimentalists) than for other residents, many of whom relish the pseudonymity provided by the virtual space. When an avatar is inexorably linked with the person who controls the account, a strong argument can be made that the reputation of the avatar is sufficiently linked to the reputation of the account owner to permit a claim based on statements about the avatar without entering into further, complex analysis. It is axiomatic that a plaintiff need not be directly named in the allegedly defamatory statement in order to have a successful claim.[6]

Bettina Chin,[7] in a law review article entitled *Regulating Your Second Life: Defamation in Virtual Worlds*, explained this as follows: "[I]f avatars are deemed to be the intellectual property of the user, then a possible assumption in the context of virtual worlds is that defaming one's property is the same as defaming one's person."[8]

But what of the situation where the avatar is not inexorably linked to someone's real-life identity? There are already avatars who are well known within a virtual world but who have chosen not to reveal their identity. Going forward, as virtual worlds become more fragmented and specialized, entertainment-based worlds—where the mystique of pseudonymity is the rule—will likely produce a number of successful artists and musicians who are known only by the identities of their avatars. Can these avatars bring defamation suits?

In the case of avatars that are essentially standard-bearers for brand names or corporate identities, the answer is almost certainly yes. We often think of avatars as associated with individuals, but in reality, there is no reason for that to be the exclusive case. It seems rather more likely that as businesses become involved in virtual worlds, they will create somewhat generic presences that can be controlled by any of a number of employees. For example, an avatar who gives concerts in virtual spaces could be managed by a business that employs a real-life singer (or even several real-life singers) to produce the music that is attributed to the avatar, as a "work for hire." This business model works in a professional context as well. A professional association, such as a law firm, could have a single "receptionist" account logged in, through which various employees who need not even be actual receptionists at the actual firm could interact with and provide information to visitors at the virtual firm's "offices." We are already seeing companies begin to associate their identities with avatars to a degree. One user, as noted earlier, has even secured a trademark registration on the appearance of her avatar and employs the image in the branding of her virtual world consulting and design business.[9]

Chin notes, "Any living person [or] entity that is capable of having a reputation and is legally competent to sue may bring an action for defamation, including corporations and partnerships," although "some courts have indicated that [companies] may recover only for statements that directly attack their finances or businesses."[10]

Avatars are not, of course, "living entities" (fictional or otherwise), but corporations and other business entities are, for legal purposes, considered persons who can possess reputations and bring suits. Thus, if an avatar is essentially the face of a corporation or other entity that can bring a suit, there is a good argument that defamation of the avatar amounts to defamation of the company.

So at least to the extent that one uses an avatar as a "face" for one's business in virtual worlds, it appears that a defamation claim is reasonable if the avatar's reputation is attacked. Chin notes:

> [C]ourts regard corporations as having no reputation in any personal sense, so one cannot defame the corporation by words that affect the "purely, personal repute of an individual." However, a corporation does demand prestige and standing in the business in which it engages, and any statement that may question the corporation's honesty or efficiency may be actionable, so long as it "tends to prejudice it in the conduct of its business or to deter others from dealing with it."[11]

This can work against a corporation as well, exposing it to liability for the potential actions of its avatar. Chin posits, "[W]here a corporation is in fact a mere instrumentality or alter ego of its owner, the actions of the sole controller, or 'shareholder,' may expose the business entity to liability, provided that the plaintiff is able to pierce the corporate veil. Accordingly, any unlawful action taken by an avatar may expose its user to liability."[12]

On the other hand, in a situation where the person or entity behind an avatar has chosen to avail herself of the pseudonymity offered by virtual worlds and has taken steps to disassociate herself from the avatar (and the avatar is not the public face of a company), a defamation claim is problematic. The key is that the defamation must be "of and concerning" the plaintiff. This inquiry is a factual inquiry, not a legal one, and depends on the circumstances. To the extent that a plaintiff has made an effort to disassociate himself from the defamed avatar (e.g., by selecting a wildly different name, physical appearance, and mode of personal presentation), it may be more difficult for the plaintiff to establish the necessary nexus between the allegedly defamatory comments and his own identity. Having an avatar that looks dramatically different from one's real-life appearance or has a completely different name or purported occupation would make little difference to the inquiry, of course, if the user revealed her real identity in her "profile" in the virtual world, or if the association between the avatar and the identity was otherwise well known.

Intentional Infliction of Emotional Distress in Virtual Worlds

Earlier in this chapter, we dismissed assault and battery as being, at least for now, impossible in virtual worlds. The law requires a touching (or the threat of one) for these torts, and current technology simply does not create that opportunity.

That said, depictions of traumatic events take place with startling regularity in virtual worlds and games, even where the designers do not intend them. The phenomenon is called "griefing" (playing a game or participating in a virtual world simply to cause grief for other players through harassment). It is a pervasive and largely uncontrollable part of the virtual world and game landscape. In extreme cases, behavior in virtual worlds and games may give rise to claims of "intentional infliction of emotional distress" (IIED).

IIED is a relatively new tort, first arising in its modern form in California in the early 1950s.[13] Although the tort has slowly garnered wider acceptance, it has proven difficult for plaintiffs to meet the test for "outrageousness" required for behavior to be actionable as intentional infliction of emotional distress. That could change with the application of the law to virtual worlds, where traditional touch-based torts do not apply, but where a surprisingly large percentage of users' behavior really is outrageous.

Many people instinctively feel that *some* liability ought to apply when one's virtual identity is subjected to attacks that would unquestionably be criminal in the real world, yet also feel that these actions do not rise to the level of their real-world counterparts. For example, "virtual rape," as we will discuss later, is undeniably traumatic to the victim, and many feel that some liability should attach, but on the other hand, classifying virtual rape the same way as physical rape minimizes the greater harm of physical rape.

It is of these sorts of divisions that new laws are often born, but here, the applicable law already exists. IIED appears perfectly suited to the sorts of malicious psychological attacks that take place in virtual worlds with surprising regularity, yet which, most people feel, should not be addressed as if they were exactly the same as their physical world counterparts.

Briefly, the elements of IIED are (1) the conduct must be heinous and "outrageous" by societal standards, (2) the behavior actually causes emotional distress, and (3) the emotional distress is severe.[14] It is the first element (outrageousness) that has proven difficult for plaintiffs to meet. Factors that have, in the past, been found necessary for a finding of outrageous include (1) a pattern of conduct (as opposed to a single incident), (2) the defendant's exploitation of a known vulnerability in the plaintiff, (3) an unequal power balance between the defendant and plaintiff, (4) use of racial epithets by the defendant, and (5) the defendant's owing of a fiduciary duty to the plaintiff.[15] The tort includes an element of causation; that is, the actions of the defendant must have actually caused the plaintiff's emotional distress.[16] Finally, the plaintiff must have experienced actual, severe, emotional distress. Courts have required evidence of the intensity, duration, and physical manifestations of the distress to prove this last element. Typically, a defendant asserting IIED establishes proof of the intensity, duration, and physical manifestations of the distress through the testimony of a treating psychiatrist and via evidence of changes in habits, behavior, and personality. Classic examples of intentional infliction of emotional distress include threats of future violence, particularly vile racial epithets, and false statements regarding the death of family members.

In the context of virtual worlds, a variety of actions could, theoretically, give rise to a valid claim for IIED. One feature of virtual worlds is the strong, personal identification that many users develop with their avatars.[17] It is notable that both game players and free-form virtual world users, myself included, regularly refer to the actions taken by their avatar on the screen in the first person (e.g., "I was visiting this great shop where I bought a new pair of shoes," or "I just got back from a quest with my guild and we got a lot of gold."). Users often form lasting friendships that sometimes cross over to the real world, and some also find short- and long-term love interests. Users regularly spend hours—sometimes many hours—logged in to these spaces as their avatars every day. It is not an exaggeration to say that many users have far more active social lives inside virtual worlds and games than outside them; it is probably not the norm, but it is hardly uncommon. For all these reasons, it should not surprise readers that many users of virtual worlds identify very closely with their avatars.

Because meeting the test for conduct that civilized society would consider "outrageous" in real life is relatively difficult, IIED has long been considered a fairly weak tort and is often viewed with some hostility by judges who see it as a secondary pleading. The New York Court of Appeals, for example, has stated that "of the intentional infliction of emotional distress claims considered by this Court, every one has failed because the alleged conduct was not sufficiently outrageous."[18] Virtual worlds could give this tort new life.

The very nature of virtual worlds in a sense encourages behavior that civilized society would consider outrageous. Several studies have shown that the greater the perception of anonymity, the more likely a party is to use aggressive behavior.[19] One study reported that "users who were anonymous were more likely to use expletives, exclamation points, capital letters, and emphasize their points. The more anonymous a user is, the more sentences containing disinhibitive indicators will be present. A higher level of anonymity thus indicates an increased likelihood of disinhibition being exhibited."[20] Another study, conducted by Microsoft, reported that "[d]eviant or 'bad' behavior is pervasive in many computer-mediated social contexts, . . . [and] chat rooms are often a venue where users make inappropriate sexual advances, swear at others or engage in other behaviors that most users deem inappropriate." The Microsoft researchers reasoned that this occurred because "[u]sers in such environments are often relatively anonymous, and [in-world] norms against such behavior do not exist or are weak."[21]

Anecdotal reports support the conclusion that people sometimes have extraordinarily close bonds to their avatars. One often-referenced article, Julian Dibbell's "A Rape in Cyberspace," discusses the psychological impact of an "attack" in which one user in a text-based virtual world made it appear to a large, public group that he had taken control of another user of the virtual world.[22] Dibbell describes the occurrence in the dispassionate tones of a reporter after the event, relating the facts, as captured by several observers. The impact is not diminished.

The facts . . . tell us that he commenced his assault entirely unprovoked, at or about 10 p.m. Pacific Standard Time. That he began by using his voodoo doll to force one of the room's occupants to sexually service him in a variety of more or less conventional ways. [His] victim was [an avatar known as] legba, a Haitian trickster spirit of indeterminate gender, brown-skinned and wearing an expensive pearl gray suit, top hat, and dark glasses. . . . That he turned his attentions now to [another avatar] Starsinger, a rather pointedly nondescript female character, tall, stout, and brown-haired, forcing her into unwanted liaisons with other individuals present in the room, among them legba. . . . That his actions grew progressively violent. That he made legba eat his/her own pubic hair. That he caused Starsinger to violate herself with a piece of kitchen cutlery. That his distant laughter echoed evilly in the living room with every successive outrage.[23]

Dibbell reported that one of the victims, "legba," subsequently wrote: "I'm not calling for policies, trials, or better jails. I'm not sure what I'm calling for. Virtual castration, if I could manage it. Mostly, [this type of thing] doesn't happen here. Mostly, perhaps I thought it wouldn't happen to me. Mostly, I trust people to conduct themselves with some veneer of civility. Mostly, I want his ass."[24]

Finally, Dibbell reported that the woman who was behind the keyboard as "legba" was forced into sexual acts against her will, and who shortly thereafter called for her attacker's "virtual castration," later told Dibbell "that as she wrote those words posttraumatic tears were streaming down her face."[25] It is clear that this user personally identified with her avatar, in a serious, meaningful way, and that the attack could easily give rise to a seemingly reasonable claim of intentional infliction of emotional distress—and this was done via text alone.

The fact that most studies and reports to date concern text-based chat is important. Graphics-based virtual worlds obviously afford greater opportunity for harassment and "outrageous" behavior. They also create much greater opportunity for a user to self-identify with an avatar, which now, instead of being represented by text, is represented by a visual, three-dimensional version of the user. Sometimes users' avatars are designed to look uncannily like the person behind the keyboard; other times, they are fanciful and largely imaginary. In either case, they are used as a projection of one's being into the virtual world space, and it is completely conceivable that severe emotional trauma could result from certain forms of attack.

As examples of the sort of behavior that, if not routinely, at least commonly takes place in modern virtual worlds, I have personally observed the following in the two years I have spent in modern three-dimensional virtual worlds while doing research for this book.

- Shortly after securing land for the first office building for the Second Life Bar Association in Second Life, I visited the plot and found two avatars engaged in simulated sexual intercourse on the roof of a building on the plot next door. I, perhaps naively, offered the avatars a tent and was cursed at. Later, one of the avatars left an object on the land that randomly shouted an audible racial epithet over and over, forcing me to turn off "spatial sound" on the Second Life Bar Association's land until the owner of the land next door, thankfully, sold the land (and thus the object) to someone else.

- While visiting a public "PG"-rated "Welcome Area" in Second Life designed to introduce new users to the virtual world, I watched a human-wolf "furry" avatar wearing a blue T-shirt, a pair of combat boots, and a large exposed phallus follow a female avatar around for several minutes apparently urinating on her.

- When visiting the web-based virtual world IMVU for the very first time, I clicked a button for a random "chat" with another user as part of the series of actions encouraged by the orientation process. I was immediately visited by an avatar wearing a motorcycle jacket who appeared as a "guest" in my new "apartment." The guest avatar then somehow— still unknown to me—caused two animations to play that involved both the guest's and my avatars. The first animation caused the guest's avatar to appear to pin my avatar's body to the ground and move up and down on top of my avatar for ten or fifteen seconds in what appeared to be a simulation of sex, and the second involved the guest avatar hitting my avatar in the stomach several times. The guest's avatar then disappeared.

- On September 11, 2007, apparently as part of an organized series of disruptions in Second Life that took place that day to "commemorate" the World Trade Center attacks, several avatars appeared in a "sandbox" (public building space) that I was visiting and, collectively, used the word "nigger" over fifty times and the word "fuck" over seventy-five times. Most of their attention was directed at a dark-skinned avatar who had been building there when they arrived. One of them followed the dark-skinned avatar around repeating this phrase over and over: "HAPPY FUCKING 9/11 BITCHES. PN ["Patriotic Nigras," a griefing group] OWNZ DA GRID, MASSIVE ATTACKS UNDERWAY. ALSO COCKS. AND CHAT-SPAMMING MAKING IT HARD TO DO ANYTHING. FUCK YOU ALL NUKKAZ!!!"

It is not simply the pseudonymous communication of most virtual worlds that encourages outrageous behavior, for that is true of message boards, e-mail, and comments on blogs (these can be bad enough, but they rarely reach the level fairly frequently observed in virtual worlds). The behavior in virtual worlds, particularly free-form virtual worlds, is much worse for two reasons. First, the tools provided by free-form virtual world creators intentionally allow users to create virtually anything that their imagination can come up with. In the hands of an unscrupulous user, this kind of creative "god" status is bound to be abused, and the results of the abuse can easily reach the "outrageous." Second, most free-form virtual worlds, and particularly the current industry leader, Second Life, pride themselves on offering a relatively hands-off world. Although Second Life's Terms of Service nominally prohibit (among other things) intolerance, harassment, assault, indecency, and disturbing the peace, the reality is that Second Life is a very big virtual world, and all but the most egregious behavior goes unpunished. Even when justice is meted out, it frequently takes the form of short-term suspensions (e.g., from Second Life's Police Blotter: "Violation: Community Standards: Assault, Scripted Objects; Action taken: Suspended 1 day").[26] Some Second Life users even see being suspended as a badge of honor. One forum poster writes, "Just for the record I play [Second Life] to troll and cause problems. I've been banned 3 times so far, and am currently working on a Nazi avatar (Nazi stuff is against the gay second life rules)."[27]

In addition, free-form virtual worlds like Second Life attract a diverse group of users who arrive with wildly differing goals. Some approach the world as a place for business, and others a place for play. That combination alone is a recipe for strife, but when mixed with the two attributes described earlier (unrestricted creation tools and relatively laissez-faire governance), the environment is simply rife with opportunities for "outrageous" behavior.

As noted earlier, judges have usually found that people's real-life behavior (where people are immediately held responsible for their actions by all who are nearby, if not society in general) is typically not sufficiently "outrageous" to trigger the protection of the doctrine of intentional infliction of emotional distress. The standard under which these claims are typically rejected is articulated in the Second Restatement of Torts. The conduct necessary to form intentional infliction of emotional distress must be "so outrageous in character, and so extreme in degree, as to go beyond all possible bounds of decency, and be regarded as atrocious, and utterly intolerable in a civilized community."[28]

It seems unlikely that there is an area of the law which is more apt to apply in virtual worlds and which has not been widely applied in the real world than this. People's behavior in virtual worlds is, frankly, often "atrocious" and would absolutely be seen as "intolerable in a civilized community."

One could conceivably argue that because "outrageous" behavior is rather more common in virtual worlds, it loses some of its "outrageousness," but that ignores the law's standard, which is objective, not subjective. Essentially, a real-life loudmouth bigot's behavior is not judged by the standards of the narrow real-life community of loudmouth bigots when evaluating whether his conduct is "outrageous," and there is no reason to use the even narrower community of loudmouth bigots in virtual worlds as the test group for the outrageousness of conduct there either. Virtual worlds, particularly free-form virtual worlds (as opposed to games), are merely another medium for expression. If the communication would be considered "outrageous" had it taken place over the telephone, or in person, or by postal letter, or by e-mail, it should, under the current standard, also be considered outrageous if it took place in a virtual world. Perhaps, as noted previously, even more so than some of these forms of communication, given that outrageous conduct in a virtual world is personally directed against a digital embodiment of the victim, rather than via a relatively less self-associated e-mail address or telephone handset.

Earlier in this chapter, *Virtual Law* posed this question: Is there a point where the law should reject the protection of the magic circle entirely? *Virtual Law* has generally taken the position that the "magic circle" ought to protect users' actions taken in virtual spaces, particularly in the context of games, which claim its protection. Certain intentional torts, however, which cannot conceivably fit within a definition of "play" (most notably intentional infliction of emotional distress) may mark a point where the magic circle should *not* offer protection.

When a user intentionally steps outside the magic circle (e.g., by circumventing the game or virtual world's mechanical restrictions, or by flagrantly violating its Terms of Service) in order to attack another user and cause extreme emotional distress that would otherwise be actionable, it is unreasonable to expect either potential plaintiffs or judges to ignore the behavior simply because it took place in what was supposed to be a play space. The defendant's cry of "it's just a game" rings hollow when the defendant willfully chooses not to treat the world as a game in the first place.

Open Questions on Tort Law and Virtual Worlds

1. In a social world which some people use as a giant role-playing game and others use to raise money for real business

ventures and nonprofit organizations, should magic circle protection apply?

2. Should the law reject the protection of the magic circle in regard to intentional torts?

Notes

1. Ultima Online, Stealing, http://guide.uo.com/skill_33.html (last visited Jan. 7, 2008).

2. FPS Gaming Vest, http://www.tngames.com/products.php (last visited Jan. 7, 2008).

3. *Teledildonics,* http://en.wikipedia.org/wiki/Teledildonics (last visited Jan. 7, 2008).

4. Chilling Effects Frequently Asked Questions, What are the elements of a defamation claim?, http://www.chillingeffects.org/question.cgi?QuestionID=408; *see also* Restatement (Second) of Torts § 558 (1977).

5. David Ziemer, *Slander Per Se Must Be Inherently Defamatory* (Sept. 29, 2004), http://www.wislawjournal.com/archive/2004/0929/slander-0929.html.

6. Restatement (Second) of Torts § 564 cmt. B (1977).

7. At the time of publication, Bettina Chin was Editor in Chief of the *Brooklyn Law Review* and was due to graduate with a JD in 2008.

8. Bettina M. Chin, *Regulating Your Second Life: Defamation in Virtual Worlds,* 72 Brook. L. Rev. 1333 (2007) (citations omitted), http://ssrn.com/abstract=1013462.

9. Trademark Application Serial No. 77110299 (filed Feb. 18, 2007), http://tarr.uspto.gov/servlet/tarr?regser=serial&entry=77110299.

10. Chin, *supra* note 8.

11. *Id.* (citations omitted).

12. *Id.* (citations omitted).

13. State Rubbish etc. Assn. v. Siliznoff, 38 Cal. 2d 330 (1952), *available at* http://login.findlaw.com/scripts/callaw?dest=ca/cal2d/38/330.html (login required; last visited Jan. 7, 2008).

14. *Id.*

15. Taylor v. Metzger, 706 A.2d 685 (N.J. 1998); GTE Southwest, Inc. v. Bruce, 998 S.W.2d 605 (Tex. 1999).

16. *GTE Southwest,* 998 S.W.2d.

17. Jessica Wolfendale, "My Avatar, My Self: Virtual Harm and Attachment," Ethics and Information Technology, Oct. 11, 2006, 111–119.

18. Howell v. New York Post, 81 N.Y.2d 115, 612 N.E.2d 699, 596 N.Y.S.2d 350 (1993) (citations omitted).

19. Michael Tresca, The Impact of Anonymity on Disinhibitive Behavior Through Computer-Mediated Communication (1998) (MA thesis, Michi-

gan State University), *available at* http://www.msu.edu/user/trescami/thesis.htm#Hypothesis%201.

20. *Id.*

21. John P. Davis, The Experience of "Bad" Behavior in Online Social Spaces: A Survey of Online Users, *available at* http://research.microsoft.com/scg/papers/Bad%20Behavior%20Survey.pdf.

22. Julian Dibbell, "A Rape in Cyberspace, or How an Evil Clown, a Haitian Trickster Spirit, Two Wizards, and a Cast of Dozens Turned a Database into a Society," Village Voice, Dec. 23, 1993, http://www.juliandibbell.com/texts/bungle_vv.html.

23. *Id.*

24. *Id.*

25. *Id.*

26. Second Life, Community: Incident Management Report, http://secondlife.com/community/blotter.php (last visited Jan. 7, 2008).

27. Forum Post: Naked Spotz and Giant Taco Havoc Dance, http://ytmnd.com/sites/profile/509834?start=1&PHPSESSID=e56c4ac2df3ff4f72ec2b640aa065f13 (last visited Jan. 7, 2008).

28. Restatement (Second) of Torts § 46 cmt. D (1965).

Criminal Law and Virtual Worlds 10

The application of criminal law to virtual worlds is the most headline-friendly aspect of virtual law. Stories regarding gambling, virtual prostitution, theft, money laundering, and fraud are much more compelling than headlines about copyright infringement. These issues do not, however, raise many novel questions in virtual worlds. Most actual crimes that occur in virtual worlds are financial crimes, and they can be addressed through simple application of existing criminal codes. The laws regarding financial fraud, money laundering, data theft, and gambling have been updated to take into account Internet-based activity, so they already cover virtual worlds and games as written. Of the remaining criminal law issues, only virtual prostitution raises novel legal questions, and, as it turns out, there simply aren't laws on the books that apply.

Although no one has yet been prosecuted in the United States for activity that took place exclusively in a virtual world, crimes unquestionably do occur. Actions that could easily give rise to charges of criminal theft and wire fraud, in particular, are fairly regularly committed in virtual worlds in the United States.

Given the size of the market for virtual property, the ever-growing user base and economy in virtual worlds, and the fact that some frauds are now netting hundreds of thousands of dollars, it is inevitable that virtual crime, particularly theft and financial fraud, will increase dramatically, and equally certain that U.S. prosecutors will eventually bring charges.

One preliminary note is necessary. There have been criminal prosecutions in other countries for activity that took place in games as well as in social virtual worlds—even where the game attempted to avoid real money trading. These prosecutions have generally been limited to activity that took place within the game world but outside the game mechanic (e.g., by using third-party software or stolen passwords to take possessions from users' accounts). These prosecutions make sense, even in light of our earlier discussion of the "magic circle," as only activity that takes place within the confines of the game mechanic would be considered protected. Thus, in games where "thief" is a formal character class[1] and scams are an acknowledged part of game play,[2] there should be no criminal prosecution whether or not the user *ultimately* intended to sell an item or in-world currency that was derived from the action. So the actions of "stealing" by the Ultima Online user via her thief character (where theft is part of the game) or "fraud" by the role-playing scam artist in Eve Online (where scams that "take advantage of your misplaced trust, temporary confusion or ignorance of game rules" are sanctioned by the rules) would not be treated as criminal acts under the "magic circle test" proposed in Chapter 4.

Reluctance of Prosecutors to Bring Charges for Crimes in Virtual Worlds

While undeniably headline-friendly, criminal activity that takes place in virtual worlds has not yet caught the eye of prosecutors in the United States. Aside from a brief visit by the FBI to Second Life's (subsequently banned) virtual casinos, the only U.S. investigations that have occurred in a virtual world have taken place in the fictional television worlds of *CSI: NY* and *Law & Order*.

Other countries have taken a much stronger stance against crimes that take place in virtual worlds and games. South Korea, where gaming is immensely popular, has had its own Cyber Crime Investigation Team since 2003. That year, the team fielded over 40,000 complaints, 22,000 of which were related to activity that took place in virtual worlds and multiuser games.[3] In 2005, Japanese police arrested a Chinese foreign exchange student who allegedly used a third-party program to exploit a bug in the code of a game called Lineage II to steal items from defeated characters.[4] And in late 2007, Dutch police arrested a seventeen-year-old who was accused of stealing nearly $6000 worth of virtual furniture from other users in the teen-oriented virtual world Habbo Hotel.[5]

There are several possible explanations for U.S. prosecutors' deciding not, to date, to pursue criminal activity that takes place in virtual worlds to as great a degree as their overseas counterparts. First, the anti-video-game-violence lobby in the United States has compiled such a lengthy and well-documented track record of defeats in court (to the general applause of First Amendment advocates and game companies) that there may now be a public perception that legislation and prosecution regarding games is generally going to fail and generate a lot of bad press from gamers.[6] It is not at all clear that the game community would *not* support prosecution of certain unsavory elements, however. In the community, there is widespread frustration with some providers' unwillingness to deal with criminal activity[7] in their virtual worlds, and recent civil cases arising from allegations of virtual world intellectual property infringement have generated largely positive reactions from both the user community,[8] the blogosphere,[9] and the mainstream press.[10] Another possible reason is that the United States, to a greater degree than many countries, relies on its civil law system to sort out minor disputes, even if they could be prosecuted as crimes. The United States has more civil lawsuits and lawyers per capita than any country in the world, and more than ninety percent of all civil lawsuits worldwide are filed in the United States.[11] In contrast, criminal prosecutors regularly report that their offices are underfunded, understaffed, and overworked.[12] Also, the lack of a centralized police force in the United States (outside of the FBI, which

■■■■■

Typical Crimes in Virtual Worlds

Money laundering

Fraud

Gambling

Stalking/Harassment

is rather unlikely to concern itself with typically misdemeanor-level petty crime), and the need to enlist local prosecution in the home jurisdiction of the typically pseudonymous defendant, discourages users from pursuing claims. Finally, the lack of prosecution creates a self-fulfilling prophesy where users simply do not report crimes and seek the help of the authorities because they have no reason to believe help would be forthcoming. Once the floodgates are opened by a single prosecution, others will likely follow.

Financial Fraud in Virtual Worlds

Financial fraud, if not rampant, is at least widespread in virtual worlds. A combination of (1) a policy of noninterference in resident disputes from some providers, (2) a lack of real-world consequences, and (3) a permissive attitude of "economic experimentation" inevitably leads to users defrauding each other.

These frauds take a variety of guises, most of which have been seen time and time again in the real world. They are most prominent in free-form virtual worlds that give residents an unfettered ability to build and script objects. In some cases, one suspects that the perpetrators do not understand that their actions are illegal.

Before Linden Lab banned unlicensed "banks" in Second Life in early 2008, simple Ponzi schemes were rampant there. A user would start a "bank," promising an exorbitant interest rate on deposits—some offered as much as 150% a year with interest compounded daily.[13] The scammer would set up an impressive-looking virtual building with marble floors and brass railings and big windows. He would also build an ATM network so that people could make deposits from anywhere on the "grid."

Deposits would start coming in, and the software the scammer was running would increase the apparent balance of each depositor every day by the agreed-upon amount. Investors saw the apparent returns in their accounts, and word of mouth quickly spread, encouraging more and more people to deposit. There was usually some pseudo-legal-sounding verbiage on a secondary web page or in an in-world statement given to users at some point in the process saying that some risk was involved and that there might be a delay in withdrawing funds, but the user was also told that a daily "interest rate" applied, and the user was shown an ever-increasing account balance that comported with that daily interest rate. Particularly when a virtual world was in rapid growth mode (as Second Life was from 2005 to 2007, when it grew from 100,000[14] to nearly 12,000,000[15] registered users), new deposits were more than enough to cover the periodic withdrawals. And some accounts were abandoned or forgotten, further creating a cushion.

Of course, unless the bank's manager was an extraordinarily smart or lucky investor, there was simply no way to consistently make the promised 100% a year on deposits, so the bank inexorably went farther and farther into the red with each passing day. This slide was hidden from users until the inevitable day when withdrawals outpaced deposits, and the scheme crashed. The largest such self-styled "bank" in Second Life, an institution known as "Ginko Financial," collapsed in the summer of 2007. On the day that it first halted withdrawals, it owed depositors over US$750,000. Most of that money was nominal interest (which it probably never had the ability to pay in the first place), but a significant portion of it came from deposits. Several users reported losing more than US$1000 in the collapse, and a few reported losing close to $10,000. The head of Ginko Financial was unapologetic to the end, posting the following statement in the official Second Life forums well after the nature of the scheme had become obvious to all but the most obtuse observers:

People's account balances represent money I owe them, nothing more. The accusations of ponzi and fraud don't even apply. This would be true even if I had taken all the money deposited and burned it in my backyard, which I have not. I did not take deposits under a false pretense. I did not promise to do anything specific with the money, or to keep anyone informed of what I was doing. I did not promise any specific time frame within which the loans would be repaid. I have no obligation to release information on my off-world ventures, period. I have no obligation to release information on my in-world ventures, period. I have no obligation to meet any withdrawal request under any specific time frame, period. When I do any of these things, it's as a convenience to those who choose to do business with me and this convenience needs to be balanced against a variety of things, such as my long term ability to honor this debt and my need for privacy. I regard privacy as important, as such I am unlikely to release information from my off-world ventures. I regard the long term as important, as such I will not be liquidating assets to ensure that a few can withdraw "RIGHT NOW". You don't have to trust or do business with me. I will honor my obligations, but I cannot do miracles. Either be patient or cash out (sell your balance to a third party, buy bonds and the [sic] sell them on the WSE or keep trying the ATM until you get lucky).[16]

As *Virtual Law* went to print, eight months after this post, no one had recovered any significant amount of money, no charges had been filed, and no civil suit had been initiated.

There had been broad speculation that Ginko Financial was a Ponzi scheme ever since it opened its doors, roughly two and a half years before its spectacular collapse. A Ponzi scheme (traditionally prosecuted as either mail or wire fraud, depending on the mechanism used to advertise the offering and transfer funds) is defined, very simply, as a scheme and artifice to defraud that was insolvent from its inception.[17]

By promising a rate of return and representing that return as debt owed to depositors from the beginning (rather than, say, by offering an "investment plan" where the manager would try to hit certain targets, but accounts were only credited after success), most self-styled virtual world banks fit this description of insolvency at inception, and, as such, most are Ponzi schemes. Although "banks" have since been functionally banned in Second Life, financial institutions in the virtual world have shown a remarkable resilience, and new schemes, some legal and some probably not, appear daily. One suspects that the collapse of Ginko, or the inevitable collapse of whatever institution replaces it, or the one after *that*, will eventually attract the attention of a U.S. prosecutor. The amounts of money being lost are not insignificant, and while the alleged crimes took place in a virtual world, the damage done, both to individuals and the grid as a whole, is very real.

Other financial frauds abound in Second Life and, to a lesser degree, in other virtual worlds. Some users offer "empty boxes" for sale, where goods are promised and never delivered.[18] Some users sell nonexistent property.[19] Some users run classic pyramid schemes (one charmingly ironic scam actually involved the sale of tiny pyramids).[20] Some users set up invisible objects in front of legitimate sales displays, so that when other users try to buy goods, they accidentally pay the scammer for a nonexistent product.[21] As noted in Chapter 12, "Securities Law and Virtual Worlds," most, if not all, sales of "stock" in virtual companies in virtual worlds are illegal, and the exchanges themselves are riddled with accusations of insider trading, self-dealing, and fraud. Within months this list will be dated, and there will be a whole new crop of scams. Not a week goes by that there is not a report of in-world activity that would likely be actionable as either theft or fraud, and it is only a matter of time before prosecution becomes commonplace.

The prospect of money laundering via virtual worlds may also provide the first criminal prosecution, as it tends to attract more serious federal enforcement attention in a post-9/11 world. Money laundering in virtual worlds is certainly possible, as one site explains:

> [O]ne can set up an account, send in identification, such as a bogus drivers' license and altered utility receipts, fund the account with the proceeds of crime, and have an associate on the other side of the world withdraw funds as profits, or even as working capital for a criminal enterprise. One

even has the option of withdrawing the funds from a financial institution. This is playing with fire. . . . Is this a great way to move criminal profits? You bet it is.[22]

Virtual Worlds as Terrorism Simulators

One should not give much credibility to breathless reports of terrorists using virtual worlds as training areas, because it makes little technological sense. As discussed elsewhere in *Virtual Law*, there is little expectation of privacy in virtual worlds, a significant data record accompanies every action, and the physics are so poor as to make any simulation a farce. The idea has, however, received mainstream press attention, including an unattributed statement that "experts say, jihadists have also started to create 'residents' in the virtual world of Second Life" from the usually reliable *Economist*.[23] The idea should, at least for the moment, be discounted. There are many reasonable criticisms of virtual worlds from a criminal law perspective; the idea they could be used to train terrorists is not currently one of them.[24] Virtual worlds do, however, represent a large collection of semi-anonymous users, many of whom are young people who feel somewhat disassociated from mainstream society, so recruitment to terrorist organizations is a somewhat (though not much) less unrealistic potential danger.

Stalking in Virtual Worlds

Allegations of "stalking" and "harassment" are relatively common in virtual worlds, and almost universally not actionable. Most are simply escalations of squabbles between residents and do not rise to the level of criminal stalking. Stalking laws vary by state, but almost all require "the intent to place [the subject] in fear of death or serious bodily injury."[25] In most virtual world "stalking" claims, there is no real possibility of any fear of death or serious bodily injury, because the two participants (1) do not actually know each other's identities, and (2) are anywhere from hundreds of miles to half a globe away from each other. Absent the ability to carry out the necessary threat, it seems implausible that these statutes would apply. That said, it is certainly possible that where users do know real-life details about each other, and other circumstances do suggest that a threat is real, these statutes could be applied to virtual world activity.

Gambling in Virtual Worlds

Although legislation is constantly percolating that would change this, running (or at least accepting funds for) an online casino is currently illegal in the United States under 2006's Unlawful Internet Gambling Enforcement Act (UIGEA). Specifically, one is not allowed to "[accept] credit cards, checks, or other bank instruments from American gamblers who illegally bet over the Internet."[26] Most commentators agreed that the Act applies not only to users who actually operated casinos in virtual worlds but also to virtual world providers, at least to the extent that they offered the ability to "cash out" users' virtual world currency as real money.[27] From a user perspective, there is little doubt that the Department of Justice interprets gambling in a virtual world as a criminal act.[28]

Sexual Ageplay and Virtual Child Pornography

A form of role-play called "sexual ageplay" occasionally makes the headlines and has caused Linden Lab to take a rare public stance against certain interactions between residents. The practice involves users (theoretically adults) using childlike avatars to engage in sexual role-play. It has given rise to a number of questions regarding the legality of "virtual child pornography," or computer-generated images that appear to depict children in sexual situations.

The practice first became an issue in early 2007, when a German television news show reported an undercover investigation that included footage, shot in Second Life, of apparent in-world sexual contact between adult avatars and avatars with childlike appearances. The report also claimed that photographs of real-life child sexual abuse had been made available in Second Life. Linden Lab banned the accounts of two users (a twenty-seven-year-old woman and a fifty-four-year-old man) who controlled avatars that appeared to be involved in the simulated sexual acts on the video.[29] After a few somewhat clumsy attempts at articulating a policy (one of which purported to ban "broadly offensive" content without defining that term) and in the face of general protest from much of the grid,[30] Linden Lab released the following fairly clear statement, roughly six months later, effectively banning the practice.[31]

(1) participation by Residents in lewd or sexual acts in which one or more of the avatars appears to represent minors (or the depiction of such acts in images, video, textures, or text) is a violation of the Community Standards;

(2) promoting or catering to such behavior or representations violates our Community Standards. For instance, the placement of avatars appearing to represent minors in proximity to "sex beds" or other sexualized graphics, objects, or scripts, would violate our Community Standards, as would the placement of sexualized "pose balls" or other content in areas depicting playgrounds or children's spaces;

(3) the graphic depiction of children in a sexual or lewd manner violates our Community Standards.[32]

Although many countries, including Germany (where the report aired), criminalize virtual child pornography, it is actually protected on First Amendment grounds in the United States.[33] Linden Lab, of course, is a private company and is free to restrict whatever it wants to. For the most part, the Second Life community appeared to support the restriction, once it was articulated clearly.

Virtual Prostitution

It should come as no surprise to readers that a thriving avatar-based escort industry exists in Second Life.[34] Similar services also exist, albeit in more clandestine form, in most other virtual worlds. Users are, essentially, selling erotic chat and visual stimulation. The erotic chat is typically conducted via text or voice, while scripts that cause the avatars in question to engage in apparent sexual acts provide accompanying visual stimulation.

Like all criminal law matters, the act is legal if no governmental body has made it *illegal*. Because no laws currently on the books specifically prohibit virtual prostitution, the question becomes this: What, if any, current laws might apply to virtual escort services?

Phone sex laws could cover virtual escort work, especially if voice is involved, but most are narrowly focused on telephone communication.[35] Similarly, laws against real-life prostitution are too specific to the act in question, typically referring directly to actual acts of intercourse involving real human bodies.[36] State obscenity laws generally prohibit material that "depicts or describes sexual conduct in a patently offensive way."[37] One could argue that as long as the avatars on-screen are engaged in nothing that is more "patently offensive" than what appears in videos that are sold legally in the relevant jurisdiction, the avatar's "act" isn't prohibited there either. In sum, like most questions of the application of criminal law to virtual world activity, the answer is fairly straightforward. The virtual world's oldest profession appears to be perfectly legal under current law.

Open Questions on Criminal Law and Virtual Worlds

1. Are there some crimes that should never be accepted as "part of the game"? Should some "crimes" be punished only within a game or virtual world?

2. Are virtual worlds sufficiently different from the Internet generally, and from the real world, that existing criminal laws should not apply unless they have been rewritten specifically to cover virtual world behavior?

Notes

1. Ultima Online, Stealing, http://guide.uo.com/skill_33.html (last visited Jan. 7, 2008).

2. Eve Online, Support: Scams and Exploits, http://kb.eve-online.com/Pages/KB/Article.aspx?id=34 (last visited Jan. 7, 2008).

3. Posting of Ian Douglas to Telegraph blog, Virtual Criminals Are Just Human, http://blogs.telegraph.co.uk/technology/iandouglas/nov2007/habbo-thefts.htm (Nov. 15, 2007, 17:34).

4. Posting of John Andersen to Gamespot blog, Lineage II Fraud Results in Arrest http://uk.gamespot.com/news/2005/08/16/news_6131205.html (Aug. 17, 2005, 12:02 AM GMT).

5. *"Virtual Theft" Leads to Arrest*, BBC News, Nov. 14, 2007, *available at* http://news.bbc.co.uk/2/hi/technology/7094764.stm.

6. Kyle Orland, *Oklahoma Violent Game Law Overturned* (Sept. 17, 2007), http://www.joystiq.com/2007/09/17/oklahoma-violent-game-law-overturned/.

7. *Play Money, Real Fraud* (Aug. 9, 2007), http://brokentoys.org/2007/08/09/play-money-real-fraud/.

8. *Big News: New Six-Plaintiff Creator Lawsuit Filed* (Oct. 27, 2007), http://www.sluniverse.com/php/vb/showthread.php?t=2058.

9. *The Landscape May Be Changing . . .* (July 13, 2007), http://www.gridgrind.com/?p=141.

10. Emil Steiner, *Second Life Players Bring Virtual Reality to Court* (Oct. 29, 2007), http://blog.washingtonpost.com/offbeat/2007/10/second_life_players_bring_virt.html.

11. *Asset Protection Group News—Bill Reed Starts New Syndicated Column*, http://netmillionaire.blogmatrix.com/:entry:netmillionaire-2006-02-28-0000/ (last visited Jan. 7, 2008).

12. Sarena Straus, On Being a Prosecutor, http://sarenastraus.blogspot.com/2007/08/on-being-prosecutor-while-back-i-posted.html (Aug. 15, 2007).

13. *Play Money, Real Fraud, supra* note 7.

14. *Wooot! 100K Dormant Alts*, SECOND LIFE HERALD, http://www.secondlifeherald.com/slh/2005/12/wooot_100k_dorm.html (Dec. 22, 2005).

15. http://secondlife.com/whatis/economy_stats.php.

16. Forum Post: Ginko Has Not Allowed Withdraws for Over a Day Now. . . ., http://forums.secondlife.com/showthread.php?p=1612530 (Aug. 2, 2007; login required).

17. *See* Merrill v. Abbott, 77 B.R. 843, 871 (D. Utah 1987); *In re* Taubman, 160 B.R. 964, 978 (Bankr. S.D. Ohio 1993); Martino v. Edison Worldwide Capital, 189 B.R. 425, 441 (Bankr. N.D. Ill. 1995); Emerson v. Maples, 161 B.R. 644, 650 (Bankr. W.D. Tenn. 1993); and Dicello v. Jenkins, 160 B.R. 1, 12 n.15 (Bankr. D.C. 1993).

18. Therese Carfagno, *Alleged Scammer Escapes After Selling Empty Boxes of Celebrity Skins* (May 5, 2007), http://www.slnn.com/article/skinscam/.

19. Myst Panther, *Scam Alert: New Pyramid Scam (Literally!)* (Nov. 23, 2006), http://slcaveatemptor.blogspot.com/2006/11/scam-alert-new-pyramid-scam-literally_23.html.

20. Pixeleen Mistral, *Island Land Scamming, Anyone?*, SECOND LIFE HERALD, Feb. 18, 2007, http://www.secondlifeherald.com/slh/2007/02/island_land_sca.html.

21. Myst Panther, *Scam Alert: Invisible Prim over Vendor (Now with Fastpay!)* (June 20, 2007), http://slcaveatemptor.blogspot.com/2006/06/scam-alert-invisible-prim-over-vendor.html.

22. Kenneth Rijock, *Virtual Money Laundering Now Available on the World Wide Web* (Jan. 2, 2007), http://www.world-check.com/articles/2007/01/02/virtual-money-laundering-now-available-world-wide-/.

23. *A World Wide Web of Terror,* Economist, July 12, 2007, *available at* http://www.economist.com/world/displaystory.cfm?story_id=9472498.

24. Joey Seiler, *Economist Claims Terrorists in Second Life* (July 12, 2007), http://www.virtualworldsnews.com/2007/07/economist-claim.html.

25. *Stalking Laws by State,* http://members.aol.com/lrfuzz1/StalkingLaws/StateLaws.html (last visited Jan. 7, 2008).

26. Anita Ramasastry, *Could Second Life Be in Serious Trouble? The Risk of Real-Life Legal Consequences for Hosting Virtual Gambling* (Apr. 11, 2007), http://writ.lp.findlaw.com/ramasastry/20070411.html.

27. *Id.; see also* Christine Hurt, *From Virtual Tax to Virtual Gambling* (Apr. 9, 2007), http://www.theconglomerate.org/2007/04/from_virtual_ta.html.

28. Hurt, *id.*

29. Posting of Robin Linden to Second Life blog, Accusations Regarding Child Pornography in Second Life, http://blog.secondlife.com/2007/05/09/accusations-regarding-child-pornography-in-second-life/ (May 9, 2007, 22:32 PST).

30. Posting of Daniel Linden to Second Life blog, Keeping Second Life Safe, Together, http://blog.secondlife.com/2007/05/31/keeping-second-lifesafe-together/ (May 31, 2007, 18:00 PST).

31. Posting of Ken D. Linden to Second Life blog, Clarification of Policy Disallowing "Ageplay," http://blog.secondlife.com/2007/11/13/clarification-of-policy-disallowing-ageplay/ (Nov. 13, 2007, 17:10 PST).

32. *Id.*

33. Ashcroft v. Free Speech Coalition, 535 U.S. 234 (2002).

34. Mitch Wagner, *Sex in Second Life* (May 26, 2007), http://www.informationweek.com/news/showArticle.jhtml?articleID=199701944.

35. 47 U.S.C. 223.

36. Idaho Statutes 18-5613; Nebraska Statutes 28-317; Kansas Statutes 21-3512.

37. Mary Minow, Features—Constitutional, Federal and State Legal Definitions of Child Pornography, Obscenity and "Harmful to Minors" of Interest to California Libraries (Sept. 30, 2002), http://www.llrx.com/features/obscenitylaws.htm.

Privacy Law and Virtual Worlds

11

Justice Louis Brandeis, in *Olmstead v. United States*, famously wrote (in dissent) of "the right to be left alone—the most comprehensive of rights, and the right most valued by a free people."[1] Justice Brandeis's words, which ring true to many attorneys and privacy advocates, run nearly perpendicular to the stated goal of most virtual worlds, which is emphatically to bring people together. Virtual worlds thrive, and thus make money, when fertilized with a healthy dose of social interaction. That social interaction leads, inevitably, to the creation of a gold mine of personal data. The data generated by interactions in virtual worlds can appear in support of hidden business models, as evidence in lawsuits, as responses to government requests, and (in the hands of unscrupulous users) in crimes ranging from blackmail to identity theft.

As a result, serious privacy law concerns are implicated by the data virtual world providers intentionally and inadvertently accumulate on a daily basis that go well beyond the concerns raised even by data collected on most websites. The sheer volume of information that is available to virtual world providers, their business partners, other users, and ultimately the government may surprise many readers and could easily, in the long run, lead to specialized privacy laws explicitly dealing with virtual worlds, similar to the privacy laws that target the health care industry (e.g., HIPAA). A comprehensive overview of privacy law is well beyond the scope of this book, but readers contemplating these questions are advised to keep in mind at minimum the existence of Fourth Amendment protections against unreasonable search and seizure, various state laws governing online privacy and data storage, and the body of law governing the protection of data collected from minors (to the degree that the question may arise in the context of virtual worlds for children).

Threats to Privacy in Virtual Worlds

One commentator, Tal Zarsky, has written at some length about the potential privacy implications of virtual worlds and has graciously extended permission to reprint excerpts from his article, *Privacy and Data Collection in Virtual Worlds*.[2] Zarsky divides the concerns into three major areas: threats to privacy by other users, threats to privacy by the government, and threats to privacy by the provider.[3] Regarding threats from the government, Zarsky writes:

> The government's collection and use of personal information in virtual worlds, and its attempts to connect virtual and physical identities create significant privacy concerns. Government agents may gather information by maintaining a presence in a virtual world—for example, by posing as other players. The government could analyze this information, and, if it generates suspicion, try to deduce the identity of the offline persona that stands behind the online avatar from the data it gathered.
>
> Avatars/persons subjected to this form of government surveillance can rarely argue that their privacy has been breached according to today's law, because all the information the government collects and uses has been viewed and gathered in an open, public forum where there is little expectation of privacy. However, virtual worlds offer a new

twist. Unlike the real world, where manpower constraints limit the government's ability to engage in ongoing undercover activities and surveillance, virtual worlds might provide almost limitless opportunities for the employment of "bots"—automated programs that can interact in virtual settings—while "eavesdropping" or soliciting information that the government finds helpful. Should these practices of automated intelligence gathering become commonplace, legislators and courts might reconsider the legality of these forms of data collection in virtual worlds.[4]

Regarding threats from other users, Zarsky notes:

> Actions by other game users also raise special privacy concerns. Other players in virtual worlds may learn of the real-world identity of a virtual persona from data they gather while playing. They might publicize or threaten to publicize this information in order to harm or gain advantage over a player.[5]

Finally, regarding threats from providers, which may have access to greater stores of information than even they realize, Zarsky comments:

> [V]irtual worlds may create a special form of privacy concerns stemming from the collection and use of personal information exclusively within virtual worlds themselves. The game controller can collect information about a specific player and, even without linking it back to the physical user, use it to the player's detriment. This results from the fact that game controllers have the ability to collect vast amounts of interesting data about every user, such as data regarding the times of the day the user plays; the parts of the virtual world the user visits and the goods he or she buys, exchanges and consumes; the other avatars he or she chooses to interact with, and the times and duration of these interactions.[6]

Zarsky may even be understating the amount and variety of data collected by virtual world providers and their ability to use it. For example, Second Life provider Linden Lab requires that users grant Linden Lab "a royalty-free, worldwide, fully paid-up, perpetual, irrevocable, non-exclusive, sublicensable right and license to exercise the copyright, publicity, and database rights you have in your account information, including any data or other information generated by your account activity, in any media now known or not currently known" in accordance with Linden Lab's privacy policy. The referenced privacy policy states that "Linden Lab does not disclose personal information you provide it to any third parties without your permission."[7] In turn, "personal information" is defined as "any information that may be used to identify an individual, including, but not limited to, a first and last name, home or other physical address, an email address, phone number or other contact information, whether at work or at home."

The result is that Linden Lab receives a broad license to the database rights, right of publicity, and copyright of all *nonpersonal* information—that is, anything that does not identify your real-life information. To the extent that a company wishes to market directly to your avatar, it appears that the policy does not restrict Linden Lab from providing any information to anyone they choose, so long as no "personal information" is given—this includes information regarding items purchased, social interactions, the amount of money in users' accounts, and more.

Technological Tools and Invasions of Privacy

Consider the expectation of privacy that most human beings have in their day-to-day lives. If someone wants privacy, he or she generally need take no greater precaution than closing the curtains to his or her home. Not so in virtual worlds. In many virtual worlds, it is not even possible to conceal the contents of one's home from other users, let alone from the provider. Voyeurs find Second Life's freely movable camera particularly useful, as it allows them to leave their avatars in one place, but move their camera great distances and zoom in on other users from afar. With "voice" tied to camera focus in some virtual worlds, users can eavesdrop on spoken communication between other avatars at great distance with relative ease.

Moving beyond the *intended* uses of the software, users who are not aware of the technical possibilities of virtual worlds would be surprised to learn what data collection tools their fellow users have created and regularly deploy in these spaces. This is, of course, a much greater problem in free-form virtual worlds that allow unfettered scripting. In Second Life, for example, users can create and program tools limited only by their imagination. Dozens of companies sell "chat monitors" that remotely monitor and record conversations. Some are placed and left in locations that the user wants to monitor, and others can be attached to avatars or hidden in clothing and body parts that users purchase for their avatars. Although the practice is against Linden Lab's Terms of Service, the devices are sufficiently popular that it seems unlikely that the provision is regularly enforced; searching for "chat spy" typically generates hundreds of hits on these products, and they regularly appear in the most popular product lists at one well-known shopping website.[8]

There are no easy answers to the questions raised here, but it is worth noting that as virtual worlds become more complex, and as user-programmed content becomes the norm rather than the exception, lawmakers may wish to consider stronger privacy protection legislation than currently exists. Virtual worlds represent a completely new set of privacy challenges. They combine four elements in a brand new, and potentially dangerous, form: (1) indefinite data storage, (2) widespread availability of invasive technology, (3) widespread pseudonymity, and (4) widespread availability of forums for social experimentation. Together, these elements will lead to users disclosing far more data about themselves than they intended. This, in turn, will lead to other users, providers, and law enforcement officers easily capturing that data.

Open Questions on Privacy Law and Virtual Worlds

1. Is legislation needed to address privacy concerns in virtual worlds?

2. What technological solutions might help alleviate privacy concerns in virtual worlds?

Notes

1. Olmstead v. United States, 277 U.S. 438 (1928).

2. Tal Zarsky, *Privacy and Data Collection in Virtual Worlds,* in STATE OF PLAY—LAW, GAMES AND VIRTUAL WORLDS (Jack M. Balkin & Beth Simone Noveck eds., 2006), *available at* http://ssrn.com/abstract=963889.

3. *Id.* at 2.

4. *Id.* at 3.

5. *Id.* at 4.

6. *Id.* at 5.

7. Linden Lab Privacy Policy, http://secondlife.com/corporate/privacy .php (last visited Jan. 7, 2008).

8. *See* SLExchange, http://www.slexchange.com/ (last visited Jan. 7, 2008).

Securities Law and Virtual Worlds **12**

One might imagine that of all areas of law unlikely to have a virtual world component, securities law would top the list. However, the introduction of real cash economies into games and social virtual worlds, the encouragement some virtual world providers give users to treat the worlds as economic playgrounds, and the pseudonymous nature of these spaces combine to create an almost unavoidable collision between securities regulation and virtual worlds.

Given the boldness with which virtual world "markets" are managed and promoted, and the inevitable ethical lapses that accompany a complete lack of oversight, it is only a matter of time before the SEC (Securities and Exchange Commission) takes action against a virtual world user for activities that violate U.S. securities regulations.

Virtual World Market Activity

Readers who are not familiar with the extent of the financial sector that is developing in virtual worlds will be surprised at its complexity and maturity. Most of this activity is currently focused on Second Life, which gives users nearly unfettered object and script creation rights, allowing users to build literally anything. Additionally, Second Life's provider, Linden Lab, encourages economic experimentation and entrepreneurship (e.g., "Make real money in a virtual world. That's right, **real money** . . . businesses succeed by the ingenuity, artistic ability, entrepreneurial acumen, and good reputation of their owners.").[1] A number of users have elected to exercise their "ingenuity" and "entrepreneurial acumen" by building full-scale stock exchanges, replicating every key aspect of a real-life stock exchange—except compliance with securities laws.

These exchanges offer virtual business owners the ability to sell shares in their companies, and offer all other users the ability to buy and trade these shares. One advertises itself as follows: "Welcome to the World Stock Exchange, a fictional securities exchange with a fully integrated banking system. The WSE enables virtual companies to raise capital while providing a chance for investors to build their wealth using the fictional Linden Dollar and World Internet Currency that can be sold for real US Dollars."[2]

There are typically at least two or three stock exchanges operating in Second Life, which occasionally buy each other, merge, split, and are renamed. They are housed in massive, imposing virtual buildings with shiny marble floors. Avatars dressed as "security guards" stand around the lobby. Besides their in-world presences, some exchanges run websites where users can manage their accounts and buy and sell shares in Second Life companies without even logging in to Second Life.

All the stock exchanges offer a disclaimer regarding the lack of "reality" in what they are doing. A sidebar on the World Stock Exchange's website contains a link to "Policies," where readers learn that in order to use World Stock Exchange services, they "acknowledge that all 'Fictional' services provided by Hope Capital on the World Stock Exchange are an imaginative creation in a simulated gaming environment that are without basis in reality and hold no legal monetary or asset value."[3] On the other hand, the front page, as noted, states that users can "build their wealth using the fictional Linden Dollar and World Internet Currency that can be sold for real US Dollars."[4] A ticker on the front page indicates that at least US$300,000 per year changes hands in "Lindens" via the World Stock Exchange.

Do Real-World Securities Laws Apply to In-World Activity?

The threshold question here is whether real-world securities laws apply to in-world activity. Securities law is rather inclusive in its definition.

> The term "security" means any note, stock, treasury stock, security future, bond, debenture, evidence of indebtedness, certificate of interest or participation in any profit-sharing agreement, collateral-trust certificate, preorganization certificate or subscription, transferable share, investment contract, voting-trust certificate, certificate of deposit for a security, fractional undivided interest in oil, gas, or other mineral rights, any put, call, straddle, option, or privilege on any security, certificate of deposit, or group or index of securities (including any interest therein or based on the value thereof), or any put, call, straddle, option, or privilege entered into on a national securities exchange relating to foreign currency, or, in general, any interest or instrument commonly known as a "security", or any certificate of interest or participation in, temporary or interim certificate for, receipt for, guarantee of, or warrant or right to subscribe to or purchase, any of the foregoing.[5]

One commentator, Caroline Bradley, notes that "[t]hese definitions include both specific terms, and terms which are more general. It should not be possible to avoid the application of the statutes by calling something which is really a security by a different name. So, for example, calling something which is really a security a 'game token' would not exclude the application of the statutes."[6] In the case of most of the stock exchanges in virtual worlds, there is no question that the products offered are referred to as "securities." The World Stock Exchange advertises quite openly that it "offers a market for trading in securities."[7]

The current test for whether an offering is a "security" comes from the Supreme Court's decision in *SEC v. Howey*.[8] The *Howey* test finds that a security is sold when "[t]he investors provide the capital and share in the earnings and profits [and] the promoters manage, control and operate the enterprise . . . regardless of the legal terminology in which such contracts are clothed."[9] One court explained:

> Judicial efforts to delineate what is—and what is not—an investment contract are grounded in the seminal case of *SEC v. W. J. Howey Co.*, 328 U.S. 293 (1946). The *Howey* Court established a tripartite test to determine whether a particular financial instrument constitutes an investment contract (and, hence, a security). This test has proven durable. Under it, an investment contract comprises (1) the investment of money (2) in a common enterprise (3) with an expectation of profits to be derived solely from the efforts of the promoter or a third party. Id. at 298-99. This formulation must be applied in light of the economic realities of the transaction. *United Hous. Found., Inc. v. Forman*, 421 U.S. 837, 851-52 (1975); *Tcherepnin v. Knight*, 389 U.S. 332, 336 (1967); *Futura Dev. Corp. v. Centex Corp.*, 761 F.2d 33, 39 (1st Cir. 1985). In other words, substance governs form, and the substance of an investment contract is a security-like interest in a "common enterprise" that, through the efforts of the promoter or others, is expected to generate profits for the security holder, either for direct distribution or as an increase in the value of the investment.[10]

As such, the *Howey* test is a broad test and has captured as "securities" a number of seemingly nonobvious candidates, including a "sale of citrus groves, in conjunction with [a] service contract, [the] purchase of life partnership in [an] evangelical community, [a] cattle-feeding and consulting agreement, [and a] chinchilla breeding and resale arrangement."[11]

Finding that securities offered in-world for Lindens are "securities" under the *Howey* test depends on finding that Lindens have value, but it seems rather difficult to argue otherwise. Securities law refers to sales of securities "for value," which implies an exchange for anything that can be readily converted to cash, including Lindens.

Bradley notes that, at bottom, it comes down to "whether virtual world investments are really investments for the purposes of the *Howey* test or whether the fact that they are made in the course of a game excludes them automatically from being treated as investment contracts."[12] In other words, the question is the same as that which arises in most issues in virtual law: At what point does "magic circle" protection exempt in-world activity from real-life legal consequences?

In relation to securities law and the magic circle, a 2001 First Circuit ruling in the case of *SEC v. SG Ltd.* is instructive. The *SG Ltd.* case predates the popularity of virtual worlds but also involved an online investment "game," and the central defense was precisely that—the securities offering was "just a game." The court explained:

> The underlying litigation was spawned by SG's operation of a "StockGeneration" website offering on-line denizens an opportunity to purchase shares in eleven different "virtual companies" listed on the website's "virtual stock exchange." SG arbitrarily set the purchase and sale prices of each of these imaginary companies in biweekly "rounds," and guaranteed that investors could buy or sell any quantity of shares at posted prices. SG placed no upper limit on the amount of funds that an investor could squirrel away in its virtual offerings.[13]

SG argued that "the virtual shares were part of a fantasy investment game created for the personal entertainment of Internet users, and therefore, that those shares do not implicate the federal securities laws."[14]

The First Circuit, reversing a district court ruling, held that although the offering was styled as a game, "[g]iving due weight to the economic realities of the situation, . . . the SEC has alleged a set of facts which, if proven, satisfy the three-part *Howey* test and support its assertion that the opportunity to invest in the shares of the privileged company, described on SG's website, constituted an invitation to enter into an investment contract within the jurisdictional reach of the federal securities laws."[15]

The court refused to recognize a "dichotomy between business dealings, on the one hand, and games, on the other hand, as a failsafe way for determining whether a particular financial arrangement should (or should not) be characterized as an investment contract."[16] Once the *Howey* test is satisfied, the court found, "it is immaterial whether the enterprise is speculative or nonspeculative or whether there is a sale of property with or without intrinsic value [and] it is equally immaterial whether the promoter depicts the enterprise as a serious commercial venture or dubs it a game."[17] Applying this principle to the stock exchanges in virtual worlds where there is a ready market for the "fictional currency" that is offered appears to place them squarely in the coverage of the *Howey* test and thus subject to SEC enforcement.

It is notable that the currently unregulated stock exchanges in Second Life are, predictably, fraught with complaints of fraud and insider dealing. It must be stressed that it is not clear if any of these allegations is true—another hallmark of the stock exchanges in Second Life is that their owners accuse each other of outlandish crimes with some regularity. One stock exchange manager was accused of running several alternate accounts, one of which allegedly absconded with over US$20,000 shortly before the user supposedly reappeared and opened a new stock exchange with a different name.[18] One stock exchange created a special fund for "account holders who have lost their virtual shares or bonds in delisted companies."[19] According to the supplied list, eighteen companies had been delisted "due to fraud or bankruptcy," against only forty-eight that were then still active.[20] Allegations of insider dealing are so common as to be almost unremarkable,[21] and attempts to curb insider dealing are met by fierce internal resistance.[22] In sum, even if the stock exchanges were somehow *not* subject to securities law, which seems doubtful, there are serious criminal law implications to much of the activity that takes place there.

Open Questions on Securities Law and Virtual Worlds

1. To what degree do disclaimers stating that stock exchanges are merely games matter in light of the reality that the currency traded is freely exchangeable for real money?

2. What technological solutions might help the virtual world stock exchanges establish greater credibility?

3. To what degree does listing a virtual company in a potentially prohibited public offering on a virtual stock exchange forever taint the company and make real-life investment ultimately less likely?

Notes

1. Second Life, The Marketplace, http://secondlife.com/whatis/market place.php (last visited Jan. 5, 2008).

2. World Stock Exchange, http://www.wselive.com/ (last visited Jan. 7, 2008).

3. World Stock Exchange Terms of Service, http://www.wselive.com/info/tos (last visited Jan. 7, 2008).

4. World Stock Exchange, *supra* note 2.

5. 15 U.S.C. § 77b(a)(1).

6. Caroline M. Bradley, *Gaming the System: Virtual Worlds and the Securities Markets* (Oct. 2007), University of Miami Legal Studies Research Paper No. 2007-10 at 23, http://ssrn.com/abstract=1022441.

7. WSE Listing Rules, http://www.wselive.com/info/rules (last visited Jan. 7, 2008).

8. SEC v. W.J. Howey Co., 328 U.S. 293, 298 (1946).

9. Bradley, *supra* note 6.

10. Investment Contracts, SEC v. SG Ltd., 265 F.3d 42 (1st Cir. 2001).

11. *Id.*

12. Bradley, *supra* note 6 at 26.

13. Background, *SEC v. SG Ltd.*, 265 F.3d 42.

14. Introduction, *SEC v. SG Ltd.*, 265 F.3d 42.

15. Conclusion, *SEC v. SG Ltd.*, 265 F.3d 42.

16. The District Court's Rationale, *SEC v. SG Ltd.*, 265 F.3d 42.

17. *Id.*

18. Marvel Ousley, *Scam Victim Believes Suspected Stock Exchange Thief Has Re-emerged with Alt* (June 1, 2007), http://www.slnn.com/article/stock-exchange-identity/.

19. LukeConnell Vandeverre, *Hope Capital Report* (Oct. 17, 2007), https://www.wselive.com/research/announcement_detail/2712.

20. *Id.*

21. Taran Rampersad, a/k/a/ Nobody Fugazi, *Peering into the Depths of Ginko Financial (Updated)*, http://www.your2ndplace.com/node/354 (Aug. 7, 2007).

22. Taran Rampersad, a/k/a/ Nobody Fugazi, *International Stock Exchange Policy to Avoid Insider Trading Meets Resistance*, http://www.your2ndplace.com/node/436 (Aug. 20, 2007).

Tax Law and Virtual Worlds 13

Although it is widely acknowledged that profits made by selling digital items or services in a virtual world are taxable as income, several key questions are very much unsettled. Moreover, tax agencies, both in the United States and internationally, have not historically pursued collection of these taxes or set up enforcement and reporting mechanisms. That appears likely to change, and users of virtual worlds who make money in these spaces need to be aware of the tax implications of their activities.

What Is Virtual Currency?

Most virtual worlds and games allow users to keep track of their "wealth" using some form of fictional currency. World of Warcraft, as well as many other medieval and fantasy-themed worlds and games, uses "gold" as a measure of wealth. Sci-fi themed Entropia Universe uses PEDs ("Project Entropia Dollars"). Free-form virtual worlds use currency as well, of course;

Second Life residents use "Lindens" and There.com residents use "Therebucks." Even virtual worlds and games for children use currency; kids checking in to Habbo Hotel buy and spend "Habbo Coins," and Barbie Girls use "B Bucks."

In game-based virtual worlds, the game mechanic controls how characters accumulate wealth. There are generally three forms of wealth creation in game-based virtual worlds: gathering, creation, and arbitrage. First, "gathering" involves currency accumulation, either through combat (e.g., slaying a monster typically provides the player with a reward of either virtual currency or items that are readily convertible to virtual currency via a sale to another player or a non-player character) or collection (e.g., finding a particularly rare herb, which can also be sold). The frequency of occurrence and location of items is tightly controlled by the game creators. Second, consider "creation." Creation does not involve making new items that had not yet been contemplated by the designers, but, rather, involves combining static elements of the world using a recipe to make an item that has greater value than the parts do individually (e.g., two iron bars, a piece of jade, and a bronze jewelry setting can be combined by certain skilled characters in World of Warcraft to make a "Heavy Jade Ring," which provides the wearer with increases in certain skills and thus has greater value than the "ingredients" do individually).[1] Third, "arbitrage" is typically built into most game worlds as well, with one non-player character (NPC) selling virtual items for less than another is paying for them. To avoid players easily amassing huge amounts of wealth via these planned market imperfections, characters' ability to conduct such trades is typically limited by time or in-world geography.

Another less obvious method of virtual wealth creation is inherent in the game characters themselves. As characters in most games spend time accomplishing game tasks, they become more powerful. This power is typically expressed as the character's "level." Some games express this level as a single number, others track the level of dozens of different skills, but the mechanic is fundamentally the same: as a player's character repeats an action, his or her odds of success at that action increase. In addition, the character may have access to better rewards when accomplishing tasks within his or her skill set at higher levels.

For example, in Ultima Online, a character who is just beginning as a miner can only successfully mine relatively low-valued iron ore and cannot smelt the ore into more valuable (and more transportable) ingots. After mining for a while, the character will gain the ability to mine copper ore, bronze ore, and, eventually, more exotic metals, and his or her ability to convert the mined ore into more valuable ingots will increase as well.[2] This mechanic is true for every skill from swordsmanship (a character's ability to hit a target increases, making it possible to fight stronger enemies)[3] to magic use (a character with higher-level skills can cast more destructive spells, with a greater chance of success)[4] to fishing (higher-level characters catch more fish and treasure maps, and fewer boots).[5] In essence, skill increases make accumulation of more valuable in-world items more likely, so characters which are more advanced have greater potential for generating in-world wealth than characters which are less advanced.

In these game-based worlds, currency and virtual objects are typically meant to be traded only within the game, and sale of these assets for real-world cash, known as "real money trading" (RMT), is generally prohibited. In addition, accounts are not meant to be sold by one player to another. Most game-based worlds' Terms of Service and End User License Agreements explicitly do not allow players to buy or sell currency, items, or accounts for real money. So in these worlds, in theory, accomplishing game tasks (e.g., killing a monster, catching a fish, or mining some rare metal) should produce a reward (e.g., a powerful virtual sword, some gold, or an increase in your character's ability to succeed at game goals) that has no external value in the real world. It seems intuitive that when a player is enriched entirely within a game world, the increase in character strength and accumulation of gold and valuable weaponry should not be taxable, even though it does represent an investment of time, and time clearly has a certain amount of "value" to the player. The wealth, so long as it remains within the magic circle of the game world, is pretend wealth. It is not any different than the accumulation of pretend wealth while playing Monopoly in one's home with one's friends.

However, unlike Monopoly dollars, currency, virtual goods, and skill increases in game worlds *do* have value outside the game world, precisely because they do represent an investment of time, or, from another perspective, an option not to invest a certain amount of time. Some players want to be able to access higher-level content without spending the time necessary to increase their character's skills and accumulate the necessary equipment. Other players put a great deal of social emphasis on having a high-level character and wish to bypass the "newbie" stage for social reasons. Whatever the reasoning behind players' desires, at bottom, when something is scarce, it becomes valuable. Because higher-level characters using elite equipment are far scarcer than lower-level ones using entry-level equipment, players, unsurprisingly, regularly breach the provision of their agreement with the game company that prohibits buying or selling of virtual items or accounts.

The primary argument for prohibiting these transactions in game worlds is that allowing RMT undermines the game mythology (and thus the shared "common good" of the play experience) by devaluing the efforts of players who achieve game goals using conventional in-game mechanisms.[6] In essence, if anyone can simply buy, with real-world money, all the advantages that game players choose to spend months of time earning via the game mechanic, then the rewards (more powerful characters, weapons, and tools; access to additional content; and in-world social recognition of success) are cheapened. This makes them less satisfying for players to obtain and, arguably, makes the game less likely to succeed in the marketplace.

That does not, of course, prevent a great number of people from making a lot of money selling currency, items, and accounts. The only thing prohibiting the sale of virtual goods from games and virtual worlds is a click-through agreement between the player and the game company—the practice is, of course, not prohibited by law. And however much game companies may express a desire to prohibit RMT, prohibitions in End User License Agreements and Terms of Service are simply not effective. To avoid alienating customers, the only penalty most companies are willing to employ is banishment of a seller's account. Except in extreme cases (such as one well-publicized case where a particularly powerful World of Warcraft account sold for almost $10,000 and was promptly banned),[7] buyers generally suffer no penalty at all. As a result, an arms race has developed, with "gold farmers" employing increasingly sophisticated methods to avoid detection, and game companies employing ever more complex and expensive methods of tracing and banning them.

Until eBay in early 2007 banned auctions for virtual goods except where specifically allowed by game companies, it was the forum of choice for most gold, item, and account sellers.[8] Most of the activity has since moved to private auction websites, but it does not appear to have diminished—the specific five-word phrase "buy world of warcraft gold" recently generated over 500,000 individual hits on Google. In other, typically free-form virtual worlds (and a few games), however, a market for currency and items is encouraged and, in some cases, actively managed by the virtual world provider.

Key differences between wealth generation in free-form social virtual worlds and wealth generation in game-based virtual worlds can be deduced from the very nature of free-form virtual worlds. The most important distinction, from a wealth creation perspective, is that free-form virtual worlds lack goals, levels, and points. In free-form virtual worlds there is no wealth accumulation from slaying monsters, collecting ingots, or conducting arbitrage between two non-player characters. Moreover there is no particular advantage (aside from a certain amount of social credibility that comes from having an older account) to having an avatar with "experience" in these worlds rather than a brand-new avatar. All avatars have the same abilities (to walk around, talk to each other, etc.), and these abilities do not "improve" with repetition.

Instead, users increase their wealth in free-form virtual worlds in an almost infinite number of ways, most of which have real-world analogs. Some users employ the in-world tools to create and sell items to increase their wealth. These include complex scripted objects that control avatar animation, designs for homes, clothing for avatars, body parts, avatar shapes, and nearly anything else you can imagine. Other users sell services, including staffing virtual offices, stores, and clubs, organizing events, performing, consulting, and even doing legal work. Still others speculate on virtual land, invest in virtual businesses, and operate financial markets, banks, and in-world investment funds. A few, inevitably, try to make a living by scamming other users out of their possessions and assets. In short, accumulation of wealth in a free-form virtual world looks a lot like accumulation of wealth in the real world.

Unlike most games (where RMT is typically prohibited), many free-form virtual worlds emphasize that they have some form of a real cash economy. Indeed, the draw of free-form virtual worlds is largely the existence of real cash economies. As discussed elsewhere, everything from T-shirts for your avatar to castles in the sky to personal services can be purchased using Lindens in Second Life. There.com is more restrictive in terms of what residents can create, but a wide range of products is available nonetheless. Most people who provide goods and services in virtual worlds do so with an eye on eventual withdrawal of their profit as real-world money. In fact, it is hard to imagine a free-form virtual world that depended entirely on the creation of user-created content succeeding if it prohibited the sale of user-created content for real money.

Advertising regarding the Second Life marketplace makes it very clear to potential users that they can sell their content. "Make real money in a virtual world," Linden Lab advertises. "That's right, **real money.**"[10] The site explains further: "Millions of Linden Dollars change hands every month for the goods and services Residents create and provide. This unit-of-trade may then be bought and sold on LindeX (Second Life's official Linden Dollar exchange), or other unaffiliated third party sites for real currency."[11]

Linden Lab is careful not to guarantee the right to withdraw your "real money" from Linden Lab itself (the Second Life Terms of Service state, "Second Life 'currency' is a limited license right available for purchase or free distribution at Linden Lab's discretion, and is not redeemable for monetary value from Linden Lab"),[12] but the fact remains that most players do view Lindens as freely interchangeable with real-world currency.

It is undeniable that a huge market exists for virtual goods. In the popular free-form virtual world of Second Life, more than $1.3 million worth of virtual currency changes hands every day in-world for goods and services. And though nominally prohibited, mechanisms for buying and selling virtual goods and currency with real-world cash exist for every popular game world. One estimate is that in 2007, approximately $1.8 billion changed hands for virtual goods.[13] IGE, a company that sells virtual goods, predicts that the market could reach $7 billion by 2009.[14]

■■■■■

Second Life's "Real-Life" Jobs[9]

Second Life advertises: "By way of example, here are just a few in-world business occupations which Residents founded and currently run, and make part or all of their real life living from."

- party and wedding planner
- pet manufacturer
- tattooist
- nightclub owner
- automotive manufacturer
- fashion designer
- aerospace engineer
- custom avatar designer
- jewelry maker
- architect
- XML coder
- freelance scripter
- game developer
- fine artist
- machinima set designer
- tour guide
- dancer
- musician
- custom animation creator
- theme park developer
- real estate speculator
- vacation resort owner
- advertiser
- bodyguard
- magazine [sic]
- publisher
- private detective
- writer
- gamer
- landscaper
- publicist
- special effects designer
- gunsmith
- hug maker

Tax Law Basics

All tax analysis starts with *Comm'r v. Glenshaw Glass Co.*[15] Under *Glenshaw Glass*, income is "any undeniable accession to wealth, which is clearly realized by the taxpayer, over which the taxpayer has complete dominion."[16] The key terms from the decision are "accession to wealth," "clearly realized," and "complete dominion." In addition, the concept of "basis" must be understood.

An "accession to wealth" need not be in the form of money; trade can suffice. For example, if an artist trades ten hours of design work for a used car, the car is an accession to wealth for the artist. The car is considered income, and its value for tax purposes is taken as its "fair market value" at the time of transfer. The key here is that any item to be reported as income must *have* a "fair market value" in the first place in order to require that it be reported.[17] Where there is no ascertainable market value for an apparent enrichment (e.g., the joyful experience of winning $1500 in Monopoly money from a friend who lands on Park Place with a hotel), there is no reportable income, even though one's efforts (playing Monopoly skillfully) yielded a return in happiness that could, arguably, be considered an accession to wealth.

The second *Glenshaw Glass* requirement, "realization," is recognized as an administrative concept as well.[18] Realization for services rendered (e.g., labor) occurs when the service is paid for (as opposed to when the work is done).[19] Realization of income from property (here, anything owned) occurs in two ways. One is income generated while the property is owned (e.g., rental fees, dividends from stock shares), which is "realized" when it is paid. The other is through the sale of the property, which is "realized" when the property is exchanged either for cash or for "property differing materially either in kind or extent."[20]

"Dominion," the third *Glenshaw Glass* requirement, is also based on practical considerations. Dominion occurs when a person asserts a legal right to control an item of income. In the context of a sale of an item, it occurs when the seller receives payment and claims the legal right to dispose of the payment as he or she sees fit. One point worth noting in this context is that income gained from illegal activities is considered income whether the taxpayer's title to it is valid or not.[21]

Next, it is important to understand the concept of "basis." A taxpayer's "basis" is subtracted from the "amount realized" to arrive at an amount of "gross income." Brushing all other complexities aside, that principle simply means that if a taxpayer spends $1500 on an item that she then sells for $2000, she gets to subtract $1500 (her "basis") from the $2000 she received from the sale before computing gross income, leaving her with $500 in gross income that must be reported.

Finally, the concept of "imputed income" is important. Again, brushing aside all nuance, at its core, the concept is that taxpayers are not subject to tax on the fruits of the taxpayer's labor that benefit the taxpayer.[22] In other words, if you catch a rainbow trout on a weekend getaway to Idaho, you do not have to pay tax on your delicious newfound "wealth."

Taxing Income from Virtual Worlds and Games

Returning to the various ways that wealth is increased within a game or virtual world, we can examine each from a tax perspective. The spectrum we'll be considering includes:

1. increasing individual wealth by accumulating virtual goods, currency, or advanced character attributes in a game where RMT is prohibited,
2. selling the goods and currency to another player in a game world,
3. selling the goods and currency, or an account with advanced character attributes, on the open market, whether with the approval of or in violation of the game's Terms of Service,
4. accumulating wealth in a free-form virtual world with a sanctioned currency exchange by selling goods or services, or through successful investments, and
5. moving accumulated wealth from a free-form virtual world with a sanctioned currency exchange to the real world by converting the in-world currency to real-world currency.

First, consider the ramifications of increasing the value of a character in a game-based virtual world by increasing the character's "skills" or "level" through game play. For example, consider a World of Warcraft player (whom we'll call "Wendy"). While playing World of Warcraft, Wendy and her guildmates venture into the region of "Netherstorm," where Wendy slays an Ethereum Gladiator, receiving a "Night Blade" for her efforts. As an added bonus, she increases her character's "level."

Under *Glenshaw Glass*, recall, income is "any undeniable accession to wealth, which is clearly realized by the taxpayer, over which the taxpayer has complete dominion."[23] There is little argument that Wendy has dominion over the gain as she, and she alone, can access the account that is able to use the Night Blade. And while there is an argument that Wendy has not "realized" any gain due to the legal restrictions on ownership ostensibly created by the Terms of Service of most games (including World of Warcraft), that argument is fairly weak as well because, among other reasons, the provisions are largely ineffective at preventing RMT.

Bryan Camp explains this argument in his paper *The Play's the Thing: A Theory of Taxing Virtual Worlds*:

> [World of Warcraft] virtual items are routinely traded in RMT on third party sites[.] Even if Blizzard routinely enforces the EULA prohibition, the weed-like growth of RMT suggests that the contractual provisions do not operate as a true restriction on [players'] ability to convert virtual items to US$.[24]

Wendy's best argument that the event is not taxable under *Glenshaw Glass* may be that she has not experienced an "undeniable accession to wealth" on the grounds that a Night Blade does not have a discernible fair market value in U.S. dollars. Before January 2007, you could find real-world values for World of Warcraft items (like Night Blades) fairly easily by searching eBay. Since eBay banned auctions for virtual items when such auctions are prohibited by the game providers' Terms of Service, however, it has been significantly more difficult to obtain valuations for virtual items. A great deal of real money still changes hands, it just does so for gold rather than items; the item-to-gold trade then largely occurs in-world. Now, determining the fair market value of a Night Blade requires (1) determining how much gold a Night Blade is worth, and then (2) determining how much the gold is worth in real money trades on the black market. Somewhat surprisingly, the price of a Night Blade recently fluctuated from as little as 600 gold to as much as 4150 gold over a three-month span.[25] Even though the market for gold is fairly stable, the wild fluctuations in prices of in-world items raise the question of whether a Night Blade has a discernible "fair market value," which in turn raises a question as to whether it is an item of taxable income.

But what about the second situation described earlier? What if Wendy, rather than keeping the Night Blade and using it to enhance her play experience, sells it to another user in World of Warcraft using one of the in-world auction houses for, say, 1500 in-world gold, the average selling price?[26] Instead of possessing a Night Blade (for which it was difficult to obtain a fair market value), Wendy now has 1500 additional gold in her account. And we know that there is a ready market—albeit a black market that violates World of Warcraft's Terms of Service—where Wendy could easily sell the 1500 gold for about $100. While there might have been a question about the ascertainability of the value of the Night Blade itself, the conversion of the Night Blade to gold obviates that concern. Gaining 1500 gold in World of Warcraft is an undeniable accession to wealth, and there is no difficulty establishing its real-world worth.

Most players' (and commentators') instinct, however, is that the sale of the Night Blade for 1500 gold in World of Warcraft should be no more taxable than the possession of the Night Blade itself. Why? From a game design perspective, we need look no farther than Johan Huizinga's concept of the magic circle. Players and commentators alike have an instinct—a good one—that play spaces should remain separate from real life. It seems "right" that Wendy should not be taxed on her 1500 gold any more than I should be taxed on the 1500 in Monopoly money that my friend pays me if he lands on Park Place with a hotel. The existence of the black market for the 1500 gold appears to threaten the magic circle, but unless Wendy avails herself of the market, the circle—for Wendy—remains intact.

Happily, this is a situation where the law (as it stands) and the instinct of players and game designers walk hand in hand. So long as Wendy keeps her gold (or the Night Blade) inside the "magic circle" that many believe should protect World of Warcraft and play spaces like it from the real world, it should be seen as no more than "imputed income"—a personal benefit to Wendy born of her own labor—and thus not taxable. In his paper *The Play's the Thing: A Theory of Taxing Virtual Worlds*, Bryan Camp explains the analysis as follows:

> Section 61 should not reach [this income] because it represents the value of self-provided services. Like a self-prepared tax return has economic value but results from the taxpayer's own skill-set, so the loot drop results from [World of Warcraft] playing skills. Among those are planning ahead, wise use of resources, physical agility, coordination to control his avatar's moves, and interacting with other players in the virtual world environment (his Guild) to mount a successful quest. All of those skills are self-directed . . . .[27]

Moving all the way to the other end of the spectrum, let's assume that Wendy, after exchanging the Night Blade for 1500 gold, sells the 1500 gold on the black market to a gold broker for $100, and then sells her account (with the higher-level character in it) for an additional $200. Here, tax liability is created because the fruits of the labor are not being kept for personal use (which would trigger the imputed income exception just discussed) but, instead, are being sold. Camp explains:

> When a WoW . . . player receives US$ for "selling" either a player account or an in-world item on an auction site, the sale produces gross income. . . . In exchange for US$, one party agrees to help another party advance in the game by meeting in-world and transferring a game object [or an amount of currency] that will enhance game play. Similarly a player might pay another to "level up" a character. Both transactions are for services [and both] produce gross income within the meaning of § 61.[28]

Similarly, selling virtual goods created in a free-form virtual world like Second Life for real money (e.g., on eBay, which still allows Second Life cash-for-goods transactions because they are not prohibited by Second Life's Terms of Service) and withdrawing profit from an in-world business in a free-form virtual world clearly generate taxable gross income.

Not all commentators agree that "imputed income" is the best way to view "drops" in games. One, Leandra Lederman, says that drops are better seen as "taken" items, to be taxed at sale but not at collection—similar to fish caught by a professional fisherman. The distinction does not have a significant impact on the analysis, however. Whether "imputed income" or "taken" items, there is no tax implication until and unless the item is sold. Both result in the same outcome. Lederman notes:

> The "player" who is actually working online will thus not escape the imposition of tax upon his or her livelihood, while the casual seller will owe tax only on actual sales. [A player] who never sells virtual items for real money, will not be taxed on her fun, at least with regard to the drops she receives.[29]

To this point, none of the conclusions drawn regarding taxation of profits generated in virtual worlds has been particularly controversial, but one area remains unexplored, and this is where it gets interesting.

The area we've not yet explored concerns a user increasing the amount of wealth he has available in a free-form virtual world by selling goods or services or by profiting on the purchase and sale or rental of virtual land. It should be noted that our analysis diverges (if only slightly) from Camp's excellent article, so there is certainly room for debate over the point.

Let's return to Wendy. After she's finished her (apparently profitable) exploration of World of Warcraft, she turns her attention to Second Life. She, like many other users, quickly discovers that there is money (remember Second Life's advertising campaign? **"Real Money!"**) to be made selling items to other residents and renting out land. So she invests US$300 in Linden Dollars (L$). This gives her—at current L$ to US$ exchange rates—about L$80,000. Notably, her purchase of the Lindens takes place on the LindeX— a Second Life web page directly linked from Second Life's home page and managed by Linden Lab.[30] The trade also profits Linden Lab, which generates about ten percent of its income from LindeX transactions.[31]

Wendy then uses some of her Lindens to buy land from another user, and she uses more Lindens to buy several prefab apartment buildings from still another user. She puts these apartments on her new property, adds a few trees and a rental office, and starts renting her apartments to other users. She also learns to write scripts in the programming language of Second Life and creates a wildly successful line of weather effects for other landowners to use to set the mood on their parcels. She sells these weather effects for tens of thousands of Lindens. Both businesses are successful, and soon Wendy is one of the over one thousand residents of Second Life who are making more than US$1000 (around L$265,000) each month.[32]

No one seriously argues that Wendy should not pay tax on her profits when she converts them to US$ by selling them to other users. The question is whether she should be obligated to pay tax on her profits *before* she converts the L$ to US$. Camp argues that she should not, on the same grounds that she should not have to pay tax on World of Warcraft gold if she simply leaves it in the game: both are protected by the magic circle. As readers will note elsewhere, however, I do not believe that free-form virtual worlds have generally availed themselves of the protection of the magic circle. Rather, they have willfully chosen to step outside it by using such advertising statements as, in the case of Second Life, "Own Virtual Land!" and "Make real money in a virtual world."

Camp argues that—at least for the moment—Lindens, World of Warcraft gold, and casino chips all amount to the same thing—units of play. And just as it is counterintuitive to tax a blackjack player for interim winnings if he ultimately cashes out nothing, it is counterintuitive to tax a virtual world user on in-world transactions. Camp acknowledges that the more currency in free-form virtual worlds operates like currency in the real world, however, the less protection it will be afforded from Section 61's definition of gross income.

> At some point, in-world activity might well become so connected with real-world activity that what is earned or created or traded in-world ought to become "gross income" within the meaning of § 61. I suggest that that point will

occur when in-world currency ceases to be mere "units of play" and becomes instead fully functional currency.[33]

We may already be at that point. One company promises that users will soon be able to order and pay for pizzas from national chains in-world, using Lindens, and have the pizzas delivered to their real-life residences.[34] One store already offers the ability to purchase real-life consumer electronics items in Second Life using Lindens and have them delivered to a real-life address.[35] It is certain that very soon creative businesses will find many more ways to allow users to spend Lindens on real-world products.

Of course, a massive industry already exists within Second Life for sexual services that appear, in some cases, to be indistinguishable from sexual services offered on websites and via telephone lines. Many adult service providers' advertisements direct customers to pay the service providers in Lindens, and then use external websites and voice programs to interact with them. Some even offer traditional landline telephone services similar to fee-based 900 number services but which accept payment in Linden Dollars.

That is the fundamental difference between, on the one hand, World of Warcraft gold and real-world casino chips and, on the other hand, Second Life Linden Dollars—you can't buy a pizza or a CD player, or pay for phone sex, with World of Warcraft gold or casino chips . . . but you can with Linden Dollars.

This all amounts to an ongoing and irreversible erosion of what little "magic circle" protection may exist for free-form virtual worlds, and that erosion is encouraged by the people who operate many of the worlds, as they clearly have an eye on real-world business interaction as a long-term goal. One could argue that there is, in fact, a *fundamental* difference between free-form virtual worlds (like Second Life) and traditional game-based worlds (like World of Warcraft) on the game-theory grounds that the designers of the former have chosen not to avail themselves of the intuitive protection of the magic circle, while the designers of the latter have tried (albeit often unsuccessfully) to keep their games within the magic circle's confines.

In any case, there has been no real effort to enforce tax collection in virtual worlds in the U.S. to date. Businesses like Wendy's, however, which are making thousands of dollars a month in virtual worlds, would be well advised to treat that income as gross income at least at the point at which it is converted to real-world currency and, arguably, as it accumulates in their virtual world accounts. To the extent that the status of income in free-form virtual worlds as imputed rather than gross income depends on the existence of free-form virtual worlds as places of play and on currency as "units of play," it seems likely that the status will be lost shortly, if it has not been lost already.

Open Questions on Tax Law and Virtual Worlds

1. Does the growing trend toward real-world purchasing power of virtual currency undermine the argument that in-world income should not be taxed? Where is the line?

2. What enforcement or reporting mechanisms might the IRS impose to track virtual world profits?

Notes

1. Heavy Jade Ring (Recipe), http://wow.crafterstome.com/recipe/heavy -jade-ring.html (last visited Jan. 7, 2008).

2. Ultima Online: Mining, http://guide.uo.com/skill_45.html (last visited Jan. 7, 2008).

3. Ultima Online: Swordsmanship, http://guide.uo.com/skill_40.html (last visited Jan. 7, 2008).

4. Ultima Online: Magery, http://guide.uo.com/skill_25.html (last visited Jan. 7, 2008).

5. Ultima Online: Fishing, http://guide.uo.com/skill_18.html (last visited Jan. 7, 2008).

6. Richard A. Bartle, *Virtual Worldliness: What the Imaginary Asks of the Real,* 49 N.Y.L. Sch. L. Rev. 19 (2005).

7. Cristina Jimenez, *The High Cost of Playing Warcraft* (Sept. 24, 2007), *available at* http://news.bbc.co.uk/1/hi/technology/7007026.stm.

8. Daniel Terdiman, *eBay Bans Auctions of Virtual Goods* (Jan. 29, 2007), *available at* http://www.news.com/eBay-bans-auctions-of-virtual-goods/2100 -1043_3-6154372.html.

9. Second Life, Business Opportunities, http://secondlife.com/whatis/businesses.php (last visited Jan. 6, 2008).

10. Second Life, The Marketplace, http://secondlife.com/whatis/market place.php (last visited Jan. 5, 2008).

11. Second Life, Economy, http://secondlife.com/whatis/economy.php (last visited Jan. 5, 2008).

12. Second Life, Terms of Service, http://secondlife.com/corporate/tos .php (last visited Jan. 5, 2008); *see also infra* Appendix IV.

13. Julian Dibbell, *The Life of the Chinese Gold Farmer,* N.Y. TIMES, June 17, 2007, (Magazine), *available at* http://www.nytimes.com/2007/06/17/magazine/17lootfarmers-t.html.

14. IGE, Our Business, http://www.ige.com/corporate.aspx?lang=en (last visited Jan. 7, 2008).

15. Comm'r v. Glenshaw Glass Co., 348 U.S. 426 (1955).

16. *Id.*

17. Bryan T. Camp, *The Play's the Thing: A Theory of Taxing Virtual Worlds,* 59 HASTINGS L.J. 25 (2007), *available at* http://ssrn.com/abstract=980693.

18. *Id.* at 29.

19. Treas. Reg. § 1.61-2(d).

20. Treas. Reg. § 1.1001-1(a).

21. James v. United States, 366 U.S. 213 (1961).

22. Camp, *supra* note 17, at 38.

23. *Comm'r v. Glenshaw Glass Co.,* 348 U.S. 426 (1955).

24. Camp, *supra* note 17, at 57.

25. The Night Blade, http://wow.allakhazam.com/db/item.html?witem=31 331;source=live (last visited Jan. 7, 2008).

26. *Id.*

27. Camp, *supra* note 17, at 66.

28. *Id.* at 45.

29. Leandra Lederman, *"Stranger Than Fiction": Taxing Virtual Worlds,* 82 N.Y.U. L. REV. (2007), *available at* http://ssrn.com/abstract=969984.

30. LindeX, http://secondlife.com/currency/ (login required; last visited Jan. 7, 2008).

31. Grace Wong, *How Real Money Works in Second Life,* http://money.cnn .com/2006/12/08/technology/sl_lindex/index.htm (Dec. 8, 2006).

32. Jon Fortt, *Linden Lab: Second Life Entrepreneurship Is Booming,* http:// bigtech.blogs.fortune.cnn.com/2007/08/01/linden-lab-second-life-entrepre neurship-is-booming/ (Aug. 1, 2007).

33. Camp, *supra* note 17, at 67.

34. *Pizza Enters the Virtual World of Second Life,* http://www.fastpitchnet working.com/pressrelease.cfm?PRID=8734 (April 21, 2007).

35. Fabio Medby, *IWOOT Lets Avatars Buy Real Products in Second Life with Virtual Currency,* http://www.slnn.com/article/iwoot/ (July 11, 2007).

Establishing a Professional Virtual World Presence 14

Attorneys, other legal professionals, and legal scholars are rapidly becoming more visible in virtual worlds. Clients, particularly high-tech clients, will soon expect attorneys to be at least familiar with these spaces. It is likely, according to Gartner, that eighty percent of all Internet users will have a presence in a virtual world by 2011.[1] The American Bar Association has several committees that deal with virtual law, including one in the Business Law Section, one in the Intellectual Property Law Section, and one in the Science and Technology Law Section (which I currently cochair). According to the Galileo Law Directory (a fantastic guide to legal resources in Second Life, reproduced in Appendix II), over seventy firms, ranging from solo practitioners to large, international, firms, are represented in Second Life. The Second Life Bar Association (an informal professional association I started in Second Life) recently celebrated its one-year anniversary and the addition of its 200th member. Law appears to have arrived in virtual worlds.

This chapter will focus largely on Second Life, because most attorneys who are contemplating a virtual world presence will seek the most popular and entrepreneurially focused virtual world. There are good reasons to consider other virtual worlds (There.com is far more structured and offers a business-friendly PG-13 experience, which Second Life decidedly does not, for example), but overall, attorneys who are considering a virtual world presence will likely find themselves most at home in Second Life. It is impossible to predict what will come next, but many believe that Linden Lab will make its server-side Second Life software more widely available, either by making it open source (thus allowing anyone to set up a Second Life–style server) or by distributing it to selected partners. In either case, the distribution of the software would allow providers to create separately hosted Second Life–style worlds with potential crossover points into the Linden Lab–controlled mainland.

Of course, room exists in the marketplace for a number of virtual worlds, particularly to the degree that they offer different feature sets. Because the quantity and quality of user content and the number of active users have a lot to do with attracting new users, it is possible that Second Life, which holds a significant lead in the marketplace, will continue to enjoy an advantage for some time. There is near-constant speculation (fueled by some credible evidence) that Google is in the process of building a virtual world, which could certainly pose a genuine threat to Second Life. A China-based virtual world, HiPiHi, is also seen as a potential global Second Life competitor. In any case, the advice that follows will apply to whatever virtual world offers a combination of a broad user base and relatively unfettered content creation. If Second Life is surpassed by a competitor, that competitor will likely share many of Second Life's key features and will certainly absorb most of its current user base.

Beyond social virtual worlds, multiplayer online games offer good opportunities to learn about different aspects of real money trading and virtual property. It is much harder to conceptualize exactly what it means to "own" or "sell" a rare piece of virtual property until you have talked to a few users who describe (sometimes in more detail than you bargained for) the steps they went through to acquire the item. Dive in, and chalk it up to the equivalent of "professional reading" or "business development." Just don't tell your guildmates you're an attorney until you've gotten to know them.

Why Legal Professionals Should Establish Virtual World Presences Now

Many people who follow virtual worlds closely, myself included, view virtual worlds as much bigger than games, storefronts, places to run rental properties, or even government simulators. Those are all excellent uses of the technology, but this is bigger. Virtual worlds arguably represent the beginning of the next major interface evolution and the first fundamental change to the way that users interact with computers since the graphical user interface became popular over twenty years ago.

Consider this—as computers got faster, the chief effect on operating systems was to make them look more and more like reality. Not much else has changed. We've stored computer files in hierarchical files systems much longer than they've *looked* like files, but now we see those systems expressed as "file folders" inside one another. We've always been able to delete things, but now we can find them later in a "trash can" or a "recycling bin." Instead of typing "c:\programs\word\word.exe" and hitting Enter to launch my word processing program, I now click an icon that represents that program. Basically, as computers get faster and faster, they get better and better at graphically representing data to users in a way that looks like the real world.

Virtual worlds represent the leading edge of the next shift. As graphics processing power increases and hardware input devices get more sophisticated, it will be possible to represent "things" on a computer so that they look, and behave, much more like their real-world counterparts. Want to look up a word in a dictionary? Just reach for it on the shelf. Or better yet, look at the spot where you see the dictionary and say the word aloud. We are not as far from that as you might expect. Although it requires a bit of imagination to look beyond the strip clubs and thinly disguised Ponzi schemes in Second Life and see the future of the Internet—Web 3.0 or the 3-D Internet according to some commentators—that is exactly what virtual worlds represent. Recall the early days of the web, when people felt that the only businesses that could succeed in the space were those selling pornography. Then recall the second stage, when everyone thought that every business idea with "web" in the name was a sure winner. Virtual worlds are on a fast track through those two stages. They will mature faster than the 2-D Internet because, unlike the amorphous web, these platforms are all owned by companies that have a vested interest in seeing their version of the 3-D internet succeed and that will, in at least some cases, take steps to ensure that success. Moreover, the leaders of these companies saw firsthand the problems that plagued the early days of the web and will be able to avoid them, or correct for them, much faster.

From a practical perspective, many attorneys' clients are already involved in virtual worlds. Attorneys who practice intellectual property law or who have high-tech clients will increasingly find themselves expected to be familiar with these spaces. If Gartner is right and eighty percent of all Internet users have a virtual world presence by the year 2011, it will be uncommon for a law firm to not have at least an outpost in the space, and many, if not most, will have full-scale virtual world offices.

Finally, there is an advantage to being among the first wave of attorneys to start paying attention to these spaces. Currently, the ratio of attorneys who have an understanding of these spaces to potential clients who need informed counsel is extremely low. That is bound to change as more attorneys discover the space. Those who move quickly not only will position themselves better within the virtual world but will have a much deeper understanding of the history and potential of the space. That understanding will dramatically help these first-movers better represent their virtual world clients in the long run.

Client Development in a Virtual World

Attorneys who set up outposts for their practices in virtual worlds automatically put themselves in a position to meet potential clients, simply by their presence. Virtual worlds are, above all else, communications tools. People log in with a purpose. Whether their purpose is making friends, starting a business, or simply exploring content that others have created, all come to the world with an agenda. Because of that, virtual world providers focus much attention on encouraging users to adopt a role (via group membership or ownership, managing property, or even simply placing text descriptions in profiles) and share that role with the rest of the community. If virtual worlds were simply solo sandboxes without a great deal of social interaction, movement, and collaboration, they'd be pretty boring. To facilitate interaction, providers build robust search tools into the virtual world clients. Attorneys, simply by listing their profession, will attract a certain degree of attention via search.

Because there are so many unanswered legal questions related to virtual worlds, so many users who are actually facing these questions on a daily basis, and so much social interaction (giving rise to conflict), attorneys may be surprised to find themselves sought out to a greater degree than they initially expect. Virtual world meetings where lawyers speak on issues related to copyright and trademark regularly draw a large crowd, most of whom are business owners with serious questions about the application of law to these spaces.

Attorneys need to be prepared for the fact that there is not, in many cases, a great deal of money available for legal representation in these spaces, at least not yet. There is also frequently an expectation of extremely low prices for legal representation (by real-world standards) among virtual world users. Just as an attorney will be able to buy a fairly nice suit for his or her avatar for no more than two or three U.S. dollars in a virtual world, many potential clients are not prepared to pay real-world rates, or anything approaching them, for legal services. That possibility is slowly changing, but some attorneys do offer extremely low rates, or even free initial consultations, for potential clients who they meet via their presence in virtual worlds in order to build a reputation in the space and because they are learning about the space in the process. That said, an increasing number of participants in virtual worlds are prepared to pay real-world rates, because the problems they face involve sums of money large enough to justify it. According to recent statistics, more than 1000 Second Life users are making more than $1000 per month in-world, and more than 150 are making more than $5000 per month. More than 50,000 users have a positive monthly balance, reflecting, generally, successful micro-businesses that have the potential to make much more. All these people are potential clients. Attorneys may want to consider creative fee arrangements, similar to the arrangements firms sometimes make with real-world start-up clients with a great deal of potential but little ready cash. Not included in these numbers are many people who make a living as content creators and are paid in "real money," not in-world currency. Some of these content creators have fairly large-scale businesses and will certainly need attorneys with virtual world experience.

Beyond current virtual world participants, however, consider the possibilities a few years down the road. Only a few hundred mainstream companies, at most, have even begun dipping their toes in the virtual world oceans. When more arrive, and having a virtual world presence becomes as important as having a web page, companies will require attorneys who understand these spaces. Moreover, there are mainstream companies that may not have the slightest desire to participate in virtual worlds themselves, but that will want to make deals with content providers who will work on their behalf. Those deals will require scrutiny from both sides.

■■■■■

Virtual World Opportunities for Attorneys

Participating in virtual world speaker series

Staffing drop-in legal clinics

Sponsoring pro bono events

Participating in government simulators

Conducting mock trials

Volunteering for nonprofit organizations

Finally, from a client development standpoint, informal professional associations in virtual worlds are very common, and some form the core of many users' virtual world social experiences. There are dozens of legal organizations where attorneys can meet, from large groups like the Second Life Bar Association (SLBA) to narrower groups focused on particular areas of law. Beyond the legal groups are business groups that regularly invite attorneys to speak, educational centers that frequently seek attorneys as panelists, and many opportunities for attorneys inclined to write articles, from in-world publications to more traditional blogs. Outside the purely social set of users, for nearly all professionals and educators, discussion is the primary activity in virtual worlds, and legal perspectives are very much appreciated.

Can Lawyers Actually Practice Law in a Virtual World?

With the caveat that serious ethical considerations must be taken into account, attorneys can, theoretically, use virtual world software as a communications tool to enhance their practices. Virtual worlds are particularly well suited to conversations between attorneys and large groups, such as training sessions, where confidentiality is not expected and privilege would not otherwise apply. Until serious concerns regarding user identification and confidentiality of communication are resolved, however, it is my position that attorneys should not conduct sensitive communications with clients in any current virtual world and should not provide legal advice to any avatar for which they have not verified the user's real-life identity, under any circumstances. For more on this issue, see the section regarding ethical concerns later in this chapter.

That said, there are a number of interesting possibilities for attorneys who are interested in practicing law in one form or another within the virtual world, some of which do not raise significant ethical concerns. One of the most promising uses of virtual worlds is for alternative dispute resolution over great distances. Some alternative dispute resolution groups have been started in Second Life already, including one significant government project undertaken by Portugal, which is open to the public. Stanford's law school has discussed opening an alternative dispute resolution center in the virtual world and plans to compile a body of "case law" for these spaces. Private projects, as discussed in Chapter 4, "Governance of Virtual Worlds," abound. Additionally, private governments, some of which involve functioning judiciaries, are beginning to appear (see Chapter 4, "Governance of Virtual Worlds"). All these will probably have roles available for advocates and may be able to provide technical solutions to help alleviate concerns regarding confidentiality and identity.

Cost of Participation in a Virtual World

The cost of participating in a virtual world depends on your level of participation and the extent to which you wish to use the virtual world provider's resources to maintain a presence when you are off-line. Basic accounts in Second Life are free. A basic account provides the user with an infinitely customizable avatar that is indistinguishable from premium account avatars. It also includes an "inventory" feature that allows the avatar access to an essentially unlimited amount of virtual personal property (clothing, gadgets, even entire create-on-demand homes and offices can be kept in

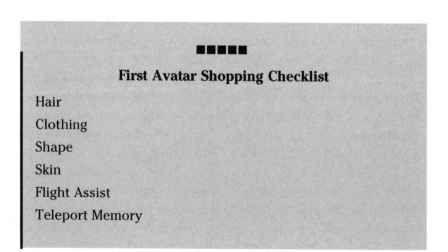

■■■■■
First Avatar Shopping Checklist

Hair

Clothing

Shape

Skin

Flight Assist

Teleport Memory

inventory). All of the personal property is nominally "carried" with the avatar and is available whenever the user is logged in.

The standard avatar you receive will be one of a handful of generic shapes. One of the first things you will want to do is change that, because an unmodified avatar is obvious to all other users and identifies you as a "newbie." People don't mind new users and are generally happy to help you get equipped, but because you will be considered a new user by everyone you meet, you'll likely feel some pressure to change the look fairly quickly. There are freebie centers all over the grid where new users can pick up a wide assortment of clothing, skins, and shapes to customize the otherwise notably "newbie" avatars. Freebies range from atrociously ugly to fairly high quality, although finding the good stuff requires a lot of patience.

If you do not wish to spend a lot of time digging through poorly organized freebie bins, you can choose to spend a little real money in Second Life (you should probably do this anyway, just to be familiar with the process). The process is simple, and the funds you deposit are instantly available as Lindens. Several forms of payment are available. A good, store-bought skin and shape and a comprehensive wardrobe collected from some of the better designers in Second Life should set you back no more than US$15, at the high end. This includes a few "tech toys" you'll find yourself wanting, such as a "flight assist" script that lets you fly higher than the default allows, and a script that will remember all the places you have teleported to. Shopping for new items for your avatar is an excellent opportunity to interact with other users and to get acquainted with the grid and the software that you are using to connect to it.

If you do not wish to purchase Lindens but still want to have money to spend in Second Life, you can look for jobs in-world through various services, or, if you have a knack for design or scripting, you can start a business selling your own products.

Premium accounts are really only necessary if you want to acquire land from Linden Lab and pay Linden Lab the monthly fees directly. They are not necessary in order to have a home or an office, as you can always rent land from another user for in-world currency. If you do plan to get land through Linden Lab, however—perhaps so that you can rent it to other users yourself—premium accounts start at $9.95 a month, discounted to $6.00 a month if you prepay for a year. The cost increases dramatically from there, depending on the amount of virtual land you own. The biggest benefit to acquiring land from Linden Lab is that it eliminates the chance that a third-party landlord will simply decide to stop renting land, or abscond with your funds, although that risk can be minimized by renting from landlords with good, long-standing reputations in the community. Another benefit to acquiring land from Linden Lab rather than from a third party is that it gives you direct access to the land management tools, such as ban lists (you can also get access to these tools from a landlord who owns her own "islands"). You can expect to spend around $5 to $10 per month on a small home or office, whether you rent it from a land baron or acquire it through Linden Lab.

The only other thing that you will be likely to spend money on is group memberships. Many groups are free, but some, including the Second Life Bar Association, charge a small sign-up fee or impose annual dues. Most groups that do have fees charge no more than a few dollars to join. The funds are generally used to pay for group projects, classified advertisements and notices, and group property.

Time Required to Participate in a Virtual World

Much like the cost of participation, you can spend as little or as much time participating in virtual worlds as your schedule allows. Your colleagues in the virtual world will adjust their expectations of your availability based on how often you are logged in, just as colleagues adjust their expectations regarding your e-mail response time based on your history of responsiveness.

There are several strategies to minimize the intrusion of virtual worlds into your real life. Second Life, for example, offers the ability to have all instant messages sent to your e-mail address. Users who have constant access to e-mail may find it easier to monitor their virtual world presence that way. There is, however, a benefit to being logged in. Users are more likely to remember you, and stay in touch, if they see you log in periodically. If you wish to remain logged in for long stretches of time and pay partial attention to the virtual world (so you see incoming instant messages, and people who walk up to you and begin talking), it can be very effective to run the virtual world software on a separate monitor, or in a separate window on large monitors, slightly out of your main work area, but still visible.

What Should a Professional's Avatar Look Like?

Just like in the real world, you will find a great variety of appearance choices among professionals in the virtual world. The possibilities are truly limitless. In selecting what your avatar will look like, the two guiding principles are (1) be yourself, and (2) be aware of the message you are sending. The first one is easy—you probably already have an idea of what you want your avatar to look like, even if it isn't fully formed, especially if you have logged in to a virtual world and seen some of the possibilities. The second is much more complex. The message sent by a user's avatar depends entirely on the nature of the virtual community the user is participating in, the history of certain appearances, and the current avatar-appearance trends there. It is impossible to predict what the trends will be in six months, let alone several years, but a few very general points seem to have stood the test of time.

First, there is a trend among some professionals (a trend of which I am a part) to have an avatar that looks as much as possible like the real-life user behind the keyboard. Some users have found that it is particularly helpful to have a look-alike avatar when dealing with people who already know them from real life or when demonstrating the capabilities of the platform to people who are not already familiar with it. The theory is that people who aren't familiar with virtual worlds will be exposed to a lot of differences—people can fly, for instance—and they do not need your appearance to be one more jarring thing to adjust to. If you can provide a touchstone to reality for your colleagues and clients, it may make it easier for them to take you seriously in what looks, to many people, like a video game or a cartoon.

Second, hypersexualized avatars (which are fairly common) tend to send the message that one is not planning to use the virtual world for professional purposes. Unfortunately, depending on the part of the virtual world fashion cycle during which you happen to join, avoiding purchasing an avatar that is more suited to a nightclub than an office is easier said than done, particularly for women. Many women professionals who attempt to have a professional appearance in virtual worlds, particularly Second Life, have expressed frustration with the difficulty of finding suitable clothing, skins, and shapes for their avatars. Many female "skins" come with the appearance of a fairly liberal application of lipstick and eye shadow, and many shapes are somewhat exaggerated in their proportions. The problem exists to a lesser degree for male avatars, but it is still an issue. Much of the clothing currently on the market for male avatars looks like it comes from *Miami Vice,* and the skins and shapes tend to make all male avatars look like superheroes. The easiest solution to this problem is to customize your avatar yourself, using the various tools provided as part of the interface. Another choice is to hire an image consultant to help you with your avatar. Image consulting is a popular "occupation" in virtual worlds and is reasonably priced.

Your avatar's height may also be an issue. Second Life has a slider that allows you to control your height in centimeters. When I set the slider at 185 cm (approximately six feet one inch tall, my real height), my avatar looks significantly shorter than nearly every other avatar in the virtual world. When real-life shorter people set their avatars to their real height, they are sometimes mistaken for users who are trying to portray children. This can be particularly problematic, given Linden Lab's ban on "sexual ageplay" and an undercurrent of general suspicion about childlike avatars. Most users set their height far taller than their real height, simply to avoid being significantly shorter than everyone else. Interestingly, this phenomenon is generally not apparent visually, as everything in the virtual world from houses to cars just gets scaled up to match. It only becomes obvious in architectural builds that are based on actual measurements, where most avatars are too tall to fit through the doors.

Finally, it is worth noting that there is a wide variety of non-human avatars available, from giant robots to "furries" (humanlike animals) to stylized anime characters. As noted in the intellectual property chapter, you can even choose a (probably infringing) avatar that looks like a celebrity or a character from a popular movie or book. Truly, if you can imagine it, someone has probably created an avatar of it. And if not, you can always create one yourself. That all said, although there is no intrinsic reason not to use a nonhuman avatar, it does send a different message than a human avatar and may project a sense of play that some attorneys wish to avoid. In the end, most professionals will probably be happier with a relatively boring avatar as their primary business identity, though bear in mind there is no reason that you can't have a secondary identity. You can even swap out your skin and shape for a more "fun" appearance when you are not doing business, although many users find that, unlike a change of clothing, dramatically altering their avatar's appearance through the use of a variety of skins and shapes "feels" odd. You get used to seeing yourself one way, it seems. Moreover, running into a business associate who knows you as your Clark Kent avatar when you're dressed as Superman could be a bit awkward. For those reasons, among others, many users maintain separate accounts for work and play.

What Kind of Virtual Office Should a Professional Have?

It is not necessary to have an office in a virtual world, although many, if not most, professionals do. If you choose not to maintain an office, you will easily be able to find places to meet with other people. The offices of the Second Life Bar Association, for example, include several conference rooms, both large and small, for members to use, and many other facilities offer private offices that can be used free of charge as well.

As noted, however, many professionals choose to have their own office. This affords somewhat greater (though still imperfect) privacy and gives the user complete control over the aesthetics of the space.

There are two ways to get land to build your office on. You can either rent land from another user (look for a land baron with a good reputation and a long history of satisfied customers), or you can pay "tier" for the land to Linden Lab by signing up for a premium account. In the former case, you own nothing and can walk away at the end of any lease period. In the latter, you will "own" the land that your office sits on and can sell it to another user at a later date.

■■■■■
Virtual Office Checklist

Neighbors?

Neighborhood?

View?

Mainland or grid?

Privacy?

Rent or buy?

The first decision you will need to make is how much land you need. The basic, $9.95 per month ($6.00 per month if a year is paid in advance) account includes "tier" on a 512-square-meter plot of land. Although the square meter area is important, as it defines the boundaries of your property, more important is the number of "prims" you are allowed to place on it. The term *prims* stands for "primitive objects," and they are the building blocks of Second Life. A basic, 512-meter plot allows you 117 prims. If you decide you would rather not pay land tier directly to Linden Lab, and want to work with a land baron instead, you can likely get a slightly better deal on a prims-per-dollar basis, though not by much, and you run some risk of the landowner simply disappearing with your money (again, look for a reputable land baron if you go this route). One advantage to renting from a land baron is that if you can find a spot with an office you like already built, you don't have to build or buy one to put there. If you end up with undeveloped land, however, there are many prefab buildings available for sale that you can "build" on your land without too much trouble.

If the idea of prims is as confusing for you as it is for most people, think of it this way—the most basic office you could possibly have that looks anything like an office consists of four walls, a floor, and a roof. Using standard building tools (which let you make basic three-dimensional shapes), that office would require six prims—one flattened cube for each wall, one for the floor, and one for the roof. If you wanted windows, that would require more prims. A door, yet more. A desk and a few chairs, and you are quickly approaching the

117 prims that you are allowed on a 512-square-meter plot. The first offices of the Second Life Bar Association were on a 512-square-meter plot, and they consisted of a fairly basic prefab building, a rug, a lamp, a desk, a small conference table, and six chairs. Every one of the 117 prims allowed was used, and when the SLBA held a reception there after one of its very early meetings, the chairs had to be picked up so that virtual beverages could be placed on the conference room table.

The number of prims in objects varies dramatically based on how complex the objects are. The chairs in the first Second Life Bar Association office used three prims. In contrast, one chair I own is a virtual version of the popular Herman Miller "Aeron" chair (these are sold by Herman Miller itself in Second Life). The chair is comprised of 63 prims, almost half the number allowed on a 512-square-meter plot of land. In other words, two of these chairs take up the same number of prims as the office, conference table, desk, rug, lamp, and six chairs that comprised the original SLBA quarters. On the other hand, they look fantastic. Generally, the best-looking objects use a lot of prims, although there is a real art to the design of high-quality low-prim furniture. Unless you have a very high prim count (which you will have to pay for), you will undoubtedly find yourself seeking low-prim furniture.

Addressing the Pitfalls Professionals May Face in Virtual Worlds

Professionals contemplating a virtual world presence often encounter a few very reasonable concerns, and we will address those in the following sections. Although none should scare you away from the space, they are worth discussing. Those of you who work in larger firms may be particularly interested, as you may need to be prepared for some skeptical inquiries from colleagues.

The Downside to Being an Early Adopter

Although being an early adopter has distinct advantages, there are some downsides. One is that there are no long-term—and really even no short-term—guarantees that the platform will stay around. At the moment, Second Life dominates the field, but that could easily change. If the company where your firm has invested itself disappears, or even if the world becomes dramatically less popular, that investment is essentially lost. And the reality is that no matter how dominant a company appears, how much user content it has in a proprietary format, and how high a percentage of all virtual world users it counts as its own, Internet users are fickle and will leave in droves if a better product comes along.

It is very likely that whatever investment is made today in a virtual world presence will need to be made all over again in a few years in a different world. Not certain, but likely. And to a degree, Second Life is a young visionary company, making young, visionary company mistakes, so you are taking some risk by getting involved in this virtual world.

Being an early adopter of complex software can also be frustrating. Although Second Life is an amazing idea, and the concept is widely loved by its residents, the software itself most definitely is not. The entire grid is down for maintenance with surprising frequency, the software uses a nonstandard interface (for example, when you right-click on your avatar, you are presented with a transparent pie-shaped menu of options, rather than a standard dropdown menu), and the client has such high graphics requirements that it simply will not run on many computers. It is, however, by far the most advanced product of its type on the market, it is managed by a talented team of people, it offers a groundbreaking intellectual property policy, and, at bottom, it is where you need to be in order to participate meaningfully in this stage of virtual world growth. If you lose the hundred or so dollars you will spend on a virtual presence over the next year, you will have learned enough to more than compensate for the loss.

Ethical Concerns in Virtual Worlds

Although none of the ethical concerns that arise in relation to virtual worlds are impossible to deal with, the issue is important. Perhaps because of the Wild West feel to virtual worlds, ethical concerns are, somewhat surprisingly, routinely being overlooked by attorneys in virtual worlds.

One concern is confidentiality of attorney-client communication. There really is no guarantee of confidentiality in virtual worlds

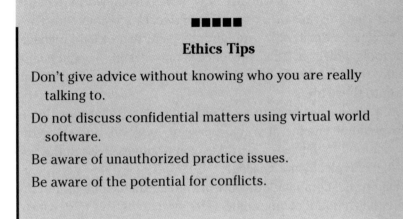

■■■■■
Ethics Tips

Don't give advice without knowing who you are really talking to.

Do not discuss confidential matters using virtual world software.

Be aware of unauthorized practice issues.

Be aware of the potential for conflicts.

at all. Whether communicating by typing or by voice, eavesdropping is easy and fairly common.

Another concern is the pseudonymity of avatars. Because there is currently no way of knowing who you are talking to in most virtual worlds, it is essentially impossible to manage conflicts of interest. Linden Lab is in the process of instituting an identity verification plan, but the details are unclear, and it seems unlikely that very many users will choose to reveal details about themselves in their profile anyway. If you do not know who you are talking to, you run a serious risk of exposing yourself to a conflict of interest.

Finally, the pseudonymity of avatars also makes it a near certainty that an attorney who fails to verify the identity and geographic location of users he or she is representing in a virtual world is engaging in the unauthorized practice of law in some jurisdiction.

As noted earlier, I recommend that attorneys refrain from conducting confidential communication in the virtual world and handle all other aspects of representation no differently than if they had been contacted by e-mail. Get identities, clear conflicts, and avoid unauthorized practice issues.

Virtual World Hassles

There are some minor hassles to participating in virtual worlds, and, in particular, Second Life. One is that the world is simply not policed by its creators, outside of responding to large-scale crises.

As such, griefers (users who are only in the virtual world to cause mayhem and disrupt other users' experience) are common. They can largely be dealt with through intelligent use of land management tools, however. Their presence is one reason to acquire land directly from Linden Lab, or via a land baron who will give you access to these tools.

Another hazard born of most providers' lack of intervention is widespread scamming. If you are careful, however, and bring the same caution to the virtual world as you would exercise in the real world, it is typically not an issue.

Finally, the combination of the prevalence of user blogs and the astounding amount of time some users seem to be able to devote to personal ax-grinding occasionally results in protracted, dramatic fights, which sometimes involve legal questions. It is better to steer wholly clear of these spats, which are typically instigated by a few well-known troublemakers. Attorneys, in particular, make tempting targets, particularly if they have the temerity to opine on legal matters—the exclusive province of whoever yells the loudest in these dustups. If you do find yourself being attacked in-world or on a blog by another resident, keep in mind that the worst of these people have already so completely undermined their own reputations that their words carry essentially no weight. Your best bet is to simply ignore them. The vast majority of the users you interact with will be among the most intelligent, technologically savvy, friendly people you will ever meet, and most will be very happy you have brought your expertise to the virtual world.

Closing Thoughts

The coming years are going to be exciting. There will be an explosion of interest in games and, particularly, free-form social virtual worlds. Social virtual worlds and multiuser games with real money components will become even more popular, bandwidth and storage will get even cheaper, and more people than ever will discover the potential of these spaces for business, recreation, and communication. The landscape will change quickly, so attorneys, legal scholars, and other legal professionals should not miss this rare opportunity to get involved at the beginning of a fascinating new intersection of law and technology.

Open Questions on Establishing a Professional Virtual World Presence

1. Why have large overseas firms established virtual world presences earlier than large U.S. firms?

2. What technological solutions might make it more reasonable to practice in-world, from an ethical perspective?

3. What lessons can people starting businesses in virtual worlds today take from early successes and failures on the 2-D web?

Note

1. *Gartner Says 80 Percent of Active Internet Users Will Have a "Second Life" in the Virtual World by the End of 2011* (Apr. 24, 2007), *available at* http://www.gartner.com/it/page.jsp?id=503861 (last visited Jan. 4, 2008).

Appendix I: Directory of Virtual Worlds, Games, and Platforms

Social Virtual Worlds

Metaversed.com, a website devoted to business and technology news related to virtual worlds, defines social virtual worlds as follows: "a social virtual world has game-like immersion and social media functionality without narrative driven goals. At its core is a sense of presence with others at the same time and place." Using that definition, here are some 3-D social virtual worlds currently in operation. This list is subjective and is not meant to be all-inclusive, but it should give you a few starting points.

Active Worlds (http://www.activeworlds.com): Active Worlds introduced the idea of 3-D social virtual worlds. According to the Active Worlds website: "Active Worlds, the web's most powerful Virtual Reality experience, lets you visit and chat in incredible 3-D worlds that are built by other users. Think you have what it takes to build your own world or Virtual Reality game? Active Worlds is the place for you, where in minutes you can create fascinating 3-D worlds that others can visit and chat in. The Active Worlds Universe is a community of hundreds of thousands of users that chat and build 3-D virtual reality environments in millions of square kilometers of virtual territory. Take a quick look at some of our satellite maps and see how our community has grown over the years. Launch the free software and come check us out for yourself. You'll be amazed at how vast our Virtual Worlds universe is."

Kaneva (http://www.kaneva.com): Kaneva is a virtual world that includes an extensive web component. From the Kaneva website: "Kaneva is the first virtual entertainment world that unifies the 2-D web with a 3-D experience. Kaneva is the first to integrate social networking, shared media, and collaborative online communities into a modern-day, immersive 3-D Virtual World. Built for the masses, Kaneva is an extension of socialization and entertainment in the real world. Kaneva has been designed from the ground up with ease-of-use, fun and entertainment top-of-mind. Kaneva is the only place where Profiles, Media and Communities are teleported from the 2-D web into a modern-day 3-D Virtual World with their own virtual spaces. Latin for 'canvas,' Kaneva's mission is to enable its members to have fun, express their interests and passions, and establish meaningful, real connections with others."

Second Life (http://www.secondlife.com): Second Life is currently the most popular social virtual world. Second Life describes itself as follows: "Second Life is a 3-D virtual world entirely created by its Residents. Since opening to the public in 2003, it has grown explosively and today is inhabited by millions of Residents from around the globe."

There.com (http://www.there.com): There.com offers a PG-13 experience and stronger content protection tools than some of its competitors, which has encouraged business partnerships. From the There.com website: "There is a beautiful virtual world where you can: create a 3-D avatar, hang out with friends, play games, build a home, [and] design and sell things."

vSide (http://www.vside.com): vSide is a virtual world that focuses on arts and entertainment. As stated on the vSide website, "vSide is an immersive, interconnected virtual city environment where you can hang out, listen to music, chat, dance, and make friends."

Although text-based and 2-D virtual worlds still exist and have devoted followings, they have not been included on this list. Special mention, however, must go to the original MUD, the very first virtual world. MUD is still in operation. You can find out more about it at http://www.british-legends.com/.

Game-Based Virtual Worlds

Many games offer aspects of the virtual world experience. Although a complete list is beyond the scope of this book, a few that are worth exploring are World of Warcraft (http://www.worldofwarcraft.com), Entropia Universe (http://www.entropiauniverse.com), Ultima Online (http://www.uo.com), Eve Online (http://www.eve-online.com), Anarchy Online (http://www.anarchyonline.com), EverQuest II (http://www.everquest2.com), and Asheron's Call (http://ac.turbine.com).

Appendix II:
Second Life's "Galileo
Law Directory"

Real-life law librarian Kate Fitz maintains an amazing resource for attorneys interested in virtual law, available at http://www.lawspotonline.com. She also, as avatar "Cat Galileo," maintains the "Galileo Law Directory" of legal resources in Second Life. She has graciously given permission to reprint her list of in-world resources here. The names listed are Second Life avatar names. "SLURL" locations are places to visit in Second Life. Note that Fitz makes it clear that she has not verified any of the information here and that the descriptions are taken from the in-world representations from profiles and group descriptions. Similarly, neither I nor the publisher of *Virtual Law* has investigated any of the representations made here.

Galileo Law Directory

No verification of claimed credentials has been conducted. Listings are based entirely on in-world representation. Discuss credentials before hiring or sharing confidential information with anyone.

Lawyers and Law Offices

Abogados/Attorney's @ Law
Founder: Franc1sco Dagostino

Abogado/Attorney's @ law nació en respuesta a las múltiples consultas legales que me formulan las personas de mi país, Chile, las que comprenden áreas diversas del derecho. Especialista en derecho laboral, civil y administrativo. Si necesitas algún tipo de orientación legal, no dudes en consultarme.

Abogados de Bilbao
Contact: Golgo MacMillan, Urien Negulesco
SLURL: Quest I 184, 169, 29 (Mature)

Abogados de Bilbao-abogadosdebilbao.es -RRHH- venta de terrenos Abogados, law, lawyers, conflictos en SL y Rl. Proximamente servicio de busqueda de empleo y trabajo en SL.

Advokat Straaf Law Office
SLURL: Rydal 38, 204, 42 (PG)

Home of Advokat Straaf - Attorney at Law

Alonzo Law Firm
SLURL: Injong 136, 73, 21 (Mature)

Disputes with vendors, sellers, landlords, or the Lindens; SL business counseling; advice and interpretation of SL Terms of Service and Community Standards.

Attorneys at LAWL (group)
Founder: Auell Villota

SL legal representatives, dealing primarily with objective decisions and settling drama.

Blackstone Lancaster - Attorney at Law
SLURL: Mullett (178, 15, 149)

Mr. Lancaster provides Second Life residents with a wide variety of professional legal services and is able to draw upon over ten years of real life civil law experience in several US States to ensure quality legal service and attention to detail for all of your matters. Blackstone Lancaster is your lawyer for your second life and can help with: General legal representation; Commercial contracts and agreements; Employment Agreements; Purchase of land; Dispute Resolution; Interactione [sic] between SL and RL legal systems.

Burney Law Firm
Founder: WebLawyer Lytton
www.burneylawfirm.com
info@burneylawfirm.com

Highly experienced lawyers in New York. Internet law; Complex litigation; Corporate law; Personal injury; Divorce; Wills and estates.

Caballeros Hospitalarios
Founder: Leso Palen

Es un pequeño bufete de juezes i abogados cuyo proposito es que nuestros clientes salgan satisfechos de sus juicios.
We are a small writing desk of judges and lawyers whose intention is that our clients leave satisfied with their judgment.

Center Tone Consultancy Trademark VIA (Very Important Avatar) (group)
Contact: Terry Rosher, Jacky Rosher
SecondLife@merkenregistratie.nl

Consultations about Intellectual Property in SecondLife and Real-Life, free for group members.

Chamber of Lawyers (group)

Founder: AvvLamberto Pera

The chamber of Lawyers is a free association between real life lawyers, whose members enjoy to share their experience with and give advices to SL users, both about RL and SL affairs or matters.

La camera degli Avvocati una libera associazione tra Avvocati reali, i cui membri hanno scelto di mettere la propria esperienza e fornire consulenza agli utenti di Second Life, sia su materie collegate a SL stesso, sia su casi relativi alla RL.

Cobalt Law (group)

Founder: Harriet Pennell

Advertising, promotions, and intellectual property law.

Crossguard IP Attorneys

SLURL: Ellesmere 59, 220, 146 (PG)
Contact: www.crossguard.info,
email: mail@crossguard.info
skype: crossguard.info

Trade Mark, Patent & Copyright Attorneys covering IP law, brand & design protection, character & personality rights, domain name dispute resolution, safeguarding know-how, intellectual property licensing & the work of the creative industries. Office is a virtual art gallery featuring classic paintings.

Cuatrecasas

Contact: Pere Seiling
SLURL: Novatierra 142, 218, 24
URL: www.cuatrecasas.com

With a team of more than 800 lawyers and a practice covering all areas of business law, Cuatrecasas is one of the leading law firms on the Iberian Peninsula. The core corporate law and litigation practices combine with exceptionally strong tax, finance and employment practices to offer Cuatrecasas clients an integrated legal service with a focus on close personal relationships and the achievement of results.

Davis LLP

Founder: Davis Sella
SLURL: Zurich City 90, 210, 25
URL: Davis LLP Video Game Law Blog

Davis LLP is an international full-service law firm, founded in 1892, with offices in Canada and Tokyo as well as here in Second Life. Areas of expertise: media, entertainment, technology and intellectual property law; ownership of virtual property; drafting of development, publication or licensing agreements; and privacy or confidentiality issues.

DivorcioWeb.com Law Office

Contact: Candela Pfeffer
SLURL: Nueva Red, 100, 50, 22
URL: http://www.DivorcioWeb.com

Drakeford & Kane LLC

SLURL: Silicon Island 184, 197, 36 (PG)

Attorneys & Consultants (Under construction.) Providing legal & business consulting services representing its clients in a multi-dimensional competitive business environment.

Elchoness Law Firm, LLC: Global Workplace Counsel

Contact: Da Etchegaray
www.globalworkplacecounsel.com

Elchoness Law Firm, LLC: Global Workplace Counsel provides employment law services and global human resources consulting. The firm typically serves clients as a virtual member of their in-house team. The firm is interested in the nexus between the virtual and real-life workplace.

Faasen & Partners

Founder: FaasenPartners Writer
SLURL: Faasen en Partners 187, 68, 27 (Mature)

advocaat, attorney, lawyer, law firm, advocatenkantoor, advocaten, ondernemingsrecht, corporate law, jurist, faasen en partners.

Field Fisher Waterhouse LLP

SLURL: depo business hub 215, 185, 35 (PG)

European Law Firm, with a strong technology, media, and IP focus.

Franklin Pierce Law (Private Group)

Founder: Nataniel Campese

For more information, IM Justice Helgerud.

Gar Hallard's Law Office

SLURL: Mill Pond 234, 113, 21 (Mature)

Licensed attorney since 1991 practicing in North Texas in both federal and state courts.

Gei Nishi

SLURL: Thayer 114, 37, 154 (Mature)

Attorney at Law. RL and SL law and business consultation.

Geri N. Kahn Law Offices

SLURL: Olivia 103, 141, 23
www.gerikahn.com

RL lawyer practicing U.S. Immigration law and Social Security Disability Law. Licensed in California. Specialist in Immigration and Nationaltiy [sic] Law, certified by the State Bar of California, Board of Legal Specialization.

Greenberg & Lieberman, LLC

Contact: Navets Potato
SLURL: Juwangsan (182, 139, 166)
SLURL: New Manhattan (189, 55, 157)

aplegal.com Law Firm - Intellectual Property Patents Trademarks Copyrights Media Prosecution Litigation Representation Escrow Services.

Hypatia Padar-Internet Law Office

Intellectual Property Resource Center
SLURL: Skiddaw (21, 200, 53)

RL attorney with 24+ years of experience. IP and Cyberlaw.

IC Abogados/Lawyers
Contact: Kydd Laval
SLURL: Fearly Beach Mall, Fearly (110, 17, 24)

Legal advice in Spanish & European laws, by IM or e-mail, from lawyer with 43 years experience, specialised in M&A, Spanish administrative law & EU competition law. Lawyers who wish to join the group may send a short CV by e-mail. General membership open to anyone who wants to improve their knowledge of law. The group also provides a forum for discussion of present subjects (no politics) or such everlasting ones as books, paintings, music & films.

InternetLitigators
Contact: www.InternetLitigators.com
SLURL: Silicon Island (63, 223, 37)

Business Lawyers for Internet Companies.

Keynes Law Firm (group)
Founder: Deon Keynes

Specializing in Divorce, Child custody, adoptions, property info, business ventures and copyright laws of SL.

Law and Lawyers (group)
Founder: WebLawyer Lytton

Dedicated to: providing high-quality legal services from licensed attorneys; discussing and debating issues of law, policy, procedure and justice; establishing an open forum for practitioners, scholars and jurists.

Law Office in French Business
SLURL: Lynnwood (177, 200, 49)

RL Lawyer. french [sic] business contracts, french [sic] commercial companies, transfer of companies, commercial lease; all formalities of registration and modifications near the commercial courts.

Legal Practionier (group)
Founder: Katrina Szondi

IM for Legal Questions in SL.

Lexis Looming Law Offices
Founder: Lexis Looming

The Law Offices of Lexis Looming are established to provide the most excellent legal services available in SL or RL. Free consultations are available. Rates are reasonable. Our attorneys have many years of experience and will provide the most discreet, professional and timely services.

LifeLog Studio Headquarters
SLURL: Lifelog island 128, 221, 26 (Mature)

Virtual Worlds Studies Centre, Legal Consulting for the Metaverse, Auditorium, Fair. Centro Studi sui Mondi Virtuali

Little Gray Law Office
SLURL: Jinn 255, 111, 76 (Mature)

SL & RL Dispute Resolution Services, Legal Consulting

Matijavich Law Offices
Founder: Juris Amat

Effective and responsive legal services in financial transactions, corporate formation, real estate and intellectual property. RL office, RL licensed attorneys ready to serve you in SL and beyond. Initial consultations are without charge.

Merv Writer Enterprises
Founder: Merv Writer
SLURL: Bowstring 204, 33, 69 (Mature)

Offers a range of businesses in Second Life, including legal advice as well as accountancy, advertising services, and more.

MMO Intellectual Property Office
Founder: Juris Amat

License and sub-license intellectual property rights with the assistance of real world IP and technology advocates. Document your creative works with our office and receive valuable assistance in developing and managing virtual intellectual property. Serious inquiries only please. Sponsored by Matijevich Law Offices.

Monday Beam & Associates, PC
SLURL: Scandium (171, 24, 32)

Criminal and civil trial litigation, as well as various Pro Bono causes. Real life (RL) contracts for "in game" (SL) business situations.

Mondrian Lykin Law Office
SLURL: Shawangunk 225, 121, 100 (Mature)

SL dispute resolution & legal consulting services.

Oldbull and Associates (group)
Founder: Xring Oldbull

Any legal business.

Perrotta, Cahn & Prieto, P.C.
Contact: Gelf Yalin
SLURL: Neufreistadt 179, 166, 173 (Mature)

SL office of a RL law firm in Atlanta, Georgia, USA. All legal needs.

Plachta Law Office, PC
SLURL: Blue Horizon 180, 80, 26 (Mature)

Plachta Law Office, P.C. (Midwest, USA). Litigation, including family law, criminal defense, native American law, defense of abuse and neglect cases, police misconduct.

Polish Legal Office (Polskie Biuro Prawne)
Founder: Lincoln Beck
email: beck.lincoln@gmail.com
URL: http://metaverselaw.blogspot.com/
SLURL: Digital Zion 36, 191, 22

Copyrights, SL law, Creative Commons, Open Source.

Praxis LLP Law Firm and The Praxis Advisory Group
SLURL: depo 6 107, 53, 30 (PG)

Legal services in California and Colorado, and strategic consultancy for the East Coast, Rocky Mountain States, West Coast and Shanghai.

PUJOL ABOGADOS ASOCIADOS // LAWYERS
Founder: Miquel Ballinger
SLURL: Quest III 32, 152, 0 (Mature)

Servicios juridicos SL y RL abogado.

Rechtsanwalt Jun

Ich bin Rechtsanwalt mit einer auf IT-Recht spezialisierten Kanzlei in Würzburg mit einer Nebenstelle in SL. Ich befasse mich sowohl aus eigenem Interesse und im Auftrag verschiedener Mandanten mit Geschäftskonzepten und Rechtsproblemen von Second Life. Beginnend bei Vertragsrecht, Jugendschutz, AGB-Recht, Kreditsicherung, geistiges Eigentum, Persönlichkeitsrechte und und und.

Richardson & Raffke Legal Associates
Contact: Alex1 Richardson

SL laws explained. Assistance with harassment or infringment. [sic] "We are NOT a RL law firm, and thus will not abide by RL Bar Association laws, however we will make an attempt to do so."

RPHaisha & Associates Consulting Offices
Contact: RPHaishaAOL Back
SLURL: Loba's paradise, Koh Miang (201, 171, 25)

Professional Public Affairs, Mediation, Business, Legal Advise [sic] and Relationship Counseling. Nearly 20 years of Real Life experience.

Second Lawyer (group)
Founder: avvocato Halderman
SLURL: Mullet 175, 12, 149
http://www.2ndlawyer.com

Second Lawyer Law firm. Sl/Rl Litigations. Experienced Lawyers.

Simpson Millar LLP-UK Law Firm
SLURL: Simtalis 18, 195, 27 (PG)

Solicitors and lawyers specialising in injury, consumer, family, employment, conveyancing and general law. UK-based SL lawyers.

SL Law Office

SLURL: Hickok (144, 59, 30)

All kinds of SL problems, group disputes, land management, IP issues, TOS interpretation, divorce mediation, regulatory issues (i.e. Gaming) and special land issues, such as acting as escrow agent in private island transfers. All SL avatar lawyers supervised by a RL lawyer.

Skaddin Lawyer & Guyot LLP

Founder: Lawyer Guyot
SLURL: Orient-Ocean View, Orient (79, 249, 47)

Offering SL service in: Citizen Disputes, Contract Drafting, Contract Disputes, Scam/Fraud Resolution, Rental Property Disputes, Landlord Disputes, Land Purchases, Gaming Issues, Porn Law, Business Development, Linden Lobbying, Second Life Advising, Camping Issues, Abuse/Harassment, Sex Crimes.

Studio Consulenza Brevetti

Welcome Center 168, 106, 21
www.studioconsulenzabrevetti.it

IP & Law Office - Patent, Trademark and Design. Marchi - European Patent Attorneys - PCT - IP and Law Office.

Tebas & Coiduras - Estudio Legal y Tributario

Founder: TClaw Auer
SLURL: Novatierra 239, 23, 38 (PG)
http://www.tebascoiduras.com

Tebas & Coiduras es una firma de asesoramiento multidisciplinar, con un alto grado de especializacin en las reas Legal y Fiscal. Contamos con oficinas propias en Madrid, Huesca, Lausana (Suiza) y prximamente en Buenos Aires (Argentina).

TRU Copyright Dept

Founder: LillyBeth Filth

Copyright agents acting on behalf of Textures R Us and its 30 artists. Representatives may issue take down notice regarding alleged copyright infringement.

Utarid & Springvale Law Offices

SLURL: Colonia Nova 56, 30, 32 (Mature)

Office space and use of private skybox offices or conference room available.

Vanguard Corporate (group)

Founder: Barnes Boa

Vanguard is a corporate group offering legal and property rights advice as well as market analysis, commercial prospecting, financial, efficiency and sustainability reporting solutions for RL and SL businesses within the SL environment.

VOYADIVORCIARME.COM - DIVORCIOS ON LINE

SLURL: ISLA MORENA - Centro Empresarial - Islamorena Bussines, Ampuria Brava (169, 105, 23)

La Primera Web de Divorcios On Line en SL. Consultas gratuitas con abogados de familia especialistas en divorcios de mutuo acuerdo y contenciosos. Actuamos en todos los juzgados de España. No dudes en consultarnos.

W. W. & W. Law Firm (group)

Contact: Jaydon Miles

Property division in SL marriage dissolution. IM one of 4 qualified Attorneys to schedule a free consultation.

Winkler Group

Founder: Charity Winkler

The Winkler group combines the practice of law with psychotherapy, helping couples equitably divide property in dissolution of marriage or partnership, and helping couples work out problems in relationships. The group has a particular interest in those whose presence in Second Life fullfills [sic] a need that cannot be satisifed [sic] in Real Life due to physical or psychological issues.

Dispute Resolution Services

16M2 District Court (group)

Founder: Felix Frankfurter

We hear disputes from any landowner or renter of 16m2 of land or greater, or claims against same. IM Justice Frankfurter for info on how to lodge a petition with the court.

Alternative Dispute Resolution Services

Contact: Bengoshi Shakkyo
SLURL: Peacemakers Training and Education Center, Coburg (85, 49, 112)

In mediation, two or more parties to a dispute meet with a trained, impartial third person to discuss issues and negotiate a resolution. ADR Services' mediators are rl professionals using sl as a tool for conflict resolution. Rates vary by mediator and nature of dispute.

Arbitration Allen

Professional arbitrator/mediator/negotiator in RL & SL helps people find a way to move past the things that are getting in the way of their peaceful coexistence both in their real lives and in their SecondLives.

Bais Din of Second Life

Founder: Jieux Shepherd

A Court of Jewish Law in Second Life. When the parties leave the Bais Din after the decision, whether as winners or losers, they are happy to have fulfilled G-d's will for the resolution of their dispute.

CONNECT: Virtual Business Professionals

Contact: Lias Leandros
SLURL: VooDoo Corp. Communications Center, VooDoo (18, 33, 38)

CONNECT is a networking and education group. Members will work together to develop a customer mediation program and publish information on best business practices in Second Life.

e-Justice Centre do Ministrio da Justia

Founder: Ministrio da Justia portugus; Universidade de Aveiro
e Universidade Nova de Lisboa
Video tour
SLURL: eJustice Centre (42, 142, 27)
15h s 18h (UTC+1), de segunda a sexta-feira (3pm-6pm
(UTC+1), M-F)
www.ejusticecenter.mj.pt

O centro disponibiliza servios de mediao e arbitragem a todos
os avatares do Second Life, para resoluo de litgios resultantes de
assentes em contrato celebrado entre partes. As mediaes e arbitra-
gens esto a cargo do Laboratrio de Resoluo Alternativa de Litgios
da Faculdade de Direito da Universidade Nova de Lisboa.

Mediation/arbitration services overseen by the ADR Lab of
Lisbon New University law faculty, available to all avatars in Sec-
ond Life to resolve contract disputes. Bilingual (Portuguese and
English).

IC Resolucion de Conflictos/ADR

Contact: Kydd Laval
Office/despacho : FEARLY BEACH MAL

Somos una alternativa a los Tribunales y al arbitraje, desde SL, en
los conflictos de toda clase tanto en SL como en RL, como mediad-
ores o consejeros de las partes, ayudando a conseguir un arreglo.
Investigamos cómo actuan otros grupos en SL y queremos coordi-
nar con ellos.

We are alternative dispute resolution (ADR) from SL to any
dispute in Sl or RL, as mediators or advisors of parties, helping
get settlement, We research activity of other groups and wish
coordination.

Olive Branch (group)

Founder: OliveEue Sholokhov
SLURL: Business Bureau Isle (133, 181, 22)

Mediation and escrow service for Second Life. Works directly with
Second Life Business Bureau. Mediates misunderstandings and
protects consumers.

Semple Solutions
SLURL: Semple Peace, Yurim (159, 99, 33)

Helps the Second Life community as a whole by providing Trust?s, [sic] Escrow, Arbitration and Contracts, establishing a contract for services between Consumers and Artisans. categories: Builders, Scripters, Animators, Artist / Sculpters and Entertainment.

SL Mediators (group)
Founder: Neal Nomad

Mediate disputes between SL residents

Services and Facilities

CC Office (lobby) ::: Legal Office (I-st floor) - aHead
SLURL: Digital Zion 31, 121, 22 (PG)

aHead: Content Creation & Sim Design, Political Marketing, We design your digital future!

IronWorks - Business Consulting
Contact: Jayson Watkin
SLURL: Limitless Central (217, 84, 42)

Offering Business related services including escrow/trusts, contract review, consulting, marketing, estate sales and business liquidation/transfers. Iron Works is not related to other outside Ironworks consulting firms.

Nota Bene - Second Life's Notary
SLURL: Nota Bene, Obscure (31, 181, 145)

At Nota Bena, [sic] you can sign documents securely in SL, any time, day or night. Notarizing guarantees everyone agreed to the same thing, and gives you a verifiable receipt with the signatures and original documents. You can also find the Creative Commons License Machine at Nota Bene.

Petrel Consulting (group)

Founder: Joe Petrel

Dedicated to Management Consulting, Leadership Skills Training, Executive Team Building, Seminars, Short Courses, Executive Meeting Facilitation, Startup Assistance, Executive Coaching, Mediation, Conflict Resolution, Relationship Building and Support.

Second Life District Court

Contact: Monday Beam & Associates, P.C.
(under remodel)

The Second Life District Court is available to Lawyers, Plaintiffs, Defendants, Prosecution, State officials, Judges, Bailiffs, Police, Federal Agents and other Law Enforcement officials are welcome [sic] to utilize the facility. Amenities include public seating, judges desk, witness box, jury box with 12 seats, and two tables for litigants and counsel.

SLPTO (SL Patent & Trademark Office)

SLURL: Indigo (93, 77, 66) (Mature)

"Real Protection for Virtual Assets."

Utarid & Springvale Law Offices

SLURL: Colonia Nova 56, 30, 32 (Mature)

Office space and use of private skybox offices or conference room available.

Virtual Intellectual Property Organization (group)

Founder: Juris Amat

Document your creative works, logos and designs with the Virtual PTO(TM) or the MMO Intellectual Property Office(TM) and receive our assistance in managing your virtual intellectual property. Participate in the structuring and establishment of IP notice and enforcement in the virtual world.

Bar Associations and Professional Groups

Abogados SL
Contact: Candela Pfeffer

Advogados (group)
Founder: Joseh Loon

Grupo criado para profissionais do ramo, com vistas a troca de experiência entre os membros, notadamente em direito eletrônico, negociação e regras dentro do SL, bem como nas demais areas. Realizamos consultoria e assesoria juridica no SL e RL!

Advogados Curitiba (group)
Founder: CesarAntonioMello Congrejo

Grupo Criado para reunir os advogados da cidade de Curitiba e Região. Também para usuários de SL que precisem de Assessoria Jurídica.

Corporate Counsel of Second Life (group)
Founder: Iorek Rasmusen
SLURL: Depo Park 2 (74, 27, 63)

The Corporate Counsel group is for those attorneys who work in RL in-house and would like to exchange their opinions and experience. Members who work in private practice or do not have a professional legal qualification can be 'affiliated' to the Corporate Counsel group.

Harvard Law Graduates
Founder: Thaumata Strangelove

IM Thaumata Strangelove for more information and an invitation.

JurisWiki
Founder: Ralf Toll
SLURL: Pixel Expo II 148, 154, 38

Gruppe für Juristen (egal ob Jurastudent, Rechtsanwalt, Richter, Staatsanwalt usw.) und andere an juristischen Themen Interessierten.

Wir treffen uns regelmäßig und diskutieren über Recht, Jura, speziell SecondLifeRecht und mehr. Wir treffen uns regelmäßig im JuraWikiBau (Pixel Expo II 148, 154, 38 (PG). Alles weitere steht auf http://jurawiki.de/WikiTreffenImSecondLife 1 L$ Eintritt. Schließlich müssen wir noch unseren Kredit i. H. v. 100 L$ für's Gruppe eröffnen abbezahlen.

Paralegal Association
Contact: Vanora McMillan

This group is for RL paralegals from all over the world, or for people who are interested in this field.

Pro Bono Second Life (group)
Founder: lorek Rasmuson
SLURL: Depo Park 2 (74, 27, 63)

A group to support, promote and encourage a commitment to pro bono across the legal profession. The group does not give legal advice itself but is a forum for lawyers who undertake or wish to undertake pro bono work in SL and/or in RL. Members who are not lawyers but work in a charitable organisation can be 'affiliated' to Pro Bono SL.

Rechtsanwalt (group)
Founder: Rip Balogh

Diese Gruppe ist für Rechtsanälte, die ihren Kanzleisitz in Deutschland haben und über eine gültige Zulassung als Rechtsanwalt verfügen.

Second Life Bar Association (SLBA)
Founder: Benjamin Noble
SLURL: Sallow (182, 242, 28)

The SLBA is an informal professional organization that helps members navigate the Second Life legal landscape. Meetings, lectures, and social events are held regularly. Attorneys, legal scholars, and other legal professionals are encouraged to join.

Second Life German Bar Association (group)

Founder: Pegasus Shamroy

This group is for those attorneys, who work in RL in Germany and/ or deal with international issues in SL or RL. Herzlich Willkommen in der Deutschen Rechtsanwaltsvereinigung von SL!

Virtual Law Association (group)

Founder: Courtroom Kidd

Dedicated to the practice of law in virtual space; researching virtual worlds' impact on existing statutory and case law; exploring use of virtual tools in the pursuit of justice and the resolution of disputes. Meeting rooms and a mock courtroom are available as well.

Business Organizations

Business Community Association (BCA) (group)

Founder: Demiurgic Mariner

Dedicated to the free exchange of ideas concerning SL commerce and all applicable rules, regulations, standards and laws. Sponsored by InternetLitigators.

CONNECT: Virtual Business Professionals

Contact: Lias Leandros
SLURL: VooDoo Corp. Communications Center, VooDoo (18, 33, 38)

New free business networking group available in Second Life, open to all retailers, venue owners, realtors and service providers. Members will work together to develop a customer mediation program and publish information on best business practices in Second Life.

Customer Protection Agency (group)

Founder: Sophos Villota

The Customer Protection Agency, also known as CPA, is a non-profit independent office which establishes norms to protect and defend

customers in SL, maintaining the public order and the social interest, issuing a list of companies whose customer disrespect have
been proven and issue a seal to reward those who "Play Fair".

Enquirer Better Business

Founder: StaceyLynn Bergman
SLURL: Hot Topics 135, 127, 24 (Mature)

To improve the quality of business here in Second Life, and assist
residents here where Lindens do not. Enquirer Better Business is
an organization of businesses working together to stop scammers,
and encourage good business ethics inside of Second Life. We also
act as a free mediation service for consumers or business owners
who have an issue that they need assistance with.

Second Life Business Bureau

Founder: OliveEue Shololkov
SLURL: Business Bureau Isle (128, 76, 22)

We are a company designed to Register Business' on the basis of
Ethical Conduct Of Business. What we do at the SLBB is lodge and
investigate your complaint and will help to resolve your issue. Each
complaint will be registered with us and a representative will contact the company/Business/Person and attempt to help you resolve
your complaint.

SL Better Business Burea [sic] and Credit

Contact: Kelli Ansett

It is the purpose of this group to present a forum for the fair business
and ethical operation of land sales and rentals. To have a means of
presenting individual concerns to linden and public knowledge.

Talksecondlife.com Members (group)

This is a business group exclusively for members of TalkSecond-
Life.com, a forum for discussing the business, economy and law
of Second Life. Register on the website to be eligible to join this
group. Membership is free.

Educational and Library Groups

Berkman Island

SLURL: Berkman (113, 70, 24)

The Berkman Center for Internet & Society at Harvard Law School "The Berkman Island is a collaboration between individuals associated with the real-life Berkman Center and Second Life citizens. Members of the community have helped landscape, enrich and create unique content." The island includes "an in-world broadcasting center and a 3D replica of the Ames Courtroom at the Harvard Law School."

CyberOne: Open Access (group)

Contact: GeoffMcG Xi

CyberOne: Open Access is a group for At-Large and enrolled participants in Harvard Law School's CyberOne: Law in the Court of Public Opinion class. We are interested in identifying interest and pairing people with projects in order to enhance the open experience of the class. Let's show what this technology can do!

Democracy Island (group)

New York Law School
SLURL: Democracy Island (122, 128, 27)

Building civic spaces in Second Life for the real and virtual world. Includes "Peer to Patent" display in cooperation with USPTO and a build of the United States Supreme Court building. Home of the Landing Lights Park 3D wiki to visualize an actual park in Queens, NY. Open enrollment.

Gone Gitmo (group)

Founder: Nonny Writer

A place to educate and discuss issues surrounding Habeas Corpus rights and the constiutionality [sic] of detention without legal recourse and interrogation as represented by Guantanamo Bay.

Info Island Bell Library LawSpot
Contact: Cat Galileo
SLURL: Info Island (210, 30, 70)

RL law librarian collects US and international legal resources, focusing on issues of law and virtual worlds.

Law Librarians of Second Life (group)
A group for law librarians and library students interested in law librarianship. Open enrollment.

Law School Student (group)
Founder: Mariotino Lungu

Open a [sic] community for those in all fields of legal academia. Our purpose is to bring the various law schools present in Sl into a community based atomosphere, [sic] in which networking and development of the legal profession in SL and RL will take place.

LSAT Games Workshop
Contact: Markie Markstein
SLURL: EduNation III (57, 31, 29)

Retail LSAT prep course instructor with a leading LSAT prep company (not Kaplan or Princeton) for over 4 years offers help with games. IM for pricing and more details.

Nova Southeastern Universary Law Library
SLURL: Cybrary City II (60, 45, 25)

General, U.S. Federal, and Florida state legal resources for law students, lawyers, and the public.

Synthetic Berkman (group)
Founder: Ansible Berkman

A social group created by the Berkman Center at Harvard Law School to explore the metaverse and research novel connections between real and synthetic worlds.

UDSL ADR Group
Founder: Tamsen Mannonen

A RL law class exploring the use of online mediation in SL.

Virtual Worlds, Study Real Businesses
Founder: Beyers Sellers

Business/econ/law educators, textbook authors and publishers, and game developers building a platform to face business challenges, and support academic research.

Governance and Law in Second Life

Al-Andalus Caliphate
Founder: Michel Manen
www.al-andalus.wetpaint.com

The Al-Andalus Caliphate Project reconstructs 13th Century Moor as a political and juridical space shaped by authentic Islamic principles, where Residents can explore the modalities of interaction between different languages, nationalities, religions and cultures. The study of Islamic law is an integral and essential element of the Al-Andalus Caliphate Project.

American Congress of SL (group)
Founder: Alann Bristol

Promote elections and congressional government in SL. To accomplish in SL what the American congress can not do, using the same circumstances, restrictions and laws. Insure continued political debate that result in solutions for the real world

Confederation of Democratic Simulators
Contact: Salzie Sachertorte
SLURL: Neufreistadt (159, 182, 172)
SLURL: Colonia Nova (63, 198, 43)

A Democratic Republic forged to provide residents with a secure environment to work, live and play in; the CDS consists of two regions, Neufreistadt and Colonia Nova.

Independent State of Caledon
Founder: Desmond Shang

A small, aristocratic, very independent 19th century Nation State.

Jurists (group)

Founder: Ashcroft Burnham

A group for those interested in in-world jurisprudence, the development of sophisticated Second Life-specific legal systems, and the legal systems of virtual nations.

Justice List (group)

Founder: Ashcroft Burnham

See listing for "Metaverse Republic."

Law and Lawyers

Founded by WebLaywer Lytton

Dedicated to: providing high-quality legal services from licensed attorneys; discussing and debating issues of law, policy, procedure and justice; establishing an open forum for practitioners, scholars and jurists.

Law Society of Second Life (group)

Founder: Frank Lardner

Dedicated to the non-political, non-commercial study of SL governing systems, study of dispute resolution and study of methods of contracting and enforcing rights/responsibilities.

Lawyers (group)

Founder: Robble Raffke

lex non distinguitur nos non distinguere debemus. "In all successful online communities there's a core group that arises that cares about and gardens effectively, gardens the environment, to keep it growing, to keep it healthy."

Local Government Study Group (group)

Founder: Ashcroft Burnham
http://lgsg.wetpaint.com/

A group to study ways of using the concept of local governments to enhance commerce, and improve organisation and law and order in

Second Life, and to lobby Linden Lab to integrate local government tools into the Second Life software. Open enrollment.

Local Governments in SL

To study and advocate fair and effective tools for use by local governments within Second Life. We strive to conduct our group as democratically as possible.

Mediation (group)

Founder: German Guru
Contact: German Zond

Group to explore the feasibility of Second Life for mediation and arbitration. Main language: German

Metaverse Republic (group)

Contact: Ashcroft Burnham
SLURL: Shawangunk 215, 89, 97
http://www.metaverserepublic.org

The Metaverse Republic, currently work in progress, will be a legal system for Second Life, with real powers of enforcement originating in user-created tools, and a democratic parliament. There are many disputes and potential disputes in Second Life that could benefit from formal resolution: disputes about broken agreements, land use, alleged griefing, extortion, etc. The Metaverse Republic aims to provide an effective and fair system for resolving such disputes.

Our World - Our Representation (group)

Contact: Anshe Chung

The Metaverse should not be ruled by a single company, but by those who actually pay for it. We demand that Linden Lab passes on the political control of Second Life to its residents, based on their monthly financial contributions. We don't believe in "One king - all votes" nor in "One alt - one vote" but in "One sqm - one vote". We deserve a democratic government based on this principle instead of a dictatorship. We also believe in maximum local autonomy of neighbourhoods within Second Life.

Parliament of Second Life (group)
Contact: Monica09 Rotaru

In direct correspondence with other policy-making bodies here in Second Life, this group maintains all the facets of a real legislature, passing the laws that the Lindens have so long ignored. Our decrees are implemented by our other organizations, so that hopefully, SL can be declared a system truly comprised of its colorful user base.

Real Life Government in Second Life (group)
Contact: Hackshaven Harford

A group designed to assist in bringing government agencies into virtual worlds.

Second Lawyer (group)
Founder: avvocato Halderman
SLURL: Mullet 175, 12, 149

Founded by a team of real life lawyers, this group's purpose is to create a Second Life Law System.

Second Life Law (group)
Founder: Everett Streeter

Dedicated to furthering legal issues raised within Second Life and other virtual worlds issues. Legal professionals and other interested parties should join. Long-term goals include the establishment of virtual "courts" or places where residents can settle disputes as well as providing services such as escrow and other services traditionally handled by attorneys.

Roleplay Groups

Law Offices (group)
Founder: Elizabeth Dailey

Law Offices group is available for those who wish to Roleplay Law, Court, Trials, Attorney, Prosecutor etc who have some knowledge with the Legal system or ways of getting information when situations arise. Of course this group is available for actual Attorneys to participate with, those studying Law.

Law Offices of Herouin & Dailey (roleplay group)
Contact: Angelina Herouin or Elizabeth Dailey
Hathian Sim (RP SIM)

Interested in legal advice? In need of a Defense Lawyer? You can be added to the group as a client if you choose to hire our team. Ease of contact and advice when in need! *Roleplaying at The Crack Den*

Night Court (group)
Founder: Wendy Cerminara

"Night Court" is a group for those interested in roleplaying the sort of legal eagle parts we've all seen in television and movie dramas. This group isn't intended for real lawyers, but their input and participation is welcomed and encouraged!

Tombstone Criminal Law (group)
Founder: Elaine Peterman

Bound by the law to uphold civility in the city as well as the courtroom. Positions include Prosecution, Defense Counsel and Judges. You may prefer one role over the rest, but you may be asked to play a different role from time to time. But will try to give you your first choices more often then [sic] none.

Appendix III: Virtual Law Resources on the Web

Kate Fitz, who graciously permitted the reprinting of her Second Life "Galileo Law Directory" in Appendix II, has also compiled a list of web resources regarding virtual law. That list is reprinted here, with a few editorial modifications.

Law and Virtual Worlds Blogs

Between Lawyers: http://betweenlawyers.corante.com/

Digital Media Law: http://digitalmedialaw.blogspot.com

Internet Cases: http://www.internetcases.com/

Law of the Game: http://lawofthegame.blogspot.com/

MetaSecurity: http://metasecurity.net/

Metaverse Law (Polish language): http://metaverse-law.blogspot.com/

PlayNoEvil Game Security News & Analysis: http://playnoevil.com/serendipity/

Terra Nova: http://terranova.blogs.com/terra_nova/

Virtual Worlds News: http://www.virtualworldsnews.com/

Virtual Worlds, Real Profits: http://www.virtualeconomies.net/blog/

Virtually Blind[1]: http://virtuallyblind.com/

Law and Virtual Worlds Primary Source Research Site

Social Science Research Network: http://www.ssrn.com/

---

1. *Virtually Blind* is edited by Benjamin Duranske, the author of *Virtual Law.*

Appendix IV: Second Life Terms of Service

Reprinted here are the current Second Life Terms of Service. They are likely to change, and updates can be found at http://secondlife.com/corporate/tos.php.

***

Welcome to Second Life! The following agreement (this "Agreement" or the "Terms of Service") describes the terms on which Linden Research, Inc. ("Linden Lab") offers you access to its services. This offer is conditioned on your agreement to all of the terms and conditions contained in the Terms of Service, including your compliance with the policies and terms linked to (by way of the provided URLs) from this Agreement. By using Second Life, you agree to these Terms of Service. If you do not so agree, you should decline this agreement, in which case you are prohibited from accessing or using Second Life. Linden Lab may amend this Agreement at any time in its sole discretion, effective upon posting the amended Agreement at the domain or subdomains of http://secondlife.com where the prior version of this Agreement was posted, or by communicating these changes through any written contact method we have established with you.

THE SERVICES AND CONTENT OF SECOND LIFE

1.1 Basic description of the service: Second Life, a multi-user environment, including software and websites.

"Second Life" is the multi-user online service offered by Linden Lab, including the software provided to you by Linden Lab (collectively, the "Linden Software") and the online environments that support the service, including without limitation: the server computation, software access, messaging and protocols that simulate the Second Life environment (the "Servers"), the software that is provided by Linden Lab and installed on the local computer or other device you use to access the Servers and thereby view or otherwise access the Second Life environment (the "Viewer"), application program interfaces provided by Linden Lab to you for use with Second Life (the "APIs"), and access to the websites and services available from the domain and subdomains of http://secondlife.com (the "Websites"). The Servers, Viewer, APIs, Websites and any other Linden Software collectively constitute the "Service" as used in this Agreement.

1.2 Linden Lab is a service provider, which means, among other things, that Linden Lab does not control various aspects of the Service.

You acknowledge that Linden Lab is a service provider that may allow people to interact online regarding topics and content chosen by users of the service, and that users can alter the service environment on a real-time basis. Linden Lab generally does not regulate the content of communications between users or users' interactions with the Service. As a result, Linden Lab has very limited control, if any, over the quality, safety, morality, legality, truthfulness or accuracy of various aspects of the Service.

1.3 Content available in the Service may be provided by users of the Service, rather than by Linden Lab. Linden Lab and other parties have rights in their respective content, which you agree to respect.

You acknowledge that: (i) by using the Service you may have access to graphics, sound effects, music, video, audio, computer programs, animation, text and other creative output (collectively, "Content"), and (ii) Content may be provided under license by independent content providers, including contributions from other users of the Service (all such independent content providers, "Content Providers"). Linden Lab does not pre-screen Content.

You acknowledge that Linden Lab and other Content Providers have rights in their respective Content under copyright and other applicable laws and treaty provisions, and that except as described in this Agreement, such rights are not licensed or otherwise transferred by mere use of the Service. You accept full responsibility and liability for your use of any Content in violation of any such rights. You agree that your creation of Content is not in any way based upon any expectation of compensation from Linden Lab.

Certain of the fonts in the Meta family of copyrighted typefaces are used in Second Life under license from FSI FontShop International. You acknowledge that you may not copy any Meta font that is included in the Viewer and that you may use any such Meta font solely to the extent necessary to use the Linden Software in Second Life and that you will not use such Meta fonts for any other purpose whatsoever.

1.4 Second Life "currency" is a limited license right available for purchase or free distribution at Linden Lab's discretion, and is not redeemable for monetary value from Linden Lab.

You acknowledge that the Service presently includes a component of in-world fictional currency ("Currency" or "Linden Dollars" or "L$"), which constitutes a limited license right to use a feature of our product when, as, and if allowed by Linden Lab. Linden Lab may charge fees for the right to use Linden Dollars, or may distribute Linden Dollars without charge, in its sole discretion.

Regardless of terminology used, Linden Dollars represent a limited license right governed solely under the terms of this Agreement, and are not redeemable for any sum of money or monetary value from Linden Lab at any time. You agree that Linden Lab has the absolute right to manage, regulate, control, modify and/or eliminate such Currency as it sees fit in its sole discretion, in any general or specific case, and that Linden Lab will have no liability to you based on its exercise of such right.

1.5 Second Life offers an exchange, called LindeX, for the trading of Linden Dollars, which uses the terms "buy" and "sell" to indicate the transfer of license rights to use Linden Dollars. Use and regulation of LindeX is at Linden Lab's sole discretion.

The Service currently includes a component called "Currency Exchange" or "LindeX," which refers to an aspect of the Service through which Linden Lab administers transactions among users for the purchase and sale of the licensed right to use Currency. Notwithstanding any other language or context to the contrary, as used in this Agreement and throughout the Service in the context of Currency transfer: (a) the term "sell" means "to transfer for consideration to another user the licensed right to use Currency in accordance with the Terms of Service," (b) the term "buy" means "to receive for consideration from another user the licensed right to use Currency in accordance with the Terms of Service," (c) the terms "buyer," "seller", "sale" and "purchase" and similar terms have corresponding meanings to the root terms "buy" and "sell," (d) "sell order" and similar terms mean a request from a user to Linden Lab to list Currency for sale on the Currency Exchange at a requested sale price, and (e) "buy order" and similar terms mean a request from a user for Linden Lab to match open sale listings with a requested purchase price and facilitate completion of the sale of Currency.

You agree and acknowledge that Linden Lab may deny any sell order or buy order individually or with respect to general volume or price limitations set by Linden Lab for any reason. Linden Lab may limit sellers or buyers to any group of users at any time. Linden Lab may halt, suspend, discontinue, or reverse any Currency Exchange transaction (whether proposed, pending or past) in cases of actual or suspected fraud, violations of other laws or regulations, or deliberate disruptions to or interference with the Service.

1.6 Second Life is subject to scheduled and unscheduled service interruptions. All aspects of the Service are subject to change or elimination at Linden Lab's sole discretion.

Linden Lab reserves the right to interrupt the Service with or without prior notice for any reason or no reason. You agree that Linden Lab will not be liable for any interruption of the Service, delay or failure to perform, and you understand that except as otherwise specifically provided in Linden Lab's billing policies posted at http://secondlife.com/corporate/billing.php, you shall not be entitled to any refunds of fees for interruption of service or failure to perform. Linden Lab has the right at any time for any reason or no reason to change and/or eliminate any aspect(s) of the Service as it sees fit in its sole discretion.

1.7 In the event you choose to use paid aspects of the Service, you agree to the posted pricing and billing policies on the Websites.

Certain aspects of the Service are provided for a fee or other charge. These fees and charges are described on the Websites, and in the event you elect to use paid aspects of the Service, you agree to the pricing, payment and billing policies applicable to such fees and charges, posted or linked at http://secondlife.com/corporate/billing.php. Linden Lab may add new services for additional fees and charges, or proactively amend fees and charges for existing services, at any time in its sole discretion.

ACCOUNT REGISTRATION AND REQUIREMENTS

2.1 You must establish an account to use Second Life, using true and accurate registration information.

You must establish an account with Linden Lab (your "Account") to use the Service, except for those portions of the Websites to which

Linden Lab allows access without registration. You agree to provide true, accurate, current and complete information about yourself as prompted by the registration form ("Registration Data") and maintain and promptly update the Registration Data to keep it true, accurate, current and complete. You may establish an Account with Registration Data provided to Linden Lab by a third party through the use of an API, in which case you may have a separate, additional account relationship with such third party. You authorize Linden Lab, directly or through third parties, to make any inquiries we consider necessary to validate your Registration Data. Linden Lab reserves all rights to vigorously pursue legal action against all persons who misrepresent personal information or are otherwise untruthful about their identity, and to suspend or cancel Accounts registered with inaccurate or incomplete information. Notwithstanding the foregoing, you acknowledge that Linden Lab cannot guarantee the accuracy of any information submitted by any user of the Service, nor any identity information about any user.

2.2 You must be 13 years of age or older to access Second Life; minors over the age of 13 are only permitted in a separate area, which adults are generally prohibited from using. Linden Lab cannot absolutely control whether minors or adults gain unauthorized access to the Service.

You must be at least 13 years of age to participate in the Service. Users under the age of 18 are prohibited from accessing the Service other than in the area designated by Linden Lab for use by users from 13 through 17 years of age (the "Teen Area"). Users age 18 and older are prohibited from accessing the Teen Area. Any user age 18 and older who gains unauthorized access to the Teen Area is in breach of this Agreement and may face immediate termination of any or all Accounts held by such user for any area of the Service. If you reside in a jurisdiction where the age of majority is greater than 18 years old, you are prohibited from accessing the Service until you have reached such age of majority.

By accepting this agreement in connection with an Account outside the Teen Area, you represent that you are an adult 18 years of age or older. By accepting this agreement in connection with an Account for use in the Teen Area, you represent that (i) you are at least 13 years of age and less than 18 years of age; (ii) you have read and accept this Agreement; (iii) your parent or legal guardian has consented to you having an Account for use of the Teen Area and participating in the Service, and to providing your personal information for your Account; and (iv) your parent or legal guardian has read and accepted this Agreement.

Linden Lab cannot absolutely control whether minors gain access to the Service other than the Teen Area, and makes no representation that users outside the Teen Area are not minors. Linden Lab cannot absolutely control whether adults gain access to the Teen Area of the Service, and makes no representation that users inside the Teen Area are not adults. Adult employees, contractors and partners of Linden Lab regularly conduct their work in the Teen Area. Linden Lab cannot ensure that other users or any non-employee of Linden Lab will not provide Content or access to Content that parents or guardians may find inappropriate or that any user may find objectionable.

2.3 You need to use an account name in Second Life which is not misleading, offensive or infringing. You must select and keep secure your account password.

You must choose an account name to identify yourself to Linden Lab staff (your "Account Name"), which will also serve as the name for the graphical representation of your body in the Service (such representation, an "Avatar"). You may not select as your Account Name the name of another person to the extent that could cause deception or confusion; a name which violates any trademark right, copyright, or other proprietary right; a name which may mislead other users to believe you to be an employee of Linden Lab; or a name which Linden Lab deems in its discretion to be vulgar or otherwise offensive. Linden Lab reserves the right to delete or change any Account Name for any reason or no reason. You are fully responsible for all activities conducted through your Account or under your Account Name.

At the time your Account is opened, you must select a password. You are responsible for maintaining the confidentiality of your password and are responsible for any harm resulting from your disclosure, or authorizing the disclosure of, your password or from use by any person of your password to gain access to your Account or Account Name. At no time should you respond to an online request for a password other than in connection with the log-on process to the Service. Your disclosure of your password to any other person is entirely at your own risk.

2.4 Account registrations are limited per unique person. Transfers of accounts are generally not permitted.

Linden Lab may require you to submit an indication of unique identity in the account registration process; e.g. credit card or other payment information, or SMS message code or other information requested by Linden Lab. When an account is created, the information given for the account must match the address, phone number, and/or other unique identifier information associated with the identification method. You may register multiple accounts per identification method only at Linden Lab's sole discretion. A single account may be used by a single legal entity at Linden Lab's sole discretion and subject to Linden Lab's requirements. Additional accounts beyond the first account per unique user may be subject to fees upon account creation. You may not transfer your Account to any third party without the prior written consent of Linden Lab; notwithstanding the foregoing, Linden Lab will not unreasonably withhold consent to the transfer of an Account in good standing by operation of valid written will to a single natural person, provided that proper notice and documentation are delivered as requested by Linden Lab.

2.5 You may cancel your account at any time; however, there are no refunds for cancellation.

Accounts may be cancelled by you at any time. Upon your election to cancel, your account will be cancelled within 24 hours, but if you have paid for a period in advance you will be allowed to use the remaining time according to these Terms of Service unless your account or this Agreement is suspended or terminated based on our belief that you have violated this Agreement. There will be no refunds for any unused time on a subscription or any prepaid fees for any portion of the Service.

2.6 Linden Lab may suspend or terminate your account at any time, without refund or obligation to you.

Linden Lab has the right at any time for any reason or no reason to suspend or terminate your Account, terminate this Agreement, and/or refuse any and all current or future use of the Service without notice or liability to you. In the event that Linden Lab suspends or terminates your Account or this Agreement, you understand and agree that you shall receive no refund or exchange for any unused time on a subscription, any license or subscription fees, any content or data associated with your Account, or for anything else.

2.7 Accounts affiliated with delinquent accounts are subject to remedial actions related to the delinquent account.

In the event an Account is suspended or terminated for your breach of this Agreement or your payment delinquency (in each case as determined in Linden Lab's sole discretion), Linden Lab may suspend or terminate the Account associated with such breach and any or all other Accounts held by you or your affiliates, and your breach shall be deemed to apply to all such Accounts.

2.8 You are responsible for your own Internet access.

Linden Lab does not provide Internet access, and you are responsible for all fees associated with your Internet connection.

LICENSE TERMS AND OTHER INTELLECTUAL PROPERTY TERMS

3.1 You have a nonexclusive, limited, revocable license to use Second Life while you are in compliance with the terms of service.

Subject to the terms of this Agreement, Linden Lab grants to you a non-exclusive, limited, fully revocable license to use the Linden Software and the rest of the Service during the time you are in full compliance with the Terms of Service. Additional terms may apply to use of the APIs or other separate elements of the Service (i.e.

elements that are not required to use the Viewer or the Servers); these terms are available where such separate elements are available for download from the Websites. Nothing in this Agreement, or on Linden Lab's websites, shall be construed as granting you any other rights or privileges of any kind with respect to the Service or to any Content. You acknowledge that your participation in the Service, including your creation or uploading of Content in the Service, does not make you a Linden Lab employee and that you do not expect to be, and will not be, compensated by Linden Lab for such activities.

3.2 You retain copyright and other intellectual property rights with respect to Content you create in Second Life, to the extent that you have such rights under applicable law. However, you must make certain representations and warranties, and provide certain license rights, forbearances and indemnification, to Linden Lab and to other users of Second Life.

Users of the Service can create Content on Linden Lab's servers in various forms. Linden Lab acknowledges and agrees that, subject to the terms and conditions of this Agreement, you will retain any and all applicable copyright and other intellectual property rights with respect to any Content you create using the Service, to the extent you have such rights under applicable law.

Notwithstanding the foregoing, you understand and agree that by submitting your Content to any area of the service, you automatically grant (and you represent and warrant that you have the right to grant) to Linden Lab: (a) a royalty-free, worldwide, fully paid-up, perpetual, irrevocable, non-exclusive right and license to (i) use, reproduce and distribute your Content within the Service as permitted by you through your interactions on the Service, and (ii) use and reproduce (and to authorize third parties to use and reproduce) any of your Content in any or all media for marketing and/or promotional purposes in connection with the Service, provided that in the event that your Content appears publicly in material under the control of Linden Lab, and you provide written notice to Linden Lab of your desire to discontinue the distribution of such Content in such material (with sufficient specificity to allow Linden Lab, in its sole discretion, to identify the relevant Content and materials), Linden Lab will make commercially reasonable efforts to cease its distribution of such Content following the receipt of such notice, although Linden Lab cannot provide any assurances regarding materials produced or distributed prior to the receipt of such notice; (b) the perpetual and irrevocable right to delete any or all of your Content from Linden Lab's servers and from the Service, whether intentionally or unintentionally, and for any reason or no reason, without any liability of any kind to you or any other party; and (c) a royalty-free, fully paid-up, perpetual, irrevocable, non-exclusive right and license to copy, analyze and use any of your Content as Linden Lab may deem necessary or desirable for purposes of debugging, testing and/or providing support services in connection with the Service. Further, you agree to grant to Linden Lab a royalty-free, worldwide, fully paid-up, perpetual, irrevocable, non-exclusive, sublicensable right and license to exercise the copyright, publicity, and database rights you have in your account information, including any data or other information generated by your account activity, in any media now known or not currently known, in accordance with our privacy policy as set forth below, including the incorporation by reference of terms posted at http://secondlife .com/corporate/privacy.php.

You also understand and agree that by submitting your Content to any area of the Service, you automatically grant (or you warrant that the owner of such Content has expressly granted) to Linden Lab and to all other users of the Service a non-exclusive, worldwide, fully paid-up, transferable, irrevocable, royalty-free and perpetual License, under any and all patent rights you may have or obtain with respect to your Content, to use your Content for all purposes within the Service. You further agree that you will not make any claims against Linden Lab or against other users of the Service based on any allegations that any activities by either of the foregoing within the Service infringe your (or anyone else's) patent rights.

You further understand and agree that: (i) you are solely responsible for understanding all copyright, patent, trademark, trade secret and other intellectual property or other laws that may apply to your Content hereunder; (ii) you are solely responsible for, and Linden Lab will have no liability in connection with, the legal consequences of any actions or failures to act on your part while using the Service, including without limitation any legal consequences relating to your intellectual property rights; and (iii) Linden Lab's acknowledgement hereunder of your intellectual property rights in your Content does not constitute a legal opinion or legal advice, but is intended solely as an expression of Linden Lab's intention not to require users of the Service to forego certain intellectual property rights with respect to Content they create using the Service, subject to the terms of this Agreement.

3.3 Linden Lab retains ownership of the account and related data, regardless of intellectual property rights you may have in content you create or otherwise own.

You agree that even though you may retain certain copyright or other intellectual property rights with respect to Content you create while using the Service, you do not own the account you use to access the Service, nor do you own any data Linden Lab stores on Linden Lab servers (including without limitation any data representing or embodying any or all of your Content). Your intellectual property rights do not confer any rights of access to the Service or any rights to data stored by or on behalf of Linden Lab.

3.4 Linden Lab licenses its textures and environmental content to you for your use in creating content in-world.

During any period in which your Account is active and in good standing, Linden Lab gives you permission to create still and/or moving media, for use only within the virtual world environment of the Service ("in-world"), which use or include the "textures" and/or "environmental content" that are both (a) created or owned by Linden Lab and (b) displayed by Linden Lab in-world.

CONDUCT BY USERS OF SECOND LIFE

4.1 You agree to abide by certain rules of conduct, including the Community Standards and other rules prohibiting illegal and other practices that Linden Lab deems harmful.

You agree to read and comply with the Community Standards posted on the Websites, (for users 18 years of age and older, at http://secondlife.com/corporate/cs.php; and for users of the Teen Area, at http://teen.secondlife.com/footer/cs

In addition to abiding at all times by the Community Standards, you agree that you shall not: (i) take any action or upload, post, e-mail or otherwise transmit Content that infringes or violates any third party rights; (ii) impersonate any person or entity without their consent, including, but not limited to, a Linden Lab employee, or falsely state or otherwise misrepresent your affiliation with a person or entity; (iii) take any action or upload, post, e-mail or otherwise transmit Content that violates any law or regulation; (iv) take any action or upload, post, e-mail or otherwise transmit Content as determined by Linden Lab at its sole discretion that is harmful, threatening, abusive, harassing, causes tort, defamatory, vulgar, obscene, libelous, invasive of another's privacy, hateful, or racially, ethnically or otherwise objectionable; (v) take any actions or upload, post, e-mail or otherwise transmit Content that contains any viruses, Trojan horses, worms, spyware, time bombs, cancelbots or other computer programming routines that are intended to damage, detrimentally interfere with, surreptitiously intercept or expropriate any system, data or personal information; (vi) take any action or upload, post, email or otherwise transmit any Content that would violate any right or duty under any law or under contractual or fiduciary relationships (such as inside information, proprietary and confidential information learned or disclosed as part of employment relationships or under nondisclosure agreements); (vii) upload, post, email or otherwise transmit any unsolicited or unauthorized advertising, or promotional materials, that are in the nature of "junk mail," "spam," "chain letters," "pyramid schemes," or any other form of solicitation that Linden Lab considers in its sole discretion to be of such nature; (viii) interfere with or disrupt the Service or servers or networks connected to the Service, or disobey any requirements, procedures, policies or regulations of networks connected to the Service; (ix) attempt to gain access to any other user's Account or password; or (x) "stalk", abuse or attempt to abuse, or otherwise harass another user. Any violation by you of the terms of the foregoing sentence may result in immediate and permanent suspension or cancellation of your Account. You agree that Linden Lab may take whatever steps it deems necessary to abridge, or prevent behavior of any sort on the Service in its sole discretion, without notice to you.

4.2 You agree to use Second Life as provided, without unauthorized software or other means of access or use. You will not make unauthorized works from or conduct unauthorized distribution of the Linden Software.

Linden Lab has designed the Service to be experienced only as offered by Linden Lab at the Websites or partner websites. Linden Lab is not responsible for any aspect of the Service that is accessed or experienced using software or other means that are not provided by Linden Lab. You agree not to create or provide any server emulators or other software or other means that provide access to or use of the Servers without the express written authorization of Linden Lab. Notwithstanding the foregoing, you may use and create software that provides access to the Servers for substantially similar function (or subset thereof) as the Viewer; provided that such software is not used for and does not enable any violation of these Terms of Service. Linden Lab is not obligated to allow access to the Servers by any software that is not provided by Linden Lab, and you agree to cease using, creating, distributing or providing any such software at the request of Linden Lab. You are prohibited from taking any action that imposes an unreasonable or disproportionately large load on Linden Lab's infrastructure.

You may not charge any third party for using the Linden Software to access and/or use the Service, and you may not modify, adapt, reverse engineer (except as otherwise permitted by applicable law), decompile or attempt to discover the source code of the Linden Software, or create any derivative works of the Linden Software or the Service, or otherwise use the Linden Software except as expressly provided in this Agreement. You may not copy or distribute any of the written materials associated with the Service. Notwithstanding the foregoing, you may copy the Viewer that Linden Lab provides to you, for backup purposes and may give copies of the Viewer to others free of charge. Further, you may use and modify the source code for the Viewer as permitted by any open source license agreement under which Linden Lab distributes such Viewer source code.

4.3 You will comply with the processes of the Digital Millennium Copyright Act regarding copyright infringement claims covered under such Act.

Our policy is to respond to notices of alleged infringement that comply with the Digital Millennium Copyright Act ("DMCA"). Copyright-infringing materials found within the world of Second Life can be identified and removed via Linden Lab's DMCA compliance process listed at http://secondlife.com/corporate/dmca.php, and you agree to comply with such process in the event you are involved in any claim of copyright infringement to which the DMCA may be applicable.

4.4 You will not use the marks of Linden Lab without authorization from Linden Lab.

You are not permitted to use the marks "Second Life", "Linden Lab", the eye-in-hand logo, or any other trade, service or other marks registered to or owned by Linden Lab, except as explicitly authorized by Linden Lab and in accordance with guidelines posted at http://secondlife.com/community/fansites_regs.php.

RELEASES, DISCLAIMERS OF WARRANTY, LIMITATION OF LIABILITY, AND INDEMNIFICATION

5.1 You release Linden Lab from your claims relating to other users of Second Life. Linden Lab has the right but not the obligation to resolve disputes between users of Second Life.

As a condition of access to the Service, you release Linden Lab (and Linden Lab's shareholders, partners, affiliates, directors, officers, subsidiaries, employees, agents, suppliers, licensees, distributors) from claims, demands and damages (actual and consequential) of every kind and nature, known and unknown, suspected and unsuspected, disclosed and undisclosed, arising out of or in any way connected with any dispute you have or claim to have with one or more users of the Service. You further understand and agree that: (a) Linden Lab will have the right but not the obligation to resolve disputes between users relating to the Service, and Linden Lab's resolution of any particular dispute does not create an obligation to resolve any other dispute; (b) to the extent Linden Lab elects to resolve such disputes, it will do so in good faith based solely on the general rules and standards of the Service and will not make judgments regarding legal issues or claims; (c) Linden Lab's resolution of such disputes will be final with respect to the virtual world of the Service but will have no bearing on any real-world legal disputes in which users of the Service may become involved; and (d) you hereby release Linden Lab (and Linden Lab's shareholders, partners, affiliates, directors, officers, subsidiaries, employees, agents, suppliers, licensees, distributors) from claims, demands and damages (actual and consequential) of every kind and nature, known and unknown, suspected and unsuspected, disclosed and undisclosed, arising out of or in any way connected with Linden Lab's resolution of disputes relating to the Service.

5.2 Other service or product providers may form contractual relationships with you. Linden Lab is not a party to your relationship with such other providers.

Subject to the terms of this Agreement, you may view or use the environment simulated by the Servers through viewer software that is not the Viewer provided by Linden Lab, and you may register for use of Second Life through websites that are not Websites owned and operated by Second Life. Linden Lab is not responsible for any software used with or in connection with Second Life other than Linden Software developed by Linden Lab. Linden Lab does not control and is not responsible for any information you provide to parties other than Linden Lab. Linden Lab is not a party to your agreement with any party that provides software, products or services to you in connection with Second Life.

5.3 All data on Linden Lab's servers are subject to deletion, alteration or transfer.

When using the Service, you may accumulate Content, Currency, objects, items, scripts, equipment, or other value or status indicators that reside as data on Linden Lab's servers. THESE DATA, AND

ANY OTHER DATA, ACCOUNT HISTORY AND ACCOUNT NAMES RESIDING ON LINDEN LAB'S SERVERS, MAY BE DELETED, ALTERED, MOVED OR TRANSFERRED AT ANY TIME FOR ANY REASON IN LINDEN LAB'S SOLE DISCRETION.

YOU ACKNOWLEDGE THAT, NOTWITHSTANDING ANY COPYRIGHT OR OTHER RIGHTS YOU MAY HAVE WITH RESPECT TO ITEMS YOU CREATE USING THE SERVICE, AND NOTWITHSTANDING ANY VALUE ATTRIBUTED TO SUCH CONTENT OR OTHER DATA BY YOU OR ANY THIRD PARTY, LINDEN LAB DOES NOT PROVIDE OR GUARANTEE, AND EXPRESSLY DISCLAIMS (SUBJECT TO ANY UNDERLYING INTELLECTUAL PROPERTY RIGHTS IN THE CONTENT), ANY VALUE, CASH OR OTHERWISE, ATTRIBUTED TO ANY DATA RESIDING ON LINDEN LAB'S SERVERS.

YOU UNDERSTAND AND AGREE THAT LINDEN LAB HAS THE RIGHT, BUT NOT THE OBLIGATION, TO REMOVE ANY CONTENT (INCLUDING YOUR CONTENT) IN WHOLE OR IN PART AT ANY TIME FOR ANY REASON OR NO REASON, WITH OR WITHOUT NOTICE AND WITH NO LIABILITY OF ANY KIND.

5.4 Linden Lab provides the Service on an "as is" basis, without express or implied warranties.

LINDEN LAB PROVIDES THE SERVICE, THE LINDEN SOFTWARE, YOUR ACCOUNT AND ALL OTHER SERVICES STRICTLY ON AN "AS IS" BASIS, PROVIDED AT YOUR OWN RISK, AND HEREBY EXPRESSLY DISCLAIMS ALL WARRANTIES OR CONDITIONS OF ANY KIND, WRITTEN OR ORAL, EXPRESS, IMPLIED OR STATUTORY, INCLUDING WITHOUT LIMITATION ANY IMPLIED WARRANTY OF TITLE, NONINFRINGEMENT, MERCHANTABILITY OR FITNESS FOR A PARTICULAR PURPOSE.

Without limiting the foregoing, Linden Lab does not ensure continuous, error-free, secure or virus-free operation of the Service, the Linden Software or your Account, and you understand that you shall not be entitled to refunds for fees based on Linden Lab's failure to provide any of the foregoing other than as explicitly provided in this Agreement. Some jurisdictions do not allow the disclaimer of implied warranties, and to that extent, the foregoing disclaimer may not apply to you.

5.5 Linden Lab's liability to you is expressly limited, to the extent allowable under applicable law.

IN NO EVENT SHALL LINDEN LAB OR ANY OF ITS SHAREHOLDERS, PARTNERS, AFFILIATES, DIRECTORS, OFFICERS, SUBSIDIARIES, EMPLOYEES, AGENTS, SUPPLIERS, LICENSEES OR DISTRIBUTORS BE LIABLE TO YOU OR TO ANY THIRD PARTY FOR ANY SPECIAL, INCIDENTAL, CONSEQUENTIAL, PUNITIVE OR EXEMPLARY DAMAGES, INCLUDING WITHOUT LIMITATION ANY DAMAGES FOR LOST PROFITS, ARISING (WHETHER IN CONTRACT, TORT, STRICT LIABILITY OR OTHERWISE) OUT OF OR IN CONNECTION WITH THE SERVICE (INCLUDING ITS MODIFICATION OR TERMINATION), THE LINDEN SOFTWARE, YOUR ACCOUNT (INCLUDING ITS TERMINA-TION OR SUSPENSION) OR THIS AGREEMENT, WHETHER OR NOT LINDEN LAB MAY HAVE BEEN ADVISED THAT ANY SUCH DAMAGES MIGHT OR COULD OCCUR AND NOTWITHSTANDING THE FAILURE OF ESSENTIAL PURPOSE OF ANY REMEDY. IN ADDITION, IN NO EVENT WILL LINDEN LAB'S CUMULATIVE LIABILITY TO YOU FOR DIRECT DAMAGES OF ANY KIND OR NATURE EXCEED FIFTY DOL-LARS (U.S. $50.00). Some jurisdictions do not allow the foregoing limitations of liability, so to the extent that any such limitation is impermissible, such limitation may not apply to you. You agree that Linden Lab cannot be held responsible or liable for anything that occurs or results from accessing or subscribing to the Service.

5.6 You will indemnify Linden Lab from claims arising from breach of this Agreement by you, from your use of Second Life, from loss of Content due to your actions, or from alleged infringement by you.

At Linden Lab's request, you agree to defend, indemnify and hold harmless Linden Lab, its shareholders, partners, affiliates, direc-tors, officers, subsidiaries, employees, agents, suppliers, licensees, distributors, Content Providers, and other users of the Service, from all damages, liabilities, claims and expenses, including with-out limitation attorneys' fees and costs, arising from any breach of this Agreement by you, or from your use of the Service. You agree to defend, indemnify and hold harmless Linden Lab, its sharehold-ers, partners, affiliates, directors, officers, subsidiaries, employees, agents, suppliers, licensees, and distributors, from all damages, liabilities, claims and expenses, including without limitation attorneys' fees and costs, arising from: (a) any action or inaction by you in connection with the deletion, alteration, transfer or other loss of Content, status or other data held in connection with your Account, and (b) any claims by third parties that your activity or Content in the Service infringes upon, violates or misappropriates any of their intellectual property or proprietary rights.

PRIVACY POLICY

6.1 Linden Lab uses your personal information to operate and improve Second Life, and will not give your personal information to third parties except to operate, improve and protect the Service.

The personal information you provide to us during registration is used for Linden Lab's internal purposes only. Linden Lab uses the information it collects to learn what you like and to improve the Service. Linden Lab will not give any of your personal information to any third party without your express approval except: as reasonably necessary to fulfill your service request, to third-party fulfillment houses, customer support, billing and credit verification services, and the like; to comply with tax and other applicable law; as otherwise expressly permitted by this Agreement or as otherwise authorized by you; to law enforcement or other appropriate third parties in connection with criminal investigations and other investigations of fraud; or as otherwise necessary to protect Linden Lab, its agents and other users of the Service. Linden Lab does not guarantee the security of any of your private transmissions against unauthorized or unlawful interception or access by third parties. Linden Lab can (and you authorize Linden Lab to) disclose any information about you to private entities, law enforcement agencies or government officials, as Linden Lab, in its sole discretion, believes necessary or appropriate to investigate or resolve possible problems or inquiries, or as otherwise required by law. If you request any technical support, you consent to Linden Lab's remote accessing and review of the computer onto which you load Linden Software for purposes of support and debugging. You agree that

Linden Lab may communicate with you via email and any similar technology for any purpose relating to the Service, the Linden Software and any services or software which may in the future be provided by Linden Lab or on Linden Lab's behalf. You agree to read the disclosures and be bound by the terms of the additional Privacy Policy information posted on our website at http://secondlife.com/corporate/privacy.php.

6.2 Linden Lab may observe and record your interaction within the Service, and may share aggregated and other general information (not including your personal information) with third parties.

You acknowledge and agree that Linden Lab, in its sole discretion, may track, record, observe or follow any and all of your interactions within the Service. Linden Lab may share general, demographic, or aggregated information with third parties about our user base and Service usage, but that information will not include or be linked to any personal information without your consent.

DISPUTE RESOLUTION

If a dispute arises between you and Linden Lab, our goal is to provide you with a neutral and cost-effective means of resolving the dispute quickly. Accordingly, you and Linden Lab agree to resolve any claim or controversy at law or in equity that arises from or relates to this Agreement or our Service (a "Claim") in accordance with one of the subsections below.

7.1 Governing Law.

This Agreement and the relationship between you and Linden Lab shall be governed in all respects by the laws of the State of California without regard to conflict of law principles or the United Nations Convention on the International Sale of Goods.

7.2 Forum for Disputes.

You and Linden Lab agree to submit to the exclusive jurisdiction and venue of the courts located in the City and County of San Francisco, California, except as provided in Subsection 7.3 below regarding optional arbitration. Notwithstanding this, you agree that Linden Lab shall still be allowed to apply for injunctive or other equitable relief in any court of competent jurisdiction.

7.3 Optional Arbitration.

For any Claim, excluding Claims for injunctive or other equitable relief, where the total amount of the award sought is less than ten thousand U.S. Dollars ($10,000.00 USD), the party requesting relief may elect to resolve the Claim in a cost-effective manner through binding non-appearance-based arbitration. A party electing arbitration shall initiate it through an established alternative dispute resolution ("ADR") provider mutually agreed upon by the parties. The ADR provider and the parties must comply with the following rules: (a) the arbitration shall be conducted, at the option of the party seeking relief, by telephone, online, or based solely on written submissions; (b) the arbitration shall not involve any personal appearance by the parties or witnesses unless otherwise mutually agreed by the parties; and (c) any judgment on the award rendered by the arbitrator may be entered in any court of competent jurisdiction.

7.4 Improperly Filed Claims.

All Claims you bring against Linden Lab must be resolved in accordance with this Dispute Resolution Section. All Claims filed or brought contrary to this Dispute Resolution Section shall be considered improperly filed. Should you file a Claim contrary to this Dispute Resolution Section, Linden Lab may recover attorneys' fees and costs up to one thousand U.S. Dollars ($1,000.00 USD), provided that Linden Lab has notified you in writing of the improperly filed Claim, and you have failed to promptly withdraw the Claim.

GENERAL PROVISIONS

The Service is controlled and operated by Linden Lab from its offices within the State of California, United States of America. Linden Lab makes no representation that any aspect of the Service is appropriate or available for use in jurisdictions outside of the United States. Those who choose to access the Service from other locations are responsible for compliance with applicable local laws.

The Linden Software is subject to all applicable export restrictions. You must comply with all export and import laws and restrictions and regulations of any United States or foreign agency or authority relating to the Linden Software and its use.

Linden Lab's failure to act with respect to a breach by you or others does not waive Linden Lab's right to act with respect to that breach or subsequent or similar breaches. No consent or waiver by Linden Lab under this Agreement shall be deemed effective unless delivered in a writing signed by a duly appointed officer of Linden Lab. All or any of Linden Lab's rights and obligations under this Agreement may be assigned to a subsequent owner or operator of the Service in a merger, acquisition or sale of all or substantially all of Linden Lab's assets. You may not assign or transfer this Agreement or any or all of your rights hereunder without the prior written consent of Linden Lab, and any attempt to do so is void. Notwithstanding anything else in this Agreement, no default, delay or failure to perform on the part of Linden Lab shall be considered a breach of this Agreement if such default, delay or failure to perform is shown to be due to causes beyond the reasonable control of Linden Lab.

This Agreement sets forth the entire understanding and agreement between you and Linden Lab with respect to the subject matter hereof. The section headings used herein, including descriptive summary sentences at the start of each section, are for convenience only and shall not affect the interpretation of this Agreement. If any provision of this Agreement shall be held by a court of competent jurisdiction to be unlawful, void, or for any reason unenforceable, then in such jurisdiction that provision shall be deemed severable from these terms and shall not affect the validity and enforceability of the remaining provisions.

Linden Lab may give notice to you by means of a general notice on our website at http://secondlife.com, through the Second Life Viewer at or after log-in to your Account, by electronic mail to your e-mail address in our records for your Account, or by written communication sent by first class mail, postage prepaid, or overnight courier to your address on record for your Account. All notices given by you or required under this Agreement shall be faxed to Linden Lab Legal Department, Attn: Dispute Resolution, at: (415) 243-9045; or mailed to us at: Linden Lab Legal Department, Attn: Dispute Resolution, 945 Battery Street, San Francisco, CA 94111.

Appendix V: World of Warcraft Terms of Use Agreement

Reprinted here is the current World of Warcraft Terms of Use Agreement. It is likely to change, and updates can be found at http://www.worldofwarcraft.com/legal/termsofuse.html.

WORLD OF WARCRAFT® TERMS OF USE AGREEMENT

Last Updated January 11, 2007

YOU SHOULD CAREFULLY READ THE FOLLOWING WORLD OF WARCRAFT TERMS OF USE AGREEMENT (THE "TERMS OF USE" OR "AGREEMENT"). IF YOU DO NOT AGREE WITH ALL OF THE TERMS OF THIS AGREEMENT, YOU MUST CLICK "REJECT." IF YOU REJECT THIS AGREEMENT WITHIN THIRTY (30)

DAYS AFTER FIRST PURCHASING THE WORLD OF WARCRAFT SOFTWARE, YOU MAY CALL (800)757-7707 TO REQUEST A FULL REFUND OF THE PURCHASE PRICE. ONCE YOU AGREE TO THE TERMS OF USE AND THE END USER LICENSE AGREEMENT (EULA), YOU WILL NO LONGER BE ELIGIBLE FOR A REFUND.

Welcome to Blizzard Entertainment, Inc.'s ("Blizzard") "World of Warcraft®" or "World of Warcraft®: The Burning Crusade™" (the "Game"). The Game includes two components: (a) the software program along with any accompanying materials or documentation (collectively, the "Program"), and (b) Blizzard's proprietary World of Warcraft online service (the "Service"). All use of the Service is governed by the terms and conditions contained in this Agreement, including any future revisions. Any use of the Service not in accordance with the Terms of Use is expressly prohibited.

Eligibility.

You represent that you are an adult in your country of residence. You agree to these Terms of Use on behalf of yourself and, at your discretion, for one (1) minor child for whom you are a parent or guardian and whom you have authorized to use the account you create on the Service.

Ownership.

All rights and title in and to the Program and the Service (including without limitation any user accounts, titles, computer code, themes, objects, characters, character names, stories, dialogue, catch phrases, locations, concepts, artwork, animations, sounds, musical compositions, audio-visual effects, methods of operation, moral rights, any related documentation, "applets" incorporated into the Program, transcripts of the chat rooms, character profile information, recordings of games played on the Program, and the Program client and server software) are owned by Blizzard or its licensors. The Program and the Service are protected by United States and international laws. The Program and the Service may contain certain licensed materials, and Blizzard's licensors may enforce their rights in the event of any violation of this Agreement.

Establishing an Account.

You may establish one (1) user account (the "Account") on the Service for each Authentication Key you receive from Blizzard. To establish an Account, you will be required to provide Blizzard with certain personal information and the Authentication Key provided to you by Blizzard. Your failure to supply accurate information to Blizzard when requested, or to update that information as it changes, shall constitute a material breach of this Agreement.

During the registration process, you will be required to select a username and a password that are unique to the Account (collectively referred to hereunder as "Login Information"). You may not share the Account or the Login Information with anyone other than as expressly set forth herein.

Notwithstanding anything to the contrary herein, you acknowledge and agree that you shall have no ownership or other property interest in the Account, and you further acknowledge and agree that all rights in and to the Account are and shall forever be owned by and inure to the benefit of Blizzard.

Limitations on Your Use of the Service.

1. Only Blizzard or its licensees have the right to host the Game. You may not host or provide matchmaking services for the Game, or intercept, emulate or redirect the proprietary communication protocols used by Blizzard in connection with the Program, regardless of the method used to do so. Such prohibited methods may include, but are not limited to, protocol emulation, reverse engineering, modifying the Program, adding unauthorized components to the Program, or using a packet sniffer while the Program is running.

2. You agree that you will not (i) modify or cause to be modified any files that are a part of the Program or the Service; (ii) create or use cheats, bots, "mods", and/or hacks, or any other third-party software designed to modify the World of Warcraft experience; or (iii) use any third-party software that

intercepts, "mines", or otherwise collects information from or through the Program or the Service. Notwithstanding the foregoing, you may update the Program with authorized patches and updates distributed by Blizzard, and Blizzard may, at its sole and absolute discretion, allow the use of certain third party user interfaces.

3. You may not disrupt or assist in the disruption of (i) any computer used to support the Service (each a "Server"); or (ii) any other player's Game experience. ANY ATTEMPT BY YOU TO DISRUPT THE SERVICE OR UNDERMINE THE LEGITIMATE OPERATION OF THE PROGRAM MAY BE A VIOLATION OF CRIMINAL AND CIVIL LAWS. You agree that you will not violate any applicable law or regulation in connection with your use of the Program or the Service.

4. Blizzard reserves the exclusive right to create derivative works based on the Program. You may not create derivative works based on the Program without Blizzard's prior written consent.

Rules of Conduct.

As with all things, your use of the Program is governed by certain rules of conduct. These rules of conduct (the "Rules of Conduct"), maintained and enforced exclusively by Blizzard, must be adhered to by all users of the Service. It is your responsibility to know, understand and abide by these Rules of Conduct. The following rules are not meant to be exhaustive, and Blizzard reserves the right to determine which conduct it considers to be outside the spirit of the Game and to take such disciplinary measures as it sees fit up to and including termination and deletion of the Account. Blizzard reserves the right to modify these Rules of Conduct at any time.

1. Rules Related to Usernames and Guild Designations.

Each user will either select a character name or allow the Program to automatically select a character name at random. Additionally, users may form "guilds" and such guilds will be required to choose a name for the guild. When you choose a character name, create a guild, or otherwise create a label that can be seen by other players using the Program, you must abide by the following guidelines as well as the rules of common decency. If Blizzard finds such a label to be offensive or improper, it may, in its sole and absolute discretion, change the name, remove the label and corresponding chat room, and/or suspend or terminate your use of the Program.

In particular, you may not use any name:

1. Belonging to another person with the intent to impersonate that person, including without limitation a "Game Master" or any other employee or agent of Blizzard;
2. That incorporates vulgar language or which are otherwise offensive, defamatory, obscene, hateful, or racially, ethnically or otherwise objectionable;
3. Subject to the rights of any other person or entity without written authorization from that person or entity;
4. That belongs to a popular culture figure, celebrity, or media personality;
5. That is, contains, or is substantially similar to a trademark or service mark, whether registered or not;
6. Belonging to any religious figure or deity;
7. Taken from Blizzard's Warcraft products, including character names from the Warcraft series of novels;
8. Related to drugs, sex, alcohol, or criminal activity;
9. Comprised of partial or complete sentence (e.g., "Inyourface", "Welovebeef", etc);
10. Comprised of gibberish (e.g., "Asdfasdf", "Jjxccm", "Hvlldrm");
11. Referring to pop culture icons or personas (e.g., "Britneyspears", "Austinpowers", "Batman")
12. That utilizes "Leet" or "Dudespeak" (e.g., "Roflcopter", "xxnewbxx", "Roxxoryou")
13. That incorporates titles. For purposes of this subsection, "titles" shall include without limitation 'rank' titles (e.g., "CorporalTed," or "GeneralVlad"), monarchistic or fantasy titles (e.g., "KingMike", "LordSanchez"), and religious titles (e.g., "ThePope," or "Reverend Al").

You may not use a misspelling or an alternative spelling to circumvent the name restrictions listed above, nor can you have a "first" and "last" name that, when combined, violate the above name restrictions.

2. Rules Related to "Chat" and Interaction With Other Users.

Communicating with other Users and Blizzard representatives is an integral part of the Program and is referred to in this document as "Chat." You understand that Blizzard may record your chat sessions and you consent to such monitoring or logging. Your Chat sessions may be subject to monitoring, logging, review, modification, disclosure, and/or deletion by Blizzard without notice to you. Additionally, you hereby acknowledge that Blizzard is under no obligation to monitor Chat, and you engage in Chat at your own risk. When engaging in Chat in the Program, or otherwise utilizing the Program, you may not:

1. Transmit or post any content or language which, in the sole and absolute discretion of Blizzard, is deemed to be offensive, including without limitation content or language that is unlawful, harmful, threatening, abusive, harassing, defamatory, vulgar, obscene, hateful, sexually explicit, or racially, ethnically or otherwise objectionable, nor may you use a misspelling or an alternative spelling to circumvent the content and language restrictions listed above;

2. Carry out any action with a disruptive effect, such as intentionally causing the Chat screen to scroll faster than other users are able to read, or setting up macros with large amounts of text that, when used, can have a disruptive effect on the normal flow of Chat;

3. Disrupt the normal flow of dialogue in Chat or otherwise act in a manner that negatively affects other users including without limitation posting commercial solicitations and/or advertisements for goods and services available outside of the World of Warcraft universe;

4. Sending repeated unsolicited or unwelcome messages to a single user or repeatedly posting similar messages in a Chat area, including but not limited to continuous advertisements to sell goods or services;

5. Communicate or post any user's personal information in the Program, or on websites or forums related to the Program,

except that a user may communicate his or her own personal information in a private message directed to a single user;

6. Use bots or other automated techniques to collect information from the Program or any forum or website owned or administered by Blizzard;

7. Harass, threaten, stalk, embarrass or cause distress, unwanted attention or discomfort to any user of the Program;

8. Cheat or utilize "exploits" while playing the Program in any way, including without limitation modification of the Program's files;

9. Participate in any action that, in the sole and absolute opinion of Blizzard, results or may result in an authorized user of the Program being "scammed" or defrauded out of gold, weapons, armor, or any other items that user has earned through authorized game play in the Program;

10. Communicate directly with players who are playing characters aligned with the opposite faction (e.g. Horde communicating with Alliance or vice versa); or

11. Impersonate any real person, including without limitation any "game master" or any other Blizzard agent or employee, nor may you communicate in the Game in any way designed to make others believe that your message constitutes a server message or was otherwise posted by any Blizzard agent or employee.

3. *Rules Related to Game Play.*

Game play is what World of Warcraft is all about, and Blizzard strictly enforces the rules that govern game play. Blizzard considers most conduct to be part of the Game, and not harassment, so player-killing the enemies of your race and/or alliance, including gravestone and/or corpse camping, is considered a part of the Game. Because the Program is a "player vs. player" game, you should always remember to protect yourself in areas where the members of hostile races can attack you, rather than contacting Blizzard's in-game customer service representatives for help when you have been killed by an enemy of your race. Nonetheless, certain acts go beyond what is "fair" and are considered serious violations of these Terms of Use. Those acts include, but are not necessarily limited to, the following:

1. Using or exploiting errors in design, features which have not been documented, and/or "program bugs" to gain access that is otherwise not available, or to obtain a competitive advantage over other players;
2. Conduct prohibited by the EULA or these Terms of Use, including without limitation that conduct prohibited by Section 2(C); and
3. Anything that Blizzard considers contrary to the "essence" of the Program.

Security of Login Information.

You are responsible for maintaining the confidentiality of your Login Information, and you will be responsible for all uses of your Login Information, whether or not authorized by you. In the event that you become aware of or reasonably suspect any breach of security, including without limitation any loss, theft, or unauthorized disclosure of your Login Information, you must immediately notify Blizzard by emailing wowaccountadmin@blizzard.com.

Blizzard's Absolute Right to Suspend, Terminate and/or Delete the Account.

BLIZZARD MAY SUSPEND, TERMINATE, MODIFY, OR DELETE THE ACCOUNT AT ANY TIME WITH ANY REASON OR NO REASON, WITH OR WITHOUT NOTICE. For purposes of explanation and not limitation, most account suspensions, terminations and/or deletions are the result of violations of this Terms of Use or the EULA.

Ownership/Selling of the Account or Virtual Items.

Blizzard does not recognize the transfer of Accounts. You may not purchase, sell, gift or trade any Account, or offer to purchase, sell, gift or trade any Account, and any such attempt shall be null and void. Blizzard owns, has licensed, or otherwise has rights to all of the content that appears in the Program. You agree that you have no right or title in or to any such content, including the virtual goods or currency appearing or originating in the Game, or any other attributes associated with the Account or stored on the Service. Blizzard does not recognize any virtual property transfers executed outside of the Game or the purported sale, gift or trade in the "real world" of anything related to the Game. Accordingly, you may not sell items for "real" money or otherwise exchange items for value outside of the Game.

Changes to the Terms of Use Agreement or the Program.

Blizzard reserves the right, at its sole and absolute discretion, to change, modify, add to, supplement or delete any of the terms and conditions of this Agreement at any time, including without limitation access policies, the availability of any feature of the Program, hours of availability, content, data, software or equipment needed to access the Program, effective with or without prior notice; provided, however, that material changes (as determined in Blizzard's sole and absolute discretion) will be disclosed as follows: Blizzard will provide you with notification of any such changes to the Program through a patch process, or by email, postal mail, website posting, pop-up screen, or in-game notice. If any future changes to this Agreement are unacceptable to you or cause you to no longer be in compliance with this Agreement, you must terminate, and immediately stop using, the Program and the Account. Your continued use of the Program following any revision to this Agreement constitute your complete and irrevocable acceptance of any and all such changes. Blizzard may change, modify, suspend, or discontinue any aspect of the Program at any time. Blizzard may also impose limits on certain features or restrict your access to parts or all of the Program without notice or liability.

Termination.

This Agreement is effective until terminated. You may terminate this Agreement by terminating the Account and deleting the Program. In the event that you terminate or breach this Agreement, you will forfeit your right to any and all payments you may have made for pre-purchased game access to World of Warcraft. You agree and acknowledge that you are not entitled to any refund for any amounts which were pre-paid on behalf of the Account prior to any termination of this Agreement. Blizzard may terminate this Agreement with or without notice by terminating your Account. The provisions of Sections 2, 4 and Sections 6-17 shall survive any termination of this Agreement.

Warranty Disclaimer.

THE PROGRAM IS PROVIDED "AS IS" AND BLIZZARD DOES NOT WARRANT THAT THE PROGRAM WILL BE UNINTERRUPTED OR ERROR-FREE, THAT DEFECTS WILL BE CORRECTED, OR THAT THE PROGRAM OR THE SERVICE ARE FREE OF VIRUSES OR OTHER HARMFUL COMPONENTS. BLIZZARD EXPRESSLY DISCLAIMS ALL WARRANTIES, EXPRESS OR IMPLIED, INCLUDING WITHOUT LIMITATION THE WARRANTIES OF MERCHANTABILITY OR FITNESS FOR ANY PARTICULAR PURPOSE OR USE, AND NON-INFRINGEMENT.

Limitation of Liability.

NEITHER BLIZZARD NOR ITS PARENT, SUBSIDIARIES, LICENSORS OR AFFILIATES SHALL BE LIABLE IN ANY WAY FOR DAMAGE OR LOSS OF ANY KIND RESULTING FROM (A) THE USE OF OR INABILITY TO USE THE PROGRAM OR SERVICE INCLUDING WITHOUT LIMITATION LOSS OF GOODWILL, WORK STOPPAGE, COMPUTER FAILURE OR MALFUNCTION; (B) THE LOSS OR DAMAGE TO PLAYER CHARACTERS, ACCOUNTS, STATISTICS, INVENTORIES, USER PROFILE INFORMATION STORED BY WORLD OF WARCRAFT; OR (C) INTERRUPTIONS OF SERVICE INCLUDING WITHOUT LIMITATION ISP DISRUPTIONS, SOFTWARE OR HARDWARE FAILURES OR ANY OTHER EVENT WHICH MAY RESULT IN A LOSS OF DATA OR DISRUPTION OF SERVICE. IN NO EVENT WILL BLIZZARD BE LIABLE TO YOU OR ANYONE ELSE FOR ANY DIRECT, INDIRECT, INCIDENTAL, SPECIAL, EXEMPLARY OR CONSEQUENTIAL DAMAGES.

Force Majeure.

Blizzard shall not be liable for any delay or failure to perform resulting from causes outside the reasonable control of Blizzard, including without limitation any failure to perform hereunder due to unforeseen circumstances or cause beyond Blizzard's control such as acts of God, war, terrorism, riots, embargoes, acts of civil or military authorities, fire, floods, accidents, strikes, or shortages of transportation facilities, fuel, energy, labor or materials.

Acknowledgments.

You hereby acknowledge and agree that:

1. WHEN RUNNING, THE PROGRAM MAY MONITOR YOUR COMPUTER'S RANDOM ACCESS MEMORY (RAM) AND/OR CPU PROCESSES FOR UNAUTHORIZED THIRD PARTY PROGRAMS RUNNING CONCURRENTLY WITH WORLD OF WARCRAFT. AN "UNAUTHORIZED THIRD PARTY PROGRAM" AS USED HEREIN SHALL BE DEFINED AS ANY THIRD PARTY SOFTWARE, INCLUDING WITHOUT LIMITATION ANY "ADDON" OR "MOD," THAT IN BLIZZARD'S SOLE DETERMINATION: (i) ENABLES OR FACILITATES CHEATING OF ANY TYPE; (ii) ALLOWS USERS TO MODIFY OR HACK THE WORLD OF WARCRAFT INTERFACE, ENVIRONMENT, AND/OR EXPERIENCE IN ANY WAY NOT EXPRESSLY AUTHORIZED BY BLIZZARD; OR (iii) INTERCEPTS, "MINES," OR OTHERWISE COLLECTS INFORMATION FROM OR THROUGH THE PROGRAM. IN THE EVENT THAT THE PROGRAM DETECTS AN UNAUTHORIZED THIRD PARTY PROGRAM, BLIZZARD MAY (a) COMMUNICATE INFORMATION BACK TO BLIZZARD, INCLUDING WITHOUT LIMITATION YOUR ACCOUNT NAME, DETAILS ABOUT THE UNAUTHORIZED THIRD PARTY PROGRAM DETECTED, AND THE TIME AND DATE THE UNAUTHORIZED THIRD PARTY PROGRAM WAS DETECTED; AND/OR (b) EXERCISE ANY OR ALL OF ITS RIGHTS UNDER SECTION 6 OF THIS AGREEMENT, WITH OR WITHOUT PRIOR NOTICE TO THE USER.

2. WHEN THE PROGRAM IS RUNNING, BLIZZARD MAY OBTAIN CERTAIN IDENTIFICATION INFORMATION ABOUT YOUR COMPUTER AND ITS OPERATING SYSTEM, INCLUDING WITHOUT LIMITATION YOUR HARD DRIVES, CENTRAL PROCESSING UNIT, IP ADDRESS(ES) AND OPERATING SYSTEM(S), FOR PURPOSES OF IMPROVING THE PROGRAM AND/OR THE SERVICE, AND TO POLICE AND ENFORCE THE PROVISIONS OF THIS AGREEMENT AND THE EULA.

3. Blizzard may, with or without notice to you, disclose your Internet Protocol (IP) address(es), personal information, and information about you and your activities in response to a written request by law enforcement, a court order or other

legal process. Blizzard may use or disclose your personal information if Blizzard believes that doing so may protect your safety or the safety of others.

4. BLIZZARD MAY RECORD YOUR CHAT SESSIONS AND OTHER ELECTRONIC COMMUNICATION TRANSMITTED OR RECEIVED THROUGH THE GAME AND YOU CONSENT TO SUCH MONITORING OR LOGGING.

5. You are wholly responsible for the cost of all telephone and Internet access charges along with all necessary equipment, servicing, repair or correction incurred in maintaining connectivity to the Servers.

Equitable Remedies.

In the event that you breach this Agreement, you hereby agree that Blizzard would be irreparably damaged if this Agreement were not specifically enforced, and therefore you agree that Blizzard shall be entitled, without bond, other security, or proof of damages, to appropriate equitable remedies with respect to breaches of this Agreement, in addition to such other remedies as Blizzard may otherwise have available to it under applicable laws. In the event any litigation is brought by either party in connection with this Agreement, the prevailing party in such litigation shall be entitled to recover from the other party all the costs, attorneys' fees and other expenses incurred by such prevailing party in the litigation.

Dispute Resolution and Governing Law.

6. Informal Negotiations. To expedite resolution and control the cost of any dispute, controversy or claim related to this Agreement ("Dispute"), you and Blizzard agree to first attempt to negotiate any Dispute (except those Disputes expressly provided below) informally for at least thirty (30) days before initiating any arbitration or court proceeding. Such informal negotiations commence upon written notice from one person to the other. Blizzard will send its notice to your billing address and email you a copy to the email address you have provided to us. You will send your notice to Blizzard Entertainment, Inc., P.O. Box 18979, Irvine CA 92623, ATTN: Legal Department.

7. Binding Arbitration. If you and Blizzard are unable to resolve a Dispute through informal negotiations, either you or Blizzard may elect to have the Dispute (except those Disputes expressly excluded below) finally and exclusively resolved by binding arbitration. Any election to arbitrate by one party shall be final and binding on the other. YOU UNDERSTAND THAT ABSENT THIS PROVISION, YOU WOULD HAVE THE RIGHT TO SUE IN COURT AND HAVE A JURY TRIAL. The arbitration shall be commenced and conducted under the Commercial Arbitration Rules of the American Arbitration Association ("AAA") and, where appropriate, the AAA's Supplementary Procedures for Consumer Related Disputes ("AAA Consumer Rules"), both of which are available that the AAA website www.adr.org. The determination of whether a Dispute is subject to arbitration shall be governed by the Federal Arbitration Act and determined by a court rather than an arbitrator. Your arbitration fees and your share of arbitrator compensation shall be governed by the AAA Rules and, where appropriate, limited by the AAA Consumer Rules. If such costs are determined by the arbitrator to be excessive, Blizzard will pay all arbitration fees and expenses. The arbitration may be conducted in person, through the submission of documents, by phone or online. The arbitrator will make a decision in writing, but need not provide a statement of reasons unless requested by a party. The arbitrator must follow applicable law, and any award may be challenged if the arbitrator fails to do so. Except as otherwise provided in this Agreement, you and Blizzard may litigate in court to compel arbitration, stay proceeding pending arbitration, or to confirm, modify, vacate or enter judgment on the award entered by the arbitrator.

8. Restrictions. You and Blizzard agree that any arbitration shall be limited to the Dispute between Blizzard and you individually. To the full extent permitted by law, (1) no arbitration shall be joined with any other; (2) there is no right or authority for any Dispute to be arbitrated on a class-action basis or to utilize class action procedures; and (3) there is no right or authority for any Dispute to be brought in a

purported representative capacity on behalf of the general public or any other persons.

9. Exceptions to Informal Negotiations and Arbitration. You and Blizzard agree that the following Disputes are not subject to the above provisions concerning informal negotiations and binding arbitration: (1) any Disputes seeking to enforce or protect, or concerning the validity of, any of your or Blizzard's intellectual property rights; (2) any Dispute related to, or arising from, allegations of theft, piracy, invasion of privacy or unauthorized use; and (3) any claim for injunctive relief.

10. Location. If you are a resident of the United States, any arbitration will take place at any reasonable location within the United States convenient for you. For residents outside the United States, any arbitration shall be initiated in the County of Los Angeles, State of California, United States of America. Any Dispute not subject to arbitration (other than claims proceeding in any small claims court), or where no election to arbitrate has been made, shall be decided by a court of competent jurisdiction within the County of Los Angeles, State of California, United States of America, and you and Blizzard agree to submit to the personal jurisdiction of that court.

11. Governing Law. Except as expressly provided otherwise, this Agreement shall be is governed by, and will be construed under, the Laws of the United States of America and the law of the State of Delaware, without regard to choice of law principles. The application of the United Nations Convention on Contracts for the International Sale of Goods is expressly excluded. For our customers who access the Service from Canada, Australia, Singapore, or New Zealand, other laws may apply if you choose not to agree to arbitrate as set forth above, and in such an event, shall affect this Agreement only to the extent required by such jurisdiction. In such a case, this Agreement shall be interpreted to give maximum effect to the terms and conditions hereof. If you access the Service from New Zealand, and are a resident of New Zealand, The New Zealand Consumer Guarantees Act

of 1993 ("Act") may apply to the Game and/or the Service as supplied by Blizzard to you. If the Act applies, then notwithstanding any other provision in this Agreement, you may have rights or remedies as set out in the Act which may apply in addition to, or, to the extent that they are inconsistent, instead of, the rights or remedies set out in this Agreement. Those who choose to access the Service from locations outside of the United States, Canada, Australia, Singapore, or New Zealand do so on their own initiative contrary to the terms of this Agreement, and are responsible for compliance with local laws if and to the extent local laws are applicable.

12. Severability. You and Blizzard agree that if any portion [of] Section 16 is found illegal or unenforceable (except any portion of 16(d)), that portion shall be severed and the remainder of the Section shall be given full force and effect. If Section 16(d) is found to be illegal or unenforceable then neither you nor Blizzard will elect to arbitrate any Dispute falling within that portion of Section 16(d) found to be illegal or unenforceable and such Dispute shall be decided by a court of competent jurisdiction within the County of Los Angeles, State of California, United States of America, and you and Blizzard agree to submit to the personal jurisdiction of that court.

Miscellaneous.

If any provision of this Agreement shall be unlawful, void, or for any reason unenforceable, then that provision shall be deemed severable from this Agreement and shall not affect the validity and enforceability of any remaining provisions. This Terms of Use Agreement is the complete and exclusive statement of the agreement between you and Blizzard concerning the Service, and this Agreement supersedes any prior or contemporaneous agreement, either oral or written, and any other communications with regard thereto between you and Blizzard; provided, however that this Agreement is in addition to, and does not replace or supplant, the EULA. This Agreement may only be modified as set forth herein.

The section headings used herein are for reference only and shall not be read to have any legal effect.

I HEREBY ACKNOWLEDGE THAT I HAVE READ AND UNDERSTAND THE FOREGOING TERMS OF USE AGREEMENT AND AGREE THAT MY USE OF THE PROGRAM AND/OR THE SERVICE IS AN ACKNOWL-EDGMENT OF MY AGREEMENT TO BE BOUND BY THE TERMS AND CONDITIONS OF THIS TERMS OF USE AGREEMENT.

Appendix VI:
Entropia Universe
End User License
Agreement

Reprinted here is the current Entropia Universe End User License Agreement. It is likely to change, and updates can be found at http://www.entropiauniverse .com/pe/en/rich/107004.html.

ENTROPIA UNIVERSE END USER LICENSE AGREEMENT (EULA)

2007-10-16

This Agreement ("Agreement") is made by and between MindArk PE AB (publ) ("MindArk") and the Participant ("Participant" and/or "You") who wishes to use the Entropia Universe.

By accepting this Agreement, the Participant agrees to it in its entirety, effective immediately.

MindArk owns the software and the system, identified as the Entropia Universe ("System").

In consideration of the promises set forth herein, the parties hereto agree as follows:

1. Arrangement

This Agreement is a legal document that details your rights and obligations as an Entropia Universe Participant, entitled to a Participant account, and access to use certain MindArk services. You cannot become an Entropia Universe Participant until you have accepted the terms of this Agreement. You hereby acknowledge that your use of the Entropia Universe constitutes your acceptance of this Agreement.

MindArk agrees to provide the Entropia Universe "as is" to the Participant. All use of the Entropia Universe is only allowed according to the terms and conditions set forth herein. All use not in accordance with this Agreement is specifically forbidden.

This Agreement is your entire agreement with MindArk and governs your use of the System. By accepting this Agreement you also agree to any additional terms and conditions that may arise from usage of affiliate systems, other MindArk systems or products, or third-party software and/or systems.

To qualify as a Participant, you must be at least 18 years old. If you are not 18 years old but you are at least 13 years old, you may still partake, but only if your account was created and registered by your parent or guardian. Any rights you might have according to this Agreement will be void and without effect, and you will not be entitled access to the Entropia Universe, if you do not satisfy the age requirement.

2. Description

MindArk provides the Entropia Universe as a service, described as a virtual universe. The Entropia Universe is not a "game".

Upon completion of the registration process, you will choose your password ("Password"), your login ("Login") and your Entropia Universe account ("Account") that are uniquely associated with your participation. A Participant may only have one Account. All of your access to the system will be through that Account, except as otherwise set forth in this Agreement. An Account supplies access to MindArk's online virtual universe. In the virtual universe you will be able to interact with other participants and online constructs. Your interactions will be through an "Avatar", or virtual persona/alter-ego, and are regulated by the Rules of Conduct section below.

You agree to obey the limits set on your Account by your category of participation. You further agree to obey the Rules of Conduct. Violation of the Rules of Conduct may result in termination of your Account.

3. Participant Account

To participate in the Entropia Universe, you must provide current, complete and accurate information, including, without limitation to, information such as your name, address, telephone number and e-mail address in each part of your Account application, and your bank account and/or credit/debit card information in the case of depositing or withdrawing funds from the Entropia Universe ("Self-Registered Personal data"). Your Personal Data will be protected by MindArk according to Section 4 of this Agreement. You agree to update any registration information that you provide whenever it is changed so that MindArk's records are also correct. MindArk reserve the right to terminate your Entropia Universe Account if you provide false or misleading information.

MindArk and its affiliates reserve the right, at their sole discretion, to refuse approval of an Account, to refuse access to an Account, to terminate an Account and to remove, edit or add content, without notice.

You are solely responsible for preserving the confidentiality of your Account, your Login and Password, and for restricting access to your Account and to your computer. MindArk never ask for this information and all communication with MindArk is conducted through the secure Support section, located at the Entropia Universe website.

You agree to accept personal liability for all actions that occur through your Account or through the use of your Login and/or Password, whether done by you or by someone else using your Account. You agree to hold MindArk free from liability for any improper or illegal use of your Account. This includes illegal or improper use by someone to whom you have given permission to use your Account. The terms of this agreement shall extend to anyone else using your Account.

If you should happen to willfully or otherwise reveal your Password and/or Login, you have relinquished your right to any assistance regarding the possible outcomes or consequences based upon your actions. Your Account may be terminated if you let someone else use it inappropriately. If your Account is terminated for any reason, MindArk is under no obligation to provide you a license to use the Entropia Universe in the future.

4. Privacy

MindArk gives access to a virtual universe to Participants all over the world. A Participant may choose to appear with his or her own name or use a nickname in the virtual universe. A Participant is able to interact with none, few or many other Participants. Mind-Ark intends to keep the identity of each Participant private to him or herself and to handle your Self-Registered Personal Data confidentially and according to MindArk's Privacy Policy, which can be found at the Entropia Universes website.

The Entropia Universe incorporates technology of Massive Incorporated ("Massive") that enables certain In-World objects (e.g. advertising) to be temporarily uploaded to your pc or console and replaced In-World while connected online. As part of that process, no personally identifiable information about you is collected and only select non-personally identifiable information is temporarily logged. No logged information is used to determine any personally identifiable information about you. For full details visit http://www.massiveincorporated.com/privacy.htm.

MindArk registers Participants Self-Registered Personal Data as well as certain automatically collected anonymous information, such as IP address and some information about your hardware and related drivers ("Automatically-Registered Personal Data") to provide a better service, for the necessity of transferring funds between MindArk and the Participant, and for the purposes of identity verification, detection and counteraction of fraud and Agreement violations and in order to balance the load on the System. By your acceptance and use of the Entropia Universe and by providing MindArk and/or MindArk affiliates with your Personal Data, you hereby consent to and approve of the collection, processing and storage of your Personal Data, its transmission to MindArk affiliates and its use for these purposes.

In any event that MindArk is requested by the proper authorities and/or other entities seeking legal remedy against you with connection to a violation made by you or alleged to have been made by your participation in the Entropia Universe, MindArk may share all information regarding you and your use of the Entropia Universe, including, but not limited to, Personal Data.

5. License

The Participant acknowledges that he or she shall have only a limited, non-exclusive, license to access and make personal use of the Entropia Universe. The Participant acknowledges and agrees that he or she will not use the Entropia Universe for any illegal purpose according to any law, local, national or international. The Participant agrees that he or she will use the Entropia Universe carefully and will not use it in any way that might result in any loss of his or her or any Third Party's property, information or other legal right. MindArk will not take any responsibility if this should occur.

The Participant agrees not to translate, modify, copy, printout, disassemble, de-compile or otherwise tamper with the Entropia Universe system, code, or any firmware, circuit board or software provided therewith. The Participant also agrees not to hack into or interfere with any data communication to or from the Entropia Universe servers, clients, and systems, as well as not to use any other software than the Entropia Universe Client to interpret or influence data sent to or from the Entropia Universe server and client systems. The Participant also agrees upon not using any Third Party software or equipment that influences the Entropia Universe in any way. The Participant agrees upon not tampering, removing (except complete uninstallation), adding, or changing the installed Entropia Universe Client Software and its associated files in any way whatsoever.

6. Account Inactivity and Account Termination

MindArk may terminate this Agreement upon notice to the Participant. Such termination may be made without reason, and may be for one or more Participants.

MindArk reserves the right, pursuant to the conditions set forth in Section 17, to terminate your Account and this Agreement without notice, at MindArk's sole discretion, if you fail to comply with the terms of this Agreement.

In the event that your Account is locked or terminated, no refund will be granted. Any delinquent or unresolved issues relating to former participation must be resolved before MindArk will permit you to have a new Account.

You acknowledge and agree that your Entropia Universe Account will be deemed inactive if it is not used for a period of three hundred and thirty (330) consecutive days. Upon verification of your identity, MindArk may, at MindArk's sole discretion, reactivate your Account.

You further acknowledge and agree that your Entropia Universe Account will be purged if [it] is not used for a period of five hundred and ten (510) consecutive days. Upon purging your Account, all your item(s) will be sold for their Trade Terminal (TT) value and the funds will be transferred to the PED balance of your Account.

In addition, your virtual real estate will be reclaimed by MindArk and your Avatar skills will be erased. You will never be able to retrieve the items, estate deeds or skills that were purged due to Account inactivity.

If you wish to cancel your Account at any time, you can do so by filing a request through the Support Section of the Entropia Universe website. MindArk reserves the right to collect fees, surcharges or costs incurred before you cancel your Account. In addition, you are responsible for any charges incurred to Third-Party vendors or content providers prior to your cancellation.

MindArk reserve the right to reactivate an Account, at MindArk's sole discretion, upon fulfillment of required identity verification or other conditions.

All provisions of this Agreement that by their nature should survive termination of this Agreement do survive its termination, including, but not limited to, provisions on ownership, proprietary rights, warranty disclaimers and liability and remedy limitations. If any provision of this Agreement shall be void or unenforceable for any reason, this will not affect the validity and enforceability of any remaining provisions of this Agreement.

7. Ownership

The System, including, but not limited to, computer code, text, graphics, audio files, logos, button icons, images, characters, items, concepts, data compilation and software, is the property of Mind-Ark and protected by Swedish and international copyright laws.

MindArk, MindArk PE, Project Entropia, Entropia Universe and other marks indicated on the Entropia Universe's website are registered trademarks of MindArk in Sweden. Any Entropia Universe design and any other MindArk graphics, logos or button icons are trademarks of MindArk.

Virtual items will often have names similar or identical to corresponding physical categories such as "people," "real estate," "possessions," and the names of specific items in those categories such as "house," "rifle," "tools," "armor," etc. Despite the similar names, all virtual items are part of the System and MindArk retains all rights, title, and interest in all parts including, but not limited to Avatars and Virtual Items; these retained rights include, without limitation, patent, copyright, trademark, trade secret and other proprietary rights throughout the world.

As part of your interactions with the System, you may acquire, create, design, or modify Virtual Items, but you agree that you will not gain any ownership interest whatsoever in any Virtual Item, and you hereby assign to MindArk all of your rights, title and interest in any such Virtual Item.

You hereby grant MindArk the worldwide, perpetual, irrevocable, royalty-free, right to exercise all intellectual property rights for any content you may upload to the Entropia universe, including, but not limited to, user-to-user communications.

8. Transactions between Participants

The Entropia Universe is fitted with an economy system that enables Participants to carry out secure transactions with other Participants, in which buyers and sellers exchange Virtual Items, Virtual Funds and Real-Life Items (the "Approved Transaction").

You acknowledge that any exchange carried out using any Non-Approved transaction procedure is at your own risk. MindArk reserves the right to take any necessary measures for the purpose of preventing and acting against frauds and Non-Approved Transactions, including, but not limited to, making a reservation against a suspected Transaction, and terminating a directly or indirectly involved Account, if MindArk judges that the Transaction was not performed in compliance to this Agreement.

Additional terms shall apply upon any transaction with Real-Life Items between you and Third Parties. For further information see Third Party's Items Purchase Agreement, available when making transactions with Real-Life items within the Entropia Universe.

9. Participant Content

The Entropia Universe allows images, videos and other communications submitted by Participants ("Participant Content") and the hosting of such Participant Contents.

In connection with Participant Content, you agree that you will not: (a) submit materials that are copyrighted, protected by trade secret or otherwise subject to third party proprietary rights, including privacy and publicity rights, unless you are the owner of such rights or have permission from their rightful owner(s) to submit the materials; (b) publish falsehoods or misrepresentations that could damage MindArk or any third party; (c) submit material that is unlawful, libelous, defamatory, obscene, threatening, pornographic, hateful, harassing, racially or ethnically offensive, or encourages conduct considered a criminal offense, give rise to civil liability, violate any law, or is otherwise inappropriate; (d) post advertisements or business solicitations not related to participation in the Entropia Universe; (e) copy materials submitted by other Participants; (f) tamper or interact with the hosting facilities provided by MindArk in any way other than through the uploading and deleting functions provided through the Entropia Universe.

MindArk reserves the right to remove Participant Content without prior notice.

MindArk does not permit copyright infracting activities and infraction of intellectual property rights in the Entropia Universe, and MindArk will remove all Participant Content when properly notified that such Participant Content infracts on another's intellectual property rights.

MindArk also reserves the right to decide whether a Participant Content is appropriate and complies with this Agreement for violations other than copyright infraction and violations of intellectual property law, such as, but not limited to, pornography, obscene or defamatory material, excessive length or any offensive behaviors described in §17 of this Agreement. MindArk may remove such Participant Content and/or terminate a Participant's access for uploading such material in violation of this Agreement at any time, without prior notice and at its sole discretion.

10. Mindark's Warranties

MINDARK REPRESENTS AND WARRANTS THAT IT HAS THE REQUISITE RIGHT AND LEGAL AUTHORITY TO GRANT THE LICENSE AND TO PROVIDE THE ENTROPIA UNIVERSE. THE ENTROPIA UNIVERSE IS PROVIDED TO YOU "AS IS". THE ENTROPIA UNIVERSE IS NOT WARRANTED BY MINDARK TO BE ERROR OR BUG FREE. MINDARK MAKES NO OTHER WARRANTY, EXPRESSED OR IMPLIED, WITH RESPECT TO THE ENTROPIA UNIVERSE. ALL WARRANTIES, WHETHER EXPRESSED OR IMPLIED, ARE HEREBY DISCLAIMED, INCLUDING, WITHOUT LIMITATION, THE IMPLIED WARRANTIES OF MERCHANTABILITY AND FITNESS FOR A PARTICULAR PURPOSE.

11. Governing Law

This Agreement is to be governed by, construed and enforced according to the laws of Sweden. You agree that any future dispute that might arise between you and MindArk is to be governed by the laws of Sweden and that any principles of conflicts of laws will not be applicable with regards to this Agreement.

12. Accounts and Funds Transfers

The Participant may deposit funds and may withdraw funds from his or her PED Card. MindArk may refuse a withdrawal, if unable to verify or authenticate any information you provide or if it is suspected that the withdrawal may involve fraudulent activity. MindArk acknowledges the responsibility to maintain records of all funds transactions. MindArk's transaction records shall be conclusive proof of the transaction carried out to or from your PED card. Account deficits in any situation apart from those described herein are the responsibility of the Participant. MindArk accepts no responsibility for funds misplaced or misused in any incidence, regardless of reason.

All funds transactions into or from the Entropia Universe must be through MindArk's Approved Transaction system. For further information please see the "Deposit" and/or "Withdrawal" sections of the Entropia Universe website.

Additional terms shall apply to any funds withdrawals using the Entropia Universe Cash Card. For further information see the Cash Card Holder Agreement at the Entropia Universe website.

13. Mindark's Limitation of Liability

MindArk provide the software platform Entropia Universe, a virtual universe where Participants are free to choose the course of action they wish to pursue.

YOU AGREE TO NOT HOLD MINDARK AND AFFILIATED SUBSIDIARIES, EMPLOYEES, CONTRACTORS, OFFICERS, DIRECTORS, TELECOMMUNICATIONS PROVIDERS AND CONTENT PROVIDERS LIABLE FOR ANY CLAIMS AND EXPENSES, INCLUDING ATTORNEYS FEES, THAT ARISE FROM A BREACH OF THIS AGREEMENT OR ARE MADE BY OTHER PARTICIPANTS RELATED TO YOUR USE OF THE ENTROPIA UNIVERSE OR THE INTERNET, OR IN CONNECTION WITH YOUR TRANSMISSION OF ANY CONTENT USING THE ENTROPIA UNIVERSE.

MINDARK SHALL, IN NO EVENT, BE LIABLE TO YOU FOR ANY DAMAGES, LOSS OR EXPENSE INCLUDING WITHOUT LIMITATION, DIRECT, INDIRECT, SPECIAL OR CONSEQUENTIAL DAMAGE, OR ECONOMIC LOSS ARISING FROM THE USE OF THE ENTROPIA UNIVERSE. MINDARK'S LIABILITY TOWARDS ANY PARTICIPANT SHALL, IF ACKNOWLEDGED, IN EACH INCIDENCE BE LIMITED TO NO MORE THAN THE INITIAL AMOUNT TRANSFERRED BY SAID PARTICIPANT INTO THE ENTROPIA UNIVERSE.

YOU ACKNOWLEDGE THAT MINDARK SHALL NOT BE LIABLE TO YOU FOR THE LOSS OF ANY DATA OR ELECTRONIC FILES, INCLUDING, BUT NOT LIMITED TO, ACCOUNT, AVATAR AND ITEMS,

FOR ANY REASON WHATSOEVER INCLUDING, BUT NOT LIMITED TO, SERVER FAILURE, INTERRUPTIONS, INTERNET LATENCY, VIRUSES, DEFECTS, ERRORS, AND NEGLIGENT ACT OF MINDARK AND/OR ITS AFFILIATES.

MindArk's failure to perform any term or condition of this Agreement as a result of conditions beyond its control such as, but not limited to, war, strikes, fires, floods, acts of God, governmental restrictions, power failures, or damage or destruction of any network facilities or servers, shall not be deemed a breach of this Agreement.

MindArk reserves the right to interrupt the Entropia Universe with or without prior notice for any reason or no reason. You agree that MindArk will not be liable for any interruption of the Entropia Universe, delay or failure to perform.

MindArk does not endorse any Participant Content or any opinion, recommendation, or advice expressed therein, and MindArk expressly disclaims any and all liability in connection with Participant Content.

MINDARK EXPRESSLY DISCLAIMS ALL REPRESENTATION AND WARRANTIES REGARDING GOODS OR SERVICES YOU OBTAIN FROM THIRD PARTIES DURING YOUR USE OF THE ENTROPIA UNIVERSE. YOU AGREE TO LOOK SOLELY TO THIRD PARTIES FOR ANY AND ALL CLAIMS REGARDING SUCH TRANSACTIONS WITH THIRD PARTIES. YOU FURTHER AGREE THAT THE SPECIAL 'THIRD PARTY'S ITEMS PURCHASE AGREEMENT' TERMS (THAT YOU ACCEPT IN THE CASE OF MAKING A THIRD PARTY ITEM PURCHASE) WILL APPLY AS A COMPLEMENT TO THIS AGREEMENT FOR ANY TRANSACTIONS OR COMMUNICATIONS BETWEEN YOU AND THE THIRD PARTY.

14. No Assignment

This Agreement is not assignable by you and shall be binding upon and inured to the benefit of the parties and their respective administrators, successors and assigns.

15. Headings

Headings used in this Agreement are provided for convenience only and shall not be used to construe meaning or intent.

16. Changes to the System

MindArk may, at any time, update, revise or change the internal data and balancing of the System, without any notice or responsibility for compensation due to loss or gain of value due to these changes.

17. Rules of Conduct

All users of the Entropia Universe are real people interacting in the form of avatars. Consider the feelings of other people in what you say and do. You are relating to a real person, not a computer character. Think before you speak and act or you may make mistakes that will prevent you from making friends and becoming part of the larger community. Treat others like you want to be treated. Show respect. Speak up for your opinions, but don't insult other people. Harassment, defamation, abuse, or threats against others through words, pictures or actions are not allowed and could result in Account suspension or termination.

AS A PARTICIPANT IN THE VIRTUAL UNIVERSE OF THE ENTROPIA UNIVERSE YOU MUST ABIDE BY THE FOLLOWING RULES. IF YOU VIOLATE ANY OF THESE RULES, YOUR POSSIBILITY TO PARTICIPATE IN ENTROPIA UNIVERSE MAY BE IMMEDIATELY TERMINATED BY MINDARK WITHOUT ANY CLAIMS WHATSOEVER.

a. You cannot impersonate any member of the MindArk staff, or fellow Participants. You cannot impersonate being a MindArk staff member, employee, or claim having association with MindArk if you don't really are/have one. You cannot create any society that would indicate such links.

b. You cannot threaten, harass, cause grief or distress to any MindArk staff in or outside the virtual universe, including, but not limited to, IRC channels or public web forums.

c. You cannot interfere with any other Participant's ability to enjoy the Entropia Universe according to its rules.

d. You cannot harass, threaten and cause grief or distress to another Participant in the Entropia Universe.

e. You are forbidden to 'spam' and/or 'flood' the communication system or abuse functions in the Entropia Universe to cause effects not intended.

f. You cannot use sexually explicit or offensive language. You cannot post or communicate any defamatory content.

g. You cannot create virtual universe avatars hosting an explicit, racist, hateful, degrading, religious, sexual or other form of offensive alias.

h. You cannot use the Entropia Universe to commit any illegal action and/or infringe any local, national or international laws intentionally or unintentionally.

i. You cannot use hateful language towards another Participant's gender, race, sexual orientation, intelligence, or religion.

j. You are not allowed to create societies that are based on any sexist, racist, degrading or hateful philosophy directed towards real life companies, persons or organizations.

k. You cannot engage in or communicate about any illegal activities, including pirated material, narcotics or contraband.

l. You cannot use the official Entropia Universe site and/or virtual environment to supply the means of access to illegal software or materials.

m. You must report errors and bugs to MindArk whenever you discover them. Neglecting to report errors or bugs, or using bugs, slow connection, Internet latency, or 'exploits' for own benefits may result in a termination of your Account, including its Virtual Items, funds, and abilities.

n. You cannot spread any rumors about MindArk, the Entropia Universe, and MindArk Staff or Partners, that can be considered potentially damaging, using the Entropia Universe, IRC or any other public forums in any media now known or not currently known, including but not limited to a web space.

o. You cannot post or convey any Entropia Universe Participant's Personal Data and/or Account information, including, but not limited to, login info, in, on or outside the Entropia Universe.

p. Gambling activities are expressly forbidden in the Entropia Universe.

You are solely responsible for any information that you provide to MindArk in the registration process, to MindArk or to another Entropia Universe Participant in any public message forum or in any other communication. You acknowledge that MindArk operates as a passive conduit for your information and communications.

YOU ACKNOWLEDGE THESE RULES AND AGREE TO ABIDE BY THEM. YOU ALSO AGREE THAT YOU ARE RESPONSIBLE FOR YOUR ENTROPIA UNIVERSE ACCOUNT AND THESE SAME RULES APPLY TO ANYBODY YOU ALLOW TO USE YOUR ACCOUNT.

18. Breach of the Agreement

Without limiting MindArk's legal remedies, if you violate any part of this Agreement or the documents it incorporates by reference, your Account may be terminated, locked, or warned in the form of a temporary lockdown. Any action taken against your Account due to a violation is the decision of MindArk and is final. Any claims, Virtual Items, funds, etc, located on a locked avatar Account will be forfeited and any fund transactions pending will be revoked. Upon verification of your identity, MindArk may, at MindArk's sole discretion, reactivate your Account.

You agree to indemnify MindArk upon its request against any liability, claim and cost arising from breach of this Agreement or in connection with the use of your Account.

19. Additional Terms

Additional terms and conditions are incorporated into this agreement by the following documents:

a. Third Party's Items Purchase Agreement
b. Cash Card Holder Agreement
c. Privacy Policy

20. Final Agreement

This Agreement terminates and supersedes all prior understandings or agreements on the subject matter hereof.

By accepting this Agreement and becoming a Participant you agree that MindArk may, at any time, update, revise or change this Agreement. If MindArk makes material changes or revisions to this Agreement, MindArk will provide notice to you, via the e-mail address you provided upon registration. Your continued participation in the Entropia Universe after notification of changes means that you have accepted the changes. If you do not want to accept the changes proposed by MindArk or any of the terms in this Agreement, your only remedy is to cancel your Account and cease using the Entropia Universe.

Appendix VII: Raph Koster's Declaration of the Rights of Avatars

A Declaration of the Rights of Avatars

Raph Koster, January 26, 2000

When a time comes that new modes and venues exist for communities, and said modes are different enough from the existing ones that question arises as to the applicability of past custom and law; and when said venues have become a forum for interaction and society for the general public regardless of the intent of the creators of said venue; and at a time when said communities and spaces are rising in popularity and are now widely exploited for commercial gain; it behooves those involved in said communities and venues to affirm and declare the inalienable rights of the members of said communities. Therefore herein have been set forth those rights which are inalienable rights of the inhabitants of virtual spaces of all sorts, in their form henceforth referred to as avatars, in order that this declaration may continually remind those who hold power over virtual spaces and the avatars contained therein of their duties and responsibilities; in order that the forms of administration of a virtual space may be at any time compared to that of other virtual spaces; and in order that the grievances of players may hereafter be judged against the explicit rights set forth, to better govern the virtual space and improve the general welfare and happiness of all.

Therefore this document holds the following truths to be self-evident: That avatars are the manifestation of actual people in an online medium, and that their utterances, actions, thoughts, and emotions should be considered to be as valid as the utterances, actions, thoughts, and emotions of people in any other forum, venue, location, or space. That the well-established rights of man approved by the National Assembly of France on August 26th of 1789 do therefore apply to avatars in full measure saving only the aspects of said rights that do not pertain in a virtual space or which must be abrogated in order to ensure the continued existence of the space in question. That by the act of affirming membership in the community within the virtual space, the avatars form a social contract with the community, forming a populace which may and must self-affirm and self-impose rights and concomitant restrictions upon their behavior. That the nature of virtual spaces is such that there must, by physical law, always be a higher power or administrator who maintains the space and has complete power over all participants, but who is undeniably part of the community formed within the space and who must therefore take action in accord with that which benefits the space as well as the participants, and who therefore also has the rights of avatars and may have other rights as well. That the ease of moving between virtual spaces and the potential transience of the community do not limit or reduce the level of emotional and social involvement that avatars may have with the community, and that therefore the ease of moving between virtual spaces and the potential transience of the community do not in any way limit, curtail, or remove these rights from avatars on the alleged grounds that avatars can always simply leave.

Articles:

1. Avatars are created free and equal in rights. Special powers or privileges shall be founded solely on the common good, and not based on whim, favoritism, nepotism, or the caprice of those who hold power. Those who act as ordinary avatars within the space shall all have only the rights of normal avatars.

2. The aim of virtual communities is the common good of its citizenry, from which arise the rights of avatars. Foremost among these rights is the right to be treated as people and not as disembodied, meaningless, soulless puppets. Inherent in this right are therefore the natural and inalienable rights of man. These rights are liberty, property, security, and resistance to oppression.

3. The principle of all sovereignty in a virtual space resides in the inalterable fact that somewhere there resides an individual who controls the hardware on which the virtual space is running, and the software with which it is created, and the database which makes up its existence. However, the body populace has the right to know and demand the enforcement of the standards by which this individual uses this power over the community, as authority must proceed from the community; a community that does not know the standards by which the administrators use their power is a community which permits its administrators to have no standards, and is therefore a community abetting in tyranny.

4. Liberty consists of the freedom to do anything which injures no one else including the weal of the community as a whole and as an entity instantiated on hardware and by software; the exercise of the natural rights of avatars are therefore limited solely by the rights of other avatars sharing the same space and participating in the same community. These limits can only be determined by a clear code of conduct.

5. The code of conduct can only prohibit those actions and utterances that are hurtful to society, inclusive of the harm that may be done to the fabric of the virtual space via hurt done to the hardware, software, or data; and likewise inclusive of the harm that may be done to the individual

who maintains said hardware, software, or data, in that harm done to this individual may result in direct harm done to the community.

6. The code of conduct is the expression of the general will of the community and the will of the individual who maintains the hardware and software that makes up the virtual space. Every member of the community has the right to contribute either directly or via representatives in the shaping of the code of conduct as the culture of the virtual space evolves, particularly as it evolves in directions that the administrator did not predict; the ultimate right of the administrator to shape and define the code of conduct shall not be abrogated, but it is clear that the administrator therefore has the duty and responsibility to work with the community to arrive at a code of conduct that is shaped by the input of the community. As a member of the community himself, the administrator would be damaging the community itself if he failed in this responsibility, for abrogation of this right of avatars could result in the loss of population and therefore damage to the common weal.

7. No avatar shall be accused, muzzled, toaded, jailed, banned, or otherwise punished except in the cases and according to the forms prescribed by the code of conduct. Any one soliciting, transmitting, executing, or causing to be executed, any arbitrary order, shall be punished, even if said individual is one who has been granted special powers or privileges within the virtual space. But any avatar summoned or arrested in virtue of the code of conduct shall submit without delay, as resistance constitutes an offense.

8. The code of conduct shall provide for such punishments only as are strictly and obviously necessary, and no one shall suffer punishment except it be legally inflicted according to the provisions of a code of conduct promulgated before the commission of the offense; save in the case where the offense endangered the continued existence of the virtual space by attacking the hardware or software that provide the physical existence of the space.

9. As all avatars are held innocent until they shall have been declared guilty, if detainment, temporary banning, jailing, gluing, freezing, or toading shall be deemed indispensable, all harshness not essential to the securing of the prisoner's person shall be severely repressed by the code of conduct.

10. No one shall be disquieted on account of his opinions, provided their manifestation does not disturb the public order established by the code of conduct.

11. The free communication of ideas and opinions is one of the most precious of the rights of man. Every avatar may, accordingly, speak, write, chat, post, and print with freedom, but shall be responsible for such abuses of this freedom as shall be defined by the code of conduct, most particularly the abuse of affecting the performance of the space or the performance of a given avatar's representation of the space.

12. The security of the rights of avatars requires the existence of avatars with special powers and privileges, who are empowered to enforce the provisions of the code of conduct. These powers and privileges are therefore granted for the good of all and not for the personal advantage of those to whom they shall be entrusted. These powers and privileges are also therefore not an entitlement, and can and should be removed in any instance where they are no longer used for the good of all, even if the offense is merely inactivity.

13. A common contribution may, at the discretion of the individual who maintains the hardware, the software, and the data that make up the virtual space, be required in order to maintain the existence of avatars who enforce the code of conduct and to maintain the hardware and the software and the continued existence of the virtual space. Avatars have the right to know the nature and amount of the contribution in advance, and said required contribution should be equitably distributed among all the citizens without regard to their social position; special rights and privileges shall never pertain to the avatar who contributes more except

insofar as the special powers and privileges require greater resources from the hardware, software, or data store, and would not be possible save for the resources obtainable with the contribution; and as long as any and all avatars are able to make this contribution and therefore gain the powers and privileges if they so choose; nor shall any articles of this declaration be contingent upon a contribution being made.

14. The community has the right to require of every administrator or individual with special powers and privileges granted for the purpose of administration, an account of his administration.

15. A virtual community in which the observance of the code of conduct is not assured and universal, nor the separation of powers defined, has no constitution at all.

16. Since property is an inviolable and sacred right, and the virtual equivalent is integrity and persistence of data, no one shall be deprived thereof except where public necessity, legally determined per the code of conduct, shall clearly demand it, and then only on condition that the avatar shall have been previously and equitably indemnified, saving only cases wherein the continued existence of the space is jeopardized by the existence or integrity of said data.

17. The administrators of the virtual space shall not abridge the freedom of assembly, save to preserve the performance and continued viability of the virtual space.

18. Avatars have the right to be secure in their persons, communications, designated private spaces, and effects, against unreasonable snooping, eavesdropping, searching and seizures, no activity pertaining thereto shall be undertaken by administrators save with probable cause supported by affirmation, particularly describing the goal of said investigations.

19. The enumeration in this document of rights shall not be construed to deny or disparage others retained by avatars.

Appendix VIII:
Eros, LLC v. John Doe
Complaint

UNITED STATES DISTRICT COURT
MIDDLE DISTRICT OF FLORIDA
TAMPA DIVISION

EROS, LLC,   CIVIL ACTION NO.:

Plaintiff,

v.   JURY TRIAL DEMANDED

JOHN DOE, a/k/a VOLKOV CATTENEO,
a/k/a AARON LONG,

Defendant.

COMPLAINT

Plaintiff Eros, LLC ("Eros") says the following by way
of Complaint:

NATURE OF THE ACTION

1. Eros is one of the most successful merchants doing business within the virtual world platform known as Second Life. Eros makes and sells virtual adult-themed objects within the Second Life platform.

2. Defendant John Doe, a/k/a Volkov Catteneo, a/k/a Aaron Long ("Defendant"), has been making and selling, and continues to make and sell numerous unauthorized copies of Eros's virtual products within Second Life using Eros's trademark in violation of the Lanham Act and the Copyright Act.

3. Eros brings this action to recover damages arising from and to enjoin defendant's violation of the Lanham and Copyright Acts.

PARTIES AND JURISDICTION

4. Eros is a limited liability corporation organized under the laws of Florida having its principal place of business at 16207 September Drive, Lutz, Florida 33549.

5. Upon information and belief, defendant John Doe a/k/a Volkov Catteneo a/k/a Aaron Long ("Defendant"), whose actual identity is presently unknown to Eros, is an individual residing in the United States.

6. This Court has original subject matter jurisdiction over this action pursuant to 28 U.S.C. § 1338(a) and 15 U.S.C. § 1121.

7. This Court has personal jurisdiction over defendant, and venue is proper within this District pursuant to 28 U.S.C. § 1391(a)(2) because defendant has purposefully directed his course of conduct and other infringing acts toward, and has injured, Eros, which is a entity having its principal place of business within this District, because a substantial part of the acts and omissions giving rise to the claims in this action occurred in this District, and because a substantial portion of the property that is the subject of this action is situated within this District.

FACTUAL BACKGROUND

8. The Second Life virtual world platform ("Second Life") is an internet hosted interactive computer simulation which

allows its participants to see, hear, use and modify the simulated objects in the computer generated environment. Second Life users adopt a Second Life name and a character or "avatar" to represent themselves virtually within Second Life.

9. Linden Research, Inc. ("Linden") owns and operates Second Life, which is currently hosted at http://secondlife.com. According to Linden, there are currently over 7 million different Second Life accounts. There are Second Life users throughout the United States and in many foreign countries.

10. At all times relevant to this Complaint and continuing to the date of the filing of this Complaint, by and through the "Terms of Service" governing users' participation in Second Life, Linden has recognized and allowed Second Life users to retain all intellectual property rights in the digital content that they create, place or otherwise own within Second Life. As a result, Second Life users conduct significant commerce within Second Life each day. According to Linden, on a typical day Second Life users conduct transactions cumulatively involving well over 1 million dollars.

11. Eros is engaged in, inter alia, the sale of a number of adult-themed virtual objects for use within Second Life in interstate commerce to Second Life users throughout the United States and foreign countries.

12. Principally through the marketing efforts of Kevin Alderman, Eros's Chief Executive Officer (known within Second Life as "Stroker Serpentine"), Eros's products have become widely known within Second Life, with Mr. Alderman, Eros and Eros's products receiving substantial coverage from national and international technologically oriented media properties such as ABCAustralia, Wired, eBay Magazine, InformationWeek, iVillage, and Huff Report.

13. Eros also routinely promotes its products throughout Second Life by placing advertisements and conducting promotional events within numerous virtual adult/social themed clubs within Second Life.

14. Eros's products have built a reputation within Second Life for performance, quality and value, and as a result, upon

information and belief, are among the best selling adult themed virtual objects within Second Life.

15. Two of these products are known as the SexGen Platinum Base Unit v4.01 (hereinafter, "Item 1") and the SexGen Platinum+Diamond Base v5.01 (hereinafter, "Item 2" and together with Item 1, the "Items"). True and correct screen shots depicting Item 1 and Item 2 as they appear within Second Life are attached as Exhibits "A" and "B", respectively.

16. Eros uses the SexGen trademark (the "Mark") to sell the Items within Second Life, and generally as a method of identifying a number of Eros's products, including but not limited to the Items.

17. Since 2005, Mr. Alderman, by and through Eros as well as a previous company that Mr. Alderman owned, has sold thousands of copies of the Items in interstate commerce to Second Life users in locations throughout the United States and in numerous foreign countries, using the Mark. Eros currently owns all rights in and to the Mark.

18. As a result of Eros's substantial sales of the Items, and Mr. Alderman's and Eros's promotional and advertising efforts, the Mark has become famous and distinctive among the relevant consuming public, serving to distinguish Eros's goods from those of its competitors and to identify Eros as the source of those goods.

19. On or about June 11, 2007, Eros filed an application to obtain federal trademark registration, serial number 77202601, for the Mark with the United States Patent and Trademark Office.

20. Eros offers the Items for sale within Second Life on a "no copy" basis, meaning that while Eros permits other Second Life users to, inter alia, transfer the Items that Eros sells to other Second Life users, Eros prohibits other Second Life users from making copies of the Items.

21. The Items are comprised of original material that is copyrightable.

22. Eros is the owner of the copyrights in the Items within the meaning of 17 U.S.C. § 101.

23. On or about June 25, 2007, Eros filed applications for copyright registrations for Item 1 and Item 2 with the United

States Copyright Office. True and correct copies of the applications and other documents associated with the applications are attached as Exhibit "C."

24. Defendant maintains one or more accounts within Second Life, and is known as Volkov Catteneo within Second Life. On information and belief, based on information obtained through Eros's investigation of Defendant's activities, defendant is an adult male who has in connection with his other on-line activities listed his name as "Aaron Long." Eros does not know whether Aaron Long is a pseudonym.

25. Despite reasonable efforts, Eros does not presently know Defendant's true identity or address but intends to obtain this information by way of subpoenas directed to one or more internet service providers that are likely to have obtained said information from Defendant.

26. Beginning no later than in or about April, 2007, defendant has made and sold, using the Mark, numerous unauthorized copies of the Items, and derivative works based on the Items, within Second Life in interstate commerce to Second Life users in locations such as Georgia, West Virginia and Great Britain. In connection with the sales of the unauthorized copies of the Items, Defendant has misrepresented the copies as authorized and legitimate copies of the Items created by Eros, resulting in actual consumer confusion regarding the origin of the copies. A true and correct screen shot depicting an unauthorized copy of the Item that Eros has been able to obtain is attached as Exhibit "D."

27. Defendant's acts as described herein have at all times been and continue to be willful, wanton, malicious, and committed in bad faith, with the deliberate intent to deceive or confuse the consuming public, to harm Eros in its business by trading off of the reputation and goodwill associated with the Mark, and to unjustly profit from the fame of and goodwill associated with the Mark.

28. As a direct and proximate result of defendant's acts, Eros has been damaged and continues to be irreparably damaged through the diversion of sales, profits and consumer

interest from Eros to Defendant, and the creation of consumer confusion and uncertainty as to the source and quality of Eros's products and its affiliation with or sponsorship of Defendant.

29. Defendant will suffer no harm as the result of a grant preliminary and/or permanent injunctive relief in Eros's favor and against Defendant, as Defendant has no legal justification for his sale of unauthorized use of the Mark and infringement of Eros's copyrights, and is making no legitimate use of Eros's Mark and copyrights.

30. There is a substantial likelihood that Eros will succeed on the merits of its Lanham Act and Copyright Act claims against Defendant.

31. The public interest favors the entry of an injunction against Defendant to protect consumers in Florida and elsewhere from the confusion, diversion, and deception that has been and is likely to continue being caused by Defendant's illegal conduct.

COUNT I

LANHAM ACT VIOLATION-UNFAIR COMPETITION AND FALSE DESCRIPTION OF ORIGIN

32. Eros incorporates the allegations of paragraphs 1 through 31 as though set forth fully herein.

33. Defendant has falsely designated the origin of the unauthorized copies of the Items defendant has sold, and made false and misleading descriptions and representations of fact in the course of selling these copies.

34. Defendant's conduct as described above has caused confusion, mistake and deception as to the origin, sponsorship or approval by Eros of defendant's goods and commercial activities.

35. Defendant's conduct was willful.

36. As a direct and proximate result of Defendant's conduct, Eros has suffered and will continue to suffer damages from lost sales, the diversion of consumer interest, and injury to its business reputation and to the goodwill associated with

its products and materials in an amount to be proven at trial.

37. Upon information and belief, Defendant continues to make unauthorized copies of the Items, and to make false and misleading descriptions and representations of fact in the course of selling these copies, and in the absence of an injunction prohibiting Defendant from doing so, intends to and will continue to do so in the future.

WHEREFORE, plaintiff Eros LLC demands judgment in its favor and against Defendant:

(a) awarding Eros an amount equal to three times the damages sustained by Eros or three times Defendant's profits, whichever amount is greater;

(b) awarding Eros interest and costs of suit;

(c) awarding Eros reasonable attorneys' fees pursuant to 15 U.S.C. § 1117(b);

(d) preliminarily and permanently enjoining Defendant from infringing the Mark, pursuant to 15 U.S.C. § 1116.

(e) requiring Defendant to deliver up for destruction all infringing copies of the Items bearing the Mark, and all articles by means of which infringing copies of the Items may be reproduced; and

(f) granting such other and further relief as the Court may deem just.

COUNT II

COPYRIGHT INFRINGEMENT

38. Eros incorporates the allegations of paragraphs 1 through 37 as though set forth fully herein.

39. By Defendant's conduct as described above, Defendant has infringed Eros's copyrights in the Items.

40. Defendant's infringement was willful.

41. As a direct and proximate result of Defendant's conduct, Eros has suffered damages.

42. Upon information and belief, Defendant is continuing to infringe Eros's copyrights in the Items by, inter alia, copying,

displaying, distributing and selling copies of the Items, and derivative works based on the Items, without Eros's authorization, and in the absence of an injunction prohibiting Defendant from doing so, intends to and will continue to do so in the future.

WHEREFORE, plaintiff Eros LLC demands judgment in its favor and against Defendant:

(a) awarding Eros an amount equal to Eros's actual damages and any additional profits of Defendant, or in the alternative, statutory damages pursuant to 17 U.S.C. § 504;

(b) awarding Eros prejudgment interest and its costs of suit;

(c) awarding Eros reasonable attorneys' fees;

(d) preliminarily and permanently enjoining Defendant from infringing Eros's copyrights in the Items;

(e) requiring the impounding and destruction of all infringing copies of the Items and of all articles by means of which infringing copies of the Items may be reproduced, pursuant to 17 U.S.C. § 503; and

(f) granting such other and further relief as the Court may deem just.

Dated: July 3, 2007

Appendix IX: Memorandum and Order Denying Motion to Dismiss (Bragg v. Linden)

United States District Court, E.D. Pennsylvania.

Marc BRAGG, Plaintiff,

v.

LINDEN RESEARCH, INC. and Philip Rosedale, Defendants.
No. CIV.A.06 4925.

MEMORANDUM

EDUARDO C. ROBRENO, J.
May 30, 2007

*1 This case is about virtual property maintained on a virtual world on the Internet. Plaintiff, Marc Bragg, Esq., claims an ownership interest in such virtual property. Bragg contends that Defendants, the operators of the virtual world, unlawfully confiscated his virtual property and denied him access to their virtual world. Ultimately at issue in this case are the novel questions of what rights and obligations grow out of the relationship between the owner and creator of a virtual world and its resident-customers. While the property and the world where it is found are "virtual," the dispute is real.

Presently before the Court are Defendants' Motion to Dismiss for Lack of Personal Jurisdiction (doc. no. 2) and Motion to Compel Arbitration (doc. no. 3). For the reasons set forth below, the motions will be denied.

I. BACKGROUND

A. Second Life

The defendants in this case, Linden Research Inc. ("Linden") and its Chief Executive Officer, Philip Rosedale, operate a multiplayer role-playing game set in the virtual world[1] known as "Second Life."[2] Participants create avatars[3] to represent themselves, and Second Life is populated by hundreds of thousands of avatars, whose interactions with one another are limited only by the human imagination.[4] According to Plaintiff, many people "are now living large portions of their lives, forming friendships with others, building and acquiring virtual property, forming contracts, substantial business relationships and forming social organizations" in virtual worlds such as Second Life. Compl. 13. Owning property in and having access to this virtual world is, moreover, apparently important to the plaintiff in this case.

B. Recognition of Property Rights

In November 2003, Linden announced that it would recognize participants' full intellectual property protection for the digital content they created or otherwise owned in Second Life. As a result, Second Life avatars may now buy, own, and sell virtual goods ranging "from cars to homes to slot machines." Compl. 7.[5] Most significantly for this case, avatars may purchase "virtual land," make improvements to that land, exclude other avatars from entering onto the land, rent the land, or sell the land to other avatars for a profit. Assertedly, by recognizing virtual property rights, Linden would distinguish itself from other virtual worlds available on the Internet and thus increase participation in Second Life.

Defendant Rosedale personally joined in efforts to publicize Linden's recognition of rights to virtual property. For example, in 2003, Rosedale stated in a press release made available on Second Life's website that:

> Until now, any content created by users for persistent state worlds, such as Everquest® or Star Wars Galaxies™, has essentially become the property of the company developing and hosting the world. . . . We believe our new policy recognizes the fact that persistent world users are making significant contributions to building these worlds and should be able to both own the content they create and share in the value that is created. The preservation of users' property rights is a necessary step toward the emergence of genuinely real online worlds.

*2 Press Release, Linden Lab, Linden Lab Preserves Real World Intellectual Property Rights of Users of its Second Life Online Services (Nov. 14, 2003). After this initial announcement, Rosedale continued to personally hype the ownership of virtual property on Second Life. In an interview in 2004, for example, Rosedale stated: "The idea of land ownership and the ease with which you can own land and do something with it . . . is intoxicating. . . . Land ownership feels important and tangible. It's a real piece of the future." Michael Learmonth, Virtual Real Estate Boom Draws Real Dollars, USA Today, June 3, 2004. Rosedale recently gave an extended interview for Inc. magazine, where he appeared on the cover stating, "What you have in Second Life is real and it is yours. It doesn't belong to us. You can make money." Michael Fitzgerald, How Philip Rosedale Created Second Life, Inc., Feb. 2007.[6]

Rosedale even created his own avatar and held virtual town hall meetings on Second Life where he made representations about the purchase of virtual land. Bragg Decl. 68. Bragg "attended" such meetings and relied on the representations that Rosedale made therein. Id.

C. Plaintiffs' Participation in Second Life

In 2005, Plaintiff Marc Bragg, Esq., signed up and paid Linden to participate in Second Life. Bragg claims that he was induced into "investing" in virtual land by representations made by Linden and Rosedale in press releases, interviews, and through the Second Life website. Bragg Decl. 4-10, 65-68. Bragg also paid Linden real money as "tax" on his land.[7] By April 2006, Bragg had not only purchased numerous parcels of land in his Second Life, he had also digitally crafted "fireworks" that he was able to sell to other avatars for a profit. Bragg also acquired other virtual items from other avatars.

The dispute ultimately at issue in this case arose on April 30, 2006, when Bragg acquired a parcel of virtual land named "Taesot" for $300. Linden sent Bragg an email advising him that Taesot had been improperly purchased through an "exploit." Linden took Taesot away. It then froze Bragg's account, effectively confiscating all of the virtual property and currency that he maintained on his account with Second Life.

Bragg brought suit against Linden and Rosedale in the Court of Common Pleas of Chester County, Pennsylvania, on October 3, 2006.[8] Linden and Rosedale removed the case to this Court (doc. no. 1) and then, within a week, moved to compel arbitration (doc. no. 3).

II. MOTION TO DISMISS FOR LACK OF PERSONAL JURISDICTION

Defendant Philip Rosedale moves to dismiss all claims asserted against him for lack of personal jurisdiction.

A. Legal Standards

A federal district court may exercise jurisdiction to the same extent as the state in which it sits; a state, in turn, may exercise jurisdiction over a non-resident defendant pursuant to its so-called "long-arm statute." Because the reach of Pennsylvania's long-arm statute "is coextensive with the limits placed on the states by the federal Constitution," the Court looks to federal constitutional doctrine to determine whether personal jurisdiction exists over Rosedale. Vetrotex Certainteed Corp. v. Consol. Fiber Glass Products Co., 75 F.3d 147, 150 (3d Cir.1996); 42 Pa.C.S.A. § 5322(b).

*3 Personal jurisdiction can be established in two different ways: specific jurisdiction and general jurisdiction. See Helicopteros Nacionales de Colombia v. Hall, 466 U.S. 408, 414-16 (1984). Specific jurisdiction is established when the basis of the "plaintiff's claim is related to or arises out of the defendant's contacts with the forum." Pennzoil Products Co. v. Colelli & Assoc., Inc., 149 F.3d 197, 201 (3d Cir.1998) (citations omitted). General jurisdiction, on the other hand, does not require the defendant's contacts with the forum state to be related to the underlying cause of action, Helicopteros, 466 U.S. at 414, but the contacts must have been "continuous and systematic." Id. at 416.

Bragg does not contend that general jurisdiction exists over Rosedale. Rather, he maintains that Rosedale's representations support specific personal jurisdiction in this case.[9] The Court therefore need only address whether specific jurisdiction exists.

In deciding whether specific personal jurisdiction is appropriate, a court must first determine whether the defendant has the minimum contacts with the forum necessary to have reasonably anticipated being haled into court there. Pennzoil, 149 F.3d at 201 (citing World-Wide Volkswagen Corp. v. Woodson, 444 U.S. 286 (1980)). Second, once minimum contacts have been established, a court may inquire whether the assertion of personal jurisdiction would comport with traditional conceptions of fair play and substantial justice. Id. at 201 (citing Burger King Corp. v. Rudzewicz, 471 U.S. 462, 476 (1985) and Int'l Shoe Co. v. Washington, 326 U.S. 310, 320 (1945)). The first step is mandatory, but the second step is discretionary. Id.

After a defendant has raised a jurisdictional defense, as Rosedale has in this case, the plaintiff bears the burden of coming forward with enough evidence to establish, with reasonable particularity, sufficient contacts between the defendant and the forum. Provident Nat'l Bank v. Cal. Fed. Savings & Loan Assoc., 819 F.2d 434, 437 (3d Cir.1987). "The plaintiff must sustain its burden of proof in establishing jurisdictional facts through sworn affidavits or other competent evidence. . . . [A]t no point may a plaintiff rely on the bare pleadings alone in order to withstand a defendant's Rule 12(b)(2) motion to dismiss for lack of in personam jurisdiction." Patterson by Patterson v. F.B.I., 893 F.2d 595, 604 (3d Cir.1990). "Once the motion is made, plaintiff must respond with actual proofs not mere allegations." Id.

B. Application

In support of the Court's exercising personal jurisdiction over Rosedale, Bragg relies on various representations that Rosedale personally made in the media "to a national audience" regarding ownership of virtual property in Second Life. Bragg maintains that Rosedale made these representations to induce Second Life participants to purchase virtual property and that such representations in fact induced Bragg to do so. Bragg also relies on the fact that he "attended" town hall meetings hosted in Second Life where he listened to Rosedale make statements about the purchase of virtual land.

1. Minimum Contacts

*4 The first question the Court must answer, then, is whether Rosedale has minimum contacts with Pennsylvania sufficient to support specific personal jurisdiction. The Court holds that Rosedale's representations—which were made as part of a national campaign to induce persons, including Bragg, to visit Second Life and purchase virtual property—constitute sufficient contacts to exercise specific personal jurisdiction over Rosedale.

Wellness Publishing v. Barefoot provides useful guidance, albeit in a non-precedential opinion. 128 Fed. App'x 266 (3d Cir.2005). In that case, the Third Circuit recognized that an advertising campaign of national scope could not, on its own, provide the basis for general jurisdiction in any state where advertisements were aired, but that under the appropriate circumstances, such contacts could provide the basis of exercising specific jurisdiction over a defendant in a particular state where the advertisements were aired. Id.[10]

In Barefoot, a group of defendants produced infomercials for calcium supplements and related products that ran nationally, including in New Jersey. Id. at 269. The defendants also processed telephone orders for products promoted in the infomercials. Id. The District Court dismissed the plaintiff's case for lack of personal jurisdiction in New Jersey. Id. at 270. On appeal, however, the Third Circuit reversed, holding that specific personal jurisdiction existed over the defendants that ran the infomercials in New Jersey. Id. In doing so, it analogized the defendants' promotional activities to the maintenance of a website. Id. (citing Toys "R" Us, Inc. v. Step Two, S.A., 318 F.3d 446, 452 (3d Cir.2003)).

Under the Third Circuit's jurisdictional analysis of websites, if a defendant website operator intentionally targets the site to the forum state and/or knowingly conducts business with forum state residents via the site, then the "purposeful availment" requirement is satisfied. Toys "R" Us, 318 F.3d at 452. In addition, a court may consider the level of interactivity of the website and the defendant's related non-Internet activities as part of the "purposeful availment" calculus. Id. at 453.

The Third Circuit applied this same jurisdictional analysis in Barefoot to hold that the defendants who ran the infomercials in New Jersey could be subject to personal jurisdiction in that state. 128 Fed. App'x at 270. First, it reasoned that, as with the mere operation of a website, "an advertising campaign with national scope does not by itself give rise to general jurisdiction in a state ' where it is broadcast." Id. That principle was inapplicable, however, because it involved precedents where the plaintiff's injuries were unrelated to the broad case of the advertisement in the forum state, which were therefore inapplicable to a specific-jurisdiction inquiry. Id. (citing Gehling v. St. George's Sch. of Med., Ltd., 773 F.2d 539 (3d Cir.1985); Giangola v. Walt Disney World Co., 753 F.Supp. 148 (D.N.J.1990)). Second, and most important for this case, the Third Circuit reasoned:

*5 [T]he advertisement in this case induced viewers to establish direct contact with [the defendant] by calling its toll-free phone number to place orders. This inducement destroys any semblance of the passive advertising addressed in Giangola, 753 F.Supp. at 155-56, which expressly distinguished advertisements in the form of direct mail solicitations. For purposes of jurisdictional analysis, an infomercial broadcast that generates telephone customers is the equivalent of an interactive web-site through which a defendant purposefully directs its commercial efforts towards residents of a forum state. Id. at 270 (some internal citations omitted).

Barefoot's analysis applies to the facts of this case. First, Bragg has provided evidence that Rosedale helped orchestrate a campaign at the national level to induce persons, including Bragg, to purchase virtual land and property on Second Life. As part of the national campaign, Bragg made representations that were distributed nationally, including in Pennsylvania. Moreover, this case does not involve "injuries unrelated to the broadcast of the advertisement in the forum state," as was the case in Gehling or Giangola.[11] Cf. Barefoot, 128 Fed. App'x at 270. Rather, Rosedale's representations constitute part of the alleged fraudulent and deceptive conduct at the heart of Bragg's claims in this case.

Second, like the role of the infomericals [sic] in Barefoot, Rosedale's personal role was to "bait the hook" for potential customers to make more interactive contact with Linden by visiting Second Life's website. Rosedale's activity was designed to generate additional traffic inside Second Life. He was the hawker sitting outside Second Life's circus tent, singing the marvels of what was contained inside to entice customers to enter. Once inside Second Life, participants could view virtual property, read additional materials about purchasing virtual property, interact with other avatars who owned virtual property, and, ultimately, purchase virtual property themselves. Significantly, participants could even interact with Rosedale's avatar on Second Life during town hall meetings that he held on the topic of virtual property.

Viewed in context, Rosedale's marketing efforts in this case are more "interactive" rather than "passive." C.f. Barefoot, 128 Fed. App'x at 270 (emphasizing that "interactive" contacts are more significant for jurisdictional purposes than "passive" contacts). Thus, they provide more than just "tangential" support for specific personal jurisdiction. See Mesalic v. Fiberfloat Corp., 897 F.2d 696, 700 n.10 (3d Cir. 1990) (noting that a defendant's marketing strategy, including advertising in national publications distributed in the forum, provided only "tangential" support for specific personal jurisdiction).[12]

The Court's decision is also consistent with the decisions of courts in other jurisdictions which have extended specific jurisdiction over defendants who have made representations in national media when the dispute arose directly from those representations. See, e.g., Indianapolis Colts, Inc. v. Metro. Baltimore Football Club Ltd. P'ship, 34 F.3d 410, 412 (7th Cir.1994) (holding that national television broadcast into the forum state was sufficient for personal jurisdiction); Caddy Prods., Inc. v. Greystone Int'l., Inc., No. 05- 301, 2005 U.S. Dist. LEXIS 34467, *4-5 (D.Minn.2005) (holding that the defendant had sufficient contacts to support the exercise of specific personal jurisdiction, which included the defendant's marketing efforts, such as attending a national trade show and advertising in a national trade publication, coupled with defendant's shipment of the product into the forum state); Hollar v. Philip Morris Inc., 43 F.Supp.2d 794, 802-03 (N.D.Ohio 1998) (holding specific personal jurisdiction existed over tobacco company that made false representations regarding smoking to a national audience, which induced plaintiffs to continue smoking; it is "axiomatic that what is distributed and broadcast nationwide will be seen and heard in all states.") (internal quotation omitted); Thomas Jackson Publ'g Inc. v. Buckner, 625 F.Supp. 1044, 1046 (D.Neb.1985) (holding that performance of songs and interviews on national television supported finding of specific personal jurisdiction over a defendant whose songs infringed the plaintiff's copyright).

*6 Rosedale relies heavily on cases from other jurisdictions for the proposition that his statements do not subject him to personal jurisdiction in Pennsylvania because none of the statements were targeted directly at Pennsylvania as opposed to the nation at large. See Dfts.' Reply at 3. Rosedale's first cited case, however, involves representations specifically targeted at one state, as opposed to a national audience, that merely could be accessed worldwide because they were available on the Internet. See Young v. New Haven Advocate, 315 F.3d 256, 263 (4th Cir.2002) ("[T]he fact that the newspapers' websites could be accessed anywhere, including Virginia, does not by itself demonstrate that the newspapers were intentionally directing their website content to a Virginia audience. Something more than posting and accessibility is needed to indicate that the newspapers purposefully (albeit electronically) directed their activity in a substantial way to the forum state. . .."). Rosedale did not target his representations at any particular state, but rather to the nation at large. The other two cases cited by Rosedale are also distinguishable, because they involved isolated statements that were not, as is the case here, an integral part of a larger publicity campaign of national scope. See Revel v. Lidov, 317 F.3d 467, 475 (5th Cir.2002) (finding that the court lacked personal jurisdiction over author of an Internet bulletin board posting "because the post to the bulletin board was presumably directed at the entire world" and was not "directed specifically at Texas"); Griffis v. Luban, 646 N.W.2d 527, 536 (Minn.2002) ("The mere fact that [the defendant], who posted allegedly defamatory statements about the plaintiff on the Internet, knew that [the plaintiff] resided and worked in Alabama is not sufficient to extend personal jurisdiction over [the defendant] in Alabama, because that knowledge does not demonstrate targeting of Alabama as the focal point of the . . . statements."). See also Growden v. Ed Bowlin & Assoc., Inc., 733 F.2d 1149, 1151-52 & n.4 (5th Cir.1984) (holding no personal jurisdiction existed based on ads in two national publications for the sale of an airplane, the crash of which was the subject of the litigation).

Accordingly, the Court finds that Rosedale has minimum contacts with Pennsylvania sufficient to support specific personal jurisdiction.

2. Fair Play and Substantial Justice

The Court also finds that the exercise of personal jurisdiction in this case would not offend due process. See Lehigh Coal, 56 F.Supp.2d at 569 (citing Burger King, 471 U.S. at 477). The factors to be considered in making this fairness determination are: (1) the burden on the defendant, (2) the forum State's interest in adjudicating the dispute, (3) the plaintiff's interest in obtaining convenient and effective relief, (4) the interstate judicial system's interest in obtaining the most efficient resolution of controversies and (5) the shared interest of the several states in furthering fundamental substantive social policies. Id.

*7 Nothing on the record counsels strongly against jurisdiction based on considerations of any undue burden to Rosedale. Rosedale has not claimed that he does not have the financial ability or that he would otherwise be irreparably prejudiced by litigating this case here in Pennsylvania. The Court also notes that Rose dale has able counsel on both coasts, i.e., in both his home state of California and here in Pennsylvania. Additionally, Pennsylvania has a substantial interest in protecting its residents from allegedly misleading representations that induce them to purchase virtual property. Pennsylvania also has an interest, more particularly, in vindicating Bragg's individual rights. Finally, Bragg may obtain convenient and effective relief in Pennsylvania, the state in which he initiated this action.

C. Fiduciary Shield Doctrine

The Court must also address Rosedale's argument that, because Rosedale made the alleged representations in his corporate capacity as Chief Executive Officer of Linden, he cannot be subject to personal jurisdiction based on those representations.

The applicability of this so called "fiduciary shield" doctrine is in dispute. Although it has not definitively spoken on the issue, the Supreme Court appears to have rejected the proposition that this doctrine is a requirement of federal due process. See Calder v. Jones, 465 U.S. 783, 790 (1984) ("[Defendants'] status as employees does not somehow shield them from jurisdiction. Each defendant's contacts with the forum state must be assessed individually."); Keeton v. Hustler, 465 U.S. 770, 781 n.13 (1984) ("We today reject the suggestion that employees who act in their official capacity are somehow shielded from suit in their individual capacity."). Moreover, neither the Pennsylvania Supreme Court nor the Third Circuit has squarely addressed the applicability of the fiduciary shield doctrine. See, e.g., Irons v. Transcor Am., 2002 WL 32348317, at *5 (E.D.Pa. 2002).

Fortunately, it is not necessary to untangle the confused knot of caselaw surrounding the fiduciary shield's status within the Third Circuit.[13] The Court will, in Gordian fashion, cut directly through the knot, because even if the doctrine did apply, the fiduciary shield would not protect Rosedale under these circumstances.

When corporate agents invoke the fiduciary shield as a protection, courts "have held that in order to hold such a defendant subject to personal jurisdiction, it must be shown that [1] the defendant had a major role in the corporate structure, [2] the quality of his contacts with the state were significant, and [3] his participation in the tortious conduct alleged was extensive." TJS Brokerage, 940 F.Supp. at 789. First, as to his role in the company, Rosedale acted as the CEO and public face of Linden. Second, as to the quality of Rosedale's contacts, Rosedale made numerous representations that were broadcast through the national media and through the Internet, via town hall meetings, that reached Pennsylvania. These were not isolated statements, but part of a national campaign to distinguish Second Life from other virtual worlds and induce the purchase of virtual property. Third, and finally, Rosedale did not simply direct others to publicize virtual property on Second Life. He personally participated in creating such publicity and its dissemination. Representations made as part of that publicity are at the heart of Bragg's case.[14]

*8 Even if the fiduciary shield doctrine were expressly recognized by the Third Circuit, Rosedale's representations, though made on the behalf of Linden, would still count as contacts in the analysis of whether the Court may exercise personal jurisdiction over him. Therefore, the Court will exercise personal jurisdiction over Rosedale.

III. MOTION TO COMPEL ARBITRATION

Defendants have also filed a motion to compel arbitration that seeks to dismiss this action and compel Bragg to submit his claims to arbitration according to the Rules of the International Chamber of Commerce ("ICC") in San Fransisco.[sic]

A. Relevant Facts

Before a person is permitted to participate in Second Life, she must accept the Terms of Service of Second Life (the "TOS") by clicking a button indicating acceptance of the TOS. Bragg concedes that he clicked the "accept" button before accessing Second Life. Compl. 126. Included in the TOS are a California choice of law provision, an arbitration provision, and forum selection clause. Specifically, located in the fourteenth line of the thirteenth paragraph under the heading "GENERAL PROVISIONS," and following provisions regarding the applicability of export and import laws to Second Life, the following language appears:

Any dispute or claim arising out of or in connection with this Agreement or the performance, breach or termination thereof, shall be finally settled by binding arbitration in San Francisco, California under the Rules of Arbitration of the International Chamber of Commerce by three arbitrators appointed in accordance with said rules. . . . Notwithstanding the foregoing, either party may apply to any court of competent jurisdiction for injunctive relief or enforcement of this arbitration provision without breach of this arbitration provision. TOS 13.

B. Legal Standards

1. Federal Law Applies

The Federal Arbitration Act ("FAA") requires that the Court apply federal substantive law here because the arbitration agreement is connected to a transaction involving interstate commerce. State Farm Mut. Auto. Ins. Co. v. Coviello, 233 F.3d 710, 713 n.1 (3d Cir.2000); Marciano v. MONY Life Ins. Co., 470 F.Supp.2d 518, 524 (E.D.Pa.2007) (Robreno, J.); see also Wright & Miller, Federal Practice and Procedure § 3569, at 173 (1984) ("[I]n a diversity suit . . ., the substantive rules contained in the [Federal Arbitration] Act, based as it is on the commerce and admiralty powers, are to be applied regardless of state law.").

Whether the arbitration agreement is connected to a transaction involving interstate commerce is a factual determination that must be made by the Court. State Farm, 233 F.3d at 713 n.1. Here, Bragg is a Pennsylvania resident. Linden is a Delaware corporation headquartered in California. Rosedale is a California resident. Bragg entered into the TOS and purchased virtual land through the Internet on Second Life as a result of representations made on the national media. The arbitration agreement is clearly connected to interstate commerce, and the Court will apply the federal substantive law that has emerged from interpretation of the FAA.

2. The Legal Standard Under the FAA

*9 Under the FAA, on the motion of a party, a court must stay proceedings and order the parties to arbitrate the dispute if the court finds that the parties have agreed in writing to do so. 9 U.S.C. §§ 3, 4, 6. A party seeking to compel arbitration must show

(1) that a valid agreement to arbitrate exists between the parties and (2) that the specific dispute falls within the scope of the agreement. Trippe Mfg. Co. v. Niles Audio Corp., 401 F.3d 529, 532 (3d Cir.2005); PaineWebber, Inc. v. Hartmann, 921 F.2d 507, 511 (3d Cir.1990).

In determining whether a valid agreement to arbitrate exists between the parties, the Third Circuit has instructed district courts to give the party opposing arbitration "the benefit of all reasonable doubts and inferences that may arise," or, in other words, to apply the familiar Federal Rule of Civil Procedure 56(c) summary judgment standard. Par-Knit Mills, Inc. v. Stockbridge Fabrics Co., Ltd., 636 F.2d 51, 54 & n.9 (3d Cir.1980); see also Berkery v. Cross Country Bank, 256 F.Supp.2d 359, 364 n.3 (E.D.Pa.2003) (Robreno, J.) (applying the summary judgment standard to a motion to compel arbitration). While there is a presumption that a particular dispute is within the scope of an arbitration agreement, Volt Info. Scis., Inc. v. Bd. of Trustees, 489 U.S. 468, 475 (1989), there is no such "presumption" or "policy" that favors the existence of a valid agreement to arbitrate. Marciano, 470 F.Supp.2d at 525-26.

C. Application

1. Unconscionability of the Arbitration Agreement
Unconscionability

Bragg resists enforcement of the TOS's arbitration provision on the basis that it is "both procedurally and substantively unconscionable and is itself evidence of defendants' scheme to deprive Plaintiff (and others) of both their money and their day in court." Pl.'s Resp. At 16.[15]

Section 2 of the FAA provides that written arbitration agreements "shall be valid, irrevocable, and enforceable, save upon such grounds as exist at law or in equity for the revocation of any contract." 9 U.S.C. § 2. Thus, "generally applicable contract defenses, such as fraud, duress, or unconscionability, may be applied to invalidate arbitration agreements without contravening § 2." Doctor's Assocs. v. Casarotto, 517 U.S. 681, 687 (1996) (citations omitted). When determining whether such defenses might apply to any purported agreement to arbitrate the dispute in question, "courts generally . . . should apply ordinary state-law principles that govern the formation of contracts." First Options of Chicago, Inc. v.

Kaplan, 514 U.S. 938, 944 (1995). Thus, the Court will apply California state law to determine whether the arbitration provision is unconscionable.[16]

Under California law, unconscionability has both procedural and substantive components. Davis v. O'Melveny & Myers, ___ F.3d ___, 2007 WL 1394530, at * 4 (9th Cir. May 14, 2007); Comb v. Paypal, Inc., 218 F.Supp.2d 1165, 1172 (N.D.Cal.2002). The procedural component can be satisfied by showing (1) oppression through the existence of unequal bargaining positions or (2) surprise through hidden terms common in the context of adhesion contracts. Comb, 218 F.Supp.2d at 1172. The substantive component can be satisfied by showing overly harsh or one-sided results that "shock the conscience." Id. The two elements operate on a sliding scale such that the more significant one is, the less significant the other need be. Id. at 743; see Armendariz v. Foundation Health Psychcare Servs., Inc., 6 P.3d 669, 690 (Cal.2000) ("[T]he more substantively oppressive the contract term, the less evidence of procedural unconscionability is required to come to the conclusion that the term is unenforceable, and vice versa."). However, a claim of unconscionability cannot be determined merely by examining the face of the contract; there must be an inquiry into the circumstances under which the contract was executed, and the contract's purpose, and effect. Comb, 218 F.Supp.2d at 1172.

(a) Procedural Unconscionability

*10 A contract or clause is procedurally unconscionable if it is a contract of adhesion. Comb, 218 F.Supp.2d at 1172; Flores v. Transamerica HomeFirst, Inc., 113 Cal.Rptr.2d 376, 381-82 (Ct.App.2001). A contract of adhesion, in turn, is a "standardized contract, which, imposed and drafted by the party of superior bargaining strength, relegates to the subscribing party only the opportunity to adhere to the contract or reject it." Comb, 218 F.Supp.2d at 1172; Armendariz, 6 P.3d at 690. Under California law, "the critical factor in procedural unconscionability analysis is the manner in which the contract or the disputed clause was presented and negotiated." Nagrampa v. MailCoups, Inc., 469 F.3d 1257, 1282 (9th Cir.2006). "When the weaker party is presented the clause and told to 'take it or leave it' without the opportunity for meaningful negotiation, oppression, and therefore procedural unconscionability, are present." Id. (internal quotation and citation omitted); see also Martinez v. Master Prot. Corp., 12 Cal.Rptr.3d 663, 669 (Ct.App.2004) ("An arbitration agreement that is an essential part of a 'take it or leave it' employment condition, without more, is procedurally unconscionable.") (citations omitted); O'Melveny & Myers, ___ F.3d ___, 2007 WL 1394530 at *6 (holding arbitration agreement presented on a take-it-or-leave-it basis was procedurally unconscionable, notwithstanding the fact that employee was provided three months to walk away from employment before agreement became effective).

The TOS are a contract of adhesion. Linden presents the TOS on a take-it-or-leave-it basis. A potential participant can either click "assent" to the TOS, and then gain entrance to Second Life's virtual world, or refuse assent and be denied access. Linden also clearly has superior bargaining strength over Bragg. Although Bragg is an experienced attorney, who believes he is expert enough to comment on numerous industry standards and the "rights" or [sic] participants in virtual worlds, see Pl.'s Resp., Ex. A 59-64, he was never presented with an opportunity to use his experience and lawyering skills to negotiate terms different from the TOS that Linden offered.

Moreover, there was no "reasonably available market alternatives [to defeat] a claim of adhesiveness." Cf. Dean Witter Reynolds, Inc. v. Superior Court, 259 Cal.Rptr. 789, 795 (Ct.App.1989) (finding no procedural unconscionability because there were other financial institutions that offered competing IRA's which lacked the challenged provision). Although it is not the only virtual world on the Internet, Second Life was the first and only virtual world to specifically grant its participants property rights in virtual land.

The procedural element of unconscionability also "focuses on . . . surprise." Gutierrez v. Autowest, Inc., 7 Cal.Rptr.3d 267, 275 (Ct.App.2003) (citations omitted). In determining whether surprise exists, California courts focus not on the plaintiff's subjective reading of the contract, but rather, more objectively, on "the extent to which the supposedly agreed-upon terms of the bargain are hidden in the prolix printed form drafted by the party seeking to enforce the disputed terms." Id. In Gutierrez, the court found such surprise where an arbitration clause was "particularly inconspicuous, printed in eight-point typeface on the opposite side of the signature page of the lease." Id.

*11 Here, although the TOS are ubiquitous throughout Second Life,[17] Linden buried the TOS's arbitration provision in a lengthy paragraph under the benign heading "GENERAL PROVISIONS." See TOS 13. Compare Net Global Mktg. v. Dialtone, Inc., No. 04-56685, 2007 U.S.App. LEXIS 674 at *7 (9th Cir. Jan. 9, 2007) (finding procedural unconscionability where "[t]here was no 'clear heading' in the Terms of Service that could refute a claim of surprise; to the contrary, the arbitration clause is listed in the midst of a long section without line breaks under the unhelpful heading of 'Miscellaneous'") and Higgins v. Superior Court, 45 Cal.Rptr.3d 293, 297 (Ct. App.2006) (holding arbitration agreement unconscionable where "[t]here is nothing in the Agreement that brings the reader's attention to the arbitration provision") with Boghos v. Certain Underwriters at Lloyd's of London, 115 P.3d 68, 70 (Cal.2005) (finding arbitration clause was enforceable where it was in bolded font and contained the heading "BINDING ARBITRATION"). Linden also failed to make available the costs and rules of arbitration in the ICC by either setting them forth in the TOS or by providing a hyper-link to another page or website where they are available. Bragg Decl. 20.

Comb is most instructive. In that case, the plaintiffs challenged an arbitration provision that was part of an agreement to which they had assented, in circumstances similar to this case, by clicking their assent on an online application page. 218 F.Supp.2d at 1169. The defendant, PayPal, was a large company with millions of individual online customers. Id. at 1165. The plaintiffs, with one exception, were all individual customers of PayPal. Id. Given the small amount of the average transaction with PayPal, the fact that most PayPal customers were private individuals, and that there was a "dispute as to whether PayPal's competitors offer their services without requiring customers to enter into arbitration agreements," the court concluded that the user agreement at issue "satisfie[d] the criteria for procedural unconscionability under California law." Id. at 1172-73. Here, as in Comb, procedural unconscionability is satisfied.

(b) Substantive Unconscionability

Even if an agreement is procedurally unconscionable, "it may nonetheless be enforceable if the substantive terms are reasonable." Id. at 1173 (citing Craig v. Brown & Root, Inc., 100 Cal.Rptr.2d 818 (Ct.App.2000) (finding contract of adhesion to arbitrate disputes enforceable)). Substantive unconscionability focuses on the one-sidedness of the contract terms. Armendariz, 6 P.3d at 690; Flores, 113 Cal.Rptr.2d at 381-82. Here, a number of the TOS's elements lead the Court to conclude that Bragg has demonstrated that the TOS are substantively unconscionable.

(i) Mutuality

Under California law, substantive unconscionability has been found where an arbitration provision forces the weaker party to arbitrate claims but permits a choice of forums for the stronger party. See, e.g., Ticknor v. Choice Hotels Int'l, Inc., 265 F.3d 931, 940-41 (9th Cir.2001); Mercuro v. Superior Court, 116 Cal.Rptr.2d 671, 675 (Ct.App.2002). In other words, the arbitration remedy must contain a "modicum of bilaterality." Armendariz, 6 P.3d at 692. This principle has been extended to arbitration provisions that allow the stronger party a range of remedies before arbitrating a dispute, such as self-help, while relegating to the weaker party the sole remedy of arbitration.[18]

*12 In Comb, for example, the court found a lack of mutuality where the user agreement allowed PayPal "at its sole discretion" to restrict accounts, withhold funds, undertake its own investigation of a customer's financial records, close accounts, and procure ownership of all funds in dispute unless and until the customer is "later determined to be entitled to the funds in dispute." 218 F.Supp.2d at 1173-74. Also significant was the fact that the user agreement was "subject to change by PayPal without prior notice (unless prior notice is required by law), by posting of the revised Agreement on the PayPal website." Id.

Here, the TOS contain many of the same elements that made the PayPal user agreement substantively unconscionable for lack of mutuality. The TOS proclaim that "Linden has the right at any time for any reason or no reason to suspend or terminate your Account, terminate this Agreement, and/or refuse any and all current or future use of the Service without notice or liability to you." TOS 7.1. Whether or not a customer has breached the Agreement is "determined in Linden's sole discretion." Id. Linden also reserves the right to return no money at all based on mere "suspicions of fraud" or other violations of law. Id. Finally, the TOS state that "Linden may amend this Agreement . . . at any time in its sole discretion by posting the amended Agreement [on its website]." TOS 1.2.

In effect, the TOS provide Linden with a variety of one-sided remedies to resolve disputes, while forcing its customers to arbitrate any disputes with Linden. This is precisely what occurred here. When a dispute arose, Linden exercised its option to use self-help by freezing Bragg's account, retaining funds that Linden alone determined were subject to dispute, and then telling Bragg that he could resolve the dispute by initiating a costly arbitration process. The TOS expressly authorized Linden to engage in such unilateral conduct. As in Comb, "[f]or all practical purposes, a customer may resolve disputes only after [Linden] has had control of the disputed funds for an indefinite period of time," and may only resolve those disputes by initiating arbitration. 218 F.Supp.2d at 1175.

Linden's right to modify the arbitration clause is also significant. "The effect of [Linden's] unilateral right to modify the arbitration clause is that it could . . . craft precisely the sort of asymmetrical arbitration agreement that is prohibited under California law as unconscionable. Net Global Mktg., 2007 U.S.App. LEXIS 674, at *9. This lack of mutuality supports a finding of substantive unconscionability.

(ii) Costs of Arbitration and Fee-Sharing

Bragg claims that the cost of an individual arbitration under the TOS is likely to exceed $13,540, with an estimated initiation cost of at least $10,000. Pl.'s Reply at 5-6. He has also submitted a Declaration of Personal Financial Information stating that such arbitration would be cost-prohibitive for him (doc. no. 41). Linden disputes Bragg's calculations, estimating that the costs associated with arbitration would total $7,500, with Bragg advancing $3,750 at the outset of arbitration. See Dfts.' Reply at 11.

*13 At oral argument, the parties were unable to resolve this dispute, even after referencing numerous provisions and charts contained within the ICC Rules. See Tran. of 2/5/07 Hrg. at 65-74. The Court's own calculations, however, indicate that the costs of arbitration, excluding arbitration, would total $17,250. With a recovery of $75,000,[19] the ICC's administrative expenses would be $2,625 (3.5% of $75,000). See ICC Rules at 28. In addition, arbitrator's fees could be set between 2.0% ($1,500) and 11.0% ($8,250) of the amount at issue per arbitrator. Id. If the ICC set the arbitrator's fees at the mid-point of this range, the arbitrator's fees would be $4,875 per arbitrator. Id. Here, however, the TOS requires that three arbitrators be used to resolve a dispute. TOS 13. Thus, the Court estimates the costs of arbitration with the ICC to be $17,250 ($2,625 + (3 x $4,875)), although they could reach as high as $27,375 ($2,625 + (3 x $8,250)).[20]

These costs might not, on their own, support a finding of substantive unconscionability. However, the ICC Rules also provide that the costs and fees must be shared among the parties, and an estimate of those costs and fees must be advanced at the initiation of arbitration. See ICC Rules of Arbitration, Ex. D to Dfts.' Reply at 28-30. California law has often been applied to declare arbitration fee-sharing schemes unenforceable. See Ting v. AT & T, 319 F.3d 1126, 1151 (9th Cir.2003). Such schemes are unconscionable where they "impose [ ] on some consumers costs greater than those a complainant would bear if he or she would file the same complaint in court." Id. In Ting, for example, the Ninth Circuit held that a scheme requiring AT & T customers to split arbitration costs with AT & T rendered an arbitration provision unconscionable. Id. See also Circuit City Stores v. Adams, 279 F.3d 889, 894 (9th Cir.2002) ("This fee allocation scheme alone would render an arbitration agreement unenforceable."); Armendariz, 6 P.3d at 687 ("[T]he arbitration process cannot generally require the employee to bear any *type* of expenses that the employee would not be required to bear if he or she were free to bring the action in court.") (emphasis in original); Ferguson v. Countrywide Credit Indus., 298 F.3d 778, 785 (9th Cir.2002) ("[A] fee allocation scheme which requires the employee to split the arbitrator's fees with the employer would *alone* render an arbitration agreement substantively unconscionable.") (emphasis added).

Here, even taking Defendants characterization of the fees to be accurate, the total estimate of costs and fees would be $7,500, which would result in Bragg having to advance $3,750 at the outset of arbitration. See Dfts.' Reply at 11. The court's own estimates place the amount that Bragg would likely have to advance at $8,625, but they could reach as high as $13,687.50. Any of these figures are significantly greater than the costs that Bragg bears by filing his action in a state or federal court. Accordingly, the arbitration costs and fee-splitting scheme together also support a finding of unconscionability.

(iii) Venue

*14 The TOS also require that any arbitration take place in San Francisco, California. TOS 13. In Comb, the Court found that a similar forum selection clause supported a finding of substantive unconscionability, because the place in which arbitration was to occur was unreasonable, taking into account "the respective circumstances of the parties." 218 F.Supp.2d at 1177. As in Comb, the record in this case shows that Linden serves millions of customers across the United States and that the average transaction through or with Second Life involves a relatively small amount. See id. In such circumstances, California law dictates that it is not "reasonable for individual consumers from throughout the country to travel to one locale to arbitrate claims involving such minimal sums." Id. Indeed, "[l]imiting venue to [Linden's] backyard appears to be yet one more means by which the arbitration clause serves to shield [Linden] from liability instead of providing a neutral forum in which to arbitrate disputes." Id.

(iv) Confidentiality Provision

Arbitration before the ICC, pursuant to the TOS, must be kept confidential pursuant to the ICC rules. See ICC Rules at 33. Applying California law to an arbitration provision, the Ninth Circuit held that such confidentiality supports a finding that an arbitration clause was substantively unconscionable. Ting, 319 F.3d at 1152. The Ninth Circuit reasoned that if the company succeeds in imposing a gag order on arbitration proceedings, it places itself in a far superior legal posture by ensuring that none of its potential opponents have access to precedent while, at the same time, the company accumulates a wealth of knowledge on how to negotiate the terms of its own unilaterally crafted contract. Id. The unavailability of arbitral decisions could also prevent potential plaintiffs from obtaining the information needed to build a case of intentional misconduct against a company. See id.

This does not mean that confidentiality provisions in an arbitration scheme or agreement are, in every instance, per se unconscionable under California law. See Mercuro v. Superior Court, 116 Cal.Rptr.2d 671, 679 (Ct.App.2002) ("While [the California] Supreme Court has taken notice of the 'repeat player effect,' the court has never declared this factor renders the arbitration agreement unconscionable per se.") (citations omitted). Here, however, taken together with other provisions of the TOS, the confidentiality provision gives rise for concern of the conscionability of the arbitration clause. See also O'Melveny & Myers, ___ F.3d ___, 2007 WL 1394530, at *11 ("The concern is not with confidentiality itself but, rather, with the scope of the language of the [arbitration agreement.]").

Thus, the confidentiality of the arbitration scheme that Linden imposed also supports a finding that the arbitration clause is unconscionable.

(v) Legitimate Business Realities

*15 Under California law, a contract may provide a "margin of safety" that provides the party with superior bargaining strength protection for which it has a legitimate commercial need. "However, unless the 'business realities' that create the special need for such an advantage are explained in the contract itself, . . . it must be factually established." Stirlen v. Supercuts, Inc., 60 Cal.Rptr.2d 138, 148 (Ct.App.1997). When a contract is alleged to be unconscionable, "the parties shall be afforded a reasonable opportunity to present evidence as to its commercial setting, purpose, and effect to aid the court in making the determination." Cal. Civ. Code § 1670.5. The statutory scheme reflects "legislative recognition that a claim of unconscionability often cannot be determined merely by examining the face of the contract, but will require inquiry into its setting, purpose, and effect." Stirlen, 60 Cal.Rptr.2d at 148 (citations and internal quotations omitted).

Here, neither in its briefing nor at oral argument did Linden even attempt to offer evidence that "business realities" justify the one-sidedness of the dispute resolution scheme that the TOS constructs in Linden's favor.

(c) Conclusion

When a dispute arises in Second Life, Linden is not obligated to initiate arbitration. Rather, the TOS expressly allow Linden, at its "sole discretion" and based on mere "suspicion," to unilaterally freeze a participant's account, refuse access to the virtual and real currency contained within that account, and then confiscate the participant's virtual property and real estate. A participant wishing to resolve any dispute, on the other hand, after having forfeited its interest in Second Life, must then initiate arbitration in Linden's place of business. To initiate arbitration involves advancing fees to pay for no less than three arbitrators at a cost far greater than would be involved in litigating in the state or federal court system. Moreover, under these circumstances, the confidentiality of the proceedings helps ensure that arbitration itself is fought on an uneven field by ensuring that, through the accumulation of experience, Linden becomes an expert in litigating the terms of the TOS, while plaintiffs remain novices without the benefit of learning from past precedent.

Taken together, the lack of mutuality, the costs of arbitration, the forum selection clause, and the confidentiality provision that Linden unilaterally imposes through the TOS demonstrate that the arbitration clause is not designed to provide Second Life participants an effective means of resolving disputes with Linden. Rather, it is a one-sided means which tilts unfairly, in almost all situations, in Linden's favor. As in Comb, through the use of an arbitration clause, Linden "appears to be attempting to insulate itself contractually from any meaningful challenge to its alleged practices." 218 F.Supp.2d at 1176.

The Court notes that the concerns with procedural unconscionability are somewhat mitigated by Bragg's being an experienced attorney. However, "because the unilateral modification clause renders the arbitration provision severely one-sided in the substantive dimension, even moderate procedural unconscionability renders the arbitration agreement unenforceable." Net Global Mktg., 2007 U.S.App. LEXIS 674, at *9 (internal citations omitted).

*16 Finding that the arbitration clause is procedurally and substantively unconscionable, the Court will refuse to enforce it.[21]

2. "Bluelining" the Arbitration Agreement

Alternatively, Linden has offered to ameliorate the one-sidedness of the TOS's arbitration provision by suggesting that Linden could waive the requirements for three arbitrators, post the initial fees of arbitration, and agree to arbitrate in Philadelphia instead of San Francisco. See Dfts.' Sur-Reply Brf. at 2-3 (doc. no. 2).

California law allows a court to "blueline" an arbitration agreement to remove an element that renders it substantively unconscionable. See Cal. Civ. Code § 1670.5(a) ("If the court as a matter of law finds the contract or any clause of the contract to have been unconscionable at the time it was made the court may refuse to enforce the contract, or it may enforce the remainder of the contract without the unconscionable clause, or it may so limit the application of any unconscionable clause as to avoid any unconscionable result."). However, a court is not obligated to blueline when an "arbitration provision is so permeated by substantive unconscionability that it cannot be cured by severance or any other action short of rewriting the contract." Nagrampa v. MailCoups, Inc., 469 F.3d 1257, 1293 (9th Cir.2006). Where an arbitration provision has "multiple defects that indicate a systematic effort to impose arbitration on [the plaintiff], not simply as an alternative to litigation, but as an inferior forum that works to [the defendant's] advantage," and there simply is "no single provision [the court] can strike or restrict in order to remove the unconscionable taint from the agreement," the court can simply refuse to enforce the arbitration provision. Id. (citing Armendariz, 6 P.3d at 696).

The arbitration clause before the Court is simply not one where a single term may be stricken to render the agreement conscionable. "The unilateral modification 'pervade[s]' and 'taint[s]' with illegality' the entire agreement to arbitrate, [and] severance of terms within the arbitration clause would not cure the problem." Net Global Mktg., 2007 U.S.App. LEXIS 674, at *9 (quoting Circuit City, 279 F.3d at 895 (citations omitted)); see also Armendariz, 6 P.3d at 697 ("[M]ultiple defects indicate a systematic effort to impose arbitration on an employee not simply as an alternative to litigation, but as an inferior forum that works to the employer's advantage. . . . Because a court is unable to cure this unconscionability through severance or restriction, and is not permitted to cure it through reformation and augmentation, it must void the entire agreement."). Davis, 2007 WL 1394530, at *15 (refusing to rewrite arbitration agreement that contained four substantively unconscionable or void terms because "[t]hese provisions cannot be stricken or excised without gutting the agreement"). Bluelining in this case will require the redrafting of the agreement.

*17 The Court declines to rewrite the agreement, at Linden's request, to save an unconscionable arbitration provision which Linden itself drafted and now seeks to enforce. Rather than provide a reasonable alternative for dispute resolution, this agreement compels a one-sided resolution of disputes between the parties.

IV. CONCLUSION

For the reasons set forth above, the Court will deny Rosedale's motion to dismiss for lack of jurisdiction. The Court will also deny Defendants' motion to compel arbitration. An appropriate order follows.

ORDER

AND NOW, this 30th day of May, 2007, it is hereby ORDERED that defendant Philip Rosedale's Motion to Dismiss for Lack of Jurisdiction (doc. no. 2) and defendant Linden Research, Inc.'s Motion to Compel Arbitration (doc. no. 3) are DENIED.

It is FURTHER ORDERED that Plaintiff's Motion for Leave to File Supplemental Briefs in Opposition to Defendants Motions to Dismiss and to Compel Arbitration to Address Issues Raised by the Court at Argument on February 5, 2007 (doc. no. 34) is DENIED as moot.

AND IT IS SO ORDERED.

Notes

1. The virtual world at issue is an interactive computer simulation which lets its participants see, hear, use, and even modify the simulated objects in the computer-generated environment. See Woodrow Barfield, Intellectual Property Rights in Virtual Environments: Considering the Rights of Owners, Programmers and Virtual Avatars, 39 Akron L.Rev. 649, 649 (2006) (defining virtual world).

2. Second Life is hosted at http://secondlife.com.

3. The term "avatar" derives etymologically from the Sanskrit word for crossing down or descent and was used originally to refer to the earthly incarnation of a Hindu deity. Webster's II New Riverside University Dictionary 141 (1998). Since the advent of computers, however, "avatar" is also used to refer to an Internet user's virtual representation of herself in a computer game, in an Internet chat room, or in other Internet fora. See Wikipedia, Definition of Avatar, available at http://en.wikipedia.org.

4. Judge Richard A. Posner has apparently made an appearance in Second Life as a "balding bespectacled cartoon rendering of himself" where he "addressed a crowd of other animated characters on a range of legal issues, including property rights in virtual reality." Alan Sipress, Where Real Money Meets Virtual Reality, the Jury is Still Out, Washington Post, Dec. 26, 2006, at A1.

5. Although participants purchase virtual property using the virtual currency of "lindens," lindens themselves are bought and sold for real U.S. dollars. Linden maintains a currency exchange that sets an exchange rate between lindens and U.S. dollars. Third parties, including ebay.com, also provide additional currency exchanges.

6. Plaintiff has inundated the Court with press releases, newspaper articles, and other media containing representations made by Rosedale regarding the ownership of property on Second Life. Plaintiff states in an affidavit that he reviewed and relied on some of these representations. Bragg Decl. 4-10, 65-68. It is of no moment that Plaintiff did not rely upon every single representation that Rosedale ever made regarding ownership of virtual property on Second Life. The immense quantity of such representations is relevant to showing that these are not isolated statements, but rather, part of a national campaign in which defendant Rosedale individually and actively participated.

7. Linden taxes virtual land. In fact, according to Bragg, by June 2004, Linden reported that its "real estate tax revenue on land sold to the participants exceeded the amount the company was generating in subscriptions." Compl. 42.

8. Bragg's complaint contains counts under the Pennsylvania Unfair Trade Practices and Consumer Protection Law, 73 P.S. § 201-1, et seq.

(Count I), the California Unfair and Deceptive Practices Act, Cal. Bus. & Prof. Code § 17200 (Count II), California Consumer Legal Remedies Act, Cal. Civ. Code § 1750, et seq. (Count III), fraud (Count IV), the California Civil Code § 1812.600, et seq. (Count V), conversion (Count VI), intentional interference with a contractual relations (Count VII), breach of contract (Count VIII), unjust enrichment (Count IX), and tortious breach of the covenant of good faith and fair dealing (Count X).

9. In the conclusion of the argument section of his brief, for example, Bragg argues that Rosedale's "representations and inducements properly form the basis of specific jurisdiction against Defendant Rosedale." Pl.'s Resp. at 14.

10. The Supreme Court has also held, under different circumstances, that defamatory statements distributed in the national media may support specific personal jurisdiction where those statements are relevant to a plaintiff's claims. In Calder v. Jones, a Californian plaintiff sued a group of Floridian defendants for placing a defamatory article about her in a nationally circulated publication. 465 U.S. 783, 788-89 (1984). The plaintiff claimed that the defendants should be subject to jurisdiction in her home state of California. Id. The Supreme Court held that, because the defendant's intentional and allegedly illegal actions were expressly aimed at California and caused harm there, jurisdiction over the defendants was "proper in California based on the 'effects' of their Florida conduct in California." Id. at 789. Here, as in Calder, Rosedale's alleged misrepresentations are relevant to Bragg's claims of fraud and deceptive practices, but Bragg has not argued that jurisdiction is proper based on Calder's effects-based jurisprudence.

11. The Third Circuit has consistently held that advertising in national publications does not subject a defendant to general jurisdiction in every state. See, e.g., Gehling, 773 F.2d 539 at 542; Giangola, 753 F.Supp. at 156 ("In an age of modern advertising and national media publications and markets, plaintiffs' argument that such conduct would make a defendant amenable to suit wherever the advertisements were aired would substantially undermine the law of personal jurisdiction."). In Giangola, for example, a district court held that plaintiffs' viewing of advertisements displaying Walt Disney World "as a must visit" on plaintiffs' vacation agenda, and which in fact induced plaintiffs to visit Disney World, did not constitute "minimum contacts" sufficient to justify personal jurisdiction in the plaintiffs' subsequent personal injury action, because the advertisements were not in any way related to the plaintiffs' personal injury action. 753 F. Supp. at 155. Moreover, as the Third Circuit noted in Barefoot, the advertisements were passive in nature and did not involve any interactivity with the plaintiffs. Id.; Barefoot, 128 Fed. App'x at 270.

12. Because the Court bases its holding on the interactive nature of the marketing scheme, the [sic] its holding does not "mean that there would be nationwide (indeed, worldwide) jurisdiction over anyone and everyone who

establishes an Internet website" or made representations posted on a website accessible throughout the world. Weber v. Jolly Hotels, 977 F. Supp. 327, 333 (D.N.J.1997).

13. Some Third Circuit precedent suggests that, where the alleged contacts involve a corporate agent's personal involvement, the "corporate shield" doctrine is obviated. See Al- Khazraji v. St. Francis College, 784 F.2d 505, 518 (3d Cir.1986) ("An individual, including a director, officer, or agent of a corporation, may be liable for injuries suffered by third parties because of his torts, regardless of whether he acted on his own account or on behalf of the corporation."). On other occasions, however, after finding personal jurisdiction has existed over a corporation, the Third Circuit has remanded to address the question of whether the individual corporate agents were not subject to personal jurisdiction because their relevant contacts were established in their roles as corporate officers. See Barefoot, 128 Fed. App'x at 269.

Numerous recent cases within this district have applied the fiduciary shield doctrine in one form or another. E.g. Schiller-Pfeiffer, Inc. v. Country Home Prods., Inc., 2004 WL 2755585 (E.D.Pa.2004) ("[A] defendant is not individually subject to personal jurisdiction merely based on his actions in a corporate capacity.") (citing TJS Brokerage & Co. v. Mahoney, 940 F.Supp. 784, 789 (E.D.Pa.1996); D & S Screen Fund II v. Ferrari, 174 F.Supp.2d 343, 347 (E.D.Pa.2001) ("As a general rule, individuals performing acts in their corporate capacity are not subject to the personal jurisdiction of the courts of that state for those acts.").

14. Defendants concede that the Court has personal jurisdiction over Linden. However, Bragg does not argue that personal jurisdiction was appropriate over Rosedale based on his direction of Linden as it made contacts with Pennsylvania. Bragg relies, instead, solely on Linden's individual contacts. Had Plaintiff argued the former, the Court's application of the fiduciary shield doctrine could have been a closer call.

15. This challenge must be determined by the Court, not an arbitrator. Bellevue Drug Co. v. Advance PCS, 333 F.Supp.2d 318 (E.D.Pa.2004) (Robreno, J.). Bragg does not challenge enforceability by claiming that a provision of the arbitration agreement will deny him a statutory right, a question of interpretation of the arbitration agreement which an arbitrator is "well situated to answer." Id. (citations omitted). Rather, Bragg claims that the arbitration agreement itself would effectively deny him access to an arbitrator, because the costs would be prohibitively expensive, a question that is more appropriately reserved for the Court to answer. Id.

16. Both parties agree that California law should govern the question of whether the arbitration provision is unconscionable.

17. For example, both the "Auctions" and the "Auctions FAQ" webpages in Second Life contain hyperlinks to the TOS. See Bragg Br., Ex. 2 at 9, 15.

18. The Court notes that the Third Circuit has found that "parties to an arbitration agreement need not equally bind each other with respect to an arbitration agreement if they have provided each other with consideration beyond the promise to arbitrate." Harris v. Green Tree Fin. Corp., 183 F.3d 173, 180-81 (3d Cir. 1999). In Green Tree, however, the Third Circuit was applying Pennsylvania law, not California law. Id. In any event, Pennsylvania courts have criticized this aspect of Green Tree's holding. E.g. Lytle v. Citifinancial Servs., 810 A.2d 643, 665 (Pa.Super.Ct.2002) (holding that, under Pennsylvania law, the reservation by a company to itself of access to the courts, to the exclusion of the consumer, created a presumption of unconscionability, "which in the absence of 'business realities' that compel inclusion of such a provision in an arbitration provision, render[ed] the arbitration provision unconscionable and unenforceable").

19. The Court's calculations are based on its finding that $75,000 is at issue, the minimum necessary to satisfy the requirements of diversity jurisdiction in this case. After a hearing on Bragg's motion to remand this case back to state court, the Court found that this jurisdictional threshold had been met (doc. no. 14).

20. At oral argument, Bragg asserted repeatedly that the schedule of arbitrator's fees in the ICC Rules represents the fee "per arbitrator," which would have to be tripled in this case as the TOS provides for three arbitrators. See Tran. of 2/5/07 Hrg. at pp. 68, 74. Defendants never refuted this point. See id.

21. Having determined that the arbitration provision is unenforceable as an unconscionable agreement, the Court need not determine whether the specific dispute in this case falls within the scope of that agreement. The Court notes, however, that the arbitration clause clearly exempts from its scope claims for "injunctive relief." See TOS 13. At the hearing on the motion to compel arbitration, the Court asked whether Bragg wanted the Court to decide the motion to compel arbitration, or allow Plaintiff [to] file an amended complaint seeking only injunctive relief. See Tran. of 2/5/07 Hrg. at pp. 89-90, 108. He elected to file an amended complaint. Id. Subsequently, however, he filed supplemental briefing in support of his original complaint, and after Defendants objected, filed a Proposed Amended Complaint "[a]s promised." Pl.s' Suppl. Brf. in Opp. to Mot. to Compel at 12 (doc. no. 43). During a telephone conference on May 8, 2007, however, Bragg finally clarified that he intended to stand on his original complaint.

Appendix X:
Hernandez v. IGE
Complaint

UNITED STATES DISTRICT COURT
SOUTHERN DISTRICT OF FLORIDA

ANTONIO HERNANDEZ, Individually and
on behalf of all others similarly situated,
                    Plaintiff,

              v.   **Amended Class**
                                    Action Complaint
INTERNET GAMING ENTERTAINMENT, LTD.
a foreign corporation, and

IGE U.S. LLC., a Delaware corporation,
                    Defendants.

Plaintiff, ANTONIO HERNANDEZ, individually, and on
behalf of all others similarly situated ("Mr. Hernandez"),
by and through undersigned counsel, hereby sues
Defendants, INTERNET GAMING ENTERTAINMENT, LTD.

and IGE U.S. LLC. (collectively, "IGE" or "Defendants"), and alleges as follows:

I. Preliminary Statement

1. This case involves IGE's calculated decision to reap substantial profits by knowingly interfering with, and substantially impairing and diminishing the intended use and enjoyment associated with consumer agreements between Blizzard Entertainment and subscribers to its virtual world called World of Warcraft® (hereinafter "Subscribers" or "Consumer-Subscribers").

2. Specifically, over the past several years IGE has received tens of millions, if not hundreds of millions, of dollars by selling *World of Warcraft*® virtual property or currency (commonly referred to as "gold") generated by cheap labor in third world countries. The process of generating virtual assets and then selling them through eBay or other industry websites is known as "gold farming," "real money trade" or "RMT."

3. IGE's gold farming activities not only substantially impair and diminish the use, enjoyment and satisfaction Consumer-Subscribers obtain by earning, through the expenditure of vast amounts of time and energy, virtual assets within *World of Warcraft*®, they also violate the express terms of agreements Subscribers enter into to participate in *World of Warcraft*®. Indeed, the express terms of Blizzard Entertainment's agreements with its Subscribers for *World of Warcraft*® specifically prohibit the sale or other commercial activity related to the sale of any *World of Warcraft*® virtual assets or property.

4. Through this lawsuit, Mr. Hernandez, both individually and on behalf of all other similarly situated Subscribers, seeks declaratory and injunctive relief, as well as damages, based on IGE's gold farming activities.

II. Parties

5. Plaintiff, Mr. Hernandez, is an individual who presently, and at all times material hereto, was a resident of Orlando, Flor-

ida. Blizzard Entertainment, Inc. is a Delaware corporation and a premier publisher of entertainment software, including the franchise that owns and operates a virtual world called *World of Warcraft®*. During the relevant time period, Mr. Hernandez: (1) was a paying subscriber to Blizzard Entertainment's *World of Warcraft®;* (2) spent hundreds of hours online in *World of Warcraft®;* (3) spent in excess of fifty dollars purchasing *World of Warcraft®* software; (4) spent in excess of fifty dollars purchasing Blizzard Entertainment's Burning Crusade expansion software; and (5) spent fifteen dollars per month in subscription fees to participate in *World of Warcraft®*.

6. Defendant, INTERNET GAMING ENTERTAINMENT, LTD., is a foreign corporation with its principal place of business in Hong Kong, China, with offices in Miami Beach, Florida and Beverly Hills, California. INTERNET GAMING ENTERTAINMENT, LTD. is a global company engaged in the business of generating and selling virtual assets.

7. Defendant, IGE U.S. LLC., is a Delaware corporation with its principal place of business at 105 N.W. 43rd Street, Boca Raton, Florida, 33431. IGE U.S. LLC. holds itself out to the world as a management service provider engaged in the business of generating and selling virtual assets. IGE U.S. LLC. is an affiliated company of Defendant, INTERNET GAMING ENTERTAINMENT, LTD.

III. Jurisdiction and Venue

8. This Court has subject matter jurisdiction pursuant to the Class Action Fairness Act of 2005, 28 U.S.C. §§ 1332(a) and 1332(d), because the amount in controversy exceeds $5 million exclusive of interest and costs, and more than two-thirds of the members of the putative Class are citizens of states different from that of Defendants.

9. This case has been filed in the Miami Division of this District because a substantial part of the acts or omissions giving rise to the claims in this action occurred in this judicial District, and Defendants may be found within this judicial District. Venue is proper pursuant to 28 U.S.C. § 1391. Indeed,

one of Defendants' three primary offices is located at 635 Euclid Avenue, Suite 222, Miami Beach, Florida, 33139.

10. Moreover, Defendants, through their employees, agents, and other representatives who reside and/or transact business in this District, implemented their fraudulent marketing and sales scheme and conspiracy in this District, and nationwide, through their Miami Beach and Boca Raton offices. Additionally, Defendants' activities affected Class Members who reside or transact business throughout the United States including this District.

11. Further, Defendants submitted themselves to the jurisdiction of this Court by committing tortious acts within this state and judicial District.

IV. Facts

A. Overview of Blizzard Entertainment's Virtual World Called World of Warcraft

12. Virtual Worlds, which are also referred to as "massively populated persistent worlds," "synthetic worlds," and "massively multiplayer online role playing games" ("MMOR-PGs"), are online computer-generated environments that a large number of consumers can access simultaneously. During the last ten (10) years, virtual worlds have grown from a relatively obscure internet phenomena [sic] into a multi-billion dollar industry with over twenty (20) million subscribers across the globe participating on a regular basis in more than 150 active virtual worlds.

13. Similar to the predictions made in the 1990s about the growth of the World Wide Web, 2007 expert predictions are that virtual worlds will continue to grow dramatically in the future. One prominent research group recently projected that "80 percent of active internet users (and Fortune 500 enterprises)" will participate in virtual worlds by the end of 2011.

14. In order to participate in a virtual world, like *World of Warcraft*®, a consumer must purchase the virtual world software and a license to use same, sign up for an account, select a username and password, and then begin paying a monthly

subscription fee to the provider/publisher. These consumers are referred to herein as "Subscribers" or "Consumer-Subscribers."

15. In addition to the items above, in order to become a *World of Warcraft®* Subscriber, a consumer must agree to be bound by the terms of Blizzard Entertainment's End User License Agreement ("EULA") and Terms of Use Agreement ("ToU"), copies of which are attached hereto as Exhibits "A" and "B." The terms of the EULA must be accepted before a Subscriber can install the *World of Warcraft®* proprietary software on his or her personal computer, and the terms of the ToU must be accepted before a Subscriber can create an account and access the *World of Warcraft®* virtual world.

16. Once the Subscriber completes the process above, he or she selects an "avatar," which is the 3-D body or "character" that represents the Subscriber in the virtual world. The Subscriber controls their avatar through their keyboard to interact with the environment. Through their avatar, Subscribers can move throughout the virtual world, communicate with other Subscribers and engage in a host of activities depending on the design of the particular virtual world.

17. An important aspect of virtual worlds is the social interaction between Subscribers. Communities of Subscribers typically develop inside a virtual world, with Subscribers forming complex social relationships with each other and larger groups.

18. Virtual worlds also have their own economies which generally include the buying and selling of virtual goods through the use of in-game virtual currency.

19. Central to the design and operation of all major virtual worlds, *World of Warcraft®* has a property system with all the familiar real-world features, such as exclusive ownership, persistence of rights and a currency system to support trade. As in the real world, property and resources are limited in virtual worlds.

20. The currency in *World of Warcraft®* is the virtual gold coin simply referred to as "gold." With this gold, a Subscriber

can purchase almost anything he or she needs, including skills, food, water, transportation, clothing and equipment. A Subscriber earns gold by performing tasks or by collecting or making goods that are then sold to other Subscribers or virtual vendors.

21. A virtual auction house inside *World of Warcraft*® is used by Subscribers to buy and sell items. This virtual auction house works much the same as eBay. To sell an item, a Subscriber sets a minimum bid and posts the item on an auction board that can be viewed by all Subscribers. Once a specified time period expires, the highest bidder wins the item and pays for it with gold. Once payment is received through *World of Warcraft's*® internal e-mail system, the item is likewise sent to the winner's *World of Warcraft*® in-world mail box.

22. As with real world economies, the cost of goods fluctuates based on: (1) supply and demand; and (2) the supply of *World of Warcraft*® gold.

23. While not necessarily the case in all virtual worlds, in order to ensure the integrity of *World of Warcraft's*® virtual world, Blizzard Entertainment's EULA and ToU expressly prohibit the sale of virtual assets for real money. This prohibition protects the integrity of *World of Warcraft*®, ensures that the competitive playing field within *World of Warcraft*® is level, and makes certain that the time, energy and effort expanded [sic] by Subscribers is not negatively impacted by others who use real money to purchase scarce and limited virtual resources.

24. Specifically, Blizzard Entertainment's ToU agreement with its Subscribers states that: [Y]ou may not sell items for "real" money or otherwise exchange items for value outside of the [virtual world]. (*See* Exhibit "B" at p. 8)

B. IGE's Illicit Gold Marketing and Sales Scheme

25. Despite the fact that gold farming within *World of Warcraft*® is expressly prohibited by Blizzard Entertainment's EULA and ToU, Defendants, by and through their employees, agents and affiliates, engage in the business of generating, marketing, distributing and selling *World of Warcraft*® gold

for real money (the "Scheme").

26. Under the Scheme, a typical transaction with Defendants for the sale and purchase of gold within *World of Warcraft*® works something like this:

   a. The buyer visits Defendants' website, www.IGE.com. The buyer is then directed to a page on Defendants' website where he or she selects the particular server (called a "realm" in *World of Warcraft*®) where the buyer's avatar is located.

   b. The buyer then selects the amount of gold they wish to buy; there is a fixed price in real dollars for various amounts of gold listed on the IGE website. Buyers are given the option of purchasing as little as 50 gold, to as much as 24,000 gold per order. For example, on the *World of Warcraft's*® Durotan server, the current price of 24,000 *World of Warcraft*® gold is $2,399.82.

   c. Once the buyer selects the amount of gold he or she wishes to buy, he or she must select the method of payment. Defendants' website gives several options for payment, including paying by credit card or PayPal.

   d. After selecting the method of payment and entering the appropriate payment information (i.e., name, address and credit card account number), the buyer must type in the name of the avatar to whom the gold should be delivered. Once the buyer gives Defendants this information, the buyer is given a receipt and told they will receive their gold within a few hours.

   e. Within the specified time period, Defendants deliver the newly purchased virtual gold to the buyer's avatar through *World of Warcraft's*® in-game mail system. To receive the gold, the buyer simply opens up the piece of mail delivered from an avatar controlled by Defendants and opens the attached virtual envelope containing the gold.

27. Since Blizzard Entertainment released *World of Warcraft*® on November 27, 2004, Defendants have sold massive quantities of *World of Warcraft*® gold for hundreds of millions of dollars.

28. Defendants engage in the fraudulent scheme and conspiracy to generate, market, distribute and sell *World of Warcraft*® gold through the efforts of hundreds of employees, agents and affiliates who work at the direction and control of, and/or for the benefit of, IGE. These employees, agents and affiliates, are commonly referred to as gold farmers ("IGE gold farmers"). IGE gold farmers are often citizens of developing third world countries who spend up to 14 hours per day, or more, logged into *World of Warcraft*® collecting resources and *World of Warcraft*® gold. IGE gold farmers log into *World of Warcraft*® through accounts paid for, and/or controlled, in whole or in part, directly or indirectly, by Defendants. At the direction of Defendants, through channels of distribution designed, established, maintained and/or controlled by Defendants, IGE gold farmers then deliver gold through the *World of Warcraft*® mail system to Subscribers who have paid real money as described above. IGE gold farmers are co-conspirators with Defendants in this fraudulent marketing and sales scheme.

C. IGE's Conspiracy

29. In addition to IGE's direct sale of *World of Warcraft*® gold through its website, IGE has entered into agreements with other individuals and/or entities not directly employed by IGE ("co-conspirators"), to:

    a. generate, or "farm" for, *World of Warcraft*® gold which IGE then sells to Subscribers for real money;

    b. promote and market the sale of *World of Warcraft*® gold owned or under the control of IGE through chat spam, virtual junk mail, pay per click campaigns, and search engine marketing;

    c. obtain labor to generate, or "farm" for, *World of Warcraft*® gold which IGE then sells to Subscribers for real money;

    d. distribute *World of Warcraft*® gold to Subscribers;

    e. sell *World of Warcraft*® gold to Subscribers for real money; and

    f. collect the proceeds from the sale of *World of Warcraft*® gold to Subscribers.

30. All the aforementioned agreements were made in furtherance of a fraudulent scheme and conspiracy to generate,
market, distribute and sell *World of Warcraft®* gold in direct
violation of: (1) Blizzard Entertainment's EULA; (2) Blizzard Entertainment's ToU; (3) Florida Statutory provisions;
(4) consumer protection statutes of the remaining 49 states,
the District of Columbia and Puerto Rico; and (5) other common law.

D. Irreparable Harm and Impact Caused by IGE's Illicit Marketing and Sales Scheme and Conspiracy

31. The volume of gold IGE sells in *World of Warcraft®* is so large
that it causes irreparable harm to Subscribers by impairing and diminishing their use and enjoyment of the *World
of Warcraft®* virtual world. Defendants' conduct also causes
substantial economic harm, above and beyond the purchase price paid by Subscribers for the software and subscription fees, including:

a. **Lost Time.** IGE gold farmers strip out already scarce
and limited virtual world resources and materials.
World of Warcraft® is designed to have limited resources
and materials, such as virtual metal ore, plants, leather
and other items ("materials"). Subscribers must harvest, or "farm," materials and sell them to earn virtual
gold. "Farming" materials is one of the primary sources
of revenue in the *World of Warcraft®* economy. IGE gold
farmers, however, systematically harvest these materials on a massive commercial scale. The result is a
shortage of materials for Subscribers who comply with
the Blizzard agreements by not buying gold from IGE,
making it vastly more time consuming for such Subscribers to earn the gold needed to participate. This
loss of time, conservatively, amounts to hundreds of
thousands of hours of Subscriber time and causes the
irreparable harm of driving Subscribers away from
World of Warcraft®. The economic harm incurred by
this loss of time is in the millions of dollars.

b. **Devaluation of Currency.** Because of IGE's infusion of
gold from its unlawful "gold farming" activities, virtual

currency held by Subscribers is constantly devalued. The devaluation of virtual currency has an economic value in real dollars, as reflected on Defendants' website. This devaluation of the *World of Warcraft®* gold currency, which is caused by Defendants' sale of gold in *World of Warcraft®*, is in the millions of dollars.

32. A virtual world like *World of Warcraft®* derives utility and benefit from the fact that it creates a fantasy world experience. Subscribers are willing to pay a substantial portion of their discretionary income for entertainment to participate in the *World of Warcraft®* fantasy. When Defendants engage in RMT, it impairs and diminishes the use, enjoyment and the fantasy experience Subscribers pay for. Such harm is irreparable and there is no adequate remedy at law to address it. Some examples of the ways the Subscriber experience is impaired and diminished include, but are not limited to, the following:

a. **Chat Spamming.** Defendants, through IGE gold farmers and other co-conspirators within their direct or indirect control, constantly "spam" advertisements to promote their illicit Scheme. Subscribers are routinely sent un-invited messages by Defendants and their agents through the *World of Warcraft®* "chat" channel and mail system advertising the sale of gold for real dollars. During the last few months the amount of chat spam has increased substantially to the point where Subscribers can receive spam messages advertising *World of Warcraft®* gold five or six times every hour. This "chat spam" destroys the fantasy experience Subscribers pay for and has caused Subscribers to surrender their subscriptions.

b. **Junk Mail.** Defendants, by and through their agents, employees, affiliates, IGE gold farmers and other co-conspirators within their direct or indirect control, routinely send junk mail advertisements to Subscribers advertising the sale of gold for real dollars. This junk mail takes up space in the Subscribers' mail boxes and causes them to waste time sorting through it. This junk mail impairs, interrupts and pollutes the use and enjoyment of the *World of Warcraft®* fantasy experience Subscribers pay for and has caused Subscribers to surrender their subscriptions.

c. **Less Time for Content.** Subscribers, like Plaintiff, have a limited amount of time in a given week available to participate in *World of Warcraft®*. Because of the additional time required to collect materials and earn currency as the result of material shortages caused by Defendants, IGE gold farmers and their co-conspirators, Subscribers have less time to participate in, and experience other content in the virtual world. This other content consists of, among other things, raids, instances, quests, battlegrounds, arena contests and world PvP. The inability to experience such other content is caused by the additional time Subscribers expend as a result of Defendants' actions.

d. **Competitively Disadvantaged.** Subscribers who do not buy gold are at a competitive disadvantage to Subscribers who purchase gold from Defendants ("Gold-Buying Subscribers") in certain aspects of *World of Warcraft®*, including, Arena competitions. These Subscribers who do not purchase gold from Defendants are held hostage by this dilemma: they must either continue to experience *World of Warcraft®* at an unfair competitive disadvantage or violate the EULA and the ToU by purchasing gold from the Defendants. This dilemma, and the resulting competitive disadvantage for Subscribers who do not buy gold from Defendants, impairs and diminishes the *World of Warcraft®* experience Subscribers pay for by purchasing software and paying monthly subscription fees.

V. Class Action Allegations

33. Pursuant to Rule 23 of the *Federal Rules of Civil Procedure,* Plaintiff brings this action on behalf of himself, a Class, and a Sub-Class defined as follows:

Subscriber Class All persons in the United States and its territories who, for purposes other than resale, purchased Blizzard Entertainment's *World of Warcraft®* software and paid subscription fees at any time from November 27, 2004 until the present.

Gold-Buying Subscribers Sub-Class All persons in the United States and its territories who, for purposes other than resale, purchased Blizzard Entertainment's *World of Warcraft®* software and paid subscription fees at any time from November 27, 2004 until the present, and who bought any *World of Warcraft®* gold for real money. Excluded from the Class are (a) Defendants and any entities in which any Defendant has a controlling interest, their legal representatives, officers, directors, assignees and successors; and (b) any co-conspirators, including any Subscribers who sold *World of Warcraft®* gold to IGE. Also excluded from the Class are any judges or justices to whom this action is assigned, as well as any relative of such judge(s) or justice(s) within the third degree of relationship, and the spouse of any such person, as well as any attorneys of record in this case.

34. Plaintiff contends that this suit is properly maintainable as a class action pursuant to Rules 23(b)(1), (b)(2), and (b)(3) of the *Federal Rules of Civil Procedure.*

A. Numerosity

35. The Class consists of numerous individuals throughout the United States, thereby making individual joinder impractical, in satisfaction of Rule 23(a)(1). Plaintiff is unable to provide an approximation of the number of potential class members, but notes that there are approximately 2 million subscribers to *World of Warcraft®* in North America. The disposition of the claims of the Class members in a single class action will provide substantial benefits to all parties and to the Court.

B. Typicality

36. The claims of the representative Plaintiff are typical of the claims of the Class, as required by Rule 23(a)(3), in that Mr. Hernandez, like all Class members, purchased Blizzard Entertainment's software and paid for subscriptions to *World of Warcraft®*. Like all Class Members, Mr. Hernandez has been damaged by Defendants' misconduct, in that, among other things, his use and enjoyment of *World of Warcraft®* has been impaired and diminished. He has thus lost the benefit of that which he paid for when he purchased Blizzard Entertainment's software and paid his monthly subscriptions to *World of Warcraft®*.

C. Common Questions of Law and Fact

37. The factual and legal basis for Defendants' fraudulent marketing and sales scheme and conspiracy is common to all members of the Class and represents a common thread of misconduct resulting in injury to Plaintiff and all members of the Class.

38. Questions of law and fact are common to Plaintiff and the Class abound in this case, and those questions predominate over any questions affecting individual Class members, within the meaning of Rule 23(a)(2) and (b)(3). These common questions of law and fact include, but are not limited to, the following:

   (a) Whether Defendants, by and through their employees, agents and affiliates, generated *World of Warcraft®* gold for re-sale with real money;

   (b) Whether Defendants, by and through their employees, agents and affiliates, marketed *World of Warcraft®* gold for re-sale with real money;

   (c) Whether Defendants, by and through their employees, agents and affiliates, distributed *World of Warcraft®* gold for re-sale with real money;

   (d) Whether Defendants, by and through their employees, agents and affiliates, sold *World of Warcraft®* gold for real money;

(e) Whether Defendants engaged in a conspiracy with others to generate, market, distribute and/or sell *World of Warcraft*® gold;

(f) Whether Defendants engaged in unfair and deceptive acts or practices of generating, marketing, distributing and/or selling *World of Warcraft*® gold as alleged herein;

(g) Whether Defendants violated Florida's or any other state's consumer protection statutes;

(h) Whether Defendants' unfair and deceptive acts or practices, or other violations of other state's [sic] consumer protection statutes, proximately caused harm to Plaintiff and the Class;

(i) Whether Plaintiff and the Class have been injured by Defendants' conduct, including both money damages and irreparable harm, for which there is no adequate remedy at law;

(j) Whether Plaintiff and other members of the Class had a business relationship with Blizzard Entertainment through their subscriptions for *World of Warcraft*® ("Business Relationship");

(k) Whether Defendants had actual or constructive knowledge of the Business Relationship;

(l) Whether Defendants intentionally and unjustifiably interfered with the Business Relationship through their generation, marketing, distribution and sales of *World of Warcraft*® gold, and their conspiracy to sell *World of Warcraft*® gold, as alleged herein;

(m) Whether Defendants' intentional and unjustified interference with the Business Relationship proximately caused injury to Plaintiff and members of the Class, including both money damages and irreparable harm with no adequate remedy at law;

(n) Whether Defendants are liable under state conspiracy and/or state concert of action and/or state aiding and abetting/facilitating laws;

(o) Whether Plaintiff and the Class are entitled to declaratory and injunctive relief, or other equitable remedy for Defendants' conduct, including an injunction;

(p) Whether Plaintiff and members of the Class are entitled to compensatory damages, and, if so, the nature of such damages;

(q) Whether Plaintiff and members of the Class are entitled to punitive damages, treble damages or exemplary damages and, if so, the nature of such damages;

(r) Whether Plaintiff and members of the Class are entitled to an award of reasonable attorneys' fees, prejudgment interest, post-judgment interest and cost of suit.

D. Adequacy

39. Plaintiff will fairly and adequately represent and protect the interests of the Class, as required by Rule 23(a)(4). Plaintiff has retained counsel with substantial experience and expertise. Plaintiff and his counsel are committed to the vigorous prosecution of this action on behalf of the Class and have the financial resources to do so. Neither Plaintiff nor his counsel has any interest adverse to the interests of the Class.

E. Class Certification under Rules 23(b)(1) and (b)(2)

40. The prosecution of separate actions by or against individual members of the Class would create a risk of inconsistent or varying adjudications with respect to individual members of the Class. The adjudications would establish incompatible standards of conduct for the Defendants which would, as a practical matter, be dispositive of the interests of the other class members not parties to the adjudications or would substantially impair or impede their ability to protect their interests. Class certification under Rule 23(b)(1) is therefore appropriate.

41. Defendants also have acted or refused to act on grounds generally applicable to all members of the Class, thereby making appropriate declaratory and injunctive relief with respect to the Class as a whole and class certification under Rule 23(b)(2).

F. Superiority

42. A class action is superior to other available methods for the fair and efficient adjudication of the controversy under Rule 23(b)(3). Absent a class action, most members of the Class likely would find the cost of litigating their claims to be prohibitive, and will have no effective remedy at law. The class treatment of common questions of law and fact is also superior to multiple individual actions or piecemeal litigation in that it conserves resources of the courts and the litigants, and promotes consistency and efficiency of adjudication.

VI. Causes of Action

CLAIM I
Breach of Third Party Beneficiary Contract

43. Plaintiff incorporates by reference thereto paragraphs 1-42 as if fully set forth herein.

44. **Valid contract.** Defendants and their co-conspirators entered into valid contracts with Blizzard Entertainment by creating *World of Warcraft®* accounts and agreeing to the EULA and the ToU. Both the EULA and ToU are standard contracts agreed to by all Subscribers.

45. **Plaintiff not a party.** Plaintiff is not a party to the contracts between Defendants and Blizzard Entertainment.

46. **Plaintiff and Class are intended beneficiaries.** Defendants and Blizzard Entertainment intended that their contracts directly benefit Plaintiff and the Class. Both the EULA and ToU prohibit real money trade and the generation, marketing, distribution and sale of *World of Warcraft®* gold for real money, and this prohibition was for the benefit of all Subscribers, including Plaintiff and the Class.

47. **The contract is breached.** Defendants and their co-conspirators breached their contracts with Blizzard Entertainment by generating, marketing, distributing and selling *World of Warcraft®* gold, and conspiring to do the same.

48. **Damages.** Plaintiff and the Class have suffered irreparable harm and damages, both of which were directly and proxi-

mately caused by Defendants' breach of the aforesaid contracts through their fraudulent scheme and conspiracy alleged herein. Such irreparable harm includes the inability to use and enjoy the *World of Warcraft®* virtual world consistent with the express terms of the EULA and ToU, for which there is no adequate remedy at law. Such money damages include compensatory, exemplary and punitive damages.

WHEREFORE, Plaintiff, on behalf of himself and the Class, respectfully seeks the relief set forth below.

CLAIM II
Conspiracy to Breach Third-Party Beneficiary Contract

49. Plaintiff incorporates by reference thereto paragraphs 1-42 as if fully set forth herein.

50. **Conspiracy between two or more parties.** Beginning at least as early as November 27, 2004, and continuing thereafter through the present time, Defendants and their co-conspirators, as described above, engaged in an ongoing fraudulent scheme and conspiracy and/or concerted action to generate, market, distribute and sell *World of Warcraft®* gold for real money.

51. **Unlawful acts by unlawful means and overt acts.** Pursuant to their scheme and conspiracy alleged herein, Defendants and their co-conspirators engaged in a wide range of activities which violated Blizzard Entertainment's EULA and ToU to the disadvantage of Plaintiff and the Class. These activities have been set forth above and throughout this Amended Complaint, and have been incorporated by reference herein, including, but not limited to the generation, marketing, distribution and sale of *World of Warcraft®* gold. These acts constitute a breach of third-party beneficiary contract with Blizzard Entertainment alleged above.

52. **Damages.** Defendants' conspiracy and concerted actions have directly and proximately caused irreparable harm and damages to Plaintiff and the Class. As a direct and proximate result of Defendants' fraudulent scheme and conspiracy

perpetrated upon Plaintiff and the Class, Defendants are jointly and severally liable to Plaintiff and the Class for all harm suffered and damages sustained, including exemplary damages, punitive damages, as well as the cost of suit and reasonable attorneys' fees.

WHEREFORE, Plaintiff, on behalf of himself and the Class, respectfully seeks the relief set forth below.

CLAIM III
Violation of the Computer Fraud and Abuse Act (18 U.S.C.A. § 1030)

53. Plaintiff incorporates by reference thereto paragraphs 1-42 as if fully set forth herein.

54. Blizzard Entertainment's *World of Warcraft*® servers and Plaintiffs and the Class' personal computers are "protected computers" as defined in the Computer Fraud and Abuse Act (18 U.S.C. § 1030), through which electronic messages are received, stored and disseminated in interstate and/or foreign commerce or communication.

55. The *World of Warcraft*® ToU specifically prohibits transmitting commercial solicitations for goods or services outside the *World of Warcraft*® universe and sending repeated unsolicited chat messages.

56. The *World of Warcraft*® EULA specifically prohibits any commercial use of the *World of Warcraft*® virtual world, including RMT and the sale of *World of Warcraft*® gold for real money.

57. By virtue of their use of *World of Warcraft*® accounts, Defendants and their co-conspirators were on notice of and agreed to the ToU and EULA.

58. Defendants and their co-conspirators have knowingly and repeatedly transmitted and/or caused to be transmitted millions of unsolicited commercial messages without authorization. Defendants have also engaged in the Scheme to sell *World of Warcraft*® gold as described above. Defen-

dants knew or should have known that these actions would impair the operation of Blizzard's protected computers, as well as the operation of Plaintiff's and the Class' protected computers, and degrade the quality of the *World of Warcraft®* virtual experience.

59. Defendants knowingly and intentionally accessed Plaintiff's and the Class' protected computers without authorization and with the intent to defraud as a result of such conduct, furthered the intended fraud, obtained something of value, and caused damages to Plaintiff and the Class in violation of 18 U.S.C. § 1030(a)(4).

60. Defendants knowingly and intentionally, caused, through the means of a computer used in interstate commerce, the transmission of information to Plaintiff's and the Class' protected computers and, as a result of such conduct, caused damage without authorization to said protected computers in violation of 18 U.S.C. § 1030(a)(5)(A)(i).

61. Defendants knowingly and intentionally accessed Plaintiff's and the Class' protected computers without authorization, and as a result of such conduct recklessly caused damage to said protected computer, in violation of 18 U.S.C. § 1030(a)(5)(A)(ii).

62. As a direct and proximate result of Defendants' actions, Plaintiffs have suffered harm in an amount to be determined at trial, but, in any event, not less than $5,000 in a one-year period.

63. Plaintiffs seek compensatory damages under 18 U.S.C. § 1030(g) in an amount within the conscious [sic] of the jury.

64. As a direct and proximate result of Defendants' actions, Plaintiff and the Class have suffered and continue to suffer irreparable harm for which there is no adequate remedy at law, and which will continue unless Defendants' actions are enjoined.

WHEREFORE, Plaintiff, on behalf of himself and the Class, respectfully seeks the relief set forth below.

CLAIM IV
Violation of Florida's Deceptive and Unfair Trade Practices Act

65. Plaintiff incorporates by reference thereto paragraphs 1-42 as if fully set forth herein.

66. Plaintiff brings this claim based upon Florida's Deceptive and Unfair Trade Practices Act (the "Act") found in Chapter 501 of the Florida Statutes.

67. **Plaintiff and the Class are Consumers Under the Act.** Plaintiff and members of the Class are "consumer[s]" and/ or "interested part[ies] or persons" within the meaning of Section 501.203(6), (7), *Florida Statutes (2006)*.

68. **Trade or Commerce.** In generating, marketing, distributing, and selling *World of Warcraft*® gold, through eBay, its proprietary websites and other avenues for real money, Defendants are engaging in "trade or commerce" within the meaning of Section 501.203(8), *Florida Statutes (2006)*.

69. **Willful Violation.** Defendants' conduct as set forth herein was "willful" and constitutes a "violation" under the Act. *See* §§501.2075 and 501.203(3), *Florida Statutes (2006)*.

70. **Unfair Acts or Practices.** As defined by Section 501.204, Defendants' conduct is unlawful as it constitutes, "unfair methods of competition," "unconscionable acts or practices," and/or "unfair or deceptive acts or practices in the conduct of any trade or commerce." *See* §501.204, *Florida Statutes (2006)*.

71. **Equitable Relief.** Plaintiff, individually and as a representative of members of the Class, seeks the entry of a judgment declaring Defendants' conduct unlawful and enjoining Defendants' unlawful conduct in the future and mandating corrective measures pursuant to Florida Statute Section 501.211, *Florida Statutes (2006)*.

72. **Money Damages.** Because Defendants' conduct has proximately caused harm to Plaintiff and the Class, as set forth above, Plaintiff, individually and as representative of the members of the Class, further requests this Court require Defendants to pay statutory damages as prescribed by Section 501.211(2) and 501.2075, *Florida Statutes (2006)*.

WHEREFORE, Plaintiff, on behalf of himself and the Class, respectfully seeks the relief set forth below.

CLAIM V
Violation of Consumer Protection Statutes of Remaining 49 States, District of Columbia and Puerto Rico

73. Plaintiff incorporates by reference thereto paragraphs 1-42 as if fully set forth herein.

74. **Plaintiff and the Class are Consumers Under Other State Statutes.** Plaintiff and the Class are individual consumers who purchased and paid for Blizzard Entertainment's *World of Warcraft®* software and paid subscription fees during the relevant time period. All 49 of the remaining states (a separate Count having been pled above for the Plaintiffs state of residence, Florida), the District of Columbia and Puerto Rico have enacted statutes to protect consumers against unfair, unconscionable, deceptive or fraudulent business practices, unfair competition and false advertising. Most states allow consumers a private right of action under these statutes.

75. **Unfair Acts or Practices.** Defendants violated Blizzard Entertainment's EULA and ToU through the fraudulent scheme and conspiracy alleged herein. This conduct constitutes unlawful, unfair, unconscionable, deceptive and fraudulent business practices within the meaning of consumer protection statutes of the remaining 49 states, the District of Columbia and Puerto Rico. This scheme and conspiracy has caused substantial detriment to Plaintiff and the Class.

76. **Irreparable Harm and Damages.** Defendants directly and proximately caused Plaintiff and the Class to suffer irreparable harm and damages, as described above, by impairing and diminishing the use and enjoyment that Plaintiff and the Class have paid for. As a direct and proximate result of Defendants' conduct, Plaintiff and the Class have suffered irreparable harm and damages in an amount to be determined at trial, and are entitled to declaratory and

injunctive relief, damages, including compensatory and treble damages, attorneys' fees and costs of suit, and any other damages provided under these statutes.

WHEREFORE, Plaintiff, on behalf of himself and the Class, respectfully seeks the relief set forth below.

CLAIM VI
Conspiracy

77. Plaintiff incorporates by reference thereto paragraphs 1-42 as if fully set forth herein.

78. **Conspiracy Between Two or More Parties.** Beginning at least as early as November 27, 2004, and continuing thereafter through the present time, Defendants, IGE gold farmers, and their co-conspirators, as described above, engaged in a continuing conspiracy and/or concerted action to generate, market, distribute and sell *World of Warcraft®* gold in violation of federal law and state law and Blizzard Entertainment's EULA and ToU. In the absence of Defendants' conspiracy and/or concerted action, the use and benefits Plaintiff and the Class paid for would not have been impaired, nor would their ability to participate in *World of Warcraft®* have been negatively affected.

79. **Unlawful Acts by Unlawful Means and Overt Acts.** Pursuant to their common plan, design, scheme, conspiracy and/or concerted action as alleged herein, Defendants and their co-conspirators engaged in numerous overt acts in furtherance of the conspiracy, encompassing a wide range of activities, the purpose and effect of which was to violate Blizzard Entertainment's EULA and ToU agreements, and the law, to the disadvantage of Plaintiff and the Class. These activities have been set forth in detail above, and throughout this Amended Complaint, and have been incorporated by reference herein, including but not limited to the generation, marketing, distribution and sale of *World of Warcraft®* gold. These acts and/or practices constitute unlawful, unfair, unconscionable, deceptive and fraudulent business practices within the meaning of Florida's Unfair and Decep-

tive Practices Act as alleged above, and the consumer protection statutes of the remaining 49 states, the District of Columbia and Puerto Rico.

80. **Irreparable Harm and Damages.** Defendants' conspiracy and concerted actions have directly and proximately caused irreparable harm and damages to Plaintiff and the Class alleged above. As a direct and proximate result of Defendants' conspiracies and/or concerted actions perpetrated upon Plaintiff and the Class, Defendants are jointly and severally liable to Plaintiff and the Class for all injury and harm Plaintiff and the Class have sustained, plus the cost of suit and reasonable attorneys' fees.

WHEREFORE, Plaintiff, on behalf of himself and the Class, respectfully seeks the relief set forth below.

CLAIM VII
Tortious Interference with Business Relationship

81. Plaintiff incorporates by reference thereto all preceding paragraphs as if fully set forth herein.

82. **Business Relationship.** Plaintiff and members of the Class have a business relationship with Blizzard Entertainment. This relationship exists through Plaintiff's and the members of the Class' monthly subscriptions with Blizzard Entertainment to participate in *World of Warcraft®,* and through their acceptance of the terms of the EULA and the ToU.

83. **Knowledge of the Relationship.** Defendants had actual or constructive knowledge of Plaintiff's relationship with Blizzard Entertainment. IGE is aware that millions of Subscribers, including Plaintiff and members of the Class, subscribe to and participate in *World of Warcraft®.* IGE also has actual or constructive knowledge that millions of Subscribers, including Plaintiff and members of the Class, have agreed to Blizzard Entertainment's EULA and the ToU.

84. **Intentional and Unjustifiable Interference.** Defendants intentionally and unjustifiably interfered with the relationship between Plaintiff (and the Class) and Blizzard Entertainment by engaging in a fraudulent scheme and conspiracy

respecting the sale of *World of Warcraft*® gold in violation of the EULA and ToU as more fully described above.

85. **Damages.** Defendants' interference with Plaintiff's and members of the Class' business relationship has caused and proximately caused irreparable harm and damages, including the money Plaintiff and the Class paid to purchase Blizzard Entertainment's software and for subscription fees.

WHEREFORE, Plaintiff, on behalf of himself and the Class, respectfully seeks the relief set forth below.

CLAIM VIII
Conspiracy to Engage in Tortious Interference with Business Relationship

86. Plaintiff incorporates by reference thereto paragraphs 1-42 as if fully set forth herein.

87. **Conspiracy between two or more parties.** Beginning at least as early as November 27, 2004, and continuing thereafter through the present time, Defendants and their co-conspirators, as described above, engaged in an ongoing fraudulent scheme and continuing conspiracy to generate, market, distribute and sell *World of Warcraft*® gold for real money through eBay and its website.

88. **Unlawful acts by unlawful means and overt acts.** Pursuant to their scheme and conspiracy alleged herein, Defendants and their co-conspirators agreed to and in fact engaged in a wide range of activities, the purpose and effect of which was to violate Blizzard Entertainment's EULA and ToU to the disadvantage of Plaintiff and the Class. These activities have been set forth in detail above and throughout this Amended Complaint, and have been incorporated by reference herein, including, but not limited to the generation, marketing, distribution and sale of *World of Warcraft*® gold. These acts constitute tortious interference with Plaintiff's business relationship with Blizzard Entertainment.

89. As part of the common design, scheme and conspiracy agreed to by Defendants and their co-conspirators, they agreed to engage in the aforesaid tortious interference.

The aforesaid acts and/or practices were in furtherance thereof.

90. **Damages.** Defendants' fraudulent scheme and conspiracy have directly and proximately caused irreparable harm and damages to Plaintiff and the Class. As a direct and proximate result of Defendants' scheme and conspiracy perpetrated upon Plaintiff and the Class, Defendants are jointly and severally liable to Plaintiff for all damages Plaintiff and the Class for all injury sustained. [sic]

WHEREFORE, Plaintiff, on behalf of himself and the Class, respectfully seeks the relief set forth below.

CLAIM IX
Trespass to Chattel

91. Plaintiff incorporates by reference thereto paragraphs 1-42 as if fully set forth herein.

92. Plaintiff and members of the Class are the owners of personal computers, servers, computer systems and associated hardware that have been interfered with by Defendants and their co-conspirators.

93. The *World of Warcraft®* ToU specifically prohibits transmitting commercial solicitations for goods or services outside the *World of Warcraft®* universe and sending unsolicited chat messages.

94. The *World of Warcraft®* EULA specifically prohibits any commercial use of the *World of Warcraft®* game.

95. At all relevant times, Defendants and/or their agents and co-conspirators intentionally and without consent used, trespassed on, and interfered with Plaintiff's and the Class' property rights by engaging in the business of generating, marketing, distributing and selling *World of Warcraft®* gold for real money and the corresponding "spam" advertisements to promote for this illicit sales scheme, thereby wrongfully exercising dominion over Plaintiffs' [sic] property and depriving Plaintiff and members of the Class [of] the legitimate use and enjoyment of their computer systems.

96. In doing so, the Defendants and their co-conspirators intentionally intermeddled with, damaged and deprived Plaintiff and members of the Class of their computer systems, or a portion thereof.

97. As a direct result of Defendants' and its co-conspirators' actions, Plaintiff and members of the Class have suffered and continue to suffer irreparable harm resulting in the loss of their personal time and the impairment and diminution of their use and enjoyment of the *World of Warcraft*® virtual world as well as the devaluation of the Class' in-game currency, for which there is no adequate remedy at law.

WHEREFORE, Plaintiff, on behalf of himself and the Class, respectfully seeks the relief set forth below.

VII. Demand for Relief

WHEREFORE, Plaintiff and the Class demand judgment against Defendants in each claim for relief, jointly and severally, and as follows:

a. Declaring the acts and practices of Defendants unlawful;

b. Enjoining Defendants from engaging in such unlawful acts and practices in the future;

c. Awarding compensatory damages, treble damages, and any other damages permitted by law, in such amounts as will be determined at trial, plus Plaintiff's costs of suit and reasonable attorneys' fees;

d. Awarding Plaintiff and the Class other appropriate equitable relief, including, but not limited to, disgorgement of all profits obtained from Defendants' wrongful conduct and declaratory relief;

e. Awarding Plaintiff and the Class pre-judgment and post-judgment interest at the maximum rate allowed by law;

f. Awarding Plaintiff and the Class their costs and expenses in this litigation, including expert fees, and reasonable attorneys' fees;

g. Awarding Plaintiff and the Class such other and further relief as may be just and proper under the circumstances.

VIII. Demand for Jury Trial

Pursuant to *Federal Rules of Civil Procedure* 38(b), Plaintiff demands a trial by jury on all issues so triable.

Dated: August 17, 2007

Appendix XI: Eros, LLC et al v. Simon *Complaint*

UNITED STATES DISTRICT COURT
FOR THE EASTERN DISTRICT OF NEW YORK

EROS, LLC, LINDA BACA   CIVIL ACTION NO.:
d/b/a RH DESIGNS, TEASA COPPRUE
d/b/a LE CADRÉ NETWORK,
SHANNON GREI d/b/a NOMINE,
KASI LEWIS d/b/a PIXEL DOLLS,
and DE DESIGNS, INC.

            Plaintiffs,

        v.   JURY TRIAL DEMANDED

THOMAS SIMON, a/k/a RASE KENZO,
and JOHN DOES 1-10,

            Defendants.

COMPLAINT

Plaintiffs Eros, LLC, DE Designs, Inc., Linda Baca d/b/a RH Designs, Teasa Copprue d/b/a Le Cadré Network, Shannon Grei d/b/a Nomine, Kasi Lewis d/b/a Pixel Dolls (collectively "Plaintiffs") say the following by way of Complaint:

NATURE OF THE ACTION

1. Plaintiffs are among the most successful merchants doing business within the virtual world platform known as Second Life. Plaintiffs make and sell some of the best-selling virtual objects within the Second Life platform.

2. Defendant Thomas Simon, known within Second Life as "Rase Kenzo" ("Simon") has been making and selling, and continues to make and sell, numerous unauthorized copies of Plaintiffs' virtual products within Second Life using Plaintiffs' trademarks in violation of the Lanham Act and the Copyright Act. On information and belief, Simon has been and continues to act in concert and conspiracy with a number of other Second Life users whose identities are currently unknown to plaintiffs, and whom plaintiffs have designated as John Does 1 through 10 for purposes of this Complaint.

3. Plaintiffs bring this action to recover damages arising from and to enjoin defendants' violation of the Lanham and Copyright Acts and ongoing civil conspiracy.

PARTIES AND JURISDICTION

4. Plaintiff Eros, LLC is a limited liability corporation organized under the laws of Florida having its principal place of business at 16207 September Drive, Lutz, Florida 33549.

5. Plaintiff Linda Baca d/b/a RH Designs is an individual residing at 7215 Braxton Drive, Noblesville, Indiana 46062.

6. Plaintiff Teasa Copprue d/b/a Le Cadré Network is an individual residing at 22532 Hessel, Detroit, Michigan 48219-1126.

7. Plaintiff Shannon Grei d/b/a Nomine is an individual residing at 420 Laurel Street, Medford, Oregon 97501.

8. Plaintiff Kasi Lewis d/b/a Pixel Dolls is an individual residing at 5627 Hickory Drive, Patterson, Georgia 31557.

9. Plaintiff DE Designs, Inc. is a corporation organized under the laws of the Commonwealth of Virginia having its principal place at 17392 Old Ridge Road, Montpelier, Virginia 23192.

10. Defendant Thomas Simon is an individual residing at 2536 120th Street, Apt. 2, Flushing, New York.

11. Upon information and belief, defendants John Does 1-10 ("Defendants") are individuals who reside in the United States.

12. This Court has original subject matter jurisdiction over the federal causes of action in this Complaint pursuant to 28 U.S.C. § 1338(a) and 15 U.S.C. § 1121, and has supplemental jurisdiction over the state law cause of action in this Complaint pursuant to 28 U.S.C. § 1367(a). This Court also has original jurisdiction over the subject matter of this action pursuant to 28 U.S.C. § 1332, in that the action is between citizens of different states and the amount in controversy exceeds the sum or value of $75,000, exclusive of interests and costs.

13. This Court has personal jurisdiction over defendants, and venue is proper within this District pursuant to 28 U.S.C. § 1391(b) because defendant Simon resides within this District, because defendants committed numerous acts in furtherance of their unlawful conspiracy within this District, because a substantial part of the acts and omissions giving rise to the claims in this action occurred in this District, and because a substantial portion of the property that is the subject of this action is situated within this District.

FACTUAL BACKGROUND

14. The Second Life virtual world platform ("Second Life") is an internet hosted interactive computer simulation which allows its participants to see, hear, use and modify the simulated objects in the computer generated environment. Second Life users adopt a Second Life name and a character

or "avatar" to represent themselves virtually within Second Life.

15. Linden Research, Inc. ("Linden") owns and operates Second Life, which is currently hosted at http://secondlife. com. According to Linden, there are currently over 9 million different Second Life accounts. There are Second Life users throughout the United States and in many foreign countries.

16. At all times relevant to this Complaint and continuing to the date of the filing of this Complaint, by and through the "Terms of Service" governing users' participation in Second Life, Linden has recognized and allowed Second Life users to retain all intellectual property rights in the digital content that they create, place or otherwise own within Second Life. As a result, Second Life users conduct significant commerce within Second Life each day. According to Linden, on a typical day Second Life users conduct transactions cumulatively involving well over 1 million dollars.

EROS LLC

17. Eros LLC ("Eros") is engaged in, *inter alia,* the sale of a number of adult-themed virtual objects for use within Second Life in interstate commerce to Second Life users throughout the United States and foreign countries.

18. Principally through the marketing efforts of Kevin Alderman, Eros's Chief Executive Officer (known within Second Life as "Stroker Serpentine"), Eros's products have become widely known within Second Life, with Mr. Alderman, Eros and Eros's products receiving substantial coverage from national and international technologically oriented media properties such as *ABC Australia, Wired, eBay Magazine, InformationWeek, iVillage,* and *Huff Report.*

19. Eros also routinely promotes its products throughout Second Life by placing advertisements and conducting promotional events within numerous virtual adult/social themed clubs within Second Life.

20. Eros's products have built a reputation within Second Life for performance, quality and value, and as a result, upon

information and belief, are among the best selling adult-themed virtual objects within Second Life.

21. Two of these products are known as the SexGen Platinum Base Unit v4.01 (hereinafter, "Eros Item 1") and the SexGen Platinum+Diamond Base v5.01 ("hereinafter, "Eros Item 2" and together with Item 1, the "Eros Items"). True and correct screen shots depicting Eros Item 1 and Eros Item 2 as they appear within Second Life are attached as Exhibits "A" and "B", respectively.

22. Eros uses the SexGen trademark (the "Eros Mark") to sell the Eros Items within Second Life, and generally as a method of identifying a number of Eros's products, including but not limited to the Eros Items.

23. Since 2005, Mr. Alderman, by and through Eros as well as a previous company that Mr. Alderman owned, has sold thousands of copies of the Eros Items in interstate commerce to Second Life users in locations throughout the United States and in numerous foreign countries, using the Eros Mark. Eros currently owns all rights in and to the Eros Marks.

24. As a result of Eros's substantial sales of the Eros Items, and Mr. Alderman's and Eros's promotional and advertising efforts, the Eros Mark has become famous and distinctive among the relevant consuming public, serving to distinguish Eros's goods from those of competitors and to identify Eros as the source of those goods.

25. On or about June 11, 2007, Eros filed an application to obtain federal trademark registration, serial number 77202601, for the Eros Mark with the United States Patent and Trademark Office.

26. The Eros Items are comprised of original material that is copyrightable.

27. Eros is the owner of the copyrights in the Eros Items within the meaning of 17 U.S.C. § 101.

28. On or about June 22, 2007, Eros filed applications for copyright registrations for the Eros Items with the United States Copyright Office. True and correct copies of the applications and other documents associated with the applications are attached as Exhibit "C."

DE DESIGNS, INC.

29. DE Designs, Inc. ("DE Designs") is engaged in, *inter alia,* the sale of a number of virtual objects, including lines of virtual clothing, for use within Second Life in interstate commerce to Second Life users throughout the United States and foreign countries.

30. Principally through the marketing efforts of Michael Hester, DE Designs' Chief Executive Officer (known within Second Life as "DoC Eldritch"), DE Designs' products have become widely known within Second Life, with Mr. Hester, DE Designs and DE Designs' products receiving coverage from media properties such as *Reuters, The Wall Street Journal, InformationWeek,* as well as numerous other web sites and blogs.

31. Mr. Hester also routinely promotes DE Designs products throughout Second Life by placing classified advertisements in Second Life-oriented publications and at various locations within Second Life.

32. DE Designs products have built a reputation within Second Life for performance, quality and value, and as a result, upon information and belief, are among the best selling virtual clothing lines within Second Life.

33. One of these products is known as the DE Day Walker 2 Resurrection (hereinafter, the "DE Item"). True and correct screen shots depicting the DE Item as it appears within Second Life are attached as Exhibit "D."

34. DE Designs uses the DE Designs trademark (the "DE Mark") to sell the DE Item within Second Life, and generally as a method of identifying a number of DE Designs products, including but not limited to the DE Item.

35. Since 2004, Mr. Hester, by and through DE Designs, has sold hundreds of thousands of virtual items, including but not limited to the DE Item, using the DE Mark in interstate commerce to Second Life users in locations throughout the United States and in numerous foreign countries. DE Designs is the exclusive licensee of Mr. Hester's rights in and to the DE Mark.

36. As a result of DE Designs' substantial sales of the DE Item and promotional and advertising efforts, the DE Mark has

become famous and distinctive among the relevant consuming public, serving to distinguish DE Designs' goods from those of its competitors and to identify DE Designs as the source of those goods.

37. On or about March 27, 2007, the United States Patent and Copyright Office placed the DE Mark on the principal United States Trademark Register, registration number 3222158.

38. The DE Item is comprised of original material that is copyrightable.

39. DE Designs is the owner of the copyrights in the DE Item within the meaning of 17U.S.C. § 101.

40. On or about September 13, 2007, DE Designs filed an application for copyright registration for the DE Item with the United States Copyright Office. True and correct copies of the application and other documents associated with the application are attached as Exhibit "E."

LINDA BACA d/b/a RH DESIGNS

41. Linda Baca, d/b/a RH Designs, is engaged in, *inter alia,* the sale of a number of virtual objects, including virtual home furnishing accent pieces, for use within Second Life in interstate commerce to Second Life users throughout the United States and foreign countries.

42. Through, *inter alia,* the marketing efforts of Ms. Baca (known within Second Life as "Rebel Hope"), RH Designs products have become widely known within Second Life, with Ms. Baca, RH Designs and RH Designs products having received coverage from Second Life related websites such as *Metaverse Messenger* and *Second Style* Magazine.

43. Ms. Baca also routinely promotes RH Designs products throughout Second Life by announcing new product offerings in-world and by internet marketing.

44. RH Designs products have built a reputation within Second Life for performance, quality and value, and as a result, upon information and belief, are among the best selling virtual home furnishing accent pieces within Second Life.

45. One of these products is known as the Classic DeVille Floor Lamp (hereinafter, "RH Item"). A true and correct copy of

a screen shot depicting the RH Item as it appears within Second Life is attached as Exhibit "F."

46. Ms. Baca uses the RH Designs trademark (the "RH Mark") to sell the RH Item within Second Life, and generally as a method of identifying a number of RH Designs products, including but not limited to the RH Item.

47. Since 2005, Ms. Baca has sold thousands of copies of RH Design products, including but not limited to the RH Item, in interstate commerce to Second Life users in locations throughout the United States and in numerous foreign countries, using the RH Mark. Ms. Baca currently owns all rights in and to the use of the RH Mark to sell the RH Item.

48. As a result of, *inter alia,* Ms. Baca's substantial sales of the RH Designs products, including but not limited to the RH Item, and substantial promotional and advertising efforts, the RH Mark has become famous and distinctive among the relevant consuming public, serving to distinguish RH Designs goods from those of competitors and to identify RH Designs as the source of those goods.

49. The RH Item is comprised of original material that is copyrightable.

50. Ms. Baca is the owner of the copyrights in the RH Item within the meaning of 17 U.S.C. § 101.

51. On or about September 18, 2007, Ms. Baca filed an application for copyright registration for the RH Item with the United States Copyright Office. True and correct copies of the application and other documents associated with the application are attached as Exhibit "G."

TEASA COPPRUE d/b/a LE CADRÉ NETWORK

52. Teasa Copprue, d/b/a Le Cadré Network, is engaged in, *inter alia,* the sale of a number of virtual objects, including virtual shoes and boots, for use within Second Life in interstate commerce to Second Life users throughout the United States and foreign countries.

53. Through, *inter alia,* through the marketing efforts of Teasa Copprue (known within Second Life as "Asri Falcone"), Le Cadré Network's products have become widely known

within Second Life, with Ms. Copprue, Le Cadré Network and Le Cadré Network's products receiving coverage from media properties such as *60 Minutes Australia* and *ABC News.*

54. Ms. Copprue also routinely promotes Le Cadré Network products throughout Second Life by advertising in Second Life related publications such [as] *Second Style* Magazine, on an in-world radio station owned by Le Cadré Network, and in various internet forums.

55. Le Cadré Network's products have built a reputation within Second Life for performance, quality and value, and as a result, upon information and belief, are among the best selling virtual shoes and boots within Second Life.

56. Two of these products are known as CFM Boots (hereinafter, "Le Cadré Item I") and Celene Boots (hereinafter, "Le Cadré Item 2" and together with Le Cadré Item I, the "Le Cadré Items"). True and correct copies of screen shots depicting Le Cadré Item I and Le Cadré Item 2 as they appear within Second Life are attached as Exhibits "H" and "I", respectively.

57. Ms. Copprue uses the Le Cadré Network trademark (the "Le Cadré Mark") to sell the Le Cadré Items within Second Life, and generally as a method of identifying a number of Le Cadré Network's products, including but not limited to the Le Cadré Items.

58. Since 2004, Ms. Copprue has sold hundreds of thousands of copies of the Le Cadré Network products, including but not limited to the Le Cadré Items, in interstate commerce to Second Life users in locations throughout the United States and in numerous foreign countries, using the Le Cadré Mark. Ms. Copprue currently is a co-owner of all rights in and to the Le Cadré Mark.

59. As a result of Ms. Copprue's substantial sales of Le Cadré Network Products, and substantial promotional and advertising efforts, the Le Cadré Mark has become famous and distinctive among the relevant consuming public, serving to distinguish Le Cadré Network's products from those of competitors and to identify Le Cadré Network as the source of those goods.

60. The Le Cadré Items are comprised of original material that is copyrightable.

61. Ms. Copprue is the owner of the copyrights in the Items within the meaning of 17 U.S.C. § 101.

62. On or about September 29, 2007, Le Cadré Network filed applications for copyright registration for the Le Cadré Items with the United States Copyright Office. True and correct copies of the applications and other documents associated with the applications are attached as Exhibit "J."

SHANNON GREI d/b/a NOMINE

63. Shannon Grei, d/b/a Nomine, is engaged in, *inter alia,* the sale of a number of virtual objects, including "skins" used to cover avatars, for use within Second Life in interstate commerce to Second Life users throughout the United States and foreign countries.

64. Principally through the marketing efforts of Ms. Grei (known within Second Life as "Munchflower Zaius"), Nomine products have become widely known within Second Life, with Ms. Grei, Nomine and Nomine products receiving coverage from media properties such as *Newsweek, Reuters* and *CBS Evening News.*

65. Ms. Grei also routinely promotes Nomine products throughout Second Life by, *inter alia,* displaying the products in her in-world store.

66. Nomine products have built a reputation within Second Life for performance, quality and value, and as a result, upon information and belief, are among the best selling avatar skin designs within Second Life.

67. One of these products is known as the Nomine Araignee Set (hereinafter, "Nomine Item"). A true and correct screen shot depicting the Nomine Item as it appears within Second Life is attached as Exhibit "K."

68. Ms. Grei uses the Nomine trademark (the "Nomine Mark") to sell the Nomine Items within Second Life, and generally as a method of identifying a number of Nomine's products, including but not limited to the Nomine Item.

69. Since 2004, Ms. Grei has sold hundreds of thousands of copies of Nomine products, including the Nomine Item, in interstate commerce to Second Life users in locations throughout the United States and in numerous foreign countries, using the Nomine Mark. Ms. Grei currently owns all rights in and to the Nomine Mark.

70. As a result of Nomine's substantial sales of the Nomine Items, and Ms. Grei's promotional and advertising efforts, the Nomine Mark has become famous and distinctive among the relevant consuming public, serving to distinguish Nomine's goods from those of its competitors and to identify Nomine as the source of those goods.

71. The Nomine Item is comprised of original material that is copyrightable.

72. Nomine is the owner of the copyrights in the Nomine Item within the meaning of 17U.S.C. § 101.

73. On or about September 19, 2007 Ms. Grei filed an application for copyright registration for the Nomine Item with the United States Copyright Office. True and correct copies of the application and other documents associated with the application are attached as Exhibit "L."

KASI LEWIS d/b/a PIXEL DOLLS AND PIXEL CHAPS

74. Kasi Lewis, d/b/a Pixel Dolls, is engaged in, *inter alia,* the sale of a number of virtual objects, including lines of virtual men's and women's clothing and avatar skins, for use within Second Life in interstate commerce to Second Life users throughout the United States and foreign countries.

75. Principally through the marketing efforts of Ms. Lewis (known within Second Life as "Nephilaine Protagonist"), Pixel Dolls products have become widely known within Second Life, with Ms. Lewis, Pixel Dolls and Pixel Dolls products having received coverage from media properties such as *Jane* Magazine, the *Associated Press,* and *PC Gamer* magazine.

76. Ms. Lewis also routinely promotes Pixel Dolls products throughout Second Life by advertising on in-world forums and by means of her website.

77. Pixel Dolls products have built a reputation within Second Life for performance, quality and value, and as a result, upon information and belief, are among the best selling virtual clothing items and avatar skins within Second Life.

78. One of these products is known as Belted Sweater Set II (hereinafter, "Pixel Item"). A true and correct copy of a screen shot depicting the Pixel Item as it appears within Second Life is attached as Exhibit "M."

79. Ms. Lewis uses the Pixel Dolls trademark (the "Pixel Mark") to sell the Pixel Item within Second Life, and generally as a method of identifying a number of Pixel Doll products, including but not limited to the Pixel Item.

80. Since 2003, Ms. Lewis has sold hundreds of thousands of Pixel Dolls products, including hut not limited to the Pixel Item, in interstate commerce to Second Life users in locations throughout the United States and in numerous foreign countries, using the Pixel Mark. Ms. Lewis currently owns all rights in and to the Pixel Mark.

81. As a result of Ms. Lewis's substantial sales of the Pixel Items, and Ms. Lewis's promotional and advertising efforts, the Pixel Mark has become famous and distinctive among the relevant consuming public, serving to distinguish Pixel Dolls products from those of competitors and to identify Pixel Dolls as the source of those products.

82. The Pixel Item is comprised of original material that is copyrightable.

83. Ms. Lewis is the Owner of the copyrights in the Pixel Item within the meaning of 17 U.S.C. § 101.

84. On or about September 19, 2007, Ms. Lewis filed an application for copyright registration for the Pixel Item with the United States Copyright Office. True and correct copies of the application and other documents associated with the application are attached as Exhibit "N."

DEFENDANTS' ILLEGAL CONDUCT

85. Simon maintains one or more accounts within Second Life, and is known as, *inter alia,* Rase Kenzo within Second Life.

86. On information and belief, Simon has been and continues to act in concert and conspiracy with a number of other Second Life users whose identities are currently unknown to plaintiffs, and to whom plaintiffs refer as John Does 1-10 for the purposes of this Complaint.

87. Upon information and belief, John Does 1-10 reside within the United States.

88. Beginning at a time currently unknown to plaintiffs and continuing to the present time, Simon has been making and selling, using the aforementioned marks of the plaintiffs (hereinafter collectively "Plaintiffs' Marks"), numerous unauthorized copies of the aforementioned items of the plaintiffs (hereinafter collectively "Plaintiffs' Items") within Second Life in interstate commerce to Second Life users. In connection with the sales of the unauthorized copies of Plaintiffs' Items Simon has misrepresented the copies as authorized and legitimate copies of Plaintiffs' Items, resulting in actual consumer confusion regarding the origin of the copies. Plaintiffs have collected a number of screen shots depicting or otherwise evidencing Simon's authorized copying of the Plaintiffs' Items at http://flickr.com/photos/kenzopics.

89. On information and belief, John Does 1-10, acting in concert and conspiracy with Simon, are reselling and/or otherwise distributing for Simon the unauthorized copies of Plaintiffs' Items for use within Second Life, through, *inter alia,* so-called Second Life "yard sales."

90. Defendants' acts as described herein have at all times been and continue to be willful, wanton, malicious, and committed in bad faith, with the deliberate intent to deceive or confuse the consuming public, to harm plaintiffs in their respective businesses by trading off of the reputation and goodwill associated with the Plaintiffs' Marks, and to unjustly profit from the fame of and goodwill associated with the Plaintiffs' Marks.

91. As a direct and proximate result of defendants' acts, plaintiffs have been damaged and continue to be irreparably

damaged through the diversion of sales, profits and consumer interest from plaintiffs to defendants, and the creation of consumer confusion and uncertainty as to the source and quality of plaintiffs' products and their affiliation with or sponsorship of defendants.

92. Defendants will suffer no harm as the result of a grant preliminary and/or permanent injunctive relief in plaintiffs' favor and against defendants, as defendants have no legal justification for their sale or unauthorized use of Plaintiffs' Marks and infringement of plaintiffs' copyrights, and are making no legitimate use of Plaintiffs' Marks and copyrights.

93. There is a substantial likelihood that plaintiffs will succeed on the merits of their respective, Lanham Act, Copyright Act and civil conspiracy claims against defendants.

94. The public interest favors the entry of an injunction against defendants to protect consumers in the United States from the confusion, diversion, and deception that has been and is likely to continue being caused by defendants' illegal conduct.

COUNT I
LANHAM ACT VIOLATION-UNFAIR COMPETITION AND FALSE DESCRIPTION OF ORIGIN

95. Plaintiffs incorporate the allegations of paragraphs 1 through 94 as though set forth fully herein.

96. Defendants have falsely designated the origin of the unauthorized copies of the Plaintiffs' Items Defendants have sold, and made false and misleading descriptions and representations of fact in the course of selling these copies.

97. Defendants' conduct as described above has caused confusion, mistake and deception as to the origin, sponsorship or approval by plaintiffs of defendants' goods and commercial activities.

98. Defendants' conduct was willful.

99. As a direct and proximate result of Defendants' conduct, Plaintiffs have suffered and will continue to suffer dam-

ages from lost sales, the diversion of consumer interest, and injury to its business reputation and to the goodwill associated with their products and materials in an amount to be proven at trial.

100. Upon information and belief, defendants continue to make unauthorized copies of the Plaintiffs' Items, and to make false and misleading descriptions and representations of fact in the course of selling these copies, and in the absence of an injunction prohibiting defendants from doing so, intend to and will continue to do so in the future.

WHEREFORE, plaintiffs Eros, LLC, Linda Baca d/b/a RH Designs, Teasa Copprue d/b/a Le Cadré Network, Shannon Grei d/b/a Nomine, Kasi Lewis d/b/a Pixel Dolls and DE Designs, Inc. demand judgment in its favor and against defendants:

(a) awarding plaintiffs an amount equal to three times the damages sustained by plaintiffs or three times defendants' profits, whichever amount is greater;

(b) awarding plaintiffs prejudgment interest and costs of suit;

(c) awarding plaintiffs reasonable attorneys' fees pursuant to 15 U.S.C. § 1117(b);

(d) preliminarily and permanently enjoining defendants from infringing the Plaintiffs' Marks, pursuant to 15 U.S.C. § 1116.

(e) requiring defendants to deliver up for destruction all infringing copies of the Plaintiffs' Items bearing the Plaintiffs' Marks, and all articles by means of which infringing copies of the Plaintiffs' Items may be reproduced; and

(f) granting such other and further relief as the Court may deem just.

COUNT II
COPYRIGHT INFRINGEMENT

101. Plaintiffs incorporate the allegations of paragraphs 1 through 100 as though set forth fully herein.

102. By defendants' conduct as described above, defendants have infringed plaintiffs' respective copyrights in the Plaintiffs' Items.

103. Defendants' infringement was willful.

104. As a direct and proximate result of defendants' conduct, Plaintiffs have suffered damages.

105. Upon information and belief, defendants are continuing to infringe plaintiffs' copyrights in the Items by, *inter alia,* copying, displaying, distributing and selling copies of the Items without plaintiffs' authorization, and in the absence of an injunction prohibiting defendants from doing so, intends to and will continue to do so in the future.

WHEREFORE, plaintiffs Eros, LLC, Linda Baca d/b/a RH Designs, Teasa Copprue d/b/a Le Cadré Network, Shannon Grei d/b/a Nomine, Kasi Lewis d/b/a Pixel Dolls and DE Designs, Inc. demand judgment in their favor and against defendants:

(a) awarding plaintiffs an amount equal to plaintiffs' actual damages and any additional profits of defendants, or in the alternative, statutory damages pursuant to 17 U.S.C. § 504;

(b) awarding plaintiffs prejudgment interest and its costs of suit;

(e) awarding plaintiffs reasonable attorneys' fees;

(d) preliminarily and permanently enjoining defendants from infringing plaintiffs' respective copyrights in the Plaintiffs' Items;

(e) requiring the impounding and destruction of all infringing copies of the Plaintiffs' Items and of all articles by means of which infringing copies of the Plaintiffs' Items may be reproduced, pursuant to 17 U.S.C. § 503; and

(f) granting such other and further relief as the Court may deem just.

COUNT III
CIVIL CONSPIRACY

106. Plaintiffs incorporate the allegations of paragraphs 1 through 105 as though set forth fully herein.

107. Through and as part of their conduct as alleged above, Defendants conspired to "palm off" the illegal copies that Simon made as items that plaintiffs had actually made, and to thereby misappropriate plaintiffs' labors and expenditures in connection with the creation of Plaintiffs' Items.

108. Defendants committed numerous overt acts in furtherance of their conspiracy, including the making, sale and distribution of thousands of unauthorized copies of Plaintiffs' Items within Second Life.

109. Defendants' conduct has caused confusion among the purchasing public within Second Life as to the origin of the unauthorized copies of Plaintiffs' Items.

110. As a direct and proximate result of defendants' conduct, plaintiffs have suffered damages.

111. Defendants' conduct was and is intentional, wanton, malicious, outrageous and of the sort warranting the imposition of punitive damages.

112. Upon information and belief, defendants are continuing to carry out their conspiracy to palm off their unauthorized copies of Plaintiffs' Items, and in the absence of an injunction prohibiting defendants from doing so, intend to and will continue to do so in the future.

WHEREFORE, plaintiffs Eros, LLC, Linda Baca d/b/a RH Designs, Teasa Copprue d/b/a Le Cadré Network, Shannon Grei d/b/a Nomine, Kasi Lewis d/b/a Pixel Dolls and DE Designs, Inc., demand judgment in its favor and against defendants:

(a) awarding plaintiffs compensatory damages in an amount to be proven at trial;

(b) awarding plaintiffs punitive damages;

(c) preliminarily and permanently enjoining defendants from continuing their illegal conspiracy;

(d) awarding plaintiffs prejudgment interest and its costs of suit;

(e) awarding Plaintiffs reasonable attorneys' fees; and

(f) granting such other and further relief as the Court may deem just.

COUNT IV
LANHAM ACT VIOLATION—COUNTERFEITING

113. Plaintiff DE Designs, Inc. ("DE Designs") incorporates the allegations of paragraphs 1 through 112 as though set forth fully herein.

114. Defendants have, without the consent of DE Designs, used in interstate commerce a reproduction, counterfeit or copy of DE Designs' registered trademark DE Designs (the "DE Mark") in connection with the sale, offering for sale, and advertisement of goods that are identical or highly similar to the goods to which DE Designs affixes the DE Mark.

115. The aforesaid use by defendants is likely to cause confusion, to cause mistake, and to deceive consumers as to the relationship or sponsorship between DE Design and defendants and/or the source and quality of their respective goods.

116. Defendants have, without the consent of DE Designs, reproduced, counterfeited, copied, or colorably imitated the DE Mark and applied such reproduction, counterfeit, copy, or colorable imitation to advertisements intended to be used in commerce upon or in connection with the sale, offering for sale, distribution, or advertising of goods or services that are identical or highly similar to the goods to which DE Designs affixes the DE Mark.

117. The aforesaid use by defendants is likely to cause confusion, to cause mistake, or to deceive consumers as to the relationship or sponsorship between DE Designs and defendants and/or the source and quality of their respective goods.

118. Defendants have committed these acts with the knowledge that such imitation and counterfeiting is intended to be used to cause confusion, to cause mistake, or to deceive.

119. Defendants' conduct constitutes a willful violation of 15 U.S.C. § 1114(1).

120. As a direct and proximate result of defendants' conduct, DE Designs has suffered and will continue to suffer damages from lost sales, the diversion of consumer interest, the blurring, dilution, and tarnishing of the DE Mark, and injury to its business reputation and to the goodwill associated with its products and materials in an amount to be proven at trial.

WHEREFORE, plaintiff DE Designs, Inc. demands judgment in its favor and against defendants:

(a) awarding plaintiff an amount equal to three times the damages sustained by plaintiff or three times defendants' profits, whichever amount is greater;

(b) awarding plaintiff prejudgment interest and costs of suit;

(c) awarding plaintiff reasonable attorneys' fees pursuant to 15 U.S.C. § 1117(b);

(d) awarding statutory damages for willful use of a counterfeit mark, pursuant to 15 U.S.C. § 1117(c);

(e) preliminarily and permanently enjoining defendants from infringing the DE Mark, pursuant to 15 U.S.C. § 1116;

(f) requiring defendants to deliver up for destruction all infringing copies of the DE Items bearing the DE Mark, and all articles by means of which infringing copies of the DE Item may be reproduced; and

(g) granting such other and further relief as the Court may deem just.

JURY DEMAND

Plaintiffs demand a jury trial on all issues so triable.

Dated: October 24, 2007

Index